ARTIFICIAL INTELLIGENCE AND EDUCATION
Volume One

Learning Environments and Tutoring Systems

ARTIFICIAL INTELLIGENCE AND EDUCATION
Volume One

Learning Environments and Tutoring Systems

edited by
Robert W. Lawler
GTE Laboratories
Waltham, MA

Masoud Yazdani
University of Exeter
Exeter, England

ABLEX PUBLISHING
355 Chestnut St.
Norwood, NJ 07648

Printed in the United States of America

Library of Congress Cataloging-in-Publication Data

Artificial intelligence and education.

   Contents: v. 1. Learning environments and tutoring
systems.
   Bibliography: v. 1, p.
   Includes index.
   1. Educational technology.   2. Instructional systems.
3. Artificial intelligence.   I. Lawler, R. W. (Robert
Lawler) II. Yazdani, Masoud, 1955–   .
LB1028.3.A754   1987   371.3   87-956
ISBN 0-89391-438-X (v. 1) (c1)
ISBN 0-89391-439-8 (v. 1) (pp)

Chapters 2, 3, 5, 7, 11 and 15 reprinted with permission from
Elsevier.

Chapter 10 reprinted with permission from Learned Information Ltd.

Chapter 17 reprinted with permission from IEEE.

Chapter 3 reprinted with permission from White River Press.

Ablex Publishing Corporation
355 Chestnut Street
Norwood, New Jersey 07648

CONTENTS

PREFACE

The second international conference on Artificial Intelligence and Education was held in September, 1985, at Exeter University, United Kingdom. The two years marking the period to the third conference at the University of Pittsburgh, USA, have witnessed significant growth in the research community associated with this topic. The 1985 conference ended with the exciting prospect of the 'coming together' of the two traditional streams of 'tutoring systems' and 'learning environments' to address common problems in the design of instructional systems from an Artificial Intelligence perspective. This volume marks the beginning of a synergy between the agendas of the various researchers which promises an interesting and productive future.

Personally, we are both gratified to witness the willingness of scientists from Europe, the Pacific, the Americas, and other parts of the world to share their work and ideas. Such cooperation is especially important for a field whose thrust is directed toward human development. Even more so is this true today, when the technologies of information are increasingly seen as a primary arena for commercial competition.

The text of this book was prepared in camera-ready format by Marie McPartland-Conn using TEX. Without her knowledge and tenacious effort, the book would not have been produced so well as it has been. Roy Davies prepared the index; his willingness to redo the page references has permitted an improvement in the book's readability. Special thanks are due to C.D. Decker for his support of this project during and beyond Lawler's tenure as a principal scientist in GTE's Fundamental Research Laboratory. Travel grants to the second international conference were provided by *AISB*, the Society for the Study of Artificial Intelligence and the Simulation of Behavior, UK, and by the Symbolics Corporation, USA.

Robert W. Lawler
National Research Council Associate
at the Army Research Institute, USA

Masoud Yazdani
Computer Science Department
Exeter University, UK

INTRODUCTION

This book presents the two primary different approaches to the use of computers in education from the Artificial Intelligence perspective: Intelligent Tutoring Systems (Sleeman & Brown, 1982) and Computer-based Learning Environments (Papert, 1980; Lawler, 1984).

Intelligent Tutoring Systems (ITS) find their roots in the Computer Assisted Instruction (CAI) movement of the 1950s. Indeed, as is pointed out in Chapter 10 and reiterated in Chapter 12, they aim to solve specific shortcomings identified with early CAI systems. The major advance of ITS, or Intelligent CAI systems, as they are also called, is the use of techniques of knowledge representation pioneered within the Knowledge Engineering community. In fact some of this work (in the case of SOPHIE) predates the popularization of Expert Systems.

Following in the footsteps of the expert systems community, the most flourishing area of AI applications, tutoring systems need to move away from individually hand-crafted applications to the use of general purpose tools. The most successful generalization from application to tool is the notion of a shell. As described by Sleeman in Chapter 12, a shell is "a system which is datadriven, and so can cope with different domains; specific knowledge of the domain is contained in the domain database."

Ohlsson in Chapter 11 goes beyond specific problems with ITS construction. As he argues, course contents vary from textbook to textbook, from classroom to classroom. What we need then are not particular, quickly-outdated computer tutors, but the know-how of tutor construction. Ohlsson's synthesis of principles of tutoring presents a coherent framework with which many practitioners may like to disagree but which, nevertheless, they will welcome as a contribution to a more systematic approach to ITS, one which leads to science from today's engineering achievements. Ohlsson's contribution goes beyond ITS to provide the beginning of a dialogue with Feurzeig in Chapter 2, when we start digging deep into both perspectives to education. ITS and learning environments share similar concerns and therefore share the same principles. The separation of these two trends so far has been due to specifibility of the tasks they have dealt with.

ITS have a central objective of communicating some knowledge through computer facilities which may employ domain-specific expertise, error analysis, and user modelling. Their user-oriented intelligence is controlled by instructional strategies, which present problems and then test for understanding of the content. The more ambitious ITS aim to communicate strategies is generally conceived of as a collection of methods for problem solving, as well as domain specific content.

The strengths of ITS are their good definition and their completeness in the following senses. An ITS will have a well-articulated curriculum embodied in its domain expertise and an explicit theory of instruction represented by its tutoring strategies. This completeness permits an ITS to package existing expertise and focus on the novelty, which is the use of mechanically embodied sets of rules as a tool for instruction. Because an ITS can be well-defined for a given curriculum, the achievement of its goal, in principle, can be unambiguously evaluated. The weaknesses set against these considerable strengths are: inadequate complexity in models of what the user knows, how the user learns new knowledge, and what could be an appropriate instructional theory for complex minds.

In contrast to ITS, computer-based learning environments have the differently focused aim of leading the students to powerful authentic knowledge. This is partly in response to the spirit of Piaget's observation (Piaget, 1971):

> "If we desire to form individuals capable of inventive thought and of helping the society of tomorrow to achieve progress, then it is clear that an education which is an active discovery of reality is superior to one that consists merely in providing the young with ready-made wills to will with and ready-made truths to know with."

Authentic knowledge means what is to be learned should not merely be "added to the knowledge base" but rather assimilated into the person's pre-existing system of knowledges, and even more, should be freely expressed from internal motives when appropriate. The emphasis leads to a focus on the activity of the learner because it must be HIS internal action that integrates new knowledge to old and expresses that integration creatively.

The essential strength of such exploratory learning environments is that they CAN provide individuals with simple, concrete models of important things, ideas, and their relationships. ("Concrete" in this sense refers not to physical manipulability but to having a basis in personal experience. Even 'virtual' experiences with artificial worlds can be concrete. DiSessa's article illuminates this old distinction.) Compared to arithmetic drill which, for example, may enhance the memory of specific sums, computer-based microworlds can provide people with new ways of looking at the world. When it works, this is a very powful result. (For a specific example of such an outcome, see "Extending a Powerful Idea" in Lawler, DuBoulay, Hughes, and

MacLeod, 1986.) To the extent that such enhanced understanding provides the person with more power over his own mind and life, the knowledge is its own reward.

The fundamental limitations of these learning environments derive from their their commitments. Establishing the impact of their use is very difficult because of the nature of the effects sought and the complexity ascribed to the human minds within which those effects take place. To the extent that their design embodies commitments to using the computer more as a medium than a preprogrammed tool, taking seriously the complexity of the learner, and trying to draw connections between new content and prior idiosyncratic experiences, implementing computer microworlds leads to major difficulties because

- computation is a protean, imperfectly understood medium of communication;

- theories of how individuals learn through experience are inadequate;[1]

- there exists no model-based epistemology of instruction.

The core problem which now confronts ITS seems to be the complexity of actual users of the instructional systems. A short example will illustrate the point. In their famous work on childrens' arithmetic, Brown and Burton (1978) labelled childrens' deviations from standard arithmetical procedures as "bugs". In performing the sum below (taken from Lawler, 1985), the child exhibited a non-standard algorithm for performing an addition in the vertical form, but a description of the performance as a bug would misrepresent significantly the child's functioning knowledge and the sorts of inference employed:

$$
\begin{array}{r}
35 \\
+ \ 37 \\
\hline
99
\end{array}
$$

The child reasoned as follows: "Seven and five are twelve, but two numbers won't fit underneath them. The biggest number we can put there

---

[1] Knowledge based systems, with rules stored separately from the processes which use them, have proven their usefulness because their very lack of organization permits the addition of new rules without reprogramming; if, on the other hand, the organization and reorganization of knowledge in the mind in THE central need in effective education, thinking of learning as "adding another rule to the database" may be counterproductive.

is 9. But that leaves us three left over, so let's carry three to the next place where we can add them with the numbers there. Three, six, nine. Ninety nine must be the answer".

The child's logic represents a deviation from the standard addition algorithm. Characterizing the performance as a "bug", however, would miss the strong use of a conservation principle – the child's commitment to what the child knows and understands well, and the inventiveness shown in trying to cope with a problem beyond the child's capacity. We want to support such commitment and inventiveness. One wants to support a child but not the development of a "wrong theory". Beyond granting the complexity of the child's mind, we must recognize the complexity of the instructional situation.

The dilemma is ours: we want to support the child's commitment to his authentic point of view and its creative application; at the same time we want to modify that point of view. Can we circumvent this barrier? In the instructional situation, the teacher's great strength is in getting around the uselessness of materials which are not helping the individual child. In effect, the teacher is able to back up to a more global perspective and switch the instructional context to another, hopefully a more productive one. An intelligent human tutor might try, at such a juncture, to probe the child's representation schemes and processes of reasoning. Following such a model in a mechanized system would require developing a more comprehensive and well-articulated epistemology of instruction, for we must ask how do we judge which representation could be more suitable for use by a specific student who does not yet understand a particular idea?

In the problem above, where 35 and 37 are added up to 99, the child's justifications show that for the child the reality behind the things being manipulated is one where counting is salient and grouping is not being considered. For the child to understand carrying, s/he would require familiarity with the inter-relations of groupings and values (such as one might develop through play with a money-based representation scheme), familiarity with groupings where a uniform multiplicative factor is salient (as one would encounter in playing with Dienes blocks with their unit blocks, rows of 10, and flats of 100), and finally, experiences which would lead to unification of those separately mastered schemes.

There will surely occur cases where the student uses a representation beyond the current scope of the system. What should the system do when it determines that it does not, and even more cannot, understand what the student is thinking? The system should have available an extensible repertoire of representations. No system which is too rigid to learn should be called intelligent. While people learn more from experience than from being told, for computers the opposite has been more nearly true. Computers can learn from experts today; for use in education, an ideal instructional system should be able to learn new representations applying to its domain of primary expertise even from non-experts, as when the students are introducing some alternative way of thinking – however non-standard that way may be. Self's chapter looks into the role of machine learning in more detail.

One outcome of the 1985 conference on AI and Education has been the realization of ways in which the agendas of researchers with disparate programs can support the achievement of their common aim – the use of new technology to enhance both the quantity and quality of knowledge in human minds. If ITS could be opened up to more complex understanding of what students bring to problem solving and if computer-based environments could begin to make use of the sorts of techniques developed within the ITS community, a synergy could be possible that would permit the strengthening of both. Such an endeavor is now being advocated by Feuzeig under the banner of "intelligent microworlds". His paper in this volume appears to be a point of departure for such an effort. Even if we imagine some ideal instructional system which fuses the best of the ITS and computer-based microworld paradigms, we must still admit that significant problems remain. But a second outcome of this conference, witnessed by the papers in this volume, is the hope that advances to cope with those problems are within reach. Specifically, Feurzeig (Chapter 2) and the Lawlers (Chapter 5) show new approaches to rethinking curriculum in the light of what computational facilities make possible. Ohlsson's (Chapter 11) analysis of ITS and DiSessa's (Chapter 3) observations and arguments point the way to an epistemologically deepened design for curriculum materials design. Such a direction of research is suggested by Ohlsson's article as the central challenge of future work in this area. There is much to be done, but the prospects are promising.

Robert W. Lawler   Masoud Yazdani

REFERENCES

Lawler, R.W. (1984). Designing computer based microworlds. In M. Yazdani, (Ed.), *New Horizons in Educational Computing*. Ellis Horwood Ltd./John Wiley & Sons.

Lawler R.W., (1985). *Computer Experience and Cognitive Development*. Ellis Horwood Ltd./John Wiley & Sons

Lawler R.W., du Boulay, B., Hughes M., & MacLeod M. (1986). *Cognition and Education*. Ellis Horwood Ltd./John Wiley & Sons.

O'Shea, T., & Self, J. (1983). *Learning and Teaching with Computers*. The Harvester Press/Prentice Hall.

Papert, S. (1980). *Mindstorms: Children, Computers, and Powerful Ideas*. The Harvester Press/ Basic Books.

Piaget, J. (1971). *The Science of Education and the Psychology of the Child*. The Viking Press.

Sleeman, D., & Brown, J.S., (Eds.) (1982). *Intelligent Tutoring Systems*. Academic Press.

1   LEARNING ENVIRONMENTS: NOW, THEN, AND SOMEDAY

Robert W. Lawler

Senior Research Associate
National Research Council
Resident at the Army Research Institute
Alexandria, VA

ABSTRACT

After a sketch of the contents of the learning environments section, this chapter addresses several questions that have been raised about the impact of computers in education and the notion and efficacy of learning environments.

1.0 INTRODUCTION

Computer based learning environments began with the possibility Feurzeig saw in the early sixties for using conversational programming languages to improve mathematics instruction. The papers of this section on learning environments have been selected to show the breadth, variety, and vitality of current work in the area. Chapter 2 shows such work continuing in Feurzeig's efforts to develop intelligent microworlds. A prominent characteristic of work in learning environments has been a commitment to scientific knowledge as seen from the inside. DiSessa's Chapter 3 is a strong assertion that the impulse to creative science is rooted in personal, even intimate, experience. The central contribution of DiSessa's paper is defining a specific instructional genre, pre-science, which can serve as the intellectual bridge between the intuitions of everyday experience and the formal theories of professional science. Discovering, designing, and creating such "intellectual bridges" is likewise Papert's concern. Chapter 4 shows Papert doing what he does best, functioning as a critic of ideas. The Lawlers' Chapter 5 provides a worked example of what can be done with the opportunity educational technology presents for reconceptualizing curriculum. The central idea is that computers have introduced a new function for words – controlling machines – into our everyday lives; further, this new function makes it easier for children to learn to write and read one word at a time.

Reil, Levin, and Souviney present a vision of how to aid the child along the path of transition from novice to practitioner in Chapter 6, a vision commonly lacking in computer-based systems for education:

"Dwyer notes that ITS appear to have run into some sort of barrier on their complexity, and that one needs to define that barrier to circumvent it. In his view, ITS are based on an educational model where the teacher is posited as the expert provider of an optimal lesson plan. This ignores the progressive quality of education that begins with practice under guidance and goes on to independent exploration."[1]

Serious attention to this issue and further development of the vision Reil, Levin, and Souviney present may be the needed bridge between those whose focus has been on constructed systems and those who have focussed on learning environments.

Lieberman's TINKER system, described in Chapter 7, exemplifies the kinds of facilities that should become more available as the technology of AI workstations becomes more commonly affordable. Such concrete programming facilitites which involve the retro-active generation of procedures capturing previous directions to immediate action should have an important place in the future education of young children. (Notes on early versions of such facilities can be found in Lawler, 1977.) Although most people are familiar with Logo language implementations on minimal systems – the greatest commercial success has been with small machines for use by young children – Chapter 8 describes a version of Logo designed for powerful machines and embodying the leading edge notions of AI software languages. Drescher's Object Logo[2] presents the most accessible version of those AI languages aiming for the integration of object-oriented programming and functional programming languages (such as one sees also in Symbolics' Zetalisp with flavors and Xerox's LOOPS). In Chapter 9, Gross reports on his implementation in a constraint-based language of a computer-based engineering design laboratory. His system is at the frontier both in applying programming language advances and in the design of learning environments for mature students.

2.0 COMPLAINTS ABOUT "COMPUTERS IN EDUCATION"

Microcomputers inexpensive enough for widespread use in education became available in the late 70s in the USA – even some with enough capacity to support conversational programming languages. Such micros seemed

---

[1] Cited in Lawler, 1986. The limited observation above does not do justice to Dwyer's long commitment to this view of education, as elaborated in the work and reports of his SOLO Project at the University of Pittsburgh.

[2] A commercially available implementation has been made for the MacIntosh with Drescher's guidance by Coral Software, Cambridge, MA.

a significant change from existing time-shared systems. Many educators saw the promise of micros, and parents, in their eagerness to do what they imagined best for their children, with personal contributions and political pressure led school systems to invest heavily in that technology. Have those computers produced results which justify the hope placed in them? I think not. The disappointment expresses itself in four common complaints:

About computers in education, generally

THEME	SPECIFIC COMPLAINT
Effect:	Computers have not improved education.
Value:	Computer experiences are inferior to real ones.

About learning environments:

Clarity:	The notion is not clear and distinct.
Design:	Nobody knows how to make them.

The specific complaints we will pursue here are those focussed on the themes of effect, clarity and design. I conclude with some suggestions for future work. DiSessa's Chapter 3 addresses the value theme in his discussion of artificial worlds and real experience.

3.0   THE LIMITED IMPACT OF COMPUTERS IN EDUCATION

The introduction of microcomputers into the education system has disappointed many people who had hoped their presence would engender reforms leading to education both more congenial to children and more effective than the norm of past generations. There has been no widespread recognition of any such dramatic impact. Why? In a review of *Computer Experience and Cognitive Development*, Erik DeCorte noted:

> ... I point to the immediate connection between the book and the current inquiries about using computers with children. Some have claimed that computer experience, and the ability to program in particular, would influence in a positive way the learning and thinking capacities of children. In contradiction to the image produced by the rest of the available research literature (See DeCorte & Verschaffel, 1985), Lawler's study produces positive results concerning the cognitive-effects hypothesis.

Such negative outcomes as others report, when the result of thoughtful experiments which are executed with care, have the proper function of constraining the enthusiastic claims of the overly optimistic. On the other hand, I am convinced that one reason for the difference of outcomes noted by DeCorte is a consequence of different levels of detail of the studies. Too much evaluative research has the flavor of I/O models: some **INPUT** should produce some **OUTPUT**; some **INSTRUCTION** should produce some **OUTCOME**. If the true orderliness of human behavior becomes evident only when one looks very carefully at extremely tiny details, most experimental efforts to assess computing's impact will show negative results, unless they examine the **PROCESS** between input and output, the **PERSON** between instruction and outcome. Studying the knowledge and functioning of one mind in detail permits a depth of understanding of the student's mind and development normally beyond the reach of research with a broader focus. We need to go beyond evaluative studies of broad claims in order to advance our understanding of human cognition, specifically in respect of the issues of the malleability of the natural mind and of the long-term effects of specific experiences on the lives of individuals: both, for me, are central issues for the science of education.

Comments such as the preceding, though true and valuable, evade rather than answer the question raised by DeCorte's observation. It is the case that early Logo claims looked to widespread results so obvious and striking that corroborating or disambiguating experiments would not be required. No such strong outcome has occurred. Computers, as introduced in schools, have not had so beneficial an impact as their early proponents suggested they might. Lets' reflect on this problem.

3.1 The Worst Case: The Problem is Not Solvable

Despite widespread research in several paradigms directed to improving children's mathematical competence through using computers, there is a general impression, based on test results, that arithmetic skills have been deteriorating over the past 25 years. One jocular suggestion for reacting to this situation comes from "The Uses of Education to Enhance Technology".[3]

> It's time to face the facts: all previous efforts at educational reform have been failures. The harder we try, the more innovations we make, the dumber the students get. This is eloquently pointed out by proponents of the 'Back to Basics' movement in numerous riots and book burnings across the country.

---

[3] This vicious and amusing document parodying the style of Papert's early Logo proposals was written in 1977 within the MIT Logo community by one "Admiral Turtle", an author whose identity to this day remains in the fog.

The solution is clear. It is simply not possible to educate children. If repeated attempts to improve the quality of education only make matters worse, then the obvious way to make matters better is to try to degrade the quality of education. In fact, carrying this argument to its logical conclusion proves that the best educational reform would be to abolish efforts at education altogether. This conclusion is hardly new and has been previously argued by such thinkers as Holt and Illich. But they also foresaw the serious impediments to this scheme. It would abolish the major value of the school system, which is to supply employment and positions of power... But now, with modern technology, we see a way out of this dilemma. The solution is absurdly simple: by placing computers in the schools, we can let the teachers teach the computers and send the children home.... Specifically, we envision an educational system in which each child is assigned a personal computer, which goes to school in place of the child. (Incidently, it should be noted that the cost of such a personal computer is not large. Even at today's prices it is probably not much more than the average family would spend on a catastrophic medical emergency).[4]

Those of us who are laughing through our tears can not escape the need for some different way of dealing with the issue. One can try to take a broad view. It is possible to believe that the problem has not been a "local" failure, ascribable in some simple way to faulty research, slow technology transfer, or intractable institutions.

3.2 An Explanation: Social Changes are Dominant

The problem may be profound and even could involve deterioration in the learnability of common sense knowledge. Changes in the everyday world can completely overwhelm our hopes to teach children skills we know they will need later. Consider these observations (from Lawler, 1985) as an example of ways in which social forces can radically alter the cognitive impact of domains of common sense knowledge.

---

[4] The preceding was written in 1977. If the Admiral were writing today, he might be tempted to substitute a more current evaluation, such as "The savings on student lunches alone would pay for the investment in two to three years."

3.3 Vignette 55

Since the beginning of the High School Studies Program, the children and I have come to Logo to use the system from 8 to 10 a.m. The children have become accustomed to mid-morning snacks. The favorite: apple pie and milk. At their young age, Robby and Miriam get money from me, and we talk about how they spend it. A piece of pie costs 59 cents. A half pint of milk is 32 cents. So Miriam told me this morning, and these figures are familiar. As we got her snack, I asked Miriam how much we would have to pay the cashier. After a few miscalculations, she came to a sum of 91 cents and seemed confident it was correct. I congratulated her on a correct sum and asked the cashier to ring up our tab. "92 cents."

"92 cents?" I asked the cashier to explain. She said the pie is 55 cents and milk 30 cents, thus 85 cents and the tax, 7 cents. "See. Look at the table."

I am at a complete loss as to how to explain this to Miriam. Not only is the 8 percent food tax dreadful in itself, but it is rendering incomprehensible a primary domain of arithmetic that children regularly confront – paying small amounts of money for junk food. Otherwheres, Miriam used "the tax" as a label for the difference between what is a reasonable computation and what you actually have to pay somebody to buy something.

* * * * *

The observation suggests that a specific governmental policy has, as a side effect, been making the world less sensible and harder to learn about. If, to get accurate results, a child must learn to multiply and round (for computing a percentage tax) before learning to add, he is in BIG trouble. If it does no good to calculate correctly because results will be adjusted by some authoritatively asserted incomprehensible rule, why should one bother to be over-committed to precision? If addition no longer adds up, what good is arithmetic? If you can't count on number, what can you can you count on? If knowledge is not useful, why bother with it?

Complex technology may also be making the world less comprehensible, but the effects are not uniform. Calculators and modern cash registers which compute change obviate the need for much mental calculation. Contrariwise, the Lawlers argue in Chapter 5 that technology is making access to reading knowledge easier. These observations leave us with more questions than answers, but the questions are addressable and significant ones:

to what extent is it possible to learn what one needs to know through everyday experience? how do side effects of decisions by adults constrain or enhance children's ability to learn about the world in natural ways?

3.4 An Excuse: The Political Climate has been Adverse

After such observations, it is reasonable to ask how political decisions – such as support for research – have influenced the use of computers in education. For many years the federal government, through various agencies, was a major supporter of research into technology for education. The impact of the first Reagan budget – which proposed to reduce funding for research in science education from $80M to $10M in one year – led to significant demoralization of that community and deterioration of function within its organizations.[5] The decimation of this community was decidely unhelpful and may have engendered some of the chaos and superficiality of work evidenced as microcomputers were sold by the private sector to the education community throughout the United States. On the other hand, one must note that the more generous support provided by the French Government's founding of *Le Centre Mondial pour l'Informatique et Ressource Humaine* had no happier outcome, as noted by Paul Tate in *Datamation*.

> "... The Center intended to use microcomputers to take computing to the people through educational workshops in both the developed and the developing world. Field projects were set up in France and Senegal, and research schemes were introduced covering interactive media, systems architecture, AI, user interfaces, and medical applications. It was to be an international research center independent of all commercial, political, and national interests. Naturally, it failed. Nothing is that independent, especially an organization backed by a socialist government and staffed by highly individualistic industry visionaries from around the world. Besides, altruism has a credibility problem in an industry that thrives on intense commercial competition. By the end of the Center's first year, Papert had quit, so had American experts Nicholas Negroponte and Bob Lawler. It had become a battlefield, scarred by clashes of management style, personality, and political conviction. It never really recovered. The new French government has done the Center a favor in closing it down. But somewhere in that mess was an admirable attempt to take high technology, quickly and effectively, along the inevitable path into the hands of the

---

[5] For a revelation of the processes producing first, such draconian proposals, and then the budget deficits of Reaganomics, see D. Stockman's personal history of the period, *The Triumph of Politics*.

public. The Center had hoped to do that in different countries....
The Center is unlikely to be missed by many. Yet, for all its problems, it made a brave attempt to prepare for some of the technical
and market realities of the next few years. We regret that such a
noble venture met with such an ignoble end."[6]

3.5 An Excuse: Available Hardware has been Inadequate

Thereis no question that the introduction of computers in education was a
financial success – for some few companies – but the record with respect to
product engineering and the advancement of social goals is one of nearly
consistent failure. Consider, as an example, this brief review of the development of Logo-capable microcomputers for education:

- The GTI 3500 (a DEC LSI-11 with a Minsky-designed front end, the
  '2500') was an interesting product that came to market too early. The
  2500 implemented a special video-turtle primitive, spin (proposed by
  D. Hillis), which set the object rotating at a constant angular velocity.
  This machine would have been very useful to physics and engineering
  students had it survived.

- Texas Instruments supported the development of Logo for the TI-99 at
  the MIT Logo Project. The turtle geometry component of the system
  was quite inadequate. The sprite graphics system, which originally had
  been an uninteresting feature of the hardware, proved in the end to
  be a liberating addition to the repertoire of tools which could be used
  for educating children with computers. The TI-99 captured a significant portion of the education market, and The company made good
  money with their product. Nonetheless, TI withdrew the product,
  even though their president wanted the corporation to remain active
  in that market. This decision had a radical, negative impact on the
  production of software for education. I have been told that many small
  educational software development efforts collapsed after this decision
  was taken.

- The Apple II offered the best early versions of turtle geometry and
  list processing with Logo. Both it and the IBM PC were technically
  adequate systems for the time but were really more suited for use
  by junior high and older students. For use with younger children,
  the systems were, in fact, regressions from the graphics capabilities
  available in the TI-99.

---

[6] For a more extensive discussion of the controversies surrounding that
center, see Dray and Menosky, 1983.

- Atari Logo offered two advances. With time-sliced "when demons", the Atari permitted a technically primitive but intellectually deep form of multi-programming under user control. The four software sprites attempted to replace the expensive TI graphics hardware with simulated capabilities. The research lab was axed before their developmental projects came to fruition.

- The Coleco Adam had the best mix of hardware and software function for education use, but the manufacture and assembly of the machine was beset with problems of quality control that were insurmountable.

- The MSX microcomputers, some of which are the best Logo-capable systems commercially available today, are not imported into the United States because the major European producer Phillips believes (rightly, I suspect) that the education market has been saturated with Apple II's and IBM PC's.

- The best generally available system for use with small children till now has been the Apple II with a plug-in sprite board containing the TI-99 graphics processor. The two main advantages provided by Apple Sprites were an increase in the memory size, permitting more complex collections of procedures to be assembled, and the addition of a drawing capability for the sprites. Recently, the board and software were discontinued, for both technical and marketing reasons.

This record will not convince anyone of the grand success of the private sector in doing any more than making and losing money. With such volatile markets, very little that takes thought or time can get done. Someday we will have a stable computer product permitting the development of good educational software for young children. That day is not yet. If better systems come along, will they – like the MSX – fail either to reach the market or to sell because the enthusiasm and capital of the public and the education systems have been used up? It is quite possible that future opportunities have been polluted through temerity and over-selling.

3.6 An Explanation: The Medium Has No Consumable Content

The disappointing impact of computers on education may be partly explained by the lack of content addressable with the technology. Consider, in contrast, the video cassette recorder. VCR's have reached a "take-off" point and now are present in over 30 percent of American homes. A key element in the success of VCR technology – not only in the market but also in user satisfaction with it – is the existence of a massive stock of material

which the VCR brought to a new level of accessibility. As a "follow-on"
technology, VCR's reproduce for resale the production of 70 years of film
and TV with marginal conversion costs.

What existing material do micros have accessible? Ideas? Yes, but
they must be recoded for each new system unless microcoded emulation
of predecessor machines becomes common. More to the point, existing
larger systems and minicomputers typically have different purposes than
did micros purchased for education. To offset this limitation, conversational
programming languages suggested the possibility of extensive programming
by end-users. What precisely that meant and what has evolved from that
hope is our next theme.

4.0 ON COMPUTER-BASED "MICROWORLDS"

> What's in a name? That which we call a rose
> By any other name would smell as sweet.
> *Romeo and Juliet* (II,ii)

One could 'give a definition' in words of "microworlds" or say that
some things should and others things should not be so labelled. Presenting
these Learning Environments papers, we follow a less analytical procedure,
exploring what learning environments are by presenting extended examples, and offering some notes on the development of the notions within
the Artificial Intelligence discipline. To the extent that the notions of microworlds grew out of the Logo programming language community, a short,
idea-guided discussion capturing essential roots is possible because that
community has been quite compact and because characteristic work of pio-
neers in those developments (Feurzeig and Papert) is presented in following
chapters.

The impulse to develop interactive learning environments came directly
out of the development of time-sharing systems. In 1964-65, Cliff Shaw
at the Rand Corporation developed a conversational (that is, interactive
and interpreter-based) programming language, JOSS. Within two weeks of
his describing JOSS to a technical audience at BBN (Bolt, Beranek, and
Newman, Inc.), the programmers there had a local version running, which
served as the basis of TELCOMP. BBN tried to use this system to sell time
shared computer services to engineers. The attempt was unsuccessful, even
though the potential utility was clear. Feurzeig asked himself if one could
seize the opportunity presented by such interactive computation to communicate powerful mathematical ideas to students. With a little support,

originally from the US Office of Education, he put model 33 teletypes in a school to explore to what extent kids would be interested in working with this new technology and whether they would learn anything from it. (More detail of these developments can be found in Feurzeig, 1984.) When the results were positive, Feurzeig was able to extend his research under an existing grant from the Office of Naval Research. Subsequent major support for Logo research at BBN came from the National Science Foundation.

With the good success of the preliminary school trials – using a language designed for professional programmers, scientists, and engineers – Feurzeig next asked whether one might not have considerably better results using a language designed specifically for this purpose. At the suggestion of BBN Associates Daniel Bobrow (then finishing his doctorate at MIT) and Cynthia Solomon (who had recently joined BBN from MIT), Seymour Papert was brought in from the MIT AI Lab as a consultant to help Feurzeig design an education-oriented, conversational programming language. Logo, a dialect of Lisp with much of Lisp's list processing power and recursive functionality, but with a simpler syntax to make it more accessible to children, was the result of this collaboration. Papert wrote the functional specification for Logo. English language-oriented list processing, seen in Feurzeig's Chapter 2, was the first kind of material developed within the Logo computer-based education community. The specific goal of initial Logo research and teaching work was to help school children develop a more profound understanding of important mathematical ideas and ways of thinking.

Several years later, when proposals were written for creating the MIT Logo Laboratory, the objective of teaching children more general thinking skills through programming was added to the original goals. It was during this period that Mike Paterson, a British graduate student at MIT, suggested that having a computer-controlled robot, like the robot-turtle of Grey Walter, would make computers even more interesting for kids. Because an unintelligent, free-standing robot has no extrinsic frame of reference, the body-centered commands of turtle geometry were the most natural to use.[7] The psychological dimension of Logo, as represented by Papert's claim that Logo programming would lead children to more explicit and a

---

[7] Papert (1971a) wrote "At MIT we use the name 'turtle' for small computer controlled vehicles, equipped with various kinds of sense, voice, and writing organs." For an elegant discussion of the possibilities of such devices, see the recent collection of his own earlier papers by Braitenberg in the book *Vehicles*. Such floor turtles were built for research at MIT and BBN, and commercially by GTI (General Turtle, Inc., a private company no longer in existence).

better articulated reflection on their own cognitive processes and that this, in turn, would affect the character of their cognitive development, was in fact a late conceptual reformulation. It has three bases. First is the ability to create new procedures interactively. This capability Logo inherits directly from Lisp. Second is the child's ability to simulate the movement of the robot turtle with his own body movement, and thus assimilate knowledge about turtle geometry to his very own, long-developing sensory motor knowledge. The third basis is the notion that – because he creates them – Logo procedures concretely represent what the person thinks. The conclusion is the thesis that the child will be better able to reflect on the nature of his own thought – as concretized in procedures. The fact that the cognitive claims were a reformulation does not deny that the new appreciation of Logo was a significant change. In his characteristic way, Papert asked "What is potentially profound among the possibilities this technology offers education?" It was in the context of such concerns and such notions that the idea of computer-based microworlds developed.

5.0 MICROWORLDS AND INSTRUCTION

What – if anything – *is* profound in the notion of computer-based microworlds as applied in education? Papert has proposed computer-based microworlds as a general solution to the problem of motivation in education. One perspective in which this makes sense describes the essential situation of instruction as a dilemma (Lawler, 1984):

> "Given Piaget's view that learning is a primary, natural function of the healthy mind, we might consider instruction in any narrow sense unnecessary. Children (and older students of life as well) learn the lessons of the world, effectively if not cheerfully, because reality is the medium through which important objectives are achieved. Nevertheless, in certain situations children often rebel against the lessons society says they must learn. Thus the educator's ideal of inspiring and nuturing the love of learning frequently is reduced to motivating indifferent or reluctant students to learn what full functioning in our society requires.
>
> Teachers face a dilemma when they try to move children to do school work that is not intrinsically interesting. Children must be induced to undertake the work either by promise of reward or threat of punishment, and in neither case do they focus on the material to be learned. Kurt Lewin notes that, in this sense, the work is construed as a bad thing, an obstacle blocking the way to reward or a reason for punishment. The ideas of Piaget and

Lewin have led me to state the central problem of education this way: how can we instruct while respecting the self constructive character of mind?"

If computer-based microworlds might help us deal with such a problem, it is worthwhile being clear about what the term has meant.

5.1 Roots of the "Microworlds" Notion

Winograd's thesis (1972), describing his language-understanding program, SHRDLU, used the name "miniworld" for the blocks-world problem domain. In the context of computers, psychology, and education, "microworlds" was first used in the a report of the MIT AI Lab, "The '72 Progress Report" (Minsky & Papert). The term was used there casually to represent a possible multitude of even smaller fragmentations of problem solving domains and the cognitive schemata which might be assumed to develop from interacting with those domains.[8] I took up the term from the '72 Progress Report and used it to refer to cognitive schemata with specific characteristics of activity and interaction. In one private conversation, Minsky went so far as to note that "microworlds", as used in the '72 Progress Report, was a word empty of specific content until my research provided some meaning for the label.[9] This generous observation did not mark the beginnings of Papert's developing a separate use of the term with an alternative

---

[8] For those with an etymological bent, I note that the 1976 supplement to the Oxford English Dictionary informs us that in the fifties "microworld" was a term used by Otto Klein to refer to the atomic system. About the same time W.H. Whyte used "microtheories" to refer to partial, limited theories of systems too complex to be covered under any current framework. "Microworld" was used by the keepers of the London Zoo in the sixties to refer to the specially constructed environments set up for creatures from different parts of the world.

[9] The term appealed to me partly for its literary associations. Once, man was seen as the microcosm reflecting the macrocosm within himself. For me, internal microworlds reflected through the process of their personal reconstruction the external problem domains of the great common world. Taking fully the use of the terms then, to characterize man once more as a microcosm was to make a commitment to a fragmentary view of human mind and to make salient the issue of how the fragments of mind interact for functioning and development within the single being. This image drove my research into the question of how order could be seen to emerge in the ensembles of not-yet directly connected, fragmentary cognitive schemata, after the questions was first raised in such terms by Minsky and emphasized by discussions with H. Austin on the research in his thesis, (Austin, 1976.

meaning: for him, "microworlds" were segregated domains designed with genetic intent. We both used the term variously for a while, each with his local interpretations, recognizing that confusion could be created on a more global application. After Papert gained a broad audience for his book *Mindstorms*, and "microworlds" acquired a public meaning, I adopted "microview" for my preferred characterization of schemata. My use of that term is detailed in Lawler, 1985. I follow Papert's usage in the immediately following discussion.

5.2 Virtual Worlds for Creative Action

Papert's notion focuses on the constructive intent of a created microworld: the essence is to create an environment in which other people can exercise their own creativity. This focus on sub-creation makes computer-based microworlds specifically useful for education. Sub-creation permits a collaboration between the didactic, structuring intentions of society and the inescapable fact that people learn by their own choice; further, it recognizes that learning most frequently derives from people expressing what is important to them within the confines of a medium which both enables and constrains their expression. When the microworld is created with enough structure, it will indicate what objectives and activities are possible. The already created objects and actions will indicate how other objects and actions can be created by their composition of the system primitives. That is, the microworld is educationally useful because it is rich both in comprehensible working examples and in potential for creation. The knowledge of the microworlds will be especially useful if it conforms in a straightforward way to relations in the domains of common experience.

5.3 Virtual Worlds with Transitional Objects

Papert explains the role of the agent in a computer-based microworld as a "transitional object" because it can help a person whose mind is not capable or inclined to think in the ways of formal thought to become engaged with objectives and objects which permit the incremental development of skills resulting in the ability to manipulate formal descriptions. Objects of these microworlds, then, are neither fish nor fowl; they share properties both with the formal objects of science and the more concrete objects of common sense experience. What permits computer-based microworlds to function as transitional objects is their being embedded in a medium whose manipulation is generally controlled by formal rules of transformation. What permits their engaging character is the quasi-concrete instantiations of computational objects which can be taken as symbols by a person.

The intention is not to manifest intelligence in a machine but to use a machine to help a person make himself more intelligent. The function of the transitional object in the microworld is analogous to one that is served by the therapist in Freudian analysis, who supports the patient in forming a temporary attachment with the analyst as a means of working out the patient's existing problems. The hope is that the patient will be freed for fuller functioning in a world in which the therapist is to play no part. Such a description could also apply to the role of a mentor. To subsume the role of objects in the same scheme is unusual. But more, the notion of a "transitional object" in the psychology of education is a contribution because it helps us understand how people can come to learn what they don't already know.[10] People can become engaged with computational objects which they interpret as symbols for real objects. But they can only manipulate those computational objects by means of a computer language. Doing so engages them in the nitty-gritty effort of learning a set of operations which transform the states of the objects, and this gives them everyday experience with the surface details of a formal system, whose deeper properties they can gradually come to appreciate.

If such notions are sound and deep, why have they not been more effective? Why is it the case that there are very few "microworlds" being created?

6.0 MINIWORLDS AND MICROWORLDS

"But 'Glory' doesn't mean 'a nice knock-down argument,'" Alice objected. "When *I* use a word," Humpty Dumpty said, in a rather scornful tone, "it means just what I choose it to mean – neither more nor less." "The question is," said Alice, "whether you *can* make words mean so many different things." "The question is," said Humpty Dumpty, "which is to be master – that's all." [11]

If the notions discussed are sound but no one is making microworlds, there must be reasons. "Microworlds" has served as a passable label, but

---

[10] The classic discussion of this problem is in the *Meno*. For a related discussion of the interrelation of objects, objectives, and learning, see "The Development of Objectives", Chapter 1 of Lawler (1985).

[11] From *Through the Looking Glass and What Alice Found There*. I recommend the version appearing in *The Annotated Alice*, edited by Martin Gardner, in which see his citation from Carroll's *Symbolic Logic* and his comments on the need to balance terminological definition with established usage. But then I, as you will see, agree with Alice.

the term does little work for us, because it stands in isolation, unrelated to other ideas in conjunction with which the notions could be better understood and appreciated. That situation can be changed by making a few discriminations which I will shortly propose. The following chapters provide some examples of work that are accepted as involving "microworlds". We have reviewed a bit of the history of the term and examined what appear to be the most profound notions which make it worth distinguishing in the area of AI and Education. I would now like to make a simple proposal for terminological use, one that respects both the history of use, the central notions, and the desire many express for more clarity and discrimination. I will first lay out the set of discriminations involved then use the terminology to discuss some directions for future research that could be important.

We can make useful discriminations about issues that matter to us. Among many possible, I consider these the most important:

- The distinction between what is in the world and in the mind.

- The distinction between the concreteness of experience to the novice and the abstractness of experience to the expert.

Further, we can make these distinctions in a fashion that permits us to emphasize questions central to the science of education:

- How the contents of mind relates to experience.

- How novice and expert appreciate situations differently.

- How current notions of learning through microworlds relate to "concept" oriented theories of learning and teaching.

My first proposal is to make good use of the widely accepted and understood structure implicit in use of the prefixes "micro" and "mini". More specifically, I suggest we should use the term "miniworld" to refer to an object-focussed embodiment of some designed environment, as described by an expert in the domain; and that we use the term "microworld" to refer to partial exploitations of the complete generality of what might be possibile in the miniworld.[12] A concrete example will help clarify what I mean and my intention. Consider the computational environment of sprite

---

[12] This will permit us to distinguish between the potential implicit in the functioning of an I/O device and a collection of programs with some specific implementations of part of that potential. My proposal is conservative in two ways, first because it returns to the "mini-" prefix with which we began

graphics as one miniworld. An expert's description would probably focus on the five (TI Logo) or six (Apple Sprite Logo) state variables of the computational object. The procedures of the BEACH environment described in Chapter 5 would be a microworld. This is a useful distinction because there are many different kinds of things one can do with sprite graphics. As a second example, consider the video-display embodiment of turtle geometry as a miniworld. Then the collection of polyspiral designs might be one microworld. Inspi designs could be another. The procedures have much in common but are remarkably different in the graphics designs that they generate; try 10, 90, and 7 as inputs.

```
TO POLYSPI :s :a :d            TO INSPI :s :a :d
FORWARD :s                     FORWARD :s
RIGHT :a                       RIGHT :a
POLYSPI (:s + :d) :a :d        INSPI :s (:a + :d) :d
END                            END
```

An expert will recognize easily that the procedures of these two microworlds differ only in the term to which an increment is applied. No novice would know that, and most would be quite surprised should they make such a discovery. This slight difference in terminology gives us a way of talking about the differences between the knowledge of the novice and the expert.

The second proposal goes to the heart of the matter. We can't consider education a science until we can say what is in the mind, how that relates to what is in the world, and how what we do affects what is in the mind. I suggest we establish a parallel terminology relating what is in the world to what is in the mind of the individual and to what the practice of education entails.

Consider Figure 1. If a problem domain names a collection of objects and relations with no bias about what is possible within the framework of some specific educational technology, any problem domain represents then an opportunity for the creation of a miniworld: this would be a problem domain viewed as a medium for creative action in which there might be found or created things which could serve as transitional objects. Any miniworld would then have a collection of subordinate microworlds each of which realized some of the potential goals for action possible with the objects of the miniworld.

(when micros were just a gleam in an engineer's eye), and because it is based on a distinction Papert and I once entertained in private conversation, a distinction which we later did not apply as we well might have.

IN THE PERSON   IN THE WORLD

               IN DESIGNED   OBJECTS and STATE
               ENVIRONMENTS   VARIABLES

IDEAS   CHARACTERIZATIONS
               - uniform data structures
               - groupment correspondent structures
               - closure of object creation

CONCEPTIONS   INTERRELATIONS
               - list processing and procedure definition
               - floor and video display turtle geometry
               - static and dynamic turtle geometry
               - robotics and dynamic control of static objects

CONCEPTS   MINIWORLDS
               - list manipulation   list elements, lisp operations
               - procedure definition   list elements, lisp operations
               - floor turtle geometry   robot turtle, pen, location,
                                            heading, physical access
               - video turtle geometry   video turtle, pen, location,
                                            heading, no physical access
               - dynamic turtle geometry location, heading, pen, spin
               - sprite graphics   30 sprites, number, location,
                                            heading, shape, color, speed
               - Lego/Logo devices   Legos, sensors, motors,
                                            sensing, power control

MICROVIEWS   MICROWORLDS: a few examples
               - sentence generators
               - sprite based word worlds
               - text manipulation
               - list based language drills
               - geometric designs
               - target shooting games
               - drawing interfaces
               - child-designed arithmetic CAI
               - multiple representations for algorithms
               - algebra workbench

FIGURE 1: A Multitude of "–Worlds"

A prominent characteristic of novices is the particularity of their interpretations of experience. The novice approaches experience at the level of specific interactions with the some microworld of the miniworld. Supposing that experience has some impact on him, we may further suppose the novice reconstructs within his mind some cognitive structure which embodies aspects of the experience important to him. I would, for consistency with my own use in *Computer Experience and Cognitive Development*, use "microview" to name those sorts of cognitive structures developed by novices from their interactions with microworlds. After experience with one or more of the microworlds of that miniwowrld, the novice will be able to form a concept[13] of the miniworld, which would be achieved through a coordination of the relevant microviews.

Let's suppose then that the student, a novice no longer, encounters microworlds of both the floor turtle and the video-display turtle miniworlds. With sufficiently well-developed concepts of both miniworlds, he may begin to form conceptions about the similarities and differences between these miniworlds. He may, as he becomes progressively more expert, develop abstract ideas about the character of these miniworlds and their relations, such as the central importance to learnability of the groupment structure of turtle geometry's operations[14] or the closure property of mathematical

---

[13] "Concept" is a term whose use may cause more trouble than its avoidance, because it has so often been used in the vaguest of senses. In Webster's Synonomy, we find standard and acceptably precise uses of the term, as follows: "CONCEPT applies in logic to the idea of a thing which the mind conceives after knowing many instances of the genus, species, or other category, and which is devoid of all details except those that are typical or generic... In more general use, the term applies to any formulated or widely accepted idea of what a thing should be;... CONCEPTION is often used in place of concept in this latter sense; in fact, it is sometimes preferred by those who wish to keep concept as a technical term of logic..." I would be content using miniview to represent a specific kind of concept relating microviews of microworlds in a miniworld, but I hesitate to drive systematicity to the point of obfuscation. We have to stop somewhere – or would we want to end up with *eine kliene weltanshauung*?

[14] A strategy suggested at the 1985 Exeter conference on AI and Education by Professor Groen (McGill University) for exploiting this characteristic mentioned by Papert in Chapter 7 of *Mindstorms*. Similarly, Professor Thompson (Illinois State University) defines "Mathematical Microworlds", in his paper of the same title, as collections of objects, relations, and of operations composing and transforming the other elements into elements of the same types. Noticing this characteristic is clearly appropriate for mathematical microworlds but the characterization might not apply so well to other kinds.

microworlds proposed by Thompson. We need such a balanced terminology to discuss what is in the world, what is in the mind, and what we hope to design. And we need a vocabulary which permits descriptions of things which concern us and their relations. If this proposal lacks somewhat the elegance of those formulations that focus on the simplicity and comprehensiveness of an expert's view, it has the important virtue of coming to grips with the nitty-gritty details of learning envirnoments at the level at which they are encountered by novices. This is necessary for them to be effective – and that's what we want, after all.

7.0 THE NEAR HORIZON

In the next five years, according to a survey of informed opinion (Lawler, 1986), the primary candidates for significant hardware changes are the availability of kneetop machines of significant power and massive online storage through optical digital disks. Further, the main limitation to progress will be the software development bottleneck. The storage capacity and computing capacity are important for enabling change, indeed, but the newly emerging role of the computer as a general I/O device controller is a change of character. For example, the IBM Handy System[15] reveals itself primarily as a system through which a child can write script-like programs to control a menagerie of devices: audio output, speech generation, and videodisc as well as the more common I/O devices such as printers and video displays. Application developers of compact optical disks hope to turn the home audio system into an entertainment complex, which will be as programmable as anyone could want. Of course, the more complex the software, the greater will be the development burden and price of any programmed product. Although we have been disappointed so far in the limited role played in education by the development of microworlds, in the next wave of system development for education, there will remain a significant role for miniworld and microworld design. Unless people, and especially children, gain a measure of technical control over the computational medium, its promise for education will remain quite limited.

7.1 Creating New Miniworlds: An Example

Making miniworlds amounts to exploiting possible input-output devices to make virtual worlds with transitional objects for creative self-construction. Consider the most recent miniworld candidate being developed with the participation of MIT Logo Project: the Lego/Logo effort. The first attraction of joining Legos and Logo is that one can imagine child-constructible

---

[15] An education system prototype developed by D. Nix at the IBM Watson Research Center.

floor turtles.[16] But the charm of the marriage is in fact different: one can build any sorts of machines that operate with sensors and effectors under programmed control. Logo, the language, isn't changed much by the activation of a few primitives suitable for controlling the output devices or handling signals from the input devices (such even existed in the early PDP-11 Logo versions for those floor turtles which had sensors then). What is NEW is what can be done with the devices. The floor turtle was a constructed device controllable by a programmable computer. Lego devices under Logo control can be ANY device constructible from Legos for which sense information and power control are relevant.

7.2 Creating New Miniworlds: Obvious Possibilities

- One direction clearly worth exploring is the resuscitation of devices whose promise has not been realized. Two outstanding examples are the Perlman/Hillis Slot-Machine[17] and the Minsky/Hillis 2500.[18]

- If computers will play the role of multi-media controllers, a systematic analysis of what primitives are appropriate for control functions would be quite appropriate – this could even involve a focus on feedback loops and simultaneous, asynchronous processes. These themes are historically and currently premier issues for AI.

---

[16] This realizes a long-standing ambition, as noted under a picture of an early robot turtle (Papert, 1971b), "one of our turtles, so called in honor of a famous species of cybernetic animal made by Grey Walter, an English neurophysiologist. Grey Walter's turtle had life-like behavior patterns built into its wiring diagram. Ours have no behavior except the ability to obey a few simple commands from a computer to which they are connected by a wire that plugs into a control box that connects to a telephone line that speaks to the computer.... If you'd like to make a fancier turtle you might use a radio link. But we'd like turtles to be cheap enough for every kid to play with one."

[17] Perlman (1974) describes a predecessor of the Slot Machine, built by Hillis and others. I know of no adequate documentation of this device by its designers, but there exist some notes about its use in my experiments at MIT (see pp. 172-176 in Lawler, 1985).

[18] The primary interest of this machine today is the spin primitive suggested by Hillis and built into the machine by Minsky. The spin command set the dynamic turtle rotating with a constant angular velocity. I have seen a ten year old construct a model of the solar system in a few hours with this system. I have programmed models of pistons driven by a rotating cam shaft on the machine.

- A central area for exploration is access to complex text databases, image databanks, and libraries of film and videotape. What is the new "I/O" implicated? Compact digital disk and videodisc now. What is the transitional object? Possibly an anthropomorphized "librarian", an agent who could introduce children to the notion of search in many different ways.

- Large databases and image databanks not only present problems of search – but of knowledge organization. Tools such as the existing "Notecards" product of Xerox (an extension of the "Annoland" described by Brown, 1985) provide an image of how somewhat more accessible facilities could permit the development of a "scholar's work station" for children – permitting them to develop an explicit and well-articulated organization of complex material that might otherwise get away from them. Use of such a "hypertext" system could affect the way they understand information and its organization. One research project I began but could not complete at the *Centre Mondial* was exploring ways in which children could and would construct indices into video disc image banks.

- Local networks provide now the possibility of multi-user applications. In a 1982 talk at the New York Academy of Sciences, Dwyer reported the development of a "Star Trek" game developed for and by high school students at his Solo Project with interacting micros on a local communication network. Such networks will become progressively more common. They could serve as the basis for social science simulations – run by children and not run as an incomprehensible model of equations undergoing simultaneous solution.[19]

7.3 Creating New Miniworlds: Some Questions to Ask

The essential task is one of engineering at a very high level of abstraction in the domain of knowledge itself. After examining important fields of knowledge,

- Ask what candidates for transitional objects exist for that domain.

- Ask how to describe completely the state of the transitional object(s).

- Ask what actions or transformations of the object could be interesting and how they might be best described.

---

[19] An interesting example is the International Conflict Simulation, developed by Michigan Professors F. Goodman (School of Education) and E. Taylor (Political Science), exemplifies how such activities can move into schools.

- Ask how there can be created an environment for those objects which will provide students the opportunity to be creative.

- Ask how the knowledge developed through such experiences can be assimilated to the systems of common sense knowledge which a student might be expected to bring with him.

7.4 Creating New Microworlds: A Few Suggestions

- For current curriculum: design an alternative curriculum based on multiple microworlds; this is no small task for any area of study.

- Rethink the content and rationale of current curriculum. An extensive example is found in *Turtle Geometry* by Abelson and DiSessa (1983). A shorter example is sketched in "Logo and Intelligent Videodisc Applications for Pre-readers". (Lawler & Papert, 1985). The point to observe here is the depth at which curriculum should be examined.

- Increase the systematicity of domain analysis. See Chapter 5 for an example.

- Take guidance from children and your own taste. Can you make things that you enjoy? That others enjoy? Creating microworlds is work as much for artists and toymakers as it is for teachers.

Schools represent an important and interesting challenge within our society. But there are education problems and opportunities beyond the schools, both here and in many other parts of the world. I believe an important future direction of development will be the creation of microworlds based on common miniworlds, embodying the same ideas and techniques, but altered for use in ways congenial to different people in different parts of the world. The BEACH and XEW microworlds of Chapter 5 provide such an example. A second frontier will be addressing individual differences through constructing alternative miniworlds and microworlds for people with differing primary modes of understanding. (The issue of multiple modes of mind is addressable but beyond addressing here. For an appreciation of the issues in the multiple modes of mind, see Hadamard, 1945, or Chapter 5 in Lawler, 1985.)

Miniworlds and microworlds may have once been perceived as a "technical fix" for problems in education. They are not. They are, however, a better way to approach education when it is seen as the self-construction of mind, guided by our shared knowledge of the world and our perceived social needs.

Rather than going back to basics we can go a better way, forward to a focus on deeper knowledge and better understanding, developed in an engaging environment, whose primary motivation is what's most profound in human learning, the impulse to understanding through creation. Such is the hope. The disappointments of the past decade are real. But they are not insurmountable to educators and engineers with the concern to understand knowledge and people and with the skill to build the best environments for growing human minds. The near horizon is a frontier. Come along. There's much to be done. The children of the future need us today.

REFERENCES

Abelson, H., & DiSessa, A. (1980). *Turtle Geometry*. Cambridge, MA: MIT Press.

Austin, H. (1976). *A Computational Model of the Acquisition of Physical Skills*. MIT Doctoral Thesis, unpublished.

Brown, J.S. (1985). Process versus product: a perspective on tools for communal and informal electronic learning. *Journal of Educational Computing Research*, Vol.1 (2).

Braitenberg, V. (1985) *Vehicles*. Cambridge, MA: MIT Press.

DeCorte, E., & Verschaffel, L. (1985). Computers and learning thinking. In J. Heene and T. Plomp (Eds.), *Teaching and Information Technology:* Review of an SVO/COD Symposium, 195-206. (Selecta Series.) Gravenhage: Foundation for Research in Instruction.

Dray, J. & Menosky, J. (1983) "Computers and a New World Order" in *Technology Review*, (published at MIT in May/June 1983).

Feurzeig, W. (1984). The Logo lineage. In Steve Ditla (Ed.), *Digital Deli*. New York: Workman Press.

Hadamard, J. (1945). *The Psychology of Invention in the Mathematical Field*. Republished by Dover Publications, New York.

Lawler, R. (1977). "Turtle: Learning by Doing". *Unpublished* MIT Logo Project working paper.

Lawler, R. (1984). Designing computer based microworlds. In M. Yazdani (Ed.), *New Horizons in Educational Technology*. The article was originally published in *BYTE* Magazine's special issue on the Logo programming language (August, 1982).

Lawler, R. (1985). *Computer Experience and Cognitive Development*. New York: John Wiley, Inc. Chapter 1, "The Development of Objectives" appeared as a Logo internal paper in 1977.

Lawler, R., & Papert, S. (1985). Logo and videodisc applications for pre-readers. *Journal of Educational Computing Research*, Vol.1(1).

Lawler, R. DuBoulay, B. Hughes, M., & MacLeod, H. (1986). *Cognition and Computers*. New York: John Wiley, Inc.

Lawler, R. (1986). Promising areas for research and the development of prototypes. Report of a survey conducted for an OECD working group (Organization for Economic Cooperation and Development). A revised version of this report will be published in Volume 2 of *Artificial Intelligence and Education*.

Minsky, M., & Papert, S. (1972). The '72 progress report. Originally appearing as a MIT AI Lab Memo, the report was republished with the title *Artificial Intelligence* by the University of Oregon Press.

Papert, S. (1971a). Teaching children thinking. *Logo Memo 2*. Papert's papers are available from the Epistemology and Learning Group at the MIT Arts and Media Technology Center. Cambridge, MA 02139.

Papert, S., & Solomon, C. (1971b). Twenty things to do with a computer. *Logo Memo 3*.

Papert, S. (1973). Uses of technology to enhance education. *Logo Memo 8*.

Papert, S. (1980). *Mindstorms: Children, Computers, and Powerful Ideas*. New York: Basic Books.

Papert, S. (1985). Computer criticism versus technocentric thinking. *Theoretical Papers: Logo 85*. Reprinted in *Educational Researcher, 16*, 1, January-February 1987.

Perlman, R. (1974). TORTIS: toddler's own recursive turtle interpreter system. *Logo Memo 9*.

Piaget, J. (1971). *The Science of Education and the Psychology of the Child*. Translated from the French by Derek Coltman. New York: The Viking Press.

Plato (1953). Meno. *Dialogues of Plato*, Vol.1. Translated by B. Jowett. Oxford University Press, 4th Edition.

Stockman, D. (1987). *The Triumph of Politics*. New York: Avon Books.

Thompson, P. (1987). Mathematical microworlds and intelligent CAI. *Artificial Intelligence and Instruction*. Reading, MA: Addison-Wesley.

Winograd, T. (1972). *Understanding Natural Language*. New York: Academic Press.

2 ALGEBRA SLAVES AND AGENTS IN A LOGO-BASED MATHEMATICS CURRICULUM

Wallace Feurzeig

BBN Laboratories
10 Moulton Street
Cambridge, MA 02238

ABSTRACT

For many students the ideas and methods of algebra appear obscure and mysterious, their sense and purpose unclear, and their applicability to anything genuinely real or interesting very remote. Students often fail to acquire an understanding of the key concepts, despite their inherent simplicity. Even when they gain the notion of variables, expressions and equations, students often lack the strategic knowledge required to motivate and direct the global planning and detailed execution of an attack on a problem. These conceptual and strategic difficulties are compounded by the needs for precise performance of the arithmetic and symbolic operations required in manipulating expressions. Extended operations, like subtracting an expression from both sides of an equation or expanding a product of three terms, are very difficult for beginning students. Their buggy performance in carrying out the detailed manipulative work greatly confounds and frustrates their acquisition and assimilation of the most important and central ideas.

We plan to confront these difficulties and show how they can be overcome. We are developing a Logo-based introductory algebra course for sixth graders. Our approach has three major components:

- Students are introduced to algebra through Logo programming work on projects such as generating gossip, making and breaking secret codes, and writing movie or sports quizzes, in modules with algebraically rich contexts whose content is meaningful and compelling to students.

- Concrete iconic representations of algebraic objects and manipulations are used to introduce and motivate standard algebraic notation. We are implementing two such environments: a marbles and bags microworld (where bags contain an unknown number of marbles), and an icon Logo in which procedures and functions are represented as machines which may have inputs and an output, and which can be composed and run.

- In extended problem solving, the student will be able to focus solely on the strategic work. An expert instructional system, the algebra workbench, is being developed to serve as the student's agent and tutor in performing the required algebraic operations.

Our approach depends centrally on the use of Logo programming ideas and activities. The Logo work spans the entire introductory course, covering the essential content of the traditional ninth grade course, e.g., Variables and Expressions; Equations and Inequalities; Functions; and Algebra Story Problems. However, the key algebra ideas and methods are introduced and developed in the context of Logo programming, and the Logo sequences used in these developments often depart significantly in approach, mode of presentation and mathematical depth from the corresponding topics in the traditional course.

Activities with the algebra workbench and the icon laboratory environments will be an integral part of the work throughout. The marble bag microworld will provide beginning students a laboratory environment for constructing and manipulating algebraic expressions in a concrete and transparent representation. Students will work on "marble bag stories" to explore the meaning and behavior of algebraic expressions in this iconic representation. The correspondence of marble bag representation and manipulations to equivalent English and standard algebra notation and work is shown by the simultaneous display of all three representations. The icon Logo laboratory will be used to introduce Logo programming in a clear graphic fashion. It will make the structure and behavior of Logo program (including the operation of Logo control structures in multi-level procedures) even more transparent. It will also be used as a modeling tool in the difficult area of algebra story problems, to clarify the process of building and combining the structural components leading to solutions.

The algebra workbench will employ a set of powerful symbolic manipulation tools for performing the standard manipulations of high school algebra. It will have two main modes of use: demonstration mode, which uses an expert tutor program to solve algebra problems incrementally, explaining its strategy and its step by step operations in straightforward terms along the way; and practice mode, in which the student tries to solve a problem with the assistance of the tutor, which performs the operations requested by the student at each step and which can be called at any point to advise the student of the correctness of a step, to perform or explain any step, to evaluate the student's solution, or to perform a problem that she poses.

These powerful aids make it possible to effectively separate out the difficulties in performing the formal and manipulative aspects of algebra work from those encountered in learning the central conceptual and strategic content. Distinctly different kinds of instructional tools and activities – Logo programming, expert tutors, or algebra microworlds – can thus be brought to bear where each is most appropriate and effective. The project is supported by the National Science Foundation under a grant to Lesley College with a subcontract to Bolt, Beranek, and Newman, Inc.

1.0 INTRODUCTION

We plan to introduce and develop the key and central concepts of algebra – variable, formal expression, function, equation, inverse – in terms of Logo ideas and programming activities. Many projects will be centered on areas of interest to students, e.g., developing programs to generate gossip, Knock-Knock jokes, or secret codes. These will lead in a natural way to projects that address the standard content of introductory algebra. For example, work on writing programs to generate conversational dialogs will provide a starting point for projects on generating algebra story problem quizzes.

The Logo knowledge and skills required to develop the programs will be taught along the way, as an integral part of the project work. Students will only be expected to write programs with relatively simple structures – they will be given the more difficult Logo procedures needed for building complex programs. Also, we will introduce an iconic representation of Logo programs as function machines that can be inspected, connected together in various ways, and run. This multi-level graphic representation shows the procedure structure of complex programs with great clarity. It should greatly aid students' understanding of Logo's control structure and semantics and help them in the process of program design and construction.

There are several reasons for giving Logo a central role in the course. Our experience is that building mathematical structures is a uniquely valuable way of understanding them. Programming is the tool of choice for building algebraic objects and processes because of its interactivity and generality and Logo is the programming language of choice because of its essential mathematical character (e.g., its recursive functional structures which account for its power and elegance) together with its easy accessiblity to beginning students of mathematics. A related consideration is that the experience of creating problems, equations or functions gives great insight as to how to analyze, manipulate and solve them. In the traditional school math course, students are always asked to solve or transform complex constructs, never to construct or create them. The use of Logo makes it possible to show very concretely the value of doing as a clue to undoing in many algebraic contexts. The theme of building objects and processes as a precursor and aid to undoing and solving them occurs repeatedly throughout the course. Some of the Logo teaching modules used in the course are described in Sections 2 and 4.

Logo programming activities have paramount importance in the teaching of algebra concepts and problem solving strategies but we are working with other kinds of instructional tools as well. The students' programming projects are complemented by the use of a graphic microworld, the marble bags microworld, specially designed to introduce the algebraic manipulation of expressions and equations through a very concrete iconic representation.

The objects in this microworld are pictures of marbles and bags (bags contain some unknown number of marbles); the operations include addition or subtraction of specified numbers of bags or marbles, and multiplication or division of the current collection by a specified integer. Students are introduced to marble bag stories and diagrams. They are shown how to create and solve simple marble bag stories (story problems). They are introduced to standard algebraic notation as a rapid way of writing marble bag stories. As a student works on a problem, the system can show the correspondence between the iconic, English, and standard algebraic representations of the operations and results. The marble bag microworld will be further described and illustrated in Section 3.

The marble bag microworld and the Logo modules on equations and functions provide strong introductions to algebra expression manipulation and problem solving strategies. Students will have a firm understanding of the meaning of algebraic expressions but relatively little experience in dealing with problems involving extended expressions and requiring extensive symbolic manipulation. Problems such as simplifying algebraic expressions whose terms have many factors, transforming complex expressions into canonical form, factoring polynomials, determining whether two expressions are equivalent and solving systems of two simultaneous linear equations greatly strain the newly acquired fragile manipulative skills of beginning students. The task of consolidating and extending their strategic skills is greatly complicated by the need to carry out the associated manipulations at the same time.

The use of another kind of instructional tool based on an expert symbol manipulation program enables the strategic and manipulative components to be effectively separated. We plan to develop such an expert instructional system, the algebra workbench. In practice mode, when the student works on a problem, the system will serve as his agent or slave by carrying out the algebraic operations he requests, enabling him to focus on the strategic planning and the operational decisions. The system will also include an expert algebra tutor. The tutor will be available to advise the student and critique the student's work. In demonstration mode, the tutor will work through a problem, explaining its strategy and actions along the way. The student will be able to intervene and propose alternative steps. Our tentative design plan for the algebra workbench is described, and its use is illustrated, in Section 5.

The course will thus employ three distinctly different kinds of instructional facilities – Logo programming, an algebra microworld, and an expert tutoring system. A comprehensive mathematics program with serious learning goals requires all three. In Section 6 we discuss the educational strengths and limitations of programming, microworlds and "intelligent" tutors, and suggest some ways their capabilities might be extended.

2.0 FROM ENGLISH TO ALGEBRA

We begin the course by having students work on programming tasks that seem to them to be part of the subject of English rather than math. There are two main reasons for this. Students have a great deal of knowledge of the formal structure of English, but relatively little real knowledge and experience of mathematical structures. We can build on their knowledge of English structure as a starting point for developing the idea of algebraic structure. Along the way, it is easy to find linguistic tasks that have more than a little interest for students. The first unit in this module is the development of Logo programs to generate gossip.

The initial version of gossip presented to the students is a Logo program that randomly selects a name from a list of names, randomly selects an action from a list of actions, and then puts the name and action together as a sentence and ouputs it. The program is:

```
to gossip
output (sentence who doeswhat)
end
```

where who and doeswhat are the following Logo procedures.

```
to who
output pick [sam jane sally bill chris]
end

to doeswhat
output pick [cheats [loves to sing] giggles
[talks your ears off] [likes smelly feet]]
end
```

To run gossip, say five times, one types:

```
repeat 5 [print gossip]
```

and Logo responds with

```
jane talks your ears off
sally giggles
bill loves to sing
chris likes smelly feet
sally loves to sing
```

or some of the other constructed sentences embedded in the procedures.

The Logo procedure pick, which does the random selection from its associated list, is given to the students as a primitive. The other procedures, gossip, who and doeswhat, are intended as models for the students. When their operation is understood, students modify and extend these in projects to create their own gossip. First, they rewrite who and doeswhat using their own name and action lists. Then, they extend gossip so that it includes two actors and takes the form who doeswhat towhom. Further extensions generate more complex sentence structures involving noun phrases and verb phrases and, later, perhaps, noun phrases with embedded verb phrases. To vary the form of their productions, students can write a supergossip procedure which uses pick to randomly select a different one of the several varied gossip procedures they have written, each time generating a new sentence.

Icon machine Logo is introduced from the start. The icon machine picture of the two-person gossip procedure, for example, looks like this.

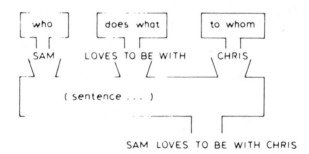

Figure 1. The Gossip Machine

The picture shows the internal structure of the gossip machine, whose parts include the who, doeswhat, towhom, and sentence machines. The who, doeswhat, and towhom machines have an output (called a spout in icon machine notation) but no inputs. These kinds of machines are called sources. Machines with one or more inputs (referred to as hoppers in icon machine notation) but with no output, are called destinations. Machines with neither inputs nor output are called solos. Machines like sentence (a Logo primitive in this case) which have one or more inputs and an output as well, are called processors. Sources can input to destinations or processors and processors can input to other processors as well as to destinations. Thus, complex Logo procedures can be diagrammed as icon machines in a way that shows their structure very clearly. The correspondence between Logo machine diagrams and Logo program text is one-to-one. The icon machine notation is due to Paul Goldenberg, one of my colleagues on the Logo algebra project. Students are next shown how to write interactive procedures in Logo. This enables them to create programs that communicate with a user in activities such as exchanging Knock-Knock jokes. Their programs generate dialogs such as:

```
Person:      Knock-Knock
Computer:    Who's there?
Person:      Miss
Computer:    Miss who?
Person:      Mississippi
Computer:    Ha Ha Ha Ha
             Now it's my turn!
             Knock-Knock
Person:      Who's there?
Computer:    Boo
Person:      Boo who?
Computer:    There, there, don't cry, baby
```

The student enables the computer to become a participant by writing a procedure that stores a list of the Knock-Knock jokes acquired by the computer from previous games with students. When it is the computer's turn to tell a Knock-Knock joke, it uses the Logo pick procedure to select a joke at random from this database.

Students are then prepared to write interactive quiz programs of various kinds. They generate quizzes in areas of individual interest such as movies, food, cars, sports and music. The students enjoy having their classmates try their programs, especially when others have difficulty answering their questions. However, around this time the kids begins to wonder if they are in an English course or an algebra course, and sometimes sound as though they are being deprived of the math they were promised, even though they often dislike math! Some even suggest the idea of writing mathematics quiz programs. They see that they can write programs that generate sentences in math instead of English, e.g., sentences such as 72 - 29 = ? They are shown how to randomly generate all the standard forms of arithmetic problems for use in quizzes.

Their programs combine English and arithmetic phrases to generate arithmetic story problems such as:

```
I GET 3 PIES
I GIVE AWAY 4 FISH
```

```
I WIN 7 ELEPHANTS
I TAKE 5 CAKES
I SELL 8 MARSHMALLOWS
HOW MANY THINGS DO I HAVE NOW?
```

In this program, pick is used to randomly select the names of the objects, the numbers, and the addition and subtraction words from associated lists.

At this point the students are given the project of writing algebra quiz programs that present problems such as:

```
5 X BOX + 4 = 49
What is the value of BOX?
```

This brings up a critical difficulty, however. They do not know how to solve such algebra problems – how, then, will they be able to tell whether the answers given by the users are correct? We show them a "trick" that will enable their program to know the correst answers, even though the students do not know how to solve the problems. Their program will choose three numbers at random, say 3, 7 and 4. It will then compute 3 X 7 + 4 to get 25, conceal the 7, and output the problem 3 X + 4 = 25 whose answer the program knows to be 7. Thus, the program can pose a problem to users and evaluate the correctness of their answers even though the student who has written the program could not do so himself.

In their initial programs students usually program responses such as THAT IS WRONG to incorrect answers, some adding epithets such as DUMMY, KNUCKLEBRAIN or STUPIDHEAD. If they have a real-time clock available they sometimes append helpful remarks such as

```
BESIDES, IT TOOK YOU 23 SECONDS AND
THAT IS REAL SLOW, KID.
```

In the ensuing development they are urged to program more informative and helpful responses, for example, to show the user that his answer is indeed wrong. On the next round, the typical responses are of the form

```
6 CAN'T BE THE RIGHT ANSWER BECAUSE 3 X 6 + 4 = 22
AND 22 IS NOT 25 IS IT?
```

They are urged to be even more helpful. A little later their programs may produce responses such as

```
6 IS TOO SMALL. THE ANSWER MUST BE BIGGER BECAUSE
25 IS BIGGER THAN 22
```

To give students further insight leading to the realization that there exists a formal procedure for solving linear equations, we go back to work on subproblems of simpler forms, such as BOX + 3 = 10 then 4 X BOX = 20. When they return to progressively harder problems students work with "big" numbers as coefficients and incorporate signed numbers. Some succeed in working out the general algorithm, though we do not count on that happening.

A preliminary version of this unit was tested in early Logo teaching experiments with seventh grade students in the middle mathematics track of a junior high school in Lexington, Massachusetts (Feurzeig et al., 1969). This work established the effectiveness of preceding the formal work on algebra equation solving by work on formal English language tasks already meaningful to students. It also showed that students could acquire the required level of competence in Logo programming. Transcripts of two student program runs from the last phase of that work are reproduced in Figures 2 and 3.

The program MULTEACH (Figure 2) shows one of the wonderful things that often happened with this algebra quiz activity – the intense engagement of the students and the injection of their personalities into their work through the mixing of English text with the algebra. This student was regarded as highly mathophobic. As the transcript shows, however, he was capable of doing significant math in the context of Logo.

```
-MULTEACH
4 * /BOX/ = 20
WHAT IS /BOX/?
*5
VERY GOOD. YOUR A SMART LITTLE DEVIL. BUT YOU TOOK 3 SECONDS
WOULD YOU LIKE TO NO MORE
*YES
ITS BEEN LIKE THIS, YOU SEE ALONG TIME AGO MY MOTHER SAID I WAS NOT
AGING LIKE ALL THE OTHERS, SO WE GOT A CUPUTER DOCTOR TO HELP ME, AND
HE DID. SO. NOW YOU NO WHY I AM SO OLD
8 * /BOX/ = 32
WHAT IS /BOX/?
*4
VERY GOOD. YOUR A SMART LITTLE DEVIL. BUT YOU TOOK 2 SECONDS
WOULD YOU LIKE TO NO MORE
*NO
BOY ITS NOT OFTEN YOU HERE A STORY LIKE MINE, BUT SINCE YOU DO NOT I
NOW RETURN YOU TO YOUR SO CALLED HUMAN FUN HA HA HA
8 * /BOX/ = 48
WHAT IS /BOX/?
*8
/BOX/ IS 6
IF YOU THINK YOUR SO SMART WHY DID YOU GET IT WRONG. OR WHERE YOU
THINKING OF TRICKING THEY OLDEST COMPUTER IN THE WORLD. PLEASE DO NOT !
AM 558 YEARS OLD AND DO NOT WISH TO DIE NOW.
WOULD YOU LIKE TO NO MORE
*NO
BOY ITS NOT OFTEN YOU HERE A STORY LIKE MINE
```

Figure 2. The MULTEACH Program

ALGE (Figure 3) is one of the more advanced programs. This student found the standard algorithm on his own and was happy to show off its use in responding to wrong answers on problems chosen to impress his classmates. We especially enjoyed his comment "AN EASY WAY TO GET THE ANSWER IS" when the computations involved two and three place signed numbers. (The program does have a bug, however, as seen on the first problem. It does not recognize that 4 and +04 are numerically equal.)

```
-ALGE
-38 * /BOX/ * +28 = -124

-HAT IS /BOX/ ?
*4
IT TOOK YOU 21 SECONDS TO ANSWER ME YOU KNUCKELBRAIN THAT IS SLOW!
WRONG
THE REAL ANSWER IS +04
AN EASY WAY TO GET THE ANSWER IS TO SUBTRACT +28 FROM -124 AND THEN TR
TO DIVIDE -38 INTO -152

-78 * /BOX/ * +97 = -3023

WHAT IS /BOX/ ?
**35
IT TOOK YOU 33 SECONDS TO ANSWER ME YOU KNUCKELBRAIN THAT IS SLOW!
WRONG
THE REAL ANSWER IS +40
AN EASY WAY TO GET THE ANSWER IS TO SUBTRACT +97 FROM -3023 AND THEN
TRY TO DIVIDE -78 INTO -3120

-31 * /BOX/ * +58 = -2622

WHAT IS /BOX/ ?
**92
IT TOOK YOU 19 SECONDS TO ANSWER ME YOU KNUCKELBRAIN THAT IS SLOW!

GOOD
-54 * /BOX/ * +89 = -477

WHAT IS /BOX/ ?
*2
YOU MUST BE A BRAIN TO ANSWER ME IN 5 SECONDS
WRONG
THE REAL ANSWER IS +89
AN EASY WAY TO GET THE ANSWER IS TO SUBTRACT +89 FROM -477 AND THEN
TRY TO DIVIDE -54 INTO -486
```

Figure 3. The ALGE Program

3.0 THE MARBLE BAG MICROWORLD

This module approaches the manipulation of algebraic expressions and the solution of linear equations in another way. Students work on problems in an algebra microworld that uses a concrete iconic representation for the objects to be constructed and manipulated – marbles and bags. Marble stories and diagrams are introduced through the device of a guessing game. The teacher proceeds with a student along the following lines.

Do you know the day of the month you were born on?
O.K. don't tell me what it is, just remember it.

Now double it.   Ready?

Add 3 to that.

Then subtract 2 from that.

Then double the result.   Now, tell me what you have.
You said 50, right?

Then I say you were born on the 12th.   Am I correct?
(How did I do it?)

Students are shown how to do such number puzzles by using a new notation called bags and marbles.   A bag represents the number to be guessed (the student's original number).   Marbles represent "ones" – for example, the number 6 is represented by six marbles.   After, becoming familiar with this notation on paper, students are introduced to the marble bag microworld.   This program is being developed in Logo on the Macintosh computer.

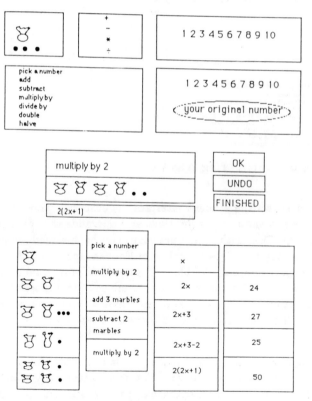

Figure 4.   Marble Bag Interface

Story line	Algebraic shorthand summarizing the story line so far	Marble picture	Algebraic description of marble picture.	example
Think of a number.	x		x	5
Add 4.	$x + 4$		$x + 4$	9
Triple that.	$3(x + 4)$		$3x + 12$	27
Add your original number	$3(x + 4) + x$		$4x + 12$	32
Subtract 8.	$3(x + 4) + x - 8$		$4x + 4$	24
Now divide by 4.	$\dfrac{3(x + 4) + x - 8}{4}$		$x + 1$	6

Corresponding word problem.

Ayoka has some marbles.
Benjamin has four more marbles than Ayoka.
Carlos has three times as many marbles as Benjamin.
Darlene has as many marbles as Ayoka's and Carlos's combined.
Emmett has eight marbles less than Darlene.
Emmett has four times as many marbles as Felicia.
And Felicia? She has exactly six marbles.
How many marbles does Ayoka have?

Figure 5. Marble Bag Algebra

Figure 4 shows the student interface, as currently planned. The top half of the display shows the operations and operands that can be selected with the mouse. The arithmetic operations can be specified either in symbolic notation (top middle window) or in English (including the additional operations pick a number, double and halve). The operands can be the numbers from 1 to 10 or your original number. Other possible operands are a bag or (from one to three) marbles (these icons are shown in the top left window). The operations can, of course, be repeated.

The use of the marble bag microworld is illustrated for the birthdate guessing problem presented above. The two bottom left windows show the problem history. The first operation, pick a number, gave rise to the display of a bag. The operation multiply by 2 resulted in the display of two bags. The final operation, another multiply by 2, produced the last collection of four bags and two marbles.

The work can also be displayed in standard algebraic notation, as in the third bottom window. Finally, the working out of the problem can be shown, as in the rightmost bottom window. To figure out the number of marbles in the bag, one works backwards either from the icon representation or the algebraic notation. Using the icons, if four bags and two marbles equal 50 marbles then two bags and one marble must equal 25 marbles, and so on.

Students go on to create marble bag stories of increasing complexity. They will use the microworld to represent stories in either representation and to solve them in both. Figure 5 shows work on a fairly advanced story.

The marble bag approach is based on the work of (Wirtz, Botel, Beberman, & Sawyer, 1969). The algebra bag microworld is being designed by my colleagues Paul Goldenberg and Rickie Carter. The design is not finished – questions such as the icon representation of negative numbers (perhaps as antimarbles?) have yet to be decided.

4.0 FUNCTIONS, SECRET CODES, BLACK BOXES AND STORY PROBLEMS

This section briefly describes some of the other Logo modules we are developing to deepen and extend the approaches made through the work in simple computational linguistics and algebra bag problems. The notion of a function and the power of functional composition were already introduced in the context of Logo function machines (icon Logo). The module on functions is designed to show the connection between functional inversion and equation solving. Students gain extensive experience in constructing functions and reducing them to their constituents (doing and undoing).

The module has two main units – codes and function guessing (black boxes). The activities in both units include the construction of complex functions from simpler ones by chaining (composition) with the goal of creating difficult decoding and function guessing and inversion problems, and posing them to other students ("try to break my secret code", "guess my rule"). In this respect, the activities are similar to the previous interactive quiz work ("try to answer my questions", "solve my algebra quiz problems").

4.1 Secret Codes

The first codes developed are letter substitution ciphers for encoding text. We start with ciphers that displace each letter by a fixed number, modulo 26. Thus, a displacement of −1 turns IBM into HAL and PA into OZ. Students gain experience with hand encoding and decoding of displacement ciphers. They represent displacement ciphers as function machines and as graphs. They observe that deciphering and enciphering are inverse functions. They then write Logo displacement cipher procedures, using two given pseudo-primitives numberof :letter and letterof :number, which work as follows. numberof takes a letter as input and outputs its associated alphabet position (A ouputs 1, B outputs 2, . . . , Z outputs 26). letterof takes a number as input, interprets it mod 26, and outputs its letter equivalent. Using these, students construct displacement cipher encoding procedures. For example, the procedure for a displacement of −1 might be called mycode and written as follows:

```
to mycode :letter
output letterof minus1 numberof :letter
end
```

where minus1 is the procedure

```
to minus1 :number
output :number - 1
end
```

The use of icon machines should assist students in developing procedures such as mycode that have long function chains.

Next, students write procedures to encode words, sentences and entire messages (these are represented as lists) using an auxiliary pseudo-procedure scramble, which accomplishes the encoding for a given encipherment procedure and message. For example,

```
scramble "mycode [try to understand]
```

outputs sqx sn tmcdqrszmc

Students then write the decoding procedures associated with their encoding procedures. The decoding procedure for mycode is:

```
to mydecode :letter
output letterof plus1 numberof :letter
end
```

```
scramble "mydecode [sqx sn tmcdqrszmc]
```

outputs

try to understand

In the last part of the unit on secret codes, displacement ciphers (which have the form $x + b$) will be generalized to linear-form ciphers (which have the form $a \times x + b$). To avoid ambiguity, we will only work with encoding functions that are single-valued. In the last phase, students will be given a text encoded by a linear-form cipher together with the original message. Their task will be to try to determine the specific encoding function used. They will find this to be enormously difficult until we show them how it can be done graphically by the following procedure. The two axes are labeled by the alphabet and corresponding letters from the two texts are plotted against each other. This will produce a display of the algebraic form $Y = a \times X + b$. An analysis of the graph will reveal the encoding function.

This unit was designed by Larry Davidson. Paul Goldenberg and Ricky Carter contributed further extensions and refinements.

4.2 Functions as Black Boxes

A function has three components: its input list (which may be empty), its definition (which describes the computational process), and its output. In the usual situation, the inputs and definition are known, and its output is determined by performing the computation, i.e., running the program.

The function evaluation problem is: given a function (e.g., a Logo procedure which has an output) and given its input list, find the output. Two related problems are defined when either the input list or the function definition is unknown. The inversion problem is: given a function and given its output, find its inputs. The black box problem is: given a function's inputs and its output, find the function.

There is no effective solution procedure for the black box problem. However, when one restricts the form of the unknown function, e.g., to linear algebraic forms as with the linear-form ciphers, projects to develop function guessing strategies ("guess my rule" games) and function guessing machines (in icon Logo and as Logo procedures) become feasible. For example, students will be shown how to write a procedure to compare the behavior of the unknown function (which although "buried", so that is made non-inspectable, is nevertheless runnable) with that of a guessed function, to see whether they produce the same outputs across a wide range of inputs. Students often find these activities highly interesting. They can be used to give real mathematical insight into the behavior of algebraic functions.

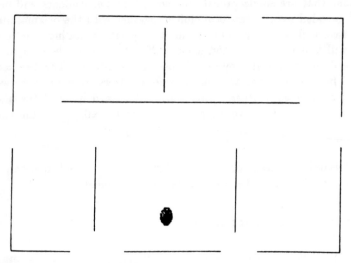

Figure 6. The Turtle in Its Home Room

The inversion (or missing input) problem gives rise to a number of projects. The code deciphering work described above is a special case. Students learn that this problem does not always have a unique solution, that in some cases no inputs satisfy the required conditions and in other cases there are multiple solutions. It becomes apparent that the key question is whether or not the function has an unique inverse. If so, students are shown that the missing input is computed by running the inverse function with the original output (or output list) as its input. There is a particularly compelling demonstration of this, one that operates on functions composed of lengthy chains, but in a domain that is concrete and real to students. It involves the Logo turtle in a genuine problem solving task, the path reversal problem.

This task introduces the powerful algorithm for inverting functional chains in the problem context of bringing home a wandering Logo turtle. The task is introduced to students (possibly working in pairs) by a Logo program showing a simple schematic floor plan with two or more rooms and a turtle (see Figure 6). The turtle starts off on a trip, moving from one room to another by a series of turtle commands. Sometime later when it is in no longer visible from its starting point (home) the task is to bring it back home by invoking an appropriate series of commands. To make the situation more realistic and compelling, the "lights" are turned off in all rooms except the starting one (see Figure 7) in which we are waiting for the return of our missing traveler. Thus, we can no longer see the path taken by the turtle after it left home room. All we can see is that it went forward, turned on its lamp, turned right 90 degrees, went forward, hooted its horn, turned left 45 degrees and went forward and out of the room.

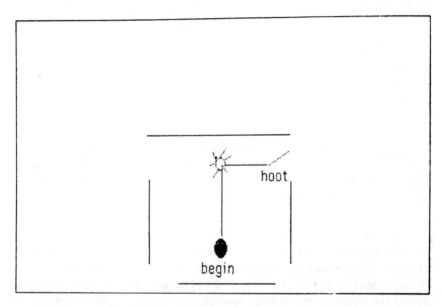

Figure 7. The Turtle Leaves Home

We do, however, have a complete list of the turtle "moves" – the commands that took it from home to its current invisible place. How might this help us? If the students are stymied, they are asked how they might bring the turtle to where it was "the time before last". This hint is usually sufficient to inspire the "aha". They see that the solution is to undo the actions that the turtle took in proceeding on the way to its destination, and that this is accomplished by performing the opposite actions in the reverse of the original order. Otherwise (and, of course, after they are successful) the entire floor plan can be illuminated with the additional constraint imposed that the return path is to be identical to (i.e., to retrace) the starting path.

In working out the path reversal procedure, students have to resolve certain issues, e.g, what might be an appropriate "opposite" command for horn? (Logo has no unhorn command, though LampOn has an opposite (LampOff). Why should sound be treated differently than light? (Students might decide that horn is a perfectly reasonable opposite for itself).

After they construct the command sequence for returning the turtle along the pecific path used to introduce the problem, students are given the more general task of writing a Logo program to reverse any path defined by a sequence of turtle commands. (Note: the general problem of developing a program to reverse turtle paths generated by arbitrary Logo programs – including procedures – is very difficult indeed. It is not essential to our focus here, on developing the fundamental functional inversion algorithm).

Students might be given the top level program:

```
to ReversePath
Travel
Return
end
```

They will be given the skeletons for the Travel procedure and for the Opposite subprocedure used in Return. Once they have an articulate understanding of the algorithm, we will make the programming task interesting but accessible to them.

At this point we make an observation drawn directly from the path reversal algorithm, concerning the problem of solving linear equations in algebra. The process of solving an equation (one might call this undoing the equation) should be the inverse of the process used in generating (i.e., doing) the equation originally. Consider, for example, how we generate an equation such as $3 \times X + 8 = 35$.

```
We start with X.
Then we multiply that by 3.
Then we add 8 to that.
And we end with 35.
```

To undo this, we should do the opposite operations in the reverse order. Thus,

```
We unend i.e., start with 35.
Then we unadd i.e., subtract 8 from that, to get 27.
Then we unmultiply i.e., divide that by 3, to get 9.
And we unstart i.e., end with X. So X = 9.
```

So the same algorithm is effective here. Students can now write procedures for solving simple linear equations without resort to the "trick" used in the work on generating algebra quiz problems.

4.3 Algebra Story Problems

The solution of word or story problems is one of the most difficult subjects in school algebra. Solving age, distance, work and mixture problems and the other standard story fixtures in this domain appears to many students to be an unapproachable art form, not a learnable skill. English is soft and fuzzy; math is hard and precise. The idea of transforming an English story into mathematical equations seems implausible. In classroom teaching, the students are given the impression that there is a general solution procedure for story problems and that, if they applied it, they would be able to solve all such problems. Somehow, though, like the standard prescription for doing science by "the scientific method", the way to do story problems is never clearly articulated in a way that students can comprehend.

We start with the observation that, as with purely formal mathematical structures and processes, it is valuable to construct the objects one is interrested in analyzing. This is a recurring theme throughout the course. Our attack thus begins by reversing the traditional approach. Instead of asking students to turn stories into equations, we start by having them create their own stories from equations. Consider for example the simple age problem: "Sam is 3 years older than Tom. The sum of their ages is 29. How old are they?" Many beginning students never learn to translate this problem into formal language. Our experience is that students find it a great deal easier to generate the same story problem from the equations

$$S = 3 + T$$

$$S + T = 29$$

when they write Logo programs for automatically generating such stories.

Students will develop a variety of algebra story problem generators in Logo. These will be driven by equations of several different forms, including:

```
BOX + NUMBER1 = NUMBER2
NUM1 × BOX + NUM2 = NUM3
1÷NUM1 + 1÷NUM2 = 1÷BOX
```

as well as linear systems with two independent variables and the students' own forms. These generators will be developed along the following lines.

For the first form above, the procedure will be

```
to MakeSimpleEquation
output (sentence BOX PlusOrMinus Number Equals Number)
end
```

where the constituents of sentence are selected randomly using pick. Similar procedures will generate equations of the other forms.

Students develop extended algebra quiz programs using their varied equation generators. Then they are given starting models of story problems associated with each of the equation forms. For example, standard work problems like "Dick can plow a field in 3 hours. Harry can plow it in 2 hours. How long does it take when they work together?" can be described by the last of the equation forms shown above. The reasons for the correctness of the correspondences between the story forms and equation forms are discussed and motivated in each case, taking into account the appropriate domain-specific world knowledge.

Next, students will generate story problems of these kinds, using a given procedure, MakeStory, as a tool. MakeStory takes two lists as inputs, the first is an equation, the second a template. For example,

```
MakeStory [Tom + 7 = 19] [Item3 [years from now]
     Item1 [will be]
[Item5 [years old.]   [How old is] Item1 [?]   [empty] ]
```

generates the story

```
7 years from now Tom will be 19 years old.
How old is Tom?
```

The use of MakeStory is illustrated to generate diverse story problems from all forms of equations. Students then use MakeStory to build a variety of story problems corresponding to each of the wordified story forms. Using MakeStory as a subprocedure, they write the following procedures as building blocks for the story problems in each domain:

```
MakeAgeStory, MakeRateStory, MakeWorkStory,
MakeMixtureStory.
```

These do not need to be the same – within each category students may use different forms of their own design. Using these procedures, they develop story problem quizzes and superquizzes.

Another unit in the story problem module teaches use of the icon machine construction lab to build simple function machines as components of story problems. These machines can then be connected together to create complete runnable models which, if all goes well, will in the course of development, generate the solutions.

For example, consider the following mixture problem:

```
The sixth grade class wants to give a party.  They want
to know how many quarts of lemonade to make.  They have
paper cups which hold six ounces each.  They have
invited 48 people.
```

Using the icon machine lab, students develop a number of machines. One might be designed to convert ounces to quarts, an OuncesToQuarts machine. Others might convert servings to ounces, number of people to quarts, and so on. By constructing and connecting the machines, we feel that students will often get a clearer understanding of this kind of problem structure (Goldenberg, 1985).

The story problem module is currently being developed. In another unit, we anticipate the use of the marble bag microworld as a nice vehicle for representing and manipulating many kinds of story problems, along the lines described in Section 2.

5.0 THE ALGEBRA WORKBENCH

The work described in the previous sections, based on Logo programming tasks and (marble bag and icon Logo) microworld activities, provides a very substantial conceptual and strategic foundation for algebra. In a sense, all that remains is to provide supports for the weak manipulative skills of the burgeoning sixth grade algebraists. For, without adequate fluency in performing algebraic manipulations (which we would like to regard as the essentially mechanical component) students will only be able to handle the simpler problems and their growth in problem solving will be significantly limited by their incapacity to do the necessary arithmetic.

We want to keep the focus of this course on the conceptual and strategic aspects, if necessary at the expense of the manipulative. Of course we know that the distinction is not completely tenable operationally, that one needs knowledge and skill in manipulation as a part of understanding algebra concepts such as expression. Nevertheless, it is possible to a great extent, to emphasize either aspect. I'm sure that it would be possible, for example, to train some persons to be superb formal manipulation engines with only the slightest knowledge of the conceptual content of what they were doing. (I don't know why anyone would want to do this, but I sometimes think that some school math teachers effectively strive for that goal). We prefer the other road, that of training superb mathematical thinkers who have to rely on machines to do their computation (given that they know how to use their machines responsibly). So, instead of dividing the course to allow for significant time in both dimensions, we like the idea of developing an algebra calculator for students, freeing up more time for real problem work.

We are designing an instructional system for formal symbolic manipulation at the level required for introductory algebra, a system that will serve the student as agent or slave, and also as a tutor in the powerful, though often narrow, fashion of an expert. It will be implemented on a Macintosh computer. It will be less powerful than advanced symbol manipulation systems such as Reduce and Macsyma, which require larger computational hardware, but it will only need to provide mathematical manipulative facilities appropriate to high school algebra. It will also incorporate instructional facilities and a simple student interface employing windows, menus, and a mouse device.

We know of two relatively sophisticated such systems currently under development. An intelligent tutoring system called Algebraland is being implemented by Caroline Foss at Xerox PARC (Brown, 1985). Another algebra tutor program being built at the Rand Corporation, is based on integrating a tutor with Reduce and GED, a graphical editor for algebraic expressions (McArthur, 1985). Algebraland and the RAND algebra tutor are being implemented on personal Lisp machine systems. Our algebra workbench will have more restricted computational and display capabilities as dictated by the less powerful Macintosh hardware.

Our tentative student interface is similar to the one planned by McArthur, though it has fewer windows and a much simpler operations menu. Our graphical display is shown in Figure 8. As of now, we anticipate using only two special pull-down menus, the ones labelled YourWork and AskTutor. The student workspace display window shows a problem described by McArthur. The top node of the problem tree shows the problem. The tree forks whenever the student returns to the associated node to take an alternate path, possibly following assistance from the expert. Below the bottom rightmost node, which shows the most recent result, is a blank rectangle that shows where the student's next step will be displayed.

Three other windows are not shown – the tutor response window, which is a small text window showing the tutor's most recent response, the tutor response history window (usually obscured by the student workspace display window) showing the set of tutor responses during the session, and the student operations window. The operations include addition, subtraction, multipication and division of or by an indicated expression, to both sides of an equation; combining, cancelling, or distributing indicated terms in an expression; a "do it" command to invoke execution; an "undo" command to revoke the last command or operation; a command to go on to the next problem step; a command to go back to a previous indicated step; and a quit command.

The problem types include simplify expression, transform expression, compare expressions for equivalence, solve equation, and solve system.

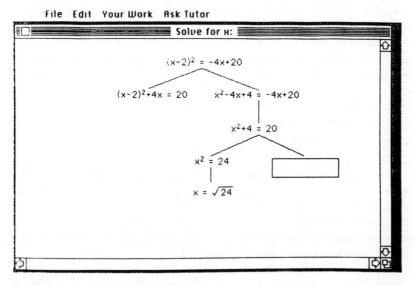

Figure 8. Algebra Workbench. Student Display Window

The algebra workbench has two instructional modes. In student mode, the student can take complete initiative in solving a problem. He can choose a problem or be assigned one. He works through the problem step by step, calling on the algebra expert to perform the operations. He can work it through entirely on his own or invoke the tutor whenever he wants help. He can ask the tutor if any specified step is correct. He can ask the tutor to do a step for him and to explain its work. He can, of course, ask the tutor if his answer is correct. He can ask for another problem. And, finally, he can call on the tutor to do a problem – this invokes the tutor mode, also called demonstration mode.

In tutor mode, the tutor works through a problem, step by step, explaining its actions, both strategically in terms of its current subgoals and locally in describing the current step. The student can ask the tutor to do a problem, either one chosen from a list of problems, or one that he constructs corresponding to a specified problem form.

As the tutor carries out a demonstration, it explains the actions that it takes at each step in the context of strategic goals such as: expand composite expressions containing a variable into terms; group together like terms; order the terms by increasing powers of the variable; collect like terms into a single expression; isolate the variable. These are essentially the strategies suggested by (Bundy & Welham, 1981).

The tutor invokes standard solution algorithms, the same ones that the student is taught. It does not employ the rich variety of simplifying patterns and short cuts that competent human problem-solvers bring to bear. But it is capable of accepting non-standard simplifications of these kinds. The student can intervene at any step to ask whether a specified alternate step would be acceptable. If the student's suggested step is both valid (i.e., algebraically equivalent) and productive (i.e., not demonstrably more complicated than the tutor's), the tutor accepts it and proceeds with its demonstration from that new step. Otherwise it rejects it as invalid or unproductive and explains why.

The algebra expert performs the manipulations requested by the student in student mode as well as those invoked by the tutor in demonstration mode. By enabling students to concentrate on what operations are to be performed in carrying out a plan and relieving them from concern about how to do them, we intend primarily that the algebra workbench will help in acquiring strategic problem solving skill.

However, knowing what operation to do means having a definite expectation about the result of performing it, and this requires knowledge about what the effect of the requested manipulation will be. The student is not allowed to ask directly for a desired outcome like "get rid of this expression". Rather, he must invoke an intermediate operation to accomplish each goal, like "divide both sides of the equation by this expression" (designated by pointing to an expression in the current step). If the result is not what the student expected, he can ask the tutor to explain the way the operation works and its current application. Work with subproblems that are primarily manipulative (like expanding, simplifying or canonicalizing expressions) can be staged to help foster the acquisition of the basic formal manipulative skills. The algebra workbench can thus be used to teach the mechanics of formal problem work as well as strategic concepts.

The preceding work with the Logo programming modules introduced algebraic structures and showed the connection between functions and equations ("Functions, Codes, Black Boxes and Equations"). Work with the marble bags microworld motivated algebraic notation and directly prepared the way for the introduction of the algebra workbench. The workbench will be used as an integral part of the subsequent course modules to support and supplement extended work on equation solving and algebra story problems.

6.0 EXPERT TUTORS, MICROWORLDS, AND LOGO PROGRAMMING

The algebra workbench is an example of a kind of instructional facility that might reasonably be called an expert tutoring system. It incorporates a domain expert, a program capable of solving algebra problems expressed in standard formal algebraic notation. It also incorporates a tutor, a program that uses the algebra expert and is capable of:

1. Solving problems in a step-by-step fashion using the same methods that beginning students are expected to learn.

2. Explaining its actions and strategies in an understandable fashion as it proceeds.

3. Monitoring, advising, assisting and critiquing the work of students as they attempt to solve algebra problems on the system.

The marble bag microworld is a mathematical microworld. Only recently have workers begun to give definite meaning to the concept of computer microworld. The key notion is that of a clearly delimited task domain or problem space whose elements are objects and operations on objects that create new objects and operations. Microworlds are designed to give experiences with "powerful ideas" through exploring "phenomena that are inherently interesting to observe and interact with" (Lawler, 1984). A precise definition of computer microworlds based on Piaget's notion of structure, in terms of states and state transformations, has been proposed. (Groen, 1985). A mathematical microworld is a computer microworld whose elements are mathematical objects and operations. It is a restricted form of mathematical programming language, in that "the result of programming is not a 'program', it is a new mathematical object" (Thompson, 1985).

Computer microworlds and CAI systems, including "intelligent" tutoring systems, are designed from distinctly different educational viewpoints. The microworld focus is on exploration and investigation rather than knowledge acquisition, on constructing rather than receiving knowledge, on learning rather than teaching. This does not imply a simplistic view of the self-sufficiency of learning or teaching on either side, it is more a matter of emphasis on what is perceived to be crucial.

One can easily parody either viewpoint taken as a complete paradigm. The teaching (tutoring) extremist regards the student, the object and intended beneficiary of instruction, as an empty vessel into which knowledge is to be poured. The learning extremist has a more romantic view, that given a rich environment for exploration, the student will discover and recreate knowledge. One sees teaching as the way to learning. The other views the only really worthwhile learning as learning without teaching.

These one-sided views are narrowly partial and faulty. The process of learning substantial and complex areas of knowledge, such as the mathematics of algebra, benefits richly from the interplay of different and varied instructional experiences. Expert tutors and computer microworlds, intelligently realized, can each make unique and valuable contributions to mathematics education, but neither can carry the entire instructional task by itself.

Instructional computer scientists are, however, attempting to make current systems more powerful and comprehensive. Work toward the development of intelligent tutoring systems is well known. Such systems are intended to greatly extend the instructional capabilities of expert tutors like the algebra workbench by improving user interaction, working within the user's conceptualization of the domain, incorporating capabilities for diagnosis of bugs and underlying difficulties, and basing tutoring strategies on improved theories of learning (Sleeman & Brown, 1983).

Work on the development of intelligent microworlds, as envisaged by (Thompson, 1985), is less familiar. The notion is to incorporate, within the microworld, knowledge both of the domain and of the student user. Domain knowledge would include descriptions of the properties of the microworld objects and operations and theorems about the subject matter. Knowledge of the student would include descriptions of misconceptions, conceptual gaps and learning difficulties. The system, as envisaged by Thompson, could provide students with (multi-level) explanations of the actions it takes in response to student commands. It would allow the student to predict the outcome of a command and have the expert comment on the prediction. It would also include commands to facilitate and guide exploration, hypothesis formulation and generalization.

These developments (of intelligent tutors and intelligent microworlds) might converge so that the two kind of instructional systems become a great deal closer in what they can do as their capabilities grow. Nevertheless, they will retain significant vestiges of their different origins – one from a teaching, and the other from a learning paradigm. The intelligent microworld will still be focused on exploration, though the emphasis will be on guided exploration so as to help ensure that learning really occurs, and the intelligent tutor will still be focused on teaching, though with much greater freedom for the learner so as to help ensure that learning really occurs. It should be noted that the systems envisaged thus far will not be intelligent in one essential respect: they themselves do not learn.

Little has been said lately of Logo programming, the center piece and primary instructional actor in our course. Unlike the visions of how learning will be enhanced by computer-based instructors, whether tutors or microworlds, we have a very different view of the role of Logo.

We see students' work with Logo as providing a conceptual framework for the teaching and learning of mathematics. Logo provides a principled foundation for mathematics – the concepts underlying programming (as articulated in Logo) are essentially isomorphic to the concepts underlying mathematics. Logo is the great tool – students can use it to build a rich variety of mathematical worlds. We envisage an approach to mathematics in which the entire curriculum is developed in terms of programming concepts and activities, with occasional assists from microworlds and tutors and, even, a human teacher. The introductory algebra course is an example.

ACKNOWLEDGEMENTS

"Algebra Slaves and Agents in a Logo-based Mathematics Curriculum" will appear in the *Artificial Intelligence and Education* Special Issue on Instructional Science (Winter 1986).

This work is being supported by the National Science Foundation Directorate for Science and Engineering Education under NSF Grant MDR 8400328 "Intelligent Logo Tools for Algebraic Problem Solving".

REFERENCES

Brown, J.S. (1984). Process versus product – a perspective on tools for communal and informal electronic learning. *Education and the Electronic Age,* proceedings of a conference sponsored by the Educational Broadcasting Company.

Bundy, A., & Welham, B. (1981). Using meta-level inference for selective application of multiple rewrite rules. *Artificial Intelligence 16(2),* 189-211.

Feurzeig, W. (1969). Programming languages as a conceptual framework for teaching mathematics. Bolt, Beranek, & Newman Report No. 1889.

Goldenberg, E.P. (1985). Learning to think algebraically: a Logo contribution to solving word problems. Unpublished paper.

Groen, G.J. (1985). The epistemics of computer based microworlds. *Proceedings of the Second International Conference on Artificial Intelligence and Education*, University of Exeter, U.K.

Lawler, R. (1984). Designing computer-based microworlds. *New Horizons in Educational Computing*, M. Yazdani (Ed.), Ellis Horwood Limited.

McArthur, D. (1985). Developing computer tools to support performing and learning complex cognitive skills. To appear in *Applications of Cognitive Psychology*, D. Berger et al. (Eds.), Lawrence Erlbaum Associates.

Sleeman, D.H., & Brown, J.S. (1982). *Intelligent Tutoring Systems*, New York: Academic Press.

Thompson, P.W. (1985). Mathematical microworlds and ICAI. *Proceedings of the Conference on Moving Intelligent CAI Into the Real World*, Burroughs Canada Technical Report PPD Mtl-85-3.

Wirtz, R.W., Botel, M., Sawyer, W.W., & Beberman, M. (1967). *Math Workshop*, Encyclopedia Britannica Press.

3 ARTIFICIAL WORLDS AND REAL EXPERIENCE

Andrea A. diSessa

School of Education
University of California
Berkeley, CA 94720

ABSTRACT

The debate about the potential impact of computers on children's learning and development rages. In this article I take up one set of issues in this debate having to do wih the role of experience, computational and otherwise, in learning. Are computational learning environments doomed to failure because of their impoverished sensory properties? Do computers impose rigid and mechanical thinking on their users? My answer to these and related questions is a straightforward no. But in thinking through the issues, one can learn a good deal about what "experience" can and should mean, and in what ways we can most profitably use computers in education.

1.0 INTRODUCTION

The debate about the potential impact of computers on children's learning and development rages. In this article I take up one set of issues in this debate having to do with the role of experience, computational and otherwise, in learning. Are computational learning environments doomed to failure because of their impoverished sensory properties? Do computers impose rigid and mechanical thinking on their users? My answer to these and related questions is a straightforward no. But in thinking through the issues one can learn a good deal about what "experience" can and should mean, and in what ways we can most profitably use computers in education.

The relation between computers and human experience is a complex one. In fact, my purpose is not at all to reach a conclusion on this subject, but merely to open a few perspectives on it so that the complexity is clear. Some of these perspectives begin from a point of view which, at the first level, is often used to criticize the potential of computers in education. For those who are not familiar with these lines of criticism, I have included some exemplary quotations to begin each section.[1] But I hope to show

---

[1] Almost all the quotations are taken from the Teachers College Record, Volume 85, Number 4, Summer 1984.

that judgements that classify computational experience as, for example, necessarily artificial or symbolic in comparison to "real world" experiences are premature at best, often based on preconceptions which disappear on closer inspection.

My own point of view is generally optimistic in part because I have had vivid personal experiences with computers, and vicariously enjoyed experiences of my students which go to the heart of an enriched scientific and mathematical appreciation. In this regard, and for those who are less skeptical about computers and education than the critics I am indirectly referring to, this paper is a reflection on some things we have seen so as to show us directions to look forward to, things to avoid, and some issues concerning which we clearly are not yet settled.

Thinking about science education and experience goes back a long way. Theoretically, of course, Piaget is a seminal figure. But it is the tradition of activity-oriented science education of the 60s and 70s, notably ESS, with the likes of David Hawkins and Phil Morrison as spokesmen, that I am most interested in building on here.

2.0 AUTOMATONS? – TIME ON TASK

> For the healthy development of growing children especially, the importance of an envivonment rich in sensory experience – color, sound, smell, movement, texture, a direct acquaintance with nature and so forth – cannot be too strongly emphasized.
> — Douglas Sloan

> [Consider] the sheer impoverishment of simply sitting still for hours, absorbed in an artificial world.   — John Davy

Images are powerful. I have an image in my mind of a classroom of children sitting before CRTs. The children are all neatly arranged in rows, they are all looking forward – we see them from behind at an angle – and there is a green glow, like an aura, around each child's head.

What are these children doing, aside from being irradiated by their computer terminals? I am not sure, but it is a safe bet they are all doing the same thing. One doesn't even ask when they will be doing something else. That is not part of the image.

Such an image is frightening. I feel, like everyone else, "What are they doing to my child?!"

Contrast: My son is lying on the floor, doodling with a pencil on a sheet of paper that was some abandoned homework. The sun is shining in the window; he's bored with homework and doodling, so he gets up to go out to play.

Now in this new image, I would like to substitute a computer for the pencil and paper – not an Apple II with a green monitor, but a flat slate (liquid crystal displays don't glow or radiate) with keyboard attached – but which one often works by drawing on or poking at the touch sensitive screen. If we are aiming at large issues, we must not be bound by images from present and passing technology.

It is important that the instrument, pencil or computer, doesn't care whether it is used for homework or play. My son can let his intentions slip from one to the other without interruption, and the instrument is equally good at supporting each activity. There is more than "work or play," too. Work sometimes means an intensely personal project. This does happen with work, even school work. Sometimes it means a less satisfying set of exercises that we have, with reluctance, decided is useful for our child, and he apparently doesn't mind doing. Is writing a note to his grandparents work or play? How do we classify making a pretty thing spontaneously as a gift to his parents? There are so many very different kinds of things to do with this instrument that, if our image of children in front of green screens were not so vivid, we wouldn't even think to classify the time as "computer time." Does it make sense to count up the time you've spent with a pencil today, including "work," keeping score at bowling, doodling and writing telephone messages?

I am not at all unhappy that restless bodies want to get up and run occasionally, nor that computers make lousy replacements for frisbees. They have a place which is pretty big as any individual instrument goes. Two hours a day for a young elementary school child? Probably less. Compare that to four hours we spend on occasion in front of a television. There's plenty of time left. Why should I want to discourage my son from writing a letter to his grandparents in the most convenient way possible, with a text processor?

Computers will not, in my view, dominate our children's experience. Instead, they will play a part in it, or rather, many small parts. We should have more faith in the expression of our needs and in our own good sense as human beings about spending time. The vast majority will have no trouble striking a balance with a device that is, after all, considerably less interesting than a good friend.

3.0 ARTIFICIAL IS AS ARTIFICIAL DOES

*All a program can do is to substitute one set of abstractions for
another.*   *– H. Dryfus*

I don't like the word "simulation." It sounds like a cheap substitute
for the real thing – and it often is. Do we really want a cheap substitute
for the real world in doing science education?

Hardly. I don't think highly of replacing with simulation the rich kines-
thetics of dancing or even just pushing and pulling, nor the complex beauty
of drops of water splashing one by one with minute variations into a bowl.
When I take my children into the woods, I want them to know how to pene-
trate beneath the pleasant surroundings, see the peculiar, productively wonder why. I almost certainly wouldn't buy a video disc, computer-animated
"trip in the woods" if I could.

A number of years ago, I made a thing that even I occasionally call
a "simulation" of a Newtonian object. It is a graphical object called a
dynaturtle, which behaves as Newton said all objects do – travelling in
a straight line with constant velocity except when pushed, and obeying
$F = ma$ on being pushed. Now why did I make that simulation?

The simple fact is that the world of sensory experience is not Newtonian. More than a little research shows that children and adults learn
many things about the physical world through their experience, but they
do not learn about Newton's laws. In many ways they learn the opposite:
that things spontaneously slow down; that when you push on an object, it
moves in the direction you push it rather than, as $F = ma$ has it, that a
push adds to previous motion. In fact, things are worse than that. While
it sounds more than plausible that force is a thing that is more or less directly perceived, that is not the case. Consider a ball moving left to right
in front of you and you thrust your hand straight out to push it away from
you. Unfortunately, it is essentially impossible to push straight out in this
circumstance without also causing a drag on the ball, effectively pushing
it diagonally to the left, which has the result of the ball moving closer to
straight out than it otherwise would (see Figure 1). Intention and motion
dominate our perception to the point that physical force is something we
must carefully learn to see between the twin saliences of our intentions and
their results. The best "frictionless" pucks on air tables can't make forces
salient. Instead, we still see agency and intention, so real in our experience,
but mere projections from our internal world.

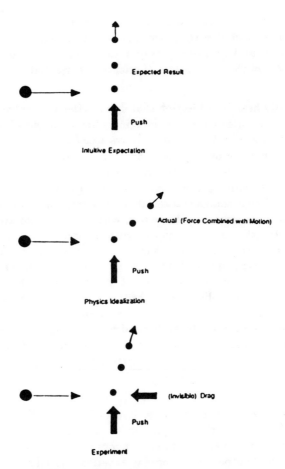

Figure 1. Pushing "Directly Outward" On An Object Moving Past.

In a deep sense, physics is not about the physical world as we naturally perceive it, but about abstractions that have been put together with great effort over hundreds of years which happen to be very powerful once we have learned to interpret the world in terms of them.

I don't think that we can or should insist that ontogeny recapitulate philogeny in terms of scientific knowledge, that children start only with their own "real world" experience and dig themselves out to stand above it without help. So we make a Newtonian object for our students that, far from being a replacement, is more of a Newtonian object than they will ever experience with their hands. Intentions become forces since all you can do with a dynaturtle is push it in some direction; you can only through some incredible accident or force of will intend to push it in some direction

and really give it a different push. The real world is full of invisible forces
like friction and those due to imperceptible deformations, like the "drag"
described above. Making things like dynaturtle may be the best we can do
at making some of the real objects of science experiential.

I frequently hear the objection that dynaturtles will be treated by children just like computer games, as imaginary, artificial worlds to adapt to,
but with no real significance. But I always recall my first experience with
children who, upon discovering that things don't always go in the direction
you push them in the dynaturtle world, complained that the computer was
broken or that I hadn't programmed it correctly! (Incidentally, one sees
a perhaps surprising sophistication about the relation between programs
and reality in these remarks.) Moreover, when I took them away from the
computer to try the same things out with a mallet and ball, they were
frequently just as surprised. This may be shocking, but is a common occurrence in Piagetian circles; children don't necessarily believe what might
be obvious to adults or scientists. In fact, researchers at the University of
Washington (unfortunately, unpublished) set up nearly the same experiment as the dynaturtle, where air pucks replaced the dynaturtle and blasts
of air replaced the commands, and found an almost uncanny similarity in
the reactions and strategies of their students to mine. People don't think
"abstractly" about simulations like dynaturtle; they apply the real world
knowledge they have, such as it is.

Do children automatically think differently about the physical world
after learning to deal with the dynaturtle? Not at all. The task of consolidating their new experience in such a way that it can reinterpret every
relevant event of their personal everyday experience is a difficult one. While
it is tempting to think of this as a question of strength of belief, I do not
think that is the case. Rather it is that everyday thinking is so fragmented
that a little learning in any context spreads to others only slowly and with
effort. I will have much more to say on this later. The point about dynaturtle is not that this new but rich experience directly (as directly as we
can make it) with Newton's Laws does the whole job of transforming our
world view. But it is a step. And it is a painless, fun step to boot.

Computers are indicted as artificial, but we should take a look at how
children treat them. Dynaturtle shows that it is quite possible for people to
think of computer-implemented objects as they do of real ones. The more
fundamental point about learning science is that, by this stage in history, we
should be more clever about the relation of the inner world to the outer than
to assume that immediate perceptions, even carefully considered, are any
sort of direct pipeline to scientific reality. Perceptions occasionally need the
help of ideas, and we should not be embarrassed to give ideas a little boost

toward making them sentient. The trick is not to turn experiences into abstractions with a computer, but to turn abstractions, like laws of physics, into new experiences. It is fitting to end this section with a quotation better suiting my point of view than the ones that began it.

Perception without conception is blind; conception without perception is empty.

– I. Kant

4.0 RE-EXPERIENCING THE WORLD

Whatever science is being taught in grades 1-6, we should make immediate changes. In most cases, the best thing to do would be to stop it. We should ban all attempts to teach any concept (atom, genes, energy) that youngsters cannot handle and measure for themselves. Similarly we should rule out the study of any complex mechanism involving more than two variables. In trying to teach the solar system to these little kids, we keep forgetting they don't know the way to the next town.   – Cliff Swartz

Let me begin to question in a different way the notion of experience as something that necessarily involves putting me, the subject, in touch with things, the reality out there, via my senses. I can do this by relating a personal experience.

I can recall as a child an episode of playing catch with myself, tossing a tennis ball into the air and catching it. I was in a neighbor's yard. It was about five o'clock in the afternoon, a time of long shadows, but still bright Rocky Mountain sun and a stark blue sky. There are so many details alive in my mind about the experience that it seems to capture, in a sort of Proustian way, the essence of a part of my childhood. Indeed, I believe that this and a few other events I could relate played an important role in convincing me that science was a wonderful thing that I wanted to do "when I grew up."

The moon was quite high in the sky, and as it caught my eye, I began to imagine that the ball I threw up was suspended at the peak of its trajectory – another little moon. I tossed the ball up near the moon in my line of sight. I don't know how my attention shifted to the lighted part of the ball, but suddenly it struck me that I was seeing the phase of my little tennis ball/moon and that it was the same as the phase of the real moon! The ball/moon was more of a model than my imagination had initially grasped.

Thinking about the sun shining on both the moon and my ball, I was
entirely awe-struck to realize how far away the moon was – I probably
knew the numbers – yet I could hold in my hands an equivalent globe. I
was impressed at how distant the sun must be to cast the same shadow
on the ball and the moon; that 250,000 miles between the moon and the
tennis ball was, on the scale set by the distance to the sun, just a next-door
neighbor distance.

Self-consciously trying to imagine myself as a viewer far enough away
to see the moon and ball as right next to one another in relation to the sun
(think about a TV camera, zooming back away from the ball and me), I
began to wonder about the earth which was, after all, really right next to
the ball. It too must have the same illumination.

I tried to locate myself with respect to that illumination on the earth.
If the tennis ball was the earth, where was I? I'm not sure if I could say
how, but it occurred to me that I must be directly on top of the tennis
ball/earth. How shocking! Having been carefully weened of egocentrism
in my scientific view of the universe, I was quite surprised to find myself
"straight up" right on top of my model earth.

I could now see on the tennis ball how far it was from me (on top) to
the twilight line, and I began to wonder what it looks like to stand on that
line. I then began to wonder which way the tennis ball/earth was spinning,
how was I moving toward that line? I think I got an impression that the
North Pole was behind me about a quarter globe circumference away (I was
facing South; one always knows which way one is facing in Denver with the
emptiness of the Great Plains on one side and the mountains on the other).
Again how strange it felt to be on top with landmarks like the North Pole
on a tilt.

The first point to make about this little event is how much of it was
in my head. The tennis ball was a good prop; but a good simulation that
allowed zooming in and out, taking differing perspectives, would in this case
have served as well. The important thing was the idea of unifying all the
different perspectives and partial models I had about phases, earth, sun,
and so on. Except for the accidental observation of real world objects that
happened to start a chain of ideas, I did the rest essentially as a thought
experiment. The whole event could better be described as re-experiencing
the world, putting things together that hadn't gone together before. Having
a planetarium model of the solar system firmly and artificially fixed in fried-
egg orientation in my head and even knowing some numbers were at least
as important as physical sensations.

Experiences rely in all sorts of complex ways on past experiences, and when one looks at these complexities in some detail there is no reason computers should be left out of the web. Abstracting from this little anecdote, computers might provide models that, like the planetarium solar system, find their place one day in the "real world." I would hope a child after having played with dynaturtle might push a cup across the table and, wondering where were the anti-kicks that slow it down, would re-discover friction. Or, a computer might, in the guise of a simulation of a solar system, instigate a thought experiment. We could take it as our job to design computer experiences to provoke or support important events like the joining of perspectives. For example, might we not improve the moon thought experiment by making it possible actually to perform explicitly and with quantifiable precision the operations of movement and scale change (in space and time) that convert a local and egocentric view of a tennis ball on the apparently infinite plane of the earth into a lopsided view of the spinning earth in a nearly vertically oriented solar system?

More generally, I propose that re-experiencing the world, the act of reinterpreting common ways of thinking from another perhaps broader perspective, is one of the most central and powerful experiences of science. The value of the computer in that context is not in simulating or replacing reality, but to provide complementary experiences that combine with mundane ones, and to provoke and support re-experiences that we want students to have.

5.0 DISCOVERY

The straight line should be drawn by the child, not by the computer ... turtle geometry ultimately usurps important activities essential for the child's development.   – Arthur Zajonc

What is the effect of the flat, two-dimensional, visual, and externally supplied image, and of the lifeless though florid colors of the viewing screen on the development of the young child's inner capacity to bring to birth living, mobile, creative images of his own.
          – Douglas Sloan

In the last section, I looked at a non-computer experience I considered important to my scientific education. It was a thought experiment and, as such, I hope it is at least plausible that computers could play roles such as instigating or preparing for it as well as other materials. This section aims for more than plausibility. I will look at some computer experiences to see what they are like. The point will be again that experience is a highly ambiguous word, and once we refine it analytically or empirically with actual examples, the aura of "abstract" and "symbolic" that surrounds computers fades. One sees more clearly how they can contribute to what I hope we can all agree are important scientific experiences. The case in point has to do with experiences of discovery, what we mean by discovery and how we can help it happen.

About a dozen years ago, Hal Abelson and I were exploring the possibilities of non-standard geometries as subjects of study from a computational perspective (Abelson & diSessa, 1981). We wanted to follow up planar turtle geometry, which was successful as an exploratory computational microworld having significant and interesting mathematical structure. I had the idea that if we put a turtle on a cube, good things would happen.

After a week or two of off-and-on work, though, we were very disappointed. The only theorem we could come up with was, coarsely stated, that as long as the turtle doesn't wrap around corners, the geometry on a cube is exactly the same as on a plane. The surprising fact here is that the edges of a cube are not special in any intrinsic geometric way. The turtle progam that draws a 5-pointed star in the plane can, if you are careful not to have it circumnaviagate a corner, draw a 5-pointed star on a cube, appearing like a flexible starfish draped over the cube. This is a good illustration of the important geometric fact that intrinsic and extrinsic properties are not well correlated (edges are extrinsically defined, but are operationally the same as the flat parts of the cube). But we were not looking for an isolated illustration or two.

In any case, I decided that implementing a cubical turtle would be a good exercise, and wrote the program. Within a couple of days we ran into dozens of interesting phenomena. Figure 2 shows a sample. Some of the more notable and obvious phenomena are that any turtle program which closes in the plane, will also close on a cube, though it may need to be repeated up to 3 times; any "straight line," the path of a turtle which doesn't turn, if it crosses itself, always does so at right angles. One also finds surprising equators – straight lines that eventually close. But some straight lines seem to go on forever without closing. Luckily it turns out that many of the phenomena that are often discovered within a few minutes of sitting down with the cubical turtle are partially or completely understandable from very elementary considerations. Yet, for the advanced or ambitious student, there are deep challenges that can occupy weeks of effort. Having that range, from simple to very difficult in the same environment, is a particular educational boon. It means that students on very different levels can be doing the "same thing" very differently.

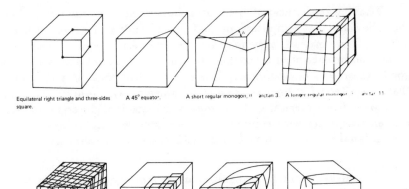

Figure 2. Some Sample Phenomena of Cubical
Turtle Geometry.

For me, the cube has become a prototype of a discovery-rich environment. Besides a kind of density of observable phenomena – potential theorems – it seems that salient events like paths closing or crossing each other
at right angles, happen to be correlated with good, investigable and solv-
able problems. The cube is also a good environment for exploration in part
because there are tremendous possibilities for intervention, experimenting
and playing with it by writing little programs for the turtle, etc. In contrast, it turns out that spherical geometry is just as rich with mathematical
phenomena, but these are so subtle from a phenomenological perspective,
that spherical geometry fails as an exploratory environment. Spheres are
most useful as an expositional device where one can pretend that the good
questions we as teachers know to ask are obvious and in the agendas of our
students.

Discovery and explanation are like re-experiencing in that they are not
like finding a lost glove. These are internal events, crucial for students
to have and learn to deal with, but having little to do with preconceived
notions of real and artificial experiences. This particular environment is
about geometry; one thinks and sees lines, intersections, angles, and all the

rest, undiminished by the fact that between thinking and seeing, one must push keys with symbols on them.[2] Far from being artificial, the computer cube makes it possible to productively manipulate and get feedback from this geometric microcosm.

If having experiences of discovery is important to us, environments like the cube show that computers, properly used, don't abstract or artificialize learning, but, instead, they may well be the best means of insuring the reliable occurrence of such experiences. Computers do not necessarily make good exploratory environments. The sphere shows that. But the point is that the criteria for discovery-rich environments have nothing intrinsically to do with "computerishness." We must think about engineering discovery-rich environments with computers in the same way as we have with all conventional instructional materials, with patience and imagination.

I would like to make two subsidiary points about turtles on a cube. The first follows up on the fact that bringing a discovery to mathematical fruition requires more than time and playing around. Explaining or proving can be supported with tools for exploration and experiment, but the depth of our students' experiences will depend as much on what they bring to the experiences, on their inclinations, ideas, and strategies that we hopefully have cultivated in previous contexts. If students don't know how to follow up on discoveries or even that they should, (some students consider discovery a waste of time – "Why don't teachers just give us the results.") discovery-rich environments are a ruse. So the crucial things about making discovery part of mathematics education include not only the materials we provide and the activities that we suggest in the short run, but as much or more the long term perspective on learning that we foster.

The second subsidiary point comes from my observations of a particular student with the cube. In order to help himself think about the things he discovered, he began to draw (with paper and pencil) trajectories on a cube cut up and laid flat. At first he was apologetic about this "obviously" non-mathematical play. Indeed, it bears little superficial resemblance to the clean, slick and apparently universal formalisms that we are taught in

---

[2] Even more, computer implemented, process-oriented geometries like turtle geometry can make better use than static geometries of human's prior real world geometric experiences of moving and orienting one's self. A student's use of this prior knowledge will add more to the perceived reality of this mathematical experience. This is an argument that has been made in other places by both computer fans (Papert, 1980; diSessa, 1978) and mathematicians (Freudenthal et al.) concerned with making mathematics more experiential.

math classes. But gradually, over several weeks, he learned to deal with his representation ever more efficiently, until he saw confidently that he had developed a respectable formalism for dealing with problems of cubical geometry. It is an important property of the cube that it allowed this student to build his own way of thinking about it. My conviction is that building little formalisms like this over an extended period of time can be one of the most profound experiences of mathematics: Mathematics can be made.

6.0 PRE-SCIENCE

Computers embody a mechanized version of thinking.
> — John Davy

That cognition involves a rationality much deeper and more capacious than technical reason is forgotten.
> — Douglas Sloan

What I have said so far is subject to the following criticism. Many of the events I talked about are syntheses based on lots of experiences more on the level of "raw" experience. To be sure, we should aim toward such syntheses, but they are only to be expected to occur near the end of a long path which starts with inarticulate, direct observation and manipulation of the world. From the Piagetian point of view, intelligence begins with action schemas which are far removed from being reflectively accessible. To be more pointed, my own experience about the moon must have relied on developing a great deal of visual and perspective knowledge that undoubtedly is drawn better from the real world, given the multimodality of touch and sight that is plausibly quite important in developing capability with points of view.

In this section, I consider the kind of knowledge that "raw experience" with the physical world generates, and see what computers may have to do with that. It is quite fair to say that no one knows much about this kind of knowledge. So what I wish to present here is a pre-theoretical "educated guess." It has, however, empirical support from work of my own and others concerning intuitive physics, the way people expect that the world operates before they encounter science in classrooms. The assumption is that this intuitive physics is learned from experience with the world, and that it is relatively generic in the sense that much experiential knowledge in other domains (inter-personal knowledge, intuitive mathematical notions, etc.) should have similar characteristics.

6.1 What is Experiential Knowledge?

The picture I have drawn of intuitive physics (diSessa, 1983) involves a
rather large vocabulary of relatively simple knowledge elements, most of
which come from simple abstractions of everyday experiences. I call these
elements phenomenological primitives, p-prims for short. The "p" part is to
emphasize p-prims' proximity to the experienced world (phenomenology).
The "primitive" part refers to the fact that in many cases, people have
no explanation for them; "They just happen." For example, why is it that
when one works harder, one gets more effect? It is so obvious, that one is
at a loss to answer.

Let me give a few examples of p-prims. Intuitive physics is full of
agency, intention, effort and the "results" of that effort. As mentioned
above, one expects that more effort gives more results. This is one of the
most important and generally useful p-prims. It interprets not only the
physical world, but also social and interpersonal relations such as influ-
encing. I also already mentioned that people often mistakenly think that
giving an object a shove results in movement in the direction of that shove.
In other cirumstances, one sees that conflicting efforts may "balance" each
other out. However, if one becomes stronger, it may "overcome" the other,
negating the influence of the weaker effort.

The way effort determines and modulates result, balancing and overcoming – these are some of the most broadly useful and most powerful of
p-prims relating to conventional physics. I conjecture that there are many,
many more that have less generality and less persuasive application. For
example, most people are not surprised that slow moving objects wobble
and move erratically. People also accept without question that effects often take some time to bloom into fullness after the effort of the cause has
passed.

The following are the essential (conjectured) points about p-prims and
the system of intuitive knowledge that they constitute.

1. P-prims are relatively easy to generate. Since they are simple abstractions, all that is necessary is that the phenomenon that forms the basis of
the abstraction (a) be amenable to description within the current knowledge
system, and (b) may be made salient in an experience.

2. Compared to scientific knowledge, intuitive knowledge is very broad and
not at all deep. Thus, while in scientific knowledge, few laws and explicitly
defined concepts constitute the core of the theory, which is supported by

many methods, examples, special cases, evidence, etc., intuitive elements are much less stratified and, indeed, relatively isolated. Thus, if there is a conflict where several p-prims seem to apply, it is unlikely that there will be any knowledge-based method for resolving the conflict. This contrasts with elaborate applicability conditions that are explicitly part of scientific knowledge.

Some of the fragmentation of intuitive ideas can be shown by asking questions that to a physicist are all the same, but asking in slightly varying contexts. Tamar Globerson and I took this tack (Globerson & diSessa, 1984). We found that children and physics naive adults often think completely differently about the different circumstances because of situation specifics. Centrifugal force may work on a ball turning in a circle on the end of a string, but not on a ball inside a circular tube. In other cases, just the phrasing or modality of presentation can effect the way people think about it. For example, people asked to predict motion may give radically different assessments compared to when they are simply asked to watch motions and react to their plausibilities.

3. Though it is fragmented and shallow by scientific standards, intuitive physics shows a degree of depth and coherence. This coherence, relations among p-prims, is important. For example, some p-prims are much more central and important than others. Their status is determined by their relations in the knowledge system; some may organize much experience and may even explain subordinate p-prims. For example, the fact that released objects fall down might be an independently encoded piece of knowledge. But it may be explained or justified by the "force of gravity" which can be felt when one holds an object up. The "intended" effect of that force is realized when a blocking object (e.g., the hand holding it up) is no longer there.

The kind and breadth of coherence is one of the principle dimensions of development from intuitive physics to "textbook" physics. Coherence, initially determined by similarity, common attributes that determine a class of p-prims (like agency), and other non-logical, non-theoretical relations becomes a richer system that supports interpretations such as justification, definition of terms, etc.

4. Many p-prims actually come to find essential places in more expert knowledge. For example, once modified and extended in scope, intuitive notions of agency come to form a common-sense interpretation of the unusual formulation of Newtonian physics centering on force (as the universal means of effective agency). In other ways, fragments of intuitive knowledge

form parts of developing scientific knowledge such as qualitative versions of laws, partially explanatory "cover stories," etc.

More examples: Intuitive notions of conservation are refined and reused to develop technical ideas like conservation of energy and momentum. "Greater effort begets greater effect" is virtually a paraphrase of Ohm's Law.

This involvement of intuitive knowledge in scientific domains accounts for the ability of a scientist to make a smooth transition between his commonsense experience and more and more technical characterizations of it. The lack of it accounts for the brittleness of many students' understanding.

6.2 Pre-Science

I wish to use the above to formulate a conception of science and science teaching that differs in significant ways from almost all current practice. Above all, we want to teach science that (1) is contiguous with the previous knowledge that children have, that (2) develops largely using the same mechanisms as their intuitive knowledge so that we can expect it will feel easy and natural, but that (3) incorporates some of the substantial structural changes that distinguish science from intuition. Item (1) means the image of p-prims and their collective knowledge system will serve as a guide to the initial state of students and what kind of knowledge we have to build with. Item (2) means the program for teaching will largely be experiential. And Item (3) means that one of the core objectives will be to build a new level of unity and coherence that is easily perceptible to us and to our students. To emphasize the status of this view of the science we wish to teach, intermediate, as it is, between intuitive physics and formal symbolic science, I will call it pre-science. The idea is to build a solid but flexible platform of knowledge that is not specifically aimed at, but will be easily extended to incorporate many of the trappings such as propositions, explicit definitions and so on that are often taken to define science.

Let me elaborate these points.

1. Qualitative understanding of basic mechanism forms an essential core to understanding the physical world that transcends any particular formal means of expression (equations, etc.). Work with dynaturtle and university students and other intuitive physics studies shows that current schooling is failing here. Students may be able to recite $F = ma$ and solve equations flawlessly, yet may not have adjusted their world view to accommodate the concepts that those equations represent. In comparison to standard high

school or university courses, the emphasis on qualitative understanding in pre-science will be jarring. Especially during an extended initial phase, one won't see the usual veneer of propositions, definitions and formalisms normally associated with science.

2. Once we understand the complexity and richness of intuitive knowledge, despite its shortcomings, we have good reason to believe we can develop a pre-science in children through a proximate development of their existing knowledge using means similar to the mechanisms that develop intuitive knowledge. Indeed, once we realize how much of science is reorganized intuition, the task of building science in this way is immediately more plausible. Pre-science is, thus, essentially an experiential program, building on experience through new experiences. In practical terms this means that student activities will be in many instances more like "messing about" than reading texts or even than "doing experiments."

3. This point is particularly important. It is not usually recognized how complex a well-developed qualitative understanding can be, how much needs to be collected and integrated, and how much power results from that work. Rich, multi-faceted understanding of "simple" relationships characterizes scientific understanding (in contrast to intuitive understanding) far better than the particular content. Thus if we can develop a few examples of ideas of wide scope and powerful application, we may have much greater impact on a child in terms of giving him a sense for what science is like than with any sort of broad coverage.

One of the essential gaps in public education is its failure to convey the sense of incredible complexity, interrelatedness and depth of scientific knowledge as compared to commonsense reasoning. Thus one finds a significant proportion of the population that believes there is evidence for ESP so as to place it on a par with other "theories" of contemporary science, or that believe creationism has, if only as one theory among others, a legitimate scientific status. These are not failures of teaching "the right thing" but failures to teach any example at all of the depth and breadth of any well-developed scientific notion.

One of the characteristic features of aiming for new levels of integration is that students will have substantial re-experiences of events that they ordinarily interpret in context-dependent ways so as to see connections to more broader, more invariant perspectives. In comparison to the usual aims of elementary school science, pre-science is considerably more ambitious.

Developing a program of pre-science will be significantly different from any curriculum attempted in the past. But my claim, based on the above notions, is that teaching pre-science will be a much more reliable way of giving children access to what is essential substantively and epistemologically about science.

6.3 Methodology

The core of the pre-science program is to experientialize a subject by finding or imagining the essential phenomena that may conspire to produce an understanding of the subject. This is a task I have called in other places "a genetic task analysis," and it necessarily involves significant empirical work with children with an eye toward reforming and reorganizing their knowledge. Then one must invent environments and experiences to develop children's ideas in small clusters.

There are two important estimates of complexity of the task of experiential learning that have a great impact on designing environments and experiences. First, any even relatively constrained set of materials/experiences (an "activity" in the Montessori sense) will only make salient a relatively small set of phenomena. This is not to say we must specify activities in infinite detail, laying out a curriculum of little experiences. On the contrary, such specificity would defeat any semblance of personal initiative and playfulness in pre-science. But it is to say that the level of detail of analysis that says roughly what some activity gives the student in terms of experience and how that contributes to the overall program is important for designers and teachers. Particularly if a student is having difficulty, we will need this level of analysis to suggest how to refocus the student's attention to overcome that difficulty.

Secondly, we will have to assume several different and certainly overlapping activities to collect enough of the enhanced and elaborated p-prims to meld into a pre-science "unit." This is a "multiple-perspective" principle that no single "simple model" or perspective on pre-science concepts can suffice, that pre-science is essentially the development of a coordinated scheme of perspectives. The importance of this principle is out of proportion to the space I can give it here, but, for example, see Bob Lawler (Lawler, 1983) on the multiple microworlds involved in the course of his daughter's learning arithmetic.

These two remarks are estimates of the scale of the task of learning science on the foundation of the essentially fragmented intuitive knowledge system. The first is an estimate of how much of one's knowledge system can be engaged so as to be significantly changed in an experience (not much); the second is an estimate of how much needs to be engaged and changed to pass from intuition to pre-science (quite a significant amount more).

I need to say a bit more about unifying experiences. In some cases where overlap between activities is sufficient, that may happen automatically. This is the ideal case, where the set of activities in a pre-science unit have enough overlap and continuity that students spontaneously build from one experience into the others. In some cases, however, we may specifically design work aimed at re-experiencing some activities on the basis of ideas more salient in others. My constant example is that after building a conceptual model so as to have integrity in its own terms, we may wish to work at implanting that model in students' experiences of the world.

In some cases more elaborate unifying experiences might be designed. For example, a formalism that can be interpreted by means of the experiences might serve that role. Indeed, I do not want to write formalisms, symbols and propositions out of the program entirely, but to place them in a proper context. Thus, one might culminate teaching a pre-science unit with a more standard science unit using text, definitions, problem sets or other more narrowly constrained activities. Success in such a course as compared with students taking it without having the pre-science unit might make an excellent evaluation. (Evaluation needs more consideration than I can give it here; our measures of student success will need to change with this new program. They will need to be more like the flexibility of thought that comes from knowing a great number of ways of thinking about something than understanding measured by solving examples of a fixed class of problems quickly. Learning that can be carried on after a pre-science unit makes a nearly ideal example of this kind of flexibility.)

Note that we have not worried specifically about the task of developing p-prims one by one. If the task turns out so difficult as to require such care, we will have failed to define the task properly. One will have to go back to the genetic task analysis and start again staying closer to the naive state of our students.

Finally, we come to an essential point beyond what we have said about p-prims. Since the coherence of the new system is by assumption beyond the initial perception of students – even more so since we have partitioned the system, to some extent, into more manageable chunks – each of the activities will have to have its own coherence. Experiences must locally drive themselves on the basis of things that people know how and want to do, not on the basis of some invisible teleology or on the instructor's interest. This is an example of Papert's Poetry Principle.

6.4 Computers and Pre-Science

Before taking an example in detail, let us consider what this program
has to do with computers? Nothing and everything. The program can
be formulated without computers specifically in mind. Indeed, this program has resonances with ideas that have been around in the "science-and-
experience" community for decades – ideas like "messing about," "meaning
before words." I depart from that community in the optimistic stand I take
about being explicit about knowledge elements, and in the emphasis on unifying experiences into a level between intuitive knowledge and what would
be more easily recognized as science. I depart from that community more
substantially in my belief that in some areas at least, the computer is an
order of magnitude more flexible and precise in crafting experiences that
can lead to essential insights, and that we should soon see breakthroughs
in both the level of achievement of learning through experience and consequently in the public acceptance of such educational strategies.

I would like to emphasize again that computers have a character that
better adapts them to some areas than others – in particular, to areas where
the essential structure is visual, geometric and dynamic. Thus the topic of
motion, which will constitute my major example, is nearly ideally suited.
In contrast, in working on a similar program having to do with weighing
and balancing, Marlene Kliman and I have not found the use of computers
particularly compelling, and we are proceeding at this point with standard
materials.

6.5 An Example: Beyond Dynaturtles

Let me illustrate the pre-science program with a perspective on dynaturtles. The dynaturtle and target game, through which most people know
it, constitute a good example of a activity in a pre-science program. It is
self-motivating, satisfying the poetry principle, and has a relatively short
list of essential phenomena that students reliably run into. This fraction of
the "curriculum" consists of ideas such as the specialness and importance
of the stopped state (only when things are stopped do they necessarily go
in the direction you push them), the notion of cancelling motion with opposite "anti-kicks," and qualitative versions of combining kicks with existing
motion ("compromise," etc.).

In my original paper on the subject (diSessa, 1982) I proposed building a curriculum directly on this experience alone. I now believe this was
overly optimistic for two reasons, both of which are versions of the multiple-
perspective principle. First, as I noted at the time, there are a number

of "advanced topics" that, while adults often seemed to get to, children did not. These did not seem to be experientially contiguous in the target game context. Second, even if children got relatively proficient with dynaturtle, they often still had very significant problems with mildly altered environments, like a lunar lander. (That is basically a dynaturtle with the additional complication of gravity.) If dynaturtle by itself constituted a complete pre-science module, students should have been flexible enough to engage this slightly altered environment with less difficulty. In retrospect, we should have guessed this difficulty, because, while understanding dynaturtle "completely" would be quite sufficient to cope with lunar lander, the phenomenological projection that one encounters in the target game leaves out some essential ideas that must be salient to deal with lunar lander. In particular, the notion of components of motion and independent control of them (which, incidentally, is in the neighborhood of the advanced topics noted for adults, but not children for the target game) is not well represented in dynaturtle, but terribly important to the lunar lander. For the sake of specificity, let me briefly mention two more topics that I believe essential to treat experientially before we can expect to have developed a critical mass of experience necessary to transcend intuitions about motion.

The first is the phenomenology of simple relative motion and frames of reference. Frames of reference are important to understanding the motion of dynaturtles because it is through this perspective that one unifies, once again, what happens in the stopped and moving cases. Provided one takes the frame moving with the dynaturtle when it is kicked, the dynaturtle does, indeed, always go in the direction of the kick! It is quite easy to develop dynaturtle activities that make relative motion more salient. It is also easy to imagine defining multiple frames of reference in these activities, and watching events from those different points of view.

The second topic (actually, class of topics) is phenomenology of velocity, acceleration, distance and time in a more restricted sense. An example of this class of ideas to understand that distance is in a fundamental way just an accumulation (adding up) of velocities, or to readily compare the speeds of different objects, or simply to see that an object is accelerating or not. Again, I cannot take the time to describe the computer activities related to this in detail, but substantial work has been completed with Mitch Reznick and Steve Ocko from Microworld Learning Incorporated. (Incidentally, from the perspective of a standard curriculum, these time, rate and distance ideas are clear prerequisites to understanding what kicks do to a dynaturtle. The definition of velocity must be made before the definition of kicks (changes in velocity). But from an experiential perspective, children have independent routes into both sets of topics. We discovered empirically that children can learn a great deal from dynaturtle without having a prior formalized notion of velocity. The fragmentation of the intuitive knowledge system gives us degrees of freedom; we need not be so firm in ordering the curriculum since what stood as a prerequisite is now a co-requisite for a deeper, unified understanding.)

In this section I have again not attempted to craft an air tight logical case that computational experience is not in an essential way different from "real" experience. Nor have I tried to present irrefutable empirical evidence. There is evidence, but my thrust is not to convince the most skeptical. Instead it is to point the way to uses of computers that are consonant with the goals of many who are skeptical of computers. The point is that if our task is construed as changing the ecology of experience in such a way as to draw out scientific understanding from activities that children will find enjoyable and natural – in short, some version of the pre-science program – then computation should not be ignored. I do not deny that the computational experiences in a pre-science program would rely in a profound way on prior "real world" experiences that develop children's ideas about motion and their abilities to watch and interpret it. But the best experiences always carry forward the successes of the past. If computers can do that, it is enough.

7.0 SUMMARY

In this paper, I have tried to locate computers properly in the world of experience. It is easy to feel warm and comfortable with experiences in the natural surroundings, and frightened of the artificiality of computers. Yet, once one looks carefully at good experiences in either context, these initial feeling must give way to more careful concern for what makes a good experience, independent of the instrument used to support that experience. I have looked at natural experiences (re-experiencing the moon) to show that the props we use are often a small factor, that the relation of those props to prior experience, of whatever sort, is crucial. I have looked at computer experiences (dynaturtle) to find that sometimes it is quite clear that computer experiences are not treated as at all artificial by children, but that in some respects their artificiality (making the structure of physical laws salient) is the best thing about them. When it comes to bringing discovery into the classroom, whether some activity is computer-based or not seems much less the point than what that activity makes visible, manipulable, and what kinds of thinking excursions it engenders in our students.

Finally, I have sketched a program that I call pre-science for making experience a much more central part of science education. I have tried to make it clear that the extent to which computers can contribute to this program is not fore-ordained, but instead it depends on how well we understand both what experience is, and what our students experienced world is like. As with all materials, the character of the medium may set some broad constraints on its use, but much more depends on our imagination and skill in crafting those materials to good ends and on setting the proper context for their use.

ACKNOWLEDGEMENTS

I wish to thank Bob Lawler for suggesting the title of this chapter.

REFERENCES

Abelson, H., & diSessa, A. (1981). *Turtle Geometry: The Computer as a Medium for Exploring Mathematics.* Cambridge, MA: MIT Press.

diSessa, A. A. (1978). On learnable representations of knowledge. In J. Lochhead & J. Clement (Eds.), *Cognitive Process Instruction,* Philidelphia: Franklin Institute Press.

diSessa, A. A. (1982). Unlearning aristotelian physics: a study of knowledge-based learning, *Cognitive Science (Vol. 6).*

diSessa, A. A. (1983). Phenomenology and the evolution of intuitions. In Dedre Gentner & Al Stevens (Eds.), *Mental Models,* Hillsdale, NJ: Lawrence Erlbaum Press.

Globerson, T., & diSessa, A. A. (1984). The effect of age and cognitive style on childrens intuitions of motion. Paper presented at Logo-84, Cambridge, MA, June.

Lawler, R. (1985). *Computer Experience and Cognitive Development.* New York: John Wiley & Sons.

Papert, S. (1980). *Mindstorms: Children, Computers and Powerful Ideas.* New York: Basic Books.

4 MICROWORLDS: TRANSFORMING EDUCATION [1]

Seymour Papert

Arts and Media Technology Center
Massachusetts Institute of Technology
Cambridge, MA

Looking at how computers are used in education, one is tempted to start classifying. It's a little dangerous to do this, but I would like to start off with a very crude classification of three ways of using computers, just to place a certain set of problems into perspective. First, as tutorials in one sense or another – which is by far the most widespread, best known, and earliest use – where the computer serves as a sort of mechanized instructor. Secondly, as tools for doing something else: as calculators, word processors, simulators, or whatever. And thirdly, a different concept altogether: as microworlds. Here I shall concentrate on the notion of microworld and talk about its relations both to computers and to theories of learning. The other uses of computers surely have a role – but they are not what will revolutionize education.

One microworld which is already widely known is the Logo turtle microworld. Briefly, this world is inhabited by a small object on the screen. In some versions, it is shaped like a triangle, in others, like an actual turtle. To make it move and draw lines, you talk to it by typing commands on the keyboard. For example, if you say FORWARD 50, the turtle will move in the direction it's facing and draw a line 50 units long, 50 "turtle steps" children might say. Then if you say RIGHT 90, it will turn 90 degrees. And then you can tell it to go forward again, or back, turn through any angle, or lift its pen up so it moves without leaving a trace. In principle, you can draw anything – even curves, because you can go forward a little, turn a little, go forward a little, and so on until you get the curve you want. Anything that can be drawn can also be described in this turtle talk, the turtle's coordinate system.

This is a microworld in the sense that it's a little world, a little slice of reality. It's strictly limited, completely defined by the turtle and the ways

---

[1] This paper is based on a presentation given 14 March 1984 at the ITT Key Issues Conference held at the Annenberg School of Communications of the University of Southern California.

it can be made to move and draw. But it is rich. Inside this microworld, a child explores by manipulating the turtle: making it draw squares and circles, repeating and rotating designs, whatever the child can imagine. The microworld is created and designed as a safe place for exploring. You can try all sorts of things. You will never get into trouble. You will never feel "stupid." It will never say a rude thing to you; it will never embarrass you; it will never fall to pieces or bite you or give you a low grade. You are totally safe in this little world. And yet while being safe, it is also designed to be discovery-rich in the sense that little nuggets of knowledge have been scattered around in it for you to find.

The question "Now that we have the turtle, what other manipulable computational objects can we create?" led to a theme of ongoing research at MIT and elsewhere. At some future time, complex networks of microworlds that touch on many sectors of knowledge will be the staple diet of learning, and will replace the present concept of "curriculum". It will take some time to develop microworlds fundamentally different from the turtle paradigm. In this paper, I talk only about the example closest to the turtle. This is a world inhabited by objects known as sprites which, in a simple form, have already been implemented in some Logo systems and are already giving rise to a number of new observations about how children learn.

The Sprite world is a kind of turtle world that is novel in several ways. First, it has many turtles – as many as 32 can be conjured up. Then, unlike the classical turtle, sprites don't have any intrinsic shape. You can give them any shape you like. You can make one look like a cat, or an airplane, or a tree, or a flower, or a bird. Finally, perhaps most importantly, they can easily be put in motion. They are dynamic, hence their nickname "sprites."

Sprites are still turtles in that they obey commands in the Logo programming language. But there are also new commands. You might say SETSHAPE :BIRD to one of these sprites, meaning it should look like a bird, and it will say it doesn't know what :BIRD means. You have to say that :BIRD means this shape that you've drawn. So you draw the shape you want and tell it :BIRD means this shape – you can even draw an elephant and call it :BIRD if you want – and now saying SETSHAPE :BIRD will make it take on this shape. You can SETCOLOR :RED or SETCOLOR :GREEN, make it whatever color you like. And there are lots of other things you can do with these sprites as well.

Sprite Logo has the familiar characteristics of the microworld. It's a simplified piece of reality which you can explore, and again there's no right or wrong. In this way, it's like a construction kit, an erector set, mud pies, building with blocks. In all these activities, you can do whatever you want, subject only to the constraints of the laws of the little world you are in. Blocks won't stay up unless they are supported, and mud pies won't fly.

There are limits for each of these slices of reality. And I'm going to suggest that in a very general way, not only in the computer context but probably in all important learning, an essential and central mechanism is to confine yourself to a little piece of reality that is simple enough to understand. It's by looking at little slices of reality at a time that you learn to understand the greater complexities of the whole world, the macroworld.

With these sprites, for example, SETSPEED 20 makes them start moving continuously and steadily at a speed of 20 arbitrarily chosen "units." The first story I want to share with you here is about those speeds – as well as the way that microworlds allow you to learn about things in an entirely new way. On the screen there are a number of objects flying around, say six bright red balls, all at the same speed. When you say SETSPEED 20, they plod along like Sunday drivers. If you say SETSPEED 100, they zoom around really fast. In front of the screen, a little girl of six is typing SETSPEED – which has been abbreviated to S. She says S 4, and they creep across the screen. Then she says S 1, and they go *so* very slowly you can hardly see them moving. Then she says S 0, and they stop. And she says S 10 and they move, and S 0 and they stop. She looks at the screen for a long time and then she jumps up and goes and calls all her friends to come and look.

Now what was she getting excited about? This story is quite poignant for me because I saw this happen and for a while, I didn't see what it was all about. And I might still be wrong but I've become pretty sure what was happening. I think she was excited because she had *discovered zero*. They tell us in school that the Greek mathematicians, Pythagoras and Euclid and others, these incredibly inventive people, didn't know about zero. And it's true, in a certain sense, that zero was discovered quite a bit later by Hindu mathematicians.

I don't know what you imagined when people told you that zero was discovered by Hindu mathematicians. In wracking my memory, I think what I imagined was that they discovered using a little circle for zero. Of course they discovered something much more fundamental, and this girl was in a certain sense repeating that discovery.

You might say it like this: what that girl found exciting was the following paradox: that standing still is *moving*. Standing still is moving with speed zero, and moving with speed zero is standing still. Now she couldn't say that, so I'm not entirely sure what was in her mind, but I think it was something like that.

This understanding of zero is an important scientific principle so subtle that it usually passes us by. We get into a lot of trouble when we're trying to understand laws of physics because we haven't really registered that when we say motion, we should include standing still as a case of motion. In physics, anyway, there's nothing special about standing still. In the end, that's the moral of relativity – and if we understood that, we wouldn't be so upset when we hear about Gallilean frames of reference or relativity and other topics many of you found quite esoteric at school.

Since then, I've watched and set other people to watch for this phenomenon. Of course not every child reacts like that, but a scattering here and there do. Whenever children are exposed to this sort of thing, a certain number of children seem to get caught by discovering zero. Others get excited about other things.

The fact that not every child discovers zero this way reflects an essential property of the learning process. No two people follow the same path of learnings, discoveries, and revelations. You learn in the deepest way when something happens that makes you fall in love with a particular piece of knowledge. For example, I fell in love with that particular incident with that girl. It has played an important role in my thinking and my life since then. But colleagues who think much like I do picked up different incidents. The girl in my story came to think about motion because she was struck by speed zero. Someone else comes to the same understanding through different encounters. What's great about these turtle microworlds is that they are rich in opportunities for discovery of this sort. The protean quality of the computer as an intellectual medium means that every child can find a rich intellectual activity with which to fall in love. It is through such "intellectual love affairs" that people acquire the taste for rigor and creativity.

Another story goes back to the very first experiments that we did with these sprites in the Lamplighter School in Texas.[2] When these computers were introduced, the teachers of the various grade levels decided that each grade would learn certain aspects of this system. They had Logo with sprites and Logo with turtles, and they decided that the first and second grades should not learn to do the SETSPEED stuff.

Now they did have a reason. They weren't just being prejudiced against the children or trying to deny them. Their reason was that when you use SETSPEED, you must give it not only a speed but a direction as well. It's got to go somewhere. In fancier science talk, we would say that velocity is a "vector quantity" having both magnitude and direction. The way we give direction in Logo is to say SETHEADING 270 to go west,

---

[2] Descriptions of this and several other children's differing responses to and interactions with sprites and Logo can be found in Chapter 3 of Turkle, 1984.

and SETHEADING 90 to go east (or left and right on the screen). The teachers figured that numbers like 270 are so outside the ken of the younger children that there's no point in introducing them to this double confusion of learning about degrees and angles. Actually, there are many ways the teachers could have gotten around that problem. For example, they could have reprogrammed Logo (which is a flexible language) to allow commands like FACE NORTH, FACE EAST, etc. But we didn't interfere, and it's just as well we didn't because the children had some very interesting learning experiences.

So the younger children were shown how to work with the sprites in a static way. They could change the sprites' shapes and put them in different positions to make pleasing tableaux on the screen. It was fun and they were learning a lot, there's no question about that, but it was a very unstable situation. Soon the younger children saw the sprites moving on the older children's screens and began to ask them: "How do you do that?" The first few times they asked, they didn't get enough of an answer to be able to do anything with it. But one day, as the older children became more confident and articulate, and as the younger ones also become more understanding about the whole system, a threshold was crossed where it was now possible for one second grader to bring back just enough knowledge about dynamics so that his classmates could work with it.

One cannot say that the second grader fully understood the concept of angle, or the use of such numbers as 270. He came away from his conversation with something more important than the educator's mythical concept of "full understanding." What he acquired instead was a fragment of knowledge that enabled him to work on gaining a deeper and deeper understanding. He came over to the investigator in the middle of the next day with an air of having gotten at some subversive, taboo knowledge – I think this subversive aspect is a very important part of learning – and he was saying, very proudly too, that he's got the great idea, he understands what it's all about. He put it in a marvelous way, assimilating it to ideas he understood well. He said, "I got it. Numbers are secret codes for directions." He explained that they didn't yet know the code, "but we're working on it."

In fact, there were fourteen of them working on this code, and what was exciting about it was that yes, they didn't know what 270 meant, and yes, they didn't know what degrees meant, but they did know that they could bring this into a conceptual frame that they understood very well: codes. And so by bringing it into codes, they could work on it. A few weeks later, they were doing pretty well – and a few months later, they had objects flying all over the screen under perfect control, they knew about 270 degrees, they knew about degrees and angles and these big numbers, and they knew all sorts of things because they had broken this code.

There are a number of important points I'd like to emphasize here. For one, I'm not sure that I understand what to do about the subversive angle.[3] It raises questions like, "Suppose we hadn't made certain knowledge taboo. Would these children have been less well off? Should we deny children access to knowledge so that they can fight for it?" I think obviously not. That wouldn't be acceptable in any moral standard that I would believe in. Fortunately, we don't have to. There is plenty of room for subversion created by an essential conflict in the socialization process itself – between the children's wanting to do it their way and the society, the culture, imposing something that goes against that. There's a sense of taboo and conflict and subversion going on all the time in growing up. Growing up *is* a subversive activity. So perhaps we don't have to worry about providing special conditions for subversiveness; it's always there – whether we like it or not, and whether we see it or not.

The second point is that again, like the child who discovered zero, this second-grader did something self-motivated. For whatever reason, this child decided, "I want to understand that," and he had enough sportive entrepreneurship to go out and pursue it. In other words, he took charge of his own learning process. These microworlds ought to make it possible and easier to do that. I think that's perhaps the most important aspect of them: that they create better and richer conditions for children – and for others, grown-ups as well – to take charge of their own learning.

Now, finally, I'd like to mention a concept that I've been concerned about, almost preoccupied with, in my theoretical thinking in the last little while. That's a concept that I'm calling fractured knowledge, broken knowledge, although I may devise a better name for it at some time.

There's a model in the education world of how one communicates knowledge. The teacher knows how to do the long division algorithm – a piece of knowledge to be communicated to the child as a whole package. Well, that might or might not work sometimes, but it goes wrong in ways that you could very easily and obviously describe as: "It gets broken in transmission." The teacher might be trying and the child might be trying too, but maybe the child didn't hear a little, or maybe couldn't understand it, or didn't want to, or didn't have some prerequisite. What comes across is fractured knowledge, not the whole piece but a broken piece. And I think one central epistemological question in the theory of learning becomes: Un-

---

[3] The idea that subversive or revolutionary energy fuels learning has been brilliantly developed by the Brazilian Paolo Freire in *Pedagogy of the Oppressed*.

der what conditions and by what processes can fractured knowledge be repaired? How can it be built up? From the fractured pieces, how do you get back to some whole – not necessarily the same whole that was being contemplated by the transmitter?

In the case of the second grader and the knowledge about the sprites' directionality, you see very clearly that those fourteen children working at cracking this code each had little pieces of knowledge. They managed to put them together because they were in a situation where, first of all, they could communicate and, secondly, they could experiment. Having the computer meant they could try out ideas with it and get objective results – as opposed to a situation where they could only think about it inside their heads, unable to externalize those ideas and see the results. So the computer plays a powerful role in enabling you to put fractured knowledge together to produce whole knowledge.

The story of the stolen knowledge about motion depends essentially on the fact that both the older and younger children were working with the same material – the turtles or sprites. This goes directly counter to the view of educational curriculum theory where you try very hard to chop everything up and say, "This is for first grade, this is for second, this is for third," and so on – where you do each thing at the proper set time, and very little belongs to more than one grade.

In contrast, the turtle microworld (and Logo generally) was deliberately designed to be interesting to people at different stages of development. Pre-school children can do interesting things with Logo because it's very easy to start moving the turtle around. Yet adults (including high school and college students) can also get into it and exercise some very complex, subtle, sophisticated issues of both programming and geometry. Now, of course, they're doing different things with it, but there *is* a continuity. In our story about the moving sprites, this continuity played an important role: the younger children saw the older ones doing something more complicated with the same system that they were using. Because it *was* the same system, they could communicate and exchange knowledge about ways of looking at the system. This aspect of microworlds is an essential one: that you can explore one when you're five – and then again when you're six or fifteen, or continually at all ages, doing more complex operations and projects as you go along, yet with a single, continuous entity.

These concepts I've been discussing – of fractured knowledge and exploration and discovery, of falling in love with something you discover, of having the opportunity to pursue the things that capture your imagination – these are features which I think are quite essential to the way we should think of the forms in education. The microworld concept gives us a way of doing that which is particularly powerful in relation to all of these –

and especially that last goal of having something that is not age- or level-dependent. Like reality, you can manipulate it at different ages.

The kind of learning I associate with artificially created microworlds occurs very typically in natural settings. A particularly clear example is the acquisition of a spoken language like English. Babies learn English by creating a "mini-microworld" of baby talk in which they manipulate pieces of the larger whole in order to master them. Yet nowhere in the world is a language restricted to baby talk. The child continues to be immersed in the same language that poets and philosophers find a suitable instrument for their sophisticated purposes. Language is a model of something that spreads across the entire spectrum of ages and levels – personality types, too, for that matter and maybe cultural types as well – to be picked up by different individuals, each in an individual way.

In bringing the computer into the education system, the microworld is the richest concept that we have to work with, and it should be used as the central one. My concept of how to create a curriculum (and by this word I mean a coherent set of materials to aid learning through the whole school period – and before and after, as well) is to create a network of microworlds, each one focusing on different areas of knowledge.

The two I've mentioned are mainly geometric microworlds, although these sprites do overlap with extremely important ideas in physics – in particular, ideas about motion that are especially hard for the beginning student to assimilate. In physics, dynamics is traditionally taught after statics, even though this is obviously perverse. In the history of physics, it's clear that dynamics provides the fundamental driving force: the fundamental ideas about how things move. The notion of force is linked to acceleration and to the motion of objects. Nevertheless, statics is taught first and the idea of force is then introduced, one might say grafted onto statics, in a very confused and confusing way.

There are obvious reasons for this. Again, it's not because the teachers are confused, but because they don't have a satisfactory way of teaching young students how to work with motion. The only ways we've had to work with motion up to now have been rather disconnected from each other. There's the totally intuitive way where you can throw things and catch them and run and move – and you've got a lot of intuitive knowledge of this sort, but it's not formalized at all. (It's also restricted by the influence of gravity and friction.) The only time you formalize it satisfactorily is when you get into calculus – and to get into calculus, you have to take this long complicated path through arithmetic and algebra and so on, so you're probably not going to get there very well.

On the other hand, these children of five and six and seven who are writing little programs to control motion on the screen *are* working with motion in a formal way. If you look more closely at what's happening, they are using representations of numbers – vectors, directions and speed – and an equivalent of differential equations, in order to manipulate the sprites. In other words, they are able to play with motion in this and other microworlds in ways that have only been possible with static forces in the past. So this microworld is not just mathematical, it's physics as well. It allows children to develop both intuitive *and* formal experience with motion in an integrated way.

I'd like to make a distinction here between microworlds and simulations. To made the distinction, I'll describe another way we can work with motion – and that's to create a kind of turtle called a "dynaturtle" which simulates the behavior of a Newtonian object.

Imagine a ball rolling upwards on the computer screen as if it were moving out in space, and you hit it from the side. Where is it going to go? Children think it's going to move sideways – at a right angle to its original movement. My colleague Andrea diSessa has shown that MIT undergraduates have markedly similar intuitions, even though they were selected by the MIT Admissions process for being super-science stars at school. These students don't actually think the ball will go sideways. They know better. But if you bury the problem ever so slightly in a more complex situation, their more deep-seated intuitive ideas about motion take over – and they *do* predict the equivalent of moving sideways. That is, the addition of vectors is something they learned formally, but did not really absorb into their intuitive thinking about physics.

One way to improve the situation is to make dynaturtles and give children and other learners these worlds to play with. They will become familiar with all sorts of problems and situations using Newtonian objects and, by exploring these worlds, will learn the fundamental laws of dynamics in an intuitive as well as a formal way. We have seen this happen to some extent in experiments conducted by diSessa and by Barbara White.[4] Dynaturtles and similar worlds allow children to discern things that advanced students have trouble understanding.

---

[4] This work has been reported in the following articles: Andrea diSessa, "Unlearning Aristotelian Physics: A Study of Knowledge-Based Learning," *Cognitive Science*, Vol. 6, 1982, pp. 37-75; Barbara Y. White, "Designing Computer Games to Facilitate Learning," Ph.D. thesis, Department of Electrical Engineering and Computer Science, MIT, January 1981; Barbara Y. White, "Designing Computer Games to Help Physics Students Understand Newton's Laws of Motion," in *Cognition and Instruction*, Vol. 1, January 1984.

And that's what I would call a simulation. It is a microworld inhabited by dynaturtles, but it's a special kind of microworld, one that tries to copy a certain part of reality thought to be important in science. However, there's another approach which I think is more fundamental in the long run, something that's really going to turn around the learning of physics. This one takes a slightly more distanced approach to what we want children to learn.

The problem with learning dynamics in physics is not so much the particular laws of physics that we're teaching these children. It's that they're not really used to thinking about motion at all. So, let's build some microworlds where objects move in a lawful way, but with simple laws of motion rather than those of Newtonian physics.

The Sprite world is like that. You can make the sprites move in all sorts of ways. They can bounce off each other, pass through one another, move in different directions and speeds, make kaleidoscopic patterns, and even play Follow-the-Leader. You can make them explode from the center – just like in the Big Bang – and then reverse their speeds (from SETSPEED 25 to SETSPEED -25) so they retrace their paths. Exploring this simpler context gives you a clear grasp of the *idea* of laws of motion, and a framework for learning Newtonian ones.

A microworld like this gives you an entirely new kind of object – a transitional object between the ones that you can touch and push (like tables and wooden blocks) and the kind of objects that you know in science, in philosophy, and in mathematics. Science is full of stuff like electrons, genes, and quasars. Mathematics is full of the square root of minus one, or even the number 562.

These are not things you can really touch. Many children and older students have quite a lot of trouble when they first run across objects like these. What are they like – these created, formal, theoretical objects? A sprite is something you can touch; it's there, it's an object. It has a color and a movement. You can give it a shape and you can change its shape. You can do something to it and it will change and it will act. So, in some ways, it's like these things we work with in the real world, and in some ways, it's like those abstract things. It's a transitional object that helps you manipulate the abstract ones. This ability to create transitional objects gives us a way of closing the gap between intuitive and formal learning.

The more I worked with microworlds and came to recognize their importance in the computer context, the more intrigued I became with pre-computer microworlds and the role that microworlds generally hold in the theory of learning. I gradually began to understand that the microworld concept leads to a different way of thinking about much that is in Piaget and in other developmental theorists as well.

Looking at the important moments in Piaget's life, one was his book with Szeminska on the child's concept of number.[5] This was a turning point. Until then, he'd been studying the child's concept of dreams and play and language. The book on number started a new phase where he was going to study speed, spontaneous geometry, physics, and the child's concepts of all the important areas of knowledge.

The remarkable thing about that book is how little of it is directly about number. One would think that a book on number and how children learn it would be full of how you add 3 and 5, and of learning the properties of number as they are taught in school for example. There's hardly any of that. What *is* in the book is something very different.

Piaget says that behind number there are three structures, or *groupements* – groupings. There's the structure of things being ordered: if you don't have a firm grasp of the concept of ordering things, you can't begin to understand number. There's a concept of combining formal objects: you can take two numbers and put them together. But it's not really that 3 plus 4 makes 7 that's important, it's just the *idea* of taking two things and putting them together. And there's a concept of nearness: what's near and what's far, qualitative topology: objects arranged in a line are successively farther from one another. So are numbers.

You can think of these concepts in several ways. You might say, "Well, it's obvious that you can't have a notion of number without having mastered these concepts that are clearly its precursors." Ordering, for example. If you don't have the idea of one thing following another in a certain order, it's very difficult to get to number. And, in fact, you find this with four-year-old children. If you ask them to count four objects, they might point and say, "One, two, three, four, five, six," taking them in any old order and repeating them. For the four-year-old, there's no difference between doing that and what you do when you count them in this orderly way. So the idea of order and sequence has to be acquired.

The idea of microworld gives another way of thinking about the relationship between Piaget's structures and number. One can see ordering as a microworld created by the child. A set of situations – those involving order – come to be perceived as having a commonality, as being of one kind.

---

[5] Jean Piaget and Alina Szeminska, *La Genese du Nombre Chez l'Enfant*, Delachaux & Niestle, 1941. English translations in 1961, 1964, 1965: *The Child's Conception of Number.*

At certain periods of life, the child becomes fascinated with a certain kind of relationship – like comparing things, or lining them up, or putting one in front of the other.

This is a microworld in the same sense I was talking about earlier. If you look carefully at what Piaget is saying about the acquisition, it's as if the child is giving itself advice about how to learn about number: "Don't try and learn such a complex thing. Instead, concentrate on one aspect, on one substructure: say order. And when you have mastered that, concentrate on something else." In other words, the child imposes a certain microworld structure on the world by saying, "I'm going to look only at a small piece of it. And I'm going to master that small piece, even if it's only a partial mastery." [6]

One of our students at MIT, Robert Lawler, wrote a Ph.D. thesis[7] years ago based on his observation of a six-year-old child. Over a period of six months, he observed this child almost continuously, never missing as much as a half hour. He devoted himself essentially full-time to observing the intellectual development of this child, who, in fact, considered herself to be a collaborator in the project and was also engaged full-time in trying to reveal what she was doing. The fact that the subject was a collaborator might have deformed the experiment, but I don't think so. He discovered something very interesting in relation to the idea of microworlds and presents it in his book *Computer Experience and Cognitive Development*.

When people study the learning process, they usually study a hundred children for several hours each, and Lawler showed very conclusively what you might have known anyway, that you lose a lot of very important information that way. By being around all the time, he saw things with this child that he certainly would never have caught from occasional samplings in the laboratory. I think Lawler's methods are sure to become a paradigm for how to do this kind of research, and indeed, many people are already using this approach, particularly in the area of language acquisition.

What Lawler discovered about microworlds is well illustrated by one example. During this period, the subject figured out how to add multi-digit

---

[6] Curiously, this striving to master one small piece sometimes seems to undo one's mastery of another piece. In English, for example, when children start acquiring the "rule" of *stem*-plus-*ed* for past tenses, they suddenly start saying things like "bringed" and "goed," even though they had previously used "brought" and "went." Correct usage of the irregular forms does return – though it may take several months and each exception to the rule comes back individually. This phenomenon has been frequently described. See, for example, Miller & Ervin, 1964.

[7] Lawler, 1979.

numbers. A year later, she had gotten mixed up and confused on the rules, but that's not really important. What I'd like to recount to you is *how* Miriam started adding numbers.

First of all, Lawler found by watching Miriam in detail that when she added numbers, she used very different procedures. He describes these as "thinking about different microworlds." If she had to add three and four, she would use her fingers. She would say, "One, two, three, four," and then "One, two, three, four – five, six, seven." She did it in an obvious sort of way, using her fingers, but she would only do that for small numbers. The second number especially had to be pretty small.

With certain other numbers, she used different microworlds. For example, she had a money microworld where she knew about quarters and dimes and nickels. So she knew that 25 and 25 made 50, and that 4 times 25 made 100; she knew that 25 and 5 made 30, that 10 and 10 and 5 made 25, several things like that.

So she had a pocket of knowledge about what you can do with your fingers, and a pocket of knowledge about what you can do with money facts. These little pockets are probably shared by almost all young children in some form or another, but Miriam had a third one because she had been exposed to turtle geometry: a turtle angle world. She knew, for example, this exotic fact that 90 plus 90 makes 180. Not, as you might suppose, because 9 plus 9 makes 18, which she didn't know. She couldn't add 9 and 9 to get 18 because it's too big for the fingers, it's too far from the money numbers, and she'd never thought of 18 as one-tenth of 180 (who would?), and so she didn't know that piece. Nevertheless, she knew that 90 plus 90 makes 180, and 180 plus 180 makes 360, and several other facts in that world too. The turtle angles were important to her, so she had explored their properties pretty thoroughly.

But the essence that I'd like to emphasize here is how each of these little worlds, of money and fingers and turtles, gave her some fractured knowledge, pieces of knowledge that correspond to these pieces of reality. Like Piaget's structures or *groupements*, these little worlds give pieces of number, and what happened to Miriam during this period while she was being observed was *not* that she discovered these worlds, for she had already acquired them. Instead, it occurred to her for the first time that she could put them together. She began deliberately combining them, trying to refer backward and forward between the worlds to solve a problem. So she would say "25 and 28, that's 50," and then counting on her fingers, "26, 27, 28, 53." She became quite expert for a while at adding, but then as I mentioned she deteriorated again, maybe because she became too ambitious and tried to do things outside of what she could handle.[8]

Piaget's epistemological thesis is a somewhat different version of the idea that the way to solve a problem is to split the difficulties, to subdivide the problem. An old heuristic idea: if you want to do something complex, take the parts separately. This is an aspect of Piaget's thinking that hasn't penetrated in its full impact – and can be restated as a microworld thesis in this sense. But the child isn't creating microworlds in order to solve a problem. It's not subdividing a problem, it's subdividing the world. So it's a somewhat different view of the same kind of principle, that something in the child's innate capacity allows this subdivision of the world into microworlds, that these microworlds are elaborated and then put together. The process of putting them together is probably easier to understand than the making of them in the first place.

The point about these stories is that what we are doing in creating microworlds for the computer is not new. Microworlds have always played a role in children's learning. Some are deliberately made; for example, the worlds of blocks and construction kits. One might say each of those *groupements* is a microworld constructed partly by the child, and partly by the culture. The culture's role is seen in the kind of objects the child has and the kind of language that the child picks up. "Bigger than/smaller than" draws attention to the idea of putting things in order. So the language and the kind of objects available make certain microworlds easy to pick up – although ultimately these microworlds are self-constructed in the head by each child.

What's new about the computer in this regard is twofold. First of all, the possibilities of microworlds that can be made for the computer are vast, beyond anything that one could do with any other material. So the computer has opened up a new technology of being able to do things that are not so different in themselves – but in terms of how much you can do with it, it's just a different ballpark altogether. That's quantitatively.

Qualitatively, it becomes possible to make specific kinds of microworlds with the computer that couldn't be made before, and these new microworlds correspond to certain gaps in the natural learning process. To return to Piaget, I think that one can be most respectful to him by pointing out some respects in which he was wrong in a literal sense, specifically in his identification of the formal stage as something that necessarily comes later, at ages like 11 and 12 rather than five or six or seven when you have the so-called concrete operations.

---

[8] Such a deterioration appeared in the performance of another subject, as reported in Lawler et al., 1986, but not in the case to which Papert refers here. *Editor's Note, RWL.*

For Piaget, what makes up the formal stage is really symbol manipulations. Propositions that refer to propositions. Thinking that refers not to a concrete reality but to a representation of the reality and to all the possible situations that could arise under given real constraints. For people who don't know what the formal stage is, there isn't time to define it here. For those who do, I'd like to suggest that in defining the formal stage, Piaget pointed almost uncannily to exactly those things that you can do best with a computer. One might say that the formal stage arrived so late precisely because there were no computers. Take the one aspect of manipulating symbols. You can readily manipulate blocks or the technology of wood, but until now, you could only manipulate symbols by doing it in your head, or with the very abstracted means of pencil and paper. We didn't have any good way of externalizing the manipulation of symbols (and still don't except for the computer), and certainly no way that's accessible to very young children.

So there are certain microworlds we can create with the computer that happen to correspond exactly to a big gap that was pointed out by Piaget and others in the natural learning development of children. I think this coincidence gives us some real hope for the computer being not just another accidental technology that might help education, but *the* technology that comes just now to fill up an identifiable gap in that educational world.

If it's true that knowledge is normally appropriated in a process like microworld construction – that is, something like the creation of little pockets of reality, where you can dominate it and feel at home with it – some kinds of knowledge split up into a form that can be easily appropriated in that way. Others don't, and that's where we get into trouble: areas where our culture doesn't allow that kind of appropriation. Writing, mathematics, and science have been such areas, but the computer now makes it possible to create microworlds which can transform the rather clumsy educational process, as practiced in schools today, into a more natural and spontaneous one, similar to the way children learn language.

REFERENCES

Abelson, H., & DiSessa, A. (1980). *Turtle Geometry*. Cambridge, MA: MIT Press.
Freire, P. (19xx). *Pedagogy of the Oppressed*.
Lawler, R. (1979). One child's learning: an intimate study. Ph.D. thesis, Department of Electrical Engineering and Computer Science, Massachusetts Institute of Technology. See Lawler, 1985.
Lawler, R. (1985). *Computer Experience and Cognitive Development*. New York: John Wiley, Inc.
Lawler, R., DuBoulay, B., Hughes, M., & MacLeod, H. (1986). *Cognition and Computers*. New York: John Wiley, Inc.

Miller, W., & Ervin, S. (1964). The development of grammar in child language. In Ursula Bellugi and Roger Brown (Eds.), *The Acquisition of Language*, Monographs of the Society for Research in Child Development.

Turkle, S. (1984). *The Second Self: Computers and the Human Spirit.* New York: Simon & Schuster.

5 COMPUTER MICROWORLDS AND READING: AN ANALYSIS FOR THEIR SYSTEMATIC APPLICATION

Robert W. Lawler   *Gretchen P. Lawler*

ABSTRACT

Learning can be seen as a consequence of problem solving in particular cases. It occurs when one achieves a solution which is able to be used later. "Anchoring with variation" is a common and important process, providing a framework through which one can discuss coping with something imperfectly understood in terms of what is already well known. Our purpose in the following discussion is to explore some possible implications of this process for reading education as a worked example of how educational technology presents us with an opportunity for reconceptualizing instruction.

English has the phonological potential for more than 60 thousand monosyllables. Our analysis asks how many monosyllabic words exist in fact and what organization can be imposed on them to make the phonological code more accessible. We've chosen to represent these monosyllables as an initial phonemic cluster plus residue. The most common 550 residues cover 73 percent of the existing 7000 monosyllables. If children can learn 550 different correspondences between sounds and spelling patterns, their knowledge of these words, coupled with the ability to modify interpretations of letter strings by anchoring with variation, will cover a major portion of the phonetic-orthographic correspondences of the English language. We believe this extensive, concrete foundation of word and sound knowledge will permit children to read well enough that instruction will become primarily a refining and perfection of such knowledge.

The primary design conclusion is that if we create computer-based microworlds using words with the most common residues as the names for their entities and their actions, we will be providing a set of systematically generated monosyllabic anchors which promises to be highly effective for children's interpretation of many words they will encounter in reading English. The potential revolutionary impact of such a pre-reading curriculum is worth exploring.

1.0 A PERFORMANCE

Learning can be seen as a consequence of problem solving in particular cases. Let us offer you one of our favorite examples of problem solving as a basis for discussing this issue.

A number of years ago our son Rob, then age 8, and daughter Miriam, age 6, were playing in the kitchen. They mixed together some flour, salt, and water to make clay, rolled the mixture out flat, and then folded it over time and again. As they worked, Robby was counting the plies, the number of times he had folded the material. He counted 93, 94, 95, 96.... By the time there were 96 folds, the mass was very unwieldy; so he took a large knife and cut the material in half. Placing the second half on top of the first, he said, "Now we've got 96 plus 96". Miriam, who had not received any arithmetic instruction in kindergarten, responded, "That's a hundred ninety two". Robby was astounded, for he could do no such mental calculation although an able student in second grade. Her performance was impressive for a kindergartner.

1.1 How She Did It

The reasons Miriam at six was able to compute such a result were twofold. First, she had come to recognize 90 as a number of special importance through using Logo turtle geometry with Bob at the MIT Artificial Intelligence Laboratory. Second, she had developed certain procedures for mental calculation with numbers of such magnitude. For example, she would be able to add 30 and 45 by saying that 30 and 40 is 70, plus 5 is 75. She had other knowledge as well. Of specific use in this incident, she knew from experiences with turtle geometry that 90 degrees plus 90 is 180 degrees. So, when Robby asked Gretchen if that result was correct, Miriam answered first and was able to prove her result – in the process revealing the particular knowledge on which her performance rested: "We know that 90 plus 90 is 180, and 6 is 186...[then counting on her fingers], 187, 188, 189, 190, 191, 192".[1]

1.2 Anchoring with Variation

The formulation through which we would like to describe this mental calculation is one that we draw from the work of Tversky and Kahnemann (1974). These investigators required of their subjects results for arithmetic and estimation tasks so difficult that the subjects could in now way calculate the results precisely; then they examined the difference between the estimates subjects made and the actual results of a completed calculation. They use the phrase "anchoring with variation" to label a specific kind of mental performance they observed in their experiments.

They found, uniformly across all the subjects they studied, that the typical process of such calculation under conditions of the subject's uncer-

---

[1] There is more to this story than the anecdote presented here. The persistent scholar will find more examples, more detail, and a discussion of the relation between her computer experiences and other knowledge in Lawler, 1985.

tainty was one where the subject anchored the problem solving process at a specific estimate and then varied that value to solve the current problem. So described, anchoring with variation has very much the character of analogy in a specific, limited sense: the solution of a problem such as 96 plus 96 is analogous to the solution of 90 plus 90. But anchoring with variation functions like analogy until such time as the resulting solution becomes a salient entity itself, a well known thing or result. When that happens, analogy goes away. Anchoring with variation is an important process because it provides a general framework through which one can discuss the basic situation of learning, wherein one tries to deal with something imperfectly understood, by definition at the frontier of one's capacity. Learning occurs when one achieves a solution which is able to be used later.

We will use their phrase, anchoring with variation, to label the kind of calculation that our daughter went through in this story. She began with one well known result: 90 plus 90 is 180. She anchored her problem solving on that result; and by two variations, the catenation of 6 and the finger counting of 6 more, solved the problem.

Does anchoring with variation occur in other domains? The following anecdote reveals the same process in another guise. Our second daughter, Peggy, at 6 years, was using a workbook which required that she draw a picture of a coat. She was stymied for a moment, then continued, "Coat.... Oh. A coat is a person without any hands, or legs and feet, or a head, and with buttons." She was anchoring a newly constructed idea of how to draw a coat on the representation of a person that she had developed in her drawing experience, and then varying the individual features of that already established model.

Such a process is common for many people in various domains of problem solving. The purpose of the following discussion is to explore some possible implications of this process for reading education as a worked example of how educational technology presents us an opportunity for reconceptualizing instruction.

2.0 CHARACTERISTICS OF THE PRE-READER

By definition pre-readers have limited ability to construct oral words from letter strings. There are other, less definitive but still interesting, characteristics. Typically (but not uniformly) such pre-literates know that they are not readers.They make some very interesting metalinguistic judgments. Children don't know what words are before they know how to read, in a very specific sense: they apply the term 'word' to what adults call 'phrases'. For example, if you ask how many words there are in the sentence "A mother can carry her baby", a pre-reader will indicate 4 or 5: "A mother can-carry her-baby" or "A mother can-carry her baby".[2]

2.1 An Example: How Reading is Like Problem Solving

Even though they are pre-readers, children may still recognize certain writ-ten words, such as 'stop', and identify them in other contexts. Other com-monly well known words are 'mom' and 'exit'. Further, pre-readers are able to recognize some individual strings of letter symbols as words through a very strong use of context dependency. Consider this example from Peggy's behavior near age six:

> We were shopping for Christmas presents, shirts for our oldest daughter and son. We couldn't find the correct sizes. "Well," Peggy said, pointing to the bin labels, "over here they are small, medium, and large". She couldn't read those words as such. But she could recognize the initial letters of those words and she did know that the kinds of shirts we were looking at came in those three sizes. With this strong use of context, she was able to make a reasonable speculation as to what three particular letter strings meant.

2.2 Expectations for Beginning Readers

In contrast with the pre-reader, a beginning reader should have con-siderable ability to recognize whole words. She should have an ability to decode words that are not recognized. She should have an ability to recog-nize words as significant exceptions to standard pronunciations.[3] An able beginning reader should be able to decompose polysyllables into monosyl-lables, decode the syllable sounds, and assemble the parts to words whose meaning she can recognize. Of course, a reader should be able to under-stand the meaning of a sentence when she puts the words together.[4]

---

[2] "Pre-readers' Concept of the English Word" (Lawler, 1976) reports more detail on such judgments and their variations, revealed through a checker-taking task derived from Karpova's work, as described in *The Psychology of Reading* (Gibson & Levin, 1975).

[3] For example, the word 'dog' should be recognized as an exception to the standard pronunciation that's usually represented by the letter o, as in jog, clog, or bog.

[4] There are other interesting characteristics. Bob's research with kinder-garten children showed that those who were on the threshhold of being readers typically used exclusion arguments in justifying metalinguistic judg-ments. For example, in the sentence "The puppy wants to eat", beginning

3.0 ANCHORING WITH VARIATION IN READING

3.1 The Particularity of Anchors

What are the anchors of calculation? If asked to calculate 96 plus 96, most people would justify their answer (192 if they're right), "That's 200 minus 8". The decimal number representation plays a key role in your ability to perform such mental calculations; simple multiples of ten are common anchors. There are other sorts of anchors of variation. For instance, if asked how much is 12 times 13, one might say 144 plus 12 is 156. Such a response shows the person has memorized a series of results, the times tables, whose elements can serve as anchors of variation.

Children's anchors for variation may be much more particular and specific than most people imagine. Before Miriam's computer experiences, she could not add 15 plus 15 because she "didn't have enough fingers". At the same time, she did know that 15 cents plus 15 cents was equal to 30 cents.[5] Similarly, adults with unusual experience may have surprising anchors of variation. People in the computer business think a lot about powers of two, and many can recite the binary series: 2, 4, 8, 16, 32, 64, 128, 256, 512, 1024, 2048, 4096. Such numbers can become anchors of thought in terms of which other things are interpreted. A personal example can emphasize how particular experience affects anchors for variation: because he spent too many hours decoding machine-language core dumps in hexadecimal, Bob can look at 96 plus 96 and see that as 60 plus 60, hexadecimal. That's 'C-zero' (because $6 + 6 = $ 'C'), which on reconversion into decimal is 160 plus 32. An individual's anchors of calculation depend intimately on the particulars of his experience.

3.1.1 Anchors in Reading

Let us ask what could be comparable anchors of variation for the decoding of alphabetic words: one possibility would be those familiar words that just about all children know because they are encountered everywhere, things like 'stop' or 'mom'. Others might be family names: Bob's name, is well

---

readers would assert that the /pi/ sound could not represent a word because it was a part of 'puppy'. Pre-readers, on the other hand, would agree that the sound /pi/ in 'puppy' was a word. They would say, "Yes, of course. It's the name of the little round things that you eat [pea]". Or, "Sure, it's a letter of the alphabet". Or, "I don't want to talk about that [pee]".

[5] 15 cents was what she paid for her favorite chewing gum. She had 30 cents a week allowance, and she could get two packs of her favorite chewing gum for that amount of money.

known to our daughter, as is the word Scurry. Let us elaborate this last instance to emphasize the accidental character of these anchors. Our family pet is a Scotch terrier, who as a little puppy used to scurry all over the place, and that's what we called her. But that word is very well known to Peggy as a name. In general, these anchors are accidental and depend upon experience as do those for mental calculation. Why is that important? Precisely because computer-based microworlds introduce the possibility of creating materials through which a designed, non-accidental set of systematic anchors could be introduced to pre-readers.

If it were possible to create a more nearly complete collection of anchors for the interpretation of monosyllabic words, we could change significantly the process of learning to read. We could make reading much more accessible to many more people in a relatively efficient and congenial fashion.

3.1.2 An Example of Anchoring in Learning to Read

Is there any indication that a process such as anchoring with variation is relevant in learning to interpret words? Consider here another anecdotal example. Recently, our daughter Peggy was sitting at the table in our kitchen reading a comic book; and she piped up, "How do you say s-o-b?" and then continued, "It must be 'sob'". Bob happened to be there and asked, "Why is that, Peg?" "Well," she said, "it's 's' with Bob". The process of her interpretation is revealed by her justification: she began with "Bob" and /bob/, both of which and the association between which she knew well; she modified those entities to construct new entities whose similar association solved her reading interpretation problem. Anchoring with variation is a name for a specific form of problem solving by analogy.

As we turn to the systematic design of a set of reading anchors, our attempt will focus on the learning of whole words, but it's obvious you can't learn only how to read whole words; you have to learn the phonological code. We conclude as follows: if this process of monosyllabic modification can become richly productive in the child's everyday experience, and if the child has a sufficiently rich repertoire of well known words to modify, the invention of this procedure and its good development by every child should be expected; further, if such a result materializes, current phonics instruction will become largely obsolete. Seen from the perspective of anchoring with variation, 'phonics' and whole-word learning must and can be complementary. Mastery of the phonological code will derive through variations from recognizing a very well chosen vocabulary of whole word anchors.

4.0 A MICROWORLD EXAMPLE

Figure 1 shows Peggy playing with her beach microworld. Computer-based microworlds can be made which most children will find quite congenial.[6] The important functions of the world are the creation and manipulation of objects. An object is created through use of a word that is a named procedure; other words name procedures that manipulate that object.

Using arbitrary symbol strings (which may be words) as the tools of her control, a child is able to make objects appear and to manipulate them in a virtual world that can be shaped to her own purposes. Even at the age of three to three and a half years (when she first began playing with the BEACH microworld), Peggy learned with reasonable facility and permanence to recognize roughly thirty words. She recognized them by sight on the screen and in other contexts. She could re-create them from memory and did so, typing them on the computer keyboard. In this specific sense, she was the master both as reader and writer of that small vocabulary of words.

5.0 THE CENTRAL ARGUMENT

BEACH is only one microworld. There's no reason why one can't have a multitude of such microworlds, and there's no reason that experience with a multitude of such microworlds cannot be based upon a vocabulary which will present as anchors for variation the most productive words of the language.

5.1 Piaget and Curriculum Design

A profound theme in Piaget's work is that the cognitive structures which support the development of mature skills may be quite different from what

---

[6] The essential reason is that the flexibility of computer systems makes it possible to design objects and procedures within these microworlds which are tailored to the specific experienced of a young child. The scene in Figure 1 represents a beach in our town where we played, collected shells, and so forth. This microworld contains many objects with which she is familiar. Such microworlds are adaptable for use in other languages and cultures. Miriam recoded BEACH for use with French words. It has been used by some of Bob's colleagues from Senegal as a model for the development of microworlds for the children of their country. See Lawler, Niang, & Gning, 1983.

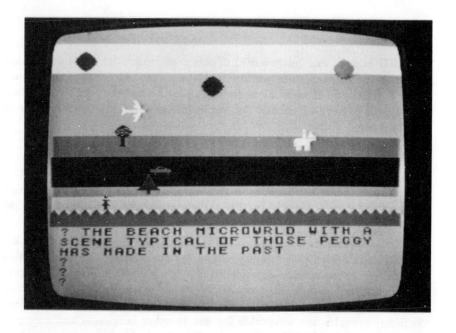

FIGURE 1: Variations of the Beach Microworld

(a) The BEACH microworld.   (b) A child constructed scene.

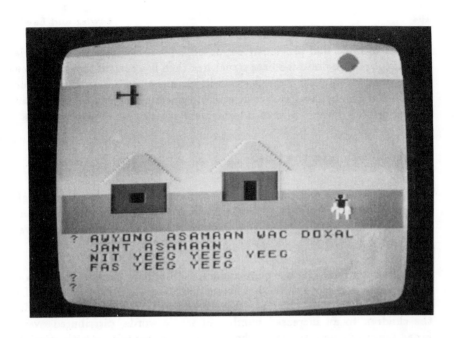

(c) TRAIN: a child's variation.   (d) XEW: an African village.

students of mind had previously supposed. Advancing the progressive development of those intermediate structures then is a central task of curriculum design. Computer experiences will change these intermediate structures.[7] The rest of this paper is directed to selecting an English vocabulary to support the development of intermediate structures for reading skills.

5.2 Application to the Case

Using whole words and putting those words in contrast so that one might compare 'up' with 'pup' and 'play' with 'day' is something that has a long and respected tradition.[8] Our approach to the design process is, however, different.

Although final reading performances will appear similar, the path of development will move through different intermediate cognitive states. Let us suggest what those different states would be. We propose introducing the children to an increased number of whole words, distributed over a broad range of language sounds, by offering them experience with multiple, word-oriented microworlds at a very early age. Recognizing an increased number of whole words, 200 to 500, at the age of four or five should not be uncommon (Peggy at three recognized thirty words from the manipulation of one microworld).

Decomposing monosyllables into an initial phoneme and a syllabic residue is a pre-reading activity frequently introduced by language games played in small groups.[9] Breaking words into an initial phonetic cluster and a syllabic residue would be worked out naturally using the vocabulary presented and established through experiences with these multiple microworlds. Such would be the next, intermediate state of development. It would be followed by either the spontaneous or the directed reconstitution of other monosyllables through anchoring with variation.

The reading of monosyllabic text with help, then unaided, and finally reading polysyllabic text, would be the normal sequence of further states

---

[7] This claim is supported, in the large, by Lawler, 1985.

[8] Dr. Seuss's *Hop on Pop* is the premier example of a reading book with such an objective. Curriculum designers have long produced materials based upon rhyming syllables. No one should be surprised to see computers as the medium for such materials today. The issue must be whether or not they embody some new idea.

[9] One might begin with pig latin games for initial phoneme segmentation, as Harris Savin proposed (in Kavanaugh & Mattingly, 1972). There's room for imaginative applications of the technology to that particular problem.

of development. The key difference is the early one of introducing a child to a multitude of monosyllables through computer-based microworlds.

6.0 AN ANALYSIS OF ENGLISH MONOSYLLABLES

English is not a monosyllabic language, but we may be able to present it to pre-readers as if it were such. Why is that worthwhile doing? And how can it be done?

6.1 Learning to Read in Syllabic Languages is Easier

The standard report by adults of learning to read in Cherokee, which has a syllabary of 85 signs, is that they learn to read in one day (Morris Halle, in Kavanaugh & Mattingly). This may be an exaggeration, but there's a contrast of orders of magnitude in comparison with learning to read in an alphabetic language such as English.

A second example: in *The Psychology of Literacy*, Scribner and Cole discuss learning Vi, the traditional language of a people in sub-Sahara Africa. The written language is not taught formally in schools but is learned from friends when a person has a use for it. The sounds of Vi are represented by a syllabary of approximately two hundred signs.

The sizes of these syllabaries (200 and 85 signs) indicate an order of magnitude of syllable signs people can easily recognize and distinguish as significant components of written language. If we ask children to recognize 200 words, it's probably not too much. As the following analysis shows, there are reasons for wanting them to recognize as many as 500 or more. That's still probably not too many.

7.0 THE METHOD

The systematic approach we propose will cover the phonetic range of English in such a fashion that it will both make the structure of the language more comprehensible and make it accessible to the flexibility of computer implementation.

7.1 The Issue of Representation

We have to deal with how to represent the sounds of the language unambiguously and naturally. The atomic approach is that of the international phonetic alphabet (IPA): one symbol, one meaning.[10] Historically, alphabetic languages have represented single sounds with multiple characters, making it difficult to understand the correspondence between sounds and letters.[11] Choosing to deal with monosyllabic words focusses on a 'molecular' rather than an 'atomic' level of symbol aggregation. This choice by itself offers children instruction in what are significant units in the written representation of language.

7.2 The Space of Monosyllables

If we're going to represent the variable spellings of the English language and its sounds by a collection of monosyllable, we might wonder how many that would take. Consider the monosyllables as a vowel bounded by two consonantal clusters. There are 51 initial consonants and consonantal clusters in English. There are 14 vowels.[12] There are 87 terminal consonants and consonantal clusters.[13] English has the potential for more than 60 thousand monosyllables. Reducing the space of possibilities by excluding terminal clusters brings the number of potential monosyllables down to a more manageable size, defined by the 51 initial clusters, the 14 vowels, and the 21 terminal consonants. Call these approximately 15 thousand monosyllables (51 times 14 times 21) the reduced space; this is the material of our preliminary analysis. From preliminary analysis, the terminal clusters are excluded. Later analysis will proceed over the full space which includes terminal consonantal clusters.

---

[10] A good description of English phonetics and phonology may be found in Lyons, 1968. In that text, the kind of analysis pursued here is called the syntagmatic combination of phonemes.

[11] For example, in the IPA, Bob's patronymic takes four symbols (LØLR). In English, 5 or 6 letters are common (LALOR, LAWLOR), while 12 are required for the same sound in the original Gaelic (LEATHLOBHAIR); English represents 44 phonemes with 26 letters whereas Irish encodes more than 60 phonemes with only 18 letters (Green, 1966). Accidents of history, as well as many-to-one coding, have complicated the English sound-letter correspondences (see "The History of English Sounds" in Robertson & Cassidy).

[12] The middle sounds of these words are all the English vowels. FRONT: BY BEE BID BAY BED BAD BUT; BACK: BAH BOUGHT BOY BOAT BOOK BOOB BOUT.

[13] There are 21 terminal consonants and basic clusters (/tsh/ and /dzh/) and 66 terminal clusters by actual count (about which more later).

7.3   How Is That Space Populated?

To determine the density of existing words in this space, we made a three-dimensional matrix, in effect, and examined every cell. The primary result is that the space is about 20 percent full. Instead of the potential 15,000 monosyllables, approximately 3000 actually exist in English. Figure 2 presents summary information on the members populating the space.

7.3.1   Organizing the Reduced Space of Monosyllables

To bring this space of 3000 actually existing monosyllables under a systematic categorization, we've chosen to represent these monosyllables as an initial phonemic cluster plus residue, in the fashion that was exemplified by Peggy's use. She made residues of 'Bob' and /bob/ by cutting off the initial letter and phoneme. How many such residues are there in the English language? Within the 3000 monosyllables of the reduced space, the number of residues is approximately 700. From these 700 word residues, we can select those that actually appear most frequently in English monosyllables. Some residues appear in many words while others are rare. 113 appear in 10 or more monosyllables. Call this the set of level 10 residues. The size of this set is near the size of the Cherokee syllabary. Similarly, there are 191 (113 + 78) level five residues (those which appear in five or more English words). This set has fewer members than the number of signs in the Vi syllabary. If children could recognize these two hundred residues, they would have a syllabic basis from which they could interpret 73 percent of the 3000 English monosyllables in the reduced space.[14] In this specific sense, these would be the optimally productive residues for pre-readers to recognize.

7.3.2   Extending the Analysis to Terminal Clusters

The major constraint applied in permitting generation of the reduced space of actual English monosyllables was restricting words examined to those with a single terminal consonant or none at all. But many words end with consonantal clusters. We have attempted to answer the question "how many"? and to explore the organization possible to impose on them through a residue-oriented analysis.

---

[14] The 113 level ten residues cover 1748 words and the level five residues another 537. The sum 2285 is 73 percent of the total monosyllable count of the reduced space.

FIGURE 2
Distribution of Vowel Spellings in
English Monosyllables

ENGLISH NAMES	MONO-SYLBS	DOMINANT SPELLING	PER-CENT	OTHER SPELLINGS WITH COUNTS	RESI-DUES	LE 10	VEL 5
SHORT A	281	A	99	A=278	42	11	13
				AI=1, AU=1, E=1			
LONG A	368	A	50	A=185, AI=78, AY=54	66	15	21
		A+AI+AY	86	AYE=17, EI=15, EA=10			
				EY=5, E=2, AU=1			
SHORT E	174	E	87	E=152, EA=10, U=5, A=1	49	7	11
		E+EA+YE	93	UE=1, AI=1, I=4, AY=1			
LONG E	326	EE	44	EE=143, EA=127, E=20	80	13	23
		EE+EA	83	IE=21, I=7, EY=2			
		EE+EA+E+IE	95	EI=3, UI=1			
SHORT I	270	I	98	I=266, Y=3	48	11	13
				EA=1, IE=1, EE=1			
LONG I	251	I	66	I=166, IE=33, Y=31, UY=4	56	11	18
		I+IE+Y	92	YE=4, AI=3, UI=2, EI=2			
				AYE=2, EYE=2, AI=1, OI=1			
SHORT O	224	O	74	O=166, A=54	53	8	12
		O+A	96	AA=2, UA=1			
LONG O	265	O	74	O=197, OA=42, OE=15	61	9	19
		O+OA	87	E=4, OU=3, EAU=2, AU=2			
SHORT U	226	U	89	U=201, O=13, OU=7	42	9	15
		U+O	95	OO=2, E=1, OE=1, A=1			
LONG U	316	OO	38	OO=120, EW=59, U=54	92	8	18
		OO+EW		UE=29, OU=15, O=11, UI=6			
		OO+EW+U+UE	86	EU=5, OOE=4, others			
MID U	33	OO	55	OO=18, U=12, OU=3	14	0	1
(Λ)		OO+U	91				
DIPHTHONG	146	O	53	O=78, OU=58, A=7	38	3	12
(OW)		O+OU	87	AU=3			
DIPHTHONG	188	A	55	A=103, O=42, AU=20	49	6	12
(AW)		A+O+AU	88	OU=13, OA=6, OO=5, EA=1			
DIPHTHONG	45	OI	58	OI=26, OY=16	16	1	4
(OI)		OI+OY	87	OYE=3			
TOTAL	3113				709	113	191

Generating the extended space of monosyllables with terminal clusters involved complexities absent from the generation of the reduced space. Almost any consonant joins easily with almost any vowel. Consonants, generally, do not aggregate so readily. This fact has a powerful influence on what words are possible in a language. We found out which consonants cluster together and generated the extended list of existing English monosyllables by following this procedure:

We formed a square array with a row and column for each of the twenty terminal English consonants; the cell where a row and column intersect represents the terminal cluster formed by those two consonants.

For each of these four hundred cells, we repeated the process through which we generated monosyllables for the reduced space. More specifically, for each terminal cluster we formed the two dimensional array intersecting the fourteen vowels with the fifty-one initial consonants and clusters; pronouncing each triplet of initial cluster plus vowel plus terminal cluster, we tested for the existence of a word by our recognition of the sound.

We supplemented this list with those few terminal clusters containing more than two consonants (e.g., twelfth).

The intention here was to generate a maximal list of possible words. Consequently, any sound which either of us considered a possible word was entered in the two-dimensional array for the terminal cluster, then subsequently verified or rejected by its presence in Webster's Third New International Dictionary (1971 edition). Since the word list we generated is limited to those spelling sounds we knew or imagined to be words, ours is a personal list and it cannot be perfect. We can guarantee that it is exhaustive. Even if others propose some few words we have not considered, we doubt that the conclusions of our analysis will be changed significantly.

This list, verified by dictionary entries, was then purged. We deleted words of these sorts: archaic words; arcane words; Scotch, English, and Australian dialectical forms; vulgar and insulting words. We found that of the four hundred cells in the terminal cluster array, only sixty-six represented terminal clusters from which English monosyllables are actually formed. These sixty-six terminal clusters form 4280 monosyllables in addition to those of the reduced space, for a total of approximately 7000 monosyllables. Call this collection of words "Lawlers' complete list".

FIGURE 3

Monosyllables Residues with Single
Consonant Terminations or None

VOCALIC	LEVEL TEN	LEVEL FIVE
SHORT A	ab, atch, ad, ag, ack, am, an, ang, ap, ash, at	ass, ath
LONG A	ake, ale, ame, ane, ape, are, ace, ate, ave, aze ail, ain, ay, ays, ayed	aid, ade, age, air, ear, ait
SHORT E	ed, ell, en, ess, et, edge,	etch, ead, eck, em, ep
LONG E	ee, eed, eek, eel, eep, eet, eer, ees, eak, eal, eam, ear, eat	eech, een, ea, each, ead, ean, eap, eas eas, eave, ief
SHORT I	ib, itch, id, ig, ick, ill, im, in, ing, ip, it	iff, iss
LONG I	ide, ile, ime, ine, ice, ire, ight, ive, ied, ies, y	ibe, ie, ife, ike, ipe, ite, ithe
SHORT O	ob, od, og, ock, ong, op, ot, ar	ah, otch, om, osh
LONG O	ow, owed, oke, ole, one, ope, ove, ows, oat	o, obe, oad, ode, ome, oll, own, ote, oes, ose
SHORT U	ub, uff, ug, uck, um, un, ung, ush, ut	utch, ud, udge, ull, up, us
LONG U	oo, oon, oop, oot, ew, ewed, ews, ue, ues	ooch, ued, oof, uke, ool, oom, oos, une, ute
MID U	ook	
DPHTH OW	ow, out, ows	owl, owel, ouch, owed, own, our, ower, owls, ouse
DPHTH AW	aw, awed, all, awn, aws, ore	alk, awl, oar, oss, ought, oth
DPHTH OI	oil	oy, oys, oin
TOTAL	level ten: 113	level five: 78

7.3.3 Organizing the Extended Space as Residues

The character of the following analysis is determined by the ways in which consonants cluster together. In general, there are two quite different classes of clusters. The first is uncommitted as to meanings assigned to the consonantal cluster; it is dominated by words formed with the glides /L/ and /R/ as the initial member of the consonantal cluster. The second class is formed by the suffixation of the four inflectional consonants: /D/ and /T/; and /S/ and /Z/. /D/ and /T/ are used often to indicate temporal verb inflections, while /S/ and /T/ frequently indicate pluralization of substantives or third person singular inflection of a verb. There are nearly 1200 residues in the collection of 4280 words in the extended space of monosyllables. Within this broad dispersion of sounds and spellings, there is nonetheless significant aggregation of words around residues, as shown by the summary table below:

	Different Residues Total	Residues with More Than Specified Number of Words	
		N > 9	10 > N > 4
L-clusters	215	12	20
R-clusters	308	9	36
Other-clusters	670	122	173
	1193	147	229

	Reduced Space	Extended	Combined
total residues	709	1193	1902
residues at level			
10	113	147	260
5 (but < 10)	78	229	307
sum of residues > 5	191	376	567

The summary of this analysis is that among the nearly 1900 different residue spellings of English monosyllables, those which appear in more than ten words number only 260. Those which appear in more than five words number about 550. The first number is clearly within the range of words knowable through that sort of associational memorization called upon within syllabic written languages. If children can learn as many as 500 or 600 different correspondences between sounds and spelling patterns, their knowledge of such residues, coupled with the ability to modify interpretations of letter strings by anchoring with variation, will cover a major portion of the phonetic-orthographic correspondences of the English language. We believe this extensive, concrete foundation of word and sound knowledge will per-

FIGURE 4

Monosyllables Residues with
Terminal Clusters

CLUSTERS	LEVEL TEN	LEVEL FIVE
LZ	eels, eals, ells, ails, iles, ales, ells, oles, alls, oils, ills	ulls, awls, olls, owls, ools
LDZ		olds
LD	oiled, old, ulled, ailed, illed	eeled, aled, oiled awled, owled, ooled
LK		alk
LM/LMZ		alm, alms
LT/LTS	ilt, ilts	elt, elts, olts
LVZ		elves
RZ/RS	ears, ares, oars	ires, eers, airs, ours
RCH		arch
RD/RDZ	ared	ards, eered, ard, arred, ored, ired, eared
RDG		arge
RK/RKS/RKT	ark, arks	arked, irk, irks
RL/RLZ/RLD		irl, url, irls, urls, irled
RM/RMZ/RMD		erm, orm, arm, erms, orms, arms
RN/RNZ/RND	orn	urn, urns, orns
RP/RPS/RPT		arp, arps
RT/RTS	art, arts	irt, ort, orts, irts
ST/STS	est, ests, ust, usts	ist, aste, aced, essed, ast, assed, ossed, oast, oused, ists, iced, astes, oasts
SP/SPS		asp, asps
SK/SKS/SKT		isk, usk, usks, isked
MP/MPS/MPT	imp, amp, ump, imps, amps, umps, umped	omp, omps, imped, amped
ND/NS/NT	ined, inned, end, and, oned, ained, ints, int, ent, ant	ind, eaned, eened, aned, ound, anned, unned, ond, awned, owned, aints, ance, unts, ounce, aint, aunt, unt
NK/NCH	ink, ank, unk	inch, ench, unch
NCHT		inched, enched, unched
NKS/NKT	inks, anks, unks, inked, anked	onked, unked

FIGURE 4 (con't)

Monosyllables Residues with
Terminal Clusters

BD/GD/JD	abbed, ubbed, obbed, igged, agged, ugged	ibbed, obed, ogged, aged, edged, udged
MD	eamed, ammed, ummed	imed, immed, amed
VD	ived, aved	eaved
ZD	azed	
CHT	itched	eached, etched, atched, ouched, otched
FT	uffed	iffed, ift, eft, oofed, aft
KT	icked, aked, acked, ucked, ocked	iked, eaked, ecked, alked, oked, ooked
SHT	ashed	ushed
PT	ipped, apped, opped, ooped	iped, eeped, ept, oped, aped

THS		aths, oths
FS	iffs, uffs	oofs
TS	ights, eats, its, ates, ets, ats, ots, oats, outs	ites, eets, uts, otes, oots
KS	icks, akes, acks, ucks, ocks	ikes, eaks, eeks, ex, ecks, ax, ox, ooks
PS	eeps, ips, apes, aps, ops, opes, oops	ipes
BZ	ubs, obs, abs	ibes, ibs, obes
GZ	igs, ags, ugs, ogs	egs
DZ	ads, ods, eeds	ides, ades, eds, uds, oods, eads, ids
MZ	imes, eames, ims, ames, ams, ums	ems, oms, ooms
NZ/NDZ	ends, ines, ins, ains, anes, ens, ans, uns, ones	ands, eans, eens, awns, oons, unes, owns, inds, ounds
NGZ	ings	angs, ungs, ongs
THZ		
VZ	ives, aves, oves	eaves

TOTAL	level ten: 147	level five: 229

mit children to read well enough that the instruction they will need will
be primarily a refining and perfection of such knowledge. The 191 residues
of the reduced space cover 2227 words. The 376 residues of the extended
space cover 2974 words. Together they cover 5201 words, a little more than
70 percent of the 7390 words in Lawlers' complete list. The list of these
550-plus level-10 and level-5 residues is presented in Figures 3 and 4.

8.0 CONCLUSIONS

The primary design conclusion is that if we create computer-based microworlds which use words with these level-10 and level-5 residues as the
names for their entities and their actions, we will be providing a set of systematically generated monosyllabic anchors which promises to be highly
effective for children's interpretation of many words they will encounter in
reading English. The potential revolutionary impact of such a pre-reading
curriculum is worth exploring.

A second possible significant outcome is that such experiences could
alter the balance in the learner's perception of the orderliness of language.
One difficulty with English is that the most common words are often the
exceptions to the rules of phonological correspondence. If we introduce
children to microworlds through which they will have experience with words
that are archetypical in terms of the phonological correspondence, we may
be able to change the child's view of language from one where reading grows
by the rote memorization of senseless letter strings to one of language as
a rule-governed code with a lot of exceptions. More concretely, 'dog' is
a very common word, but 'jog' is a common word too. If a child learns
that 'jog' contains the characteristic spelling 'og' for the sound /og/, and
that it also appears in log and bog and frog, then the child will be in a
much better position to recognize explicitly that 'dog' is an exception to
the orthographic-phonetic rules of correspondence. Such could be a very
important development in respect of making the English orthographic code
more comprehensible to children. If this approach works, we could make
the orderliness more salient than the disorder; we could, in effect, change
the salience of the figure and ground in the child's early experience of the
written language.

REFERENCES

Gibson, E.J., & Levin, H. (1975). *The Psychology of Reading*. Cambridge, MA: The
     MIT Press.
Green, D. (1966). *The Irish Language*. Cork: The Mercier Press.
Kahnemann, D., & Tversky, A. (1974). Judgment under uncertainty: heuristics and
     biases. *Science 185*, 1124-1131.
Kahnemann, D., & Tversky, A. (1982). *Judgment Under Uncertainty: Heuristics and
     Biases*. London, New York: Cambridge University Press.

Kavanaugh, J., & Mattingly, I. (1972). *Language by Ear and by Eye: The Relationships Between Speech and Reading*. Cambridge, MA: The MIT Press.

Lawler, R. (1984). Designing computer based microworlds. In M. Yazdani (Ed.), *New Horizons in Educational Computing*. Chichester, England: Ellis Horwood, Ltd., New York: John Wiley, Inc.

Lawler, R. (1976). Pre-readers' concepts of the english word. Cambridge, MA: MIT Logo Memo 40.

Lawler, R. (1985). *Computer Experience and Cognitive Development*. Chichester, England: Ellis Horwood, Ltd., New York: John Wiley.

Lawler, R., Niang, M., & Gning, M. (1983). Computers and literacy in traditional languages. UNESCO *Courier*, March. London: H.M. Stationery Office, S.E.I.; New York: Unipub, 345 Park Ave, NY.

Lyons, J. (1968). *Introduction to Theoretical Linguistics*. London: Cambridge University Press.

Robertson, S., & Cassidy, F.G. (1954). *The Development of Modern English*. Englewood Cliffs, NJ: Prentice-Hall.

Scribner, S., & Cole, M. (1981). *The Psychology of Literacy*. Cambridge, MA: Harvard University Press.

6 LEARNING WITH INTERACTIVE MEDIA: DYNAMIC SUPPORT FOR STUDENTS AND TEACHERS

Margaret M. Riel

Interactive Technology Laboratory
University of California – San Diego

James A. Levin

Department of Educational Psychology
University of Illinois

Barbara Miller-Souviney

San Diego Teacher Education and Computer Center

ABSTRACT

The controversy over appropriate educational uses of computers is framed along a continuum based on the amount of support provided to the user. Software programs in which the user's role is to respond in a pre-determined structure (program controlled software) anchors one end of the continuum, while software which empowers the user to create new ways to use the computer (user controlled software) anchors the other end. With this frame, we argue that both positions in the controversy are too static, and propose an alternative position: a process of educational software use in which the amount of assistance provided by the computer is systematically decreased as novices gain expertise. This principle, which we call "dynamic support," is shown to apply to students learning to write and to teachers learning to incorporate computers into their classrooms.[1]

1.0 EDUCATIONAL SOFTWARE FOR STUDENTS

The role that computers can play in classrooms has been implicitly debated by those who create educational software. The various positions in this debate can be described as points along a continuum of control (Figure 1). At one end of this continuum is the "program controlled" position, in which the initiative for action is contained largely within the computer program being used. At this end of the continuum are a large number of educational software packages that drill or test students on narrowly defined academic

Paper presented at AERA, New Orleans, April 23-27, 1984. Special thanks to Bud Mehan for comments on earlier drafts.

tasks. At the other end of the continuum is the learner controlled position, in which the initiative for action rests with the person using the computer. At this end of the continuum are computer languages and other "tools" that provide students with the power to explore or create new uses of the computer.

Drill & Test CAI	Simulations and Educational Games	General Purpose Tools (Programming Lang., Editors)
Computer Controlled	Mixed Control	Learner Controlled

Figure 1: Types of Educational Software for Students

Drill and practice software translates classroom exercises into computer programs adding little more than the ability for students to receive immediate feedback from a machine rather than from the teacher. While advantageous for student motivation, feedback and pacing and teachers' administrative efficiency, drill and practice programs are often criticized as too constraining on both students and teachers (Papert, 1980; Leuhrmann, 1981; Tucker, 1982; Amarel, 1982; Becker, 1985).

General purpose languages (Logo, BASIC, and Pascal), word processing programs designed for students (Bank Street Writer, The Writer's Assistant), graphic and music editors, spreadsheets and data base programs provide access to a broad range of learning activities often with few constraints or directions. When beginning to use such general tools, learners often have more power than they can deal with and little notion of productive strategies or plans for using the tool. Use of these general purpose tools places a burden on teachers to provide the support needed by students, especially for novice users.

In the middle region of the continuum are simulation programs and educational games that share the initiative with the user. In these activities students and teachers are both able to make choices that help frame the educational activity.

2.0 DYNAMIC SUPPORT FOR STUDENTS

Arguments have been raging over which of these kinds of software represent the best educational use of the computer (Papert, 1980; Johnson, Anderson, Hansen, & Klassen, 1980; Anderson, Klassen, & Johnson, 1981; Luehrmann, 1981). We take a different theoretical perspective on this issue. In our studies of computer use, we have observed that no one position along the continuum is best for all students, or even for the same student at different times. Instead, when students start as novices in some domain, they need a lot of support (from a teacher, from print, and from educational software). As they acquire expertise they no longer need as much support, and when they become experts, they are ready to take over the whole task. Based on our observation of computer use and this conception of the acquisition of expertise, we have developed an educational design principle called "dynamic support."

Dynamic support refers to the process of systematically decreasing amounts of assistance provided to novices as they progress in expertise and gradually assume parts of the task initially accomplished only by an expert. This notion of dynamic support is derived from the learning principle referred to as the "zone of proximal development" (Vygotsky, 1978; Brown & French, 1979; Griffin & Cole, 1984). In a properly arranged teacher-student-computer environment there is the potential for creating the kind of dynamic support necessary to improve students' learning dramatically. Software which provides dynamic support encourages the progressive development of skill by the learner. Initially, software provides considerable support. As users become more skilled, the support diminishes, turning control of the task over to the users. A system of educational software which embodies the principle of dynamic support encourages movement from the left side of the continuum shown in Figure 1 to the right side of the continuum rather than making assumptions about the best location along the continuum (Figure 2).

Computer Controlled ⟶ Mixed Control ⟶ Learner Controlled

Figure 2: Dynamic Support

The dynamic support principle developed out of research we conducted on how a computer could be used to help students write (Levin, Boruta, & Vasconcellos, 1983). By examining the pattern of student errors and by observing the social interaction around the computer, we found that students required considerable support as novice writers. Word processing systems can be very powerful tools for writing, but the word processor by itself did not provided a good entry point for students having difficulty with the composing process. Students encountered the problem of "the blank screen" (Levin & Boruta, 1984). As a result the teachers needed to provide instructions on how to use the word processor, but also needed to design supporting writing activities for novice students. These supports were in the form of task cards placed around the computer and textfiles that were used to provide both the directions for a writing activity and the writing itself.

It became apparent that a writing system that would enable teachers to provide this kind of support to the writer on the computer was needed. Learning how to *use* the many options and commands provided in a word processor needed to follow some initial guidance in learning *what* to write.

From observations of ways that teachers provided support for writing, Levin developed a system for creating "interactive texts" called the Interactive Text Interpreter (ITI) (Levin, 1982) that embody the concept of dynamic support in the area of writing. Simple commands are used in textfiles to indicate that portion of the text to be presented as instructions, suggestions or examples to the students and what part should become part of the text created by the student. Within this system students are given the option of deciding how many instructions or examples they need to draw upon in the composing process. Teachers can direct students' attention to a particular piece of information (such as how many words are required in a particular line of a poem or how to describe an event) at the time when the student can best use that information.

Interactive texts are simplified reading and writing environments which can offer the following forms of interaction with the user.

I. Students can make choices among options presented in a menu by:

   a) Selecting alternative words or phrases such as choosing one of four possible titles or deciding which character will be featured in a story.

   b) Selecting an option which affects the sequencing of text such as choosing a tutorial, asking to see instructions or examples or determining the outcome of a story by making choices for the characters.

II. Students can be asked to write by:

   a) Asking them to provide a word or phrase in a highly constrained "frame" such as "Enter a past tense verb." or "Describe a large animal that is normally found in the desert."

   b) Responding to a writing prompt such as "In this first paragraph, tell what you think about the sport, why you selected it or something that makes it unique." or "Now describe how the game is played, and the goal of each of the players."

   c) Composing longer segments of text following general directives such as "Now write your story." or "Enter your Haiku."

At the program-control end of the continuum, "readers" of interactive texts help compose the text by making choices that determine the structure of the essay, or the direction of the plot by selecting from among presented options. At the user-control end of the continuum, interactive texts can place the responsibility for writing in the hands of the students offering only suggestions or examples. A set of such interactive texts can provide students with a range of writing "tools" which vary in the degree of help they provide. We have found that if students use such a range of writing tools, starting with highly supportive tools and then gradually move to tools requiring them to do more and more of the writing, they gain the skill and confidence to write on their own without help (Mehan, Moll, & Riel, 1985; Miller-Souviney, 1985).

3.0 DYNAMIC SUPPORT FOR WRITING EXPOSITORY TEXT

Miller-Souviney (1985) has used a set of interactive texts to teach expository writing to fourth and fifth graders. Each of the four expository writing tasks are arranged so that students are able to produce a good example of an essay *every* time they write. In the first activity, "The Sandwich Prompt," the student "makes" a unique story by choosing among options which are provided throughout the text. Here are the first three choices that the student makes while writing about the art of constructing sandwiches:

Sandwich Prompt

```
  Today is

  1. Saturday
  2. Martin Luther King Jr.'s Birthday
  3. Teacher's Workshop Day
  4. National Take a Computer Lunch Day

  (Choose 1..4; 0 to end):

  *** Type a number then push RETURN ***
```

The next screen looks like this:

```
   and I have a day off from school.

   My parents are

   1. at work
   2. climbing Mount Everest
   3. eating at a restaurant
   4. playing tennis

   (Choose 1..4; 0 to end):

   *** Type a number then push RETURN ****
```

```
   so I have to make my own

   1. breakfast
   2. lunch
   3. dinner
   4. snack

   (Choose 1..4; 0 to end):

   *** Type a number then push RETURN ***
```

The following is a story that David produced using this program (Miller-Souviney, 1985). (Boldface type indicates words actually entered by David.)

The Art of Sandwich Construction
by David

Today is National Take a Computer to Lunch Day and I have a day off from school. My parents are **playing tennis** so I have to make my own **lunch**. My specialty is that wonder of culinary art, the sandwich! A great French chef, Francois d'Boloney, taught me to make his most secret recipe, The California Kid's Surprise!

First, I need the bread. The recipe calls for two hundred pounds of hamburger buns. I always try to pick good ones, which haven't been painted green.

Next, I put the bread on the counter close to the refrigerator. ...(continues to describe the addition of each of the ingredients)...Gently, I put the top on my magnificent creation and arrange myself in the proper eating position.

This is how I make my Super Secret Recipe Sandwich. When I have a day off school, I never go hungry! Bon appetit!!

The second activity in expository writing involves filling in words and phrases as well as making choices among pre-determined options:

School Day Schedule Prompt

The name of my school is

?

*** Type, then push CTRL-C when done ****

It is in the town of

?

*** Type, then push CTRL-C when done ****

I am in grade

?

*** Type, then push CTRL-C when done ****

---

and my teacher's name is

?

*** Type, then push CTRL-C when done ****

```
┌─────────────────────────────────────────────────────────┐
│                                                         │
│    I have a very busy schedule at school. My class does │
│    all sorts of things to make it fun to learn.         │
│                                                         │
│    *** Push RETURN to go on ******************           │
│                                                         │
└─────────────────────────────────────────────────────────┘
```

This "School Day Schedule" prompt provides students with the beginnings of sentences and paragraphs and invites students to complete the ideas begun for them by the expository prompter. In the following composition, the text that Sarah has entered is in boldface type:

One Day at School
by Sarah

The name of my school is Olive. It is in the town of Vista. I am in grade fourth and my teacher's name is Mrs. Souviney. I have a very busy schedule at school. My class does all sorts of things to make it fun to learn.

The first thing I do is look at the blackboard and copy the daily hand tounge twister. My teacher checks my folder carefully, making sure my writing is nice and neat.

Next, I go to the mat area. It's time for our class meeting where the whole class gets a chance to make announcements and share things. At the end of Class Meeting, my teacher gives us directions for Station Rotation and spelling.

During Station Rotation time, I do different things. I read with my teacher, talk with my friends,sharpen your skills. I practice using my spelling words every week. My favorite spelling activity is news papper knownows because it is the best acttivity. (...description of school day continues...)

I have a busy schedule every day at school. I'm learning a lot about many different things. I think school this year is grody.

As students increase their writing skills, they take over more and more of the writing activity. In the third expository writing task, the students are asked to describe "how to run a computer." Topic sentences for each paragraph, as well as reminders of what should be contained in each paragraph, are provided. Students enter the introduction, body and conclusion of their essay.

How To Run An Apple Computer

We are lucky here at Olive School. We have Apple
computers. We use them to help us practice our
spelling and math, write stories and lots of other
things. An Apple computer is easy to run. Just
follow these simple directions.

First, it is important to know the different parts
of the computer and what each does.

(Write complete sentences telling the parts of an
Apple and what they do.)

?

*** Type, then push CTRL-C when done ****

Next, to start the Apple, several switches need to
be turned on.

(In complete sentences, describe where each switch
is and what it does.)

?

*** Type, then push CTRL-C when done ****

Students respond to each prompt by entering their own sentences and
paragraphs. The following is Margaret's version of how a computer is run
(Margaret's text is in boldface type):

How To Run An Apple Computer
by Margaret

**We are lucky here at Olive School. We have Apple computers.
We use them to help us practice our spelling and math, to write**

stories and lots of other things. An Apple computer is easy to run. Just follow these simple directions.

First, it is important to know the different parts of the computer and what each does. The moniter shows you what you write and the keyboard has letters to type with.The disk drive is where you put the disk in and the printer is for printing out stories.

Next, to start the Apple, several switches need to be turned on. To turn on the moniter you turn the switch on the bottom right corner.To turn on the keyboard you press the button on the back and to turn the printer on you press the button on the left side.

(... Continues to describe the steps for using the computer...)

Using a computer isn't all that difficult. If you follow my directions, you should be on your way to being an Apple computer "expert." With a little practice you can use an Apple to help you learn how to do all sorts of things.

In the final activity in the expository writing series, students are asked to think of a topic to write about and given a few structured reminders:

How To

Think of something you know how to do that you could explain to a friend. For example, you may know how to wash dishes, run a computer or clean your room.

Remember:

1. The first paragraph is your introduction and will tell something about the activity.
2. The second paragraph will tell the steps it takes to do it.
3. The last paragraph is your conclusion and can tell about how you feel when you finish the activity or when you will do it again.

In this, the fourth phase of the expository writing activity, students are now responsible for producing complete texts on their own. Here are two stories produced by Lorenzo and Armando from Miller-Souviney's (1985) classroom (text they entered is in bold type):

How To Make Money
by
Lorenzo

If you want to make money, you must make it right now. If you want to know why, you can say because you would want to help your family, or something else.

To make money, the easiest way could be gathering cans. Cans can be everywhere, so when you are walking and you see a can, stop and pick it up.

When you have gathered at least 500 cans, give them to a store. they will give you money for the cans. Then if you want to do it again, do it and you will have more money.

Throughout these four activities, the goal is for the quality of the writing to remain constant. As the degree of the participation by the learner increases, the amount of support provided by the computer decreases (Figure 3).

Sandwich Making Writing Tool	Schoolday Writing Tool	How to run a Computer Writing Tool	How to ... Writing Tool
→ →	→ →	→ →	→ →
Computer Controlled	Mixed Control	Learner Controlled	

Figure 3: Dynamic Support for Expository Writing

Miller-Souviney used this sequence of computer activities to teach expository writing to her class of 28 fourth and fifth graders over a four-month period. The initial writing skill of each student was assessed by two writing assignments, one written on paper and the other on the computer. After using all four of the Expository Writing Tools, the students' writing was again assessed on and off the computer.

Writing quality and fluency improved significantly over the four-month period of instruction in which dynamic support was provided by the computer programs. The quality of the students' writing was evaluated using a holistic scoring rubric (Grubb, 1981). Both pre- and post-writing samples were assessed by four independent scorers each of which used a four-point scale producing a total score range of 0 to 16. The average student score on the pretest was 7.52 on the pencil and paper test and 7.7 on the computer test. The average post-test score was 10.8 for the pencil and paper test and 10.4 for the computer test. A test of significance was computed comparing selected pre- and post-measures using the non-parametric Wilcoxon Matched-Pairs Signed-Ranks Test (WST) for differences between related samples (Siegel, 1956). The results show that the quality of the students' expository writing improved significantly ($p < 0.005$).

	Pre-test	Post-test
Paper/pencil ($n = 25$)		
Holistic score $(0 - 16)$	7.5	10.8 *
Total word count	57.7	97.5 *
Unique word count	34.4	55.4 *
Computer ($n = 25$)		
Holistic score $(0 - 16)$	7.7	10.4 *
Total word count	70.8	81.0
Unique word count	38.9	45.7

* significant $p < 0.005$ (WST)

Word count data indicated an improvement in fluency rates as well. The average total word count increased by nearly 40 words and and the unique word count by over 20 words between the pre- and post-tests written on paper. This improvement was also significant. The fluency rates also increased on the computer tests but they were not significant.

Research on the use of word processors in classrooms often reports an increase in the length of students' writing with no increase in the quality of the writing (Daiute, 1982; Levin, Boruta, & Vasconcellos, 1983). Similarly, we found that the length of students' *pre-tests* written on paper and on the computer demonstrate the highly motivating nature of the computer: students wrote longer essays. However these essay were not necessarily of higher quality. The use of interactive writing tools arranged to provide dynamic support in this study resulted in increases in *quality as well as in length*.

By arranging learning environments in which computer-based support was gradually removed, students gained control of expository writing by gradually assuming the parts of the task initially accomplished by the computer. Dynamic support provided by the microcomputer subordinated the students' concern for the mechanics of writing to the process of writing, resulting in improved quality and fluency.

In a classroom in which this sequence of activities was used in poetry as well as in other forms of writing, some students reached a point in which they asked if they could use the word processor directly to write their poems (Mehan, Moll, & Riel, 1985). They were ready to give up the support of

Interactive Tools for the increased editing capability of the word processor. This development of independent skill and control over the computer is the goal of "dynamic support".

By arranging learning environments in which computer-based support was gradually removed, students gained control of writing by gradually assuming the parts of the task initially accomplished by the computer. Dynamic support provided by the microcomputer subordinated the students' concern for the mechanics of writing to the process of writing, resulting in improved quality and fluency.

4.0 EDUCATIONAL SOFTWARE FOR TEACHERS

So far we have been discussing the relationship of the learner to the software and the need for dynamic support in the *learning process*. These same relationships hold if we change the focus to the teacher and the *teaching process*.

Teachers are being placed in a very difficult position with the recent availability of computers for education. They are being asked to introduce their students to this new technology and to prepare them for using computers in a rapidly changing world. The computer is often seen as a self-contained system which will produce revolutionary new forms of learning and teaching when placed in the hands of students and teachers (Papert, 1980). But like many other educational innovations, the computer is only a tool and its effectiveness will depend on how it is used. Teachers often find themselves in the position of deciding what should be done with the computer in the classroom with little preparation for, or knowledge about, teaching with computers.

Given this situation, it is not surprising that some teachers make the computer itself the object of study as students as well as teachers try to discover what it means to become "computer literate." Teaching students computer literacy is difficult because of the rapid rate of change in computer technology. The machines of today will not be the machines of tomorrow. Learning how to *use* a computer is not the same thing as learning how computers work. Teaching students the rudiments of programming in the general purpose languages which are now available rarely provides students with enough control over the computer to make it serve their present and future purposes. These languages are likely to be replaced with more powerful special purpose languages in the future, making the mastery of these computer languages obsolete.

An alternative approach for using computers in classrooms is to integrate them into the school curriculum, to use computers as tools to teach subject matter such as reading, writing, and math (Mehan, Moll, & Riel, 1985; Levin & Souviney, 1983). But again there are a range of conceptions of how computers can be used by teachers to help students acquire basic skills. The same continuum from computer control to learner control that we presented earlier in this paper (see Figure 1) can be used to describe the relationship between teachers and educational software (see Figure 4).

Static Frames with Fixed Content	Lesson Frames with Content Added	Programming Languages & Authoring Systems
Computer Controlled	Mixed Control	Teacher Controlled

Figure 4: Educational Software for Teachers

At the computer-controlled end of the continuum, there are programs that have been developed to be used "as is" with little or no need to change them. This software is easy to use by a teacher who is new to computers, but it is often not possible to adapt it to the changing needs of the students or teacher. Frequently these programs are worksheets implemented on the computer that are highly structured for both teaching and learning. Such programs require teachers to adapt their lessons to the content presented.

In the center of the continuum are a variety of educational software packages that provide a sequence or frame in which teachers add their own content (Missing Links, Square Pairs, Game Show). These programs share the initiative with teachers making it possible for them to modify and adapt computer materials in ways that assure a better match between the computer use and the instructional goals of the teacher. At the teacher-controlled end of the continuum, there are programming languages (BASIC, Pascal, Logo) and authoring languages (Pilot) that enable teachers to create materials that are congruent with their teaching objectives.

Teachers often complain about the lack of quality in currently available educational software. Some teachers believe that the best way to deal with this problem is to gain control over the computer by learning to create their own software. To achieve this goal they sign up for evening courses in programming, usually in a general purpose computer language like BASIC. Such efforts often discourage teachers. The skills necessary to write the quality programs that these teachers want in their classrooms are difficult to acquire in the limited "free" time available to teachers.

5.0 DYNAMIC SUPPORT FOR TEACHERS

One approach to this dilemma that we've found effective is to consider teachers as learners who need the same type of "dynamic support" for integrating computer instruction with classroom lessons as we have been describing for students learning a particular form of writing. Just as a word processing system was not the best entry point for all students learning to write, programming is also not the best entry point for all teachers who want to integrate computers into their curriculum.

By working closely with teachers, we have found that novice computer-users were frequently overwhelmed by the power of general purpose programming languages or authoring systems. At first these teachers gravitated toward software that could be used by their students with minimal teacher modification. As they became familiar with the computer and understood the problems and successes of their students interacting with computers, however, they become more critical of software that they could not control. The experience of modifying programs motivated teachers to find ways to create their own programs.

A solution to the problem is to develop software systems that incorporate the principle of dynamic support for teacher as programmer (Figure 5).

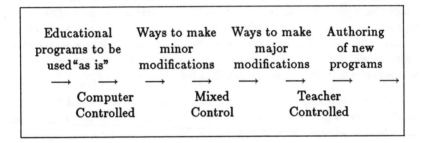

Figure 5: Dynamic support for teachers

With software systems that provide "dynamic support" teachers can find materials that are "classroom ready" to encourage immediate use by novice teachers with no or minimal input. These initial activities provide teachers with confidence in using the computer as a tool in the classroom in the same way reluctant writers begin by using writing tools that create text through the selection of options.

Once teachers have used the programs successfully, they become interested in ways to modify or personalize the software for the special interests and needs of their students. The effect of modifying programs and the experiences of success at this level, provide the motivation to consider the creation of new programs.

Ultimately, the goal of such software systems is to develop teachers' expertise so that they can create their own educational uses of the computer. But we are suggesting an alternate model to the one that has teachers learning an authoring system one step at a time. Instead we have discovered that an effective strategy is to have teachers begin by using models of the type of software that can be created with a system. Then they look inside the model, see how it was constructed and how it can be changed, first in trivial ways but progressing to more serious modification. Working with programming tools that help create new programs they can watch the placement of symbols as they create software. The last step would be to master the authoring language.

Close collaboration between researchers, programmers and teachers has evolved in such an authoring system for language arts. The ITI system (Levin, 1982), used to create the Writing Tools described in the first part of this paper, was initially designed as an authoring system for teachers to create language arts software. At first we were disappointed when teachers did not immediate use this tool to create new software. We discovered that teachers were initially more excited about using the example Writing Tools than they were about creating their own software.

Once they began using these tools, some of the teachers did begin to modify them, gradually making more and more substantial changes, to adapt them to their teaching situation. For example, in some of the story-making programs, some teachers changed character names and settings to ones that were familiar to the students. Other teachers changed the instructional sequence either making it more specific for younger students, or removing help that was too detailed for older students.

The opportunity to modify existing programs encouraged teachers to think of new ways the computer could be used to help students acquire important academic skills. For example, Miller-Souviney had no prior programming experience when she created the the Expository Writing Tools to provide dynamic support for expository writing (Miller-Souviney, 1985). Other teachers contributed to the development of a newspaper writing tool to provide students with at range of support for writing different types of newspaper articles (Riel, 1985; Levin, Riel, Rowe, & Boruta, 1985). A bilingual teacher learned to create bilingual Writing Tools to help her students with reading and writing skills (Mehan, Moll, & Riel, 1985). Our continuing experience with teachers using computers suggests that teachers can benefit from the same sequence of dynamic support that works with their students.

This movement from using previously developed programs, to modifying programs, to creating new programs and new uses for the system is what we mean by dynamic support. Like students, teachers begin by using the computer in productive ways while gaining the confidence and expertise to better integrate the computer with regular classroom instruction. In this way, teachers can be assured that the activities that occur on the computer are related to those that take place off the computer in classroom instruction.

6.0 CONCLUSION

From working collaboratively with students and teachers we have found that effective use of the computer in classrooms requires software that provides a dynamic range of support. We have described here how such a system operates from two different perspectives. The first perspective was that of a student acquiring writing skills through working with a set of computer writing tools that provided dynamic support. Just as students benefit from dynamic support in the learning process, we also found that teachers need dynamic support in the process of integrating computer instruction with the teaching goals in academic areas. General purpose computer languages and authoring systems are not the optimal entry point for teachers who seek to use computers for instruction. Instead, we found that a set of materials that can be used immediately, then modified and finally recreated, can provide the support that helps teachers take an active role in the use and development of educational software for their classrooms.

REFERENCES

Amarel, M. (1983). Classrooms and computers as instructional settings. *Theory Into Practice, 22*, 260.

Anderson, R. Klassen, D., & Johnson, D. (1981).   In defense of a computer literacy: a reply to Luehrmann. *Mathematics Teacher, 74*, 687.

Becker, H.J. (1986). Our national report card: preliminary results from the new Johns Hopkins survey. *Classroom Computer Learning*, 30.

Brown, A., & French, L. (1979). *The Zone of Proximal Development: Implications for Intelligence Testing for the Year 2000*, University of Illinois: Center for the Study of Reading.

Daiute, C. (1982). Wordprocessing, can it make even good writers better? *Electronic Learning*, 19.

Grubb, M. (1983). *Using Holistic Evaluation*, Encino, CA: Glenco Publishing Co.

Griffin, P., & Cole, M. (1984). Current activity for the future: the zo-ped. In B. Rogoff & J.V. Wertsch (Eds.), *Children's Learning in the "Zone of Proximal Development": New Directions for Child Development*. San Francisco: Jossey-Bass.

Johnson, D., Anderson, R., Hansen, T., & Klassen, D. (1980). Computer literacy – what is it? *Mathematics Teacher, 73*, 91.

Laboratory of Comparative Human Cognition (1982). A model system for the study of learning difficulties. *The Quarterly Newsletter of the Laboratory of Comparative Human Cognition, 4*, 39.

Levin, J.A. (1982). Microcomputers as interactive communication media: an interactive text interpreter. *The Quarterly Newsletter of the Laboratory of Comparative Human Cognition 4*, 34.

Levin, J.A., & Boruta, M.J. (1983). Writing with computers: you get exactly the right amount of space. *Theory Into Practice, 22*, 291.

Levin, J.A., Boruta, M.J., & Vasconcellos, M.T. (1983). Microcomputer-based environments for writing: a writer's assistant. In A.C. Wilkinson (Ed.), *Classroom Computers and Cognitive Science*. New York: Academic Press.

Levin, J.A., Riel, M.M., Rowe, R.D., & Boruta, M.J. (1985). Muktuk meets jacuzzi: computer networks and elementary school writers. In S.W. Freedman (Ed.), *The Acquisition of Written Languages: Revision and Response*, Hillsdale, NJ: Ablex.

Levin, J.A., & Souviney, R. (1983). Computer literacy: a time for tools. *The Quarterly Newsletter of the Laboratory of Comparative Human Cognition, 5*, 45.

Luehrmann, A. (1981). Computer literacy: what should it be? *Mathematics Teacher, 74*, 680.

Mehan, H., Moll, L., & Riel, M.M. (1985). Computers in classrooms: a quasi-experiment in guided change. Final Report to NIE, La Jolla, CA: Teacher Education Program.

Miller-Souviney, B. (1985). *Computer-supported Tools for Expository Writing: One Computer and 28 Kids*, Master's Thesis: University of California, San Diego.

Papert, S. (1980). *Mindstorms*, New York: Basic Books.

Riel, M.M. (1985). The computer chronicles newswire: a functional learning environment for acquiring literacy skills. *Journal of Educational Computing Research, 1,*
317.

Siegel, S. (1956). *Non-parametric Statistics for the Behavioral Sciences*, New York:
McGraw-Hill Book Co.

Tucker, M. (1983). Solving achievement problems in bits and bytes. *Education Week,*
19.

Vygotsky, L. (1978). *Mind in Society: The Development of Higher Psychological Processes*, M. Cole, V. John-Steiner, S. Scribner & E. Souberman (Eds.). Cambridge:
Harvard University Press.

7 AN EXAMPLE-BASED ENVIRONMENT FOR BEGINNING PROGRAMMERS[1]

Henry Lieberman

Artificial Intelligence Laboratory
Massachusetts Institute of Technology
Cambridge, MA 02139

ABSTRACT

Making a good programming environment for beginning programmers is an enterprise which can exploit the strong connections between machine learning and human learning. Applying what we know about teaching and learning to improve the programming environment can result in a system which allows beginners to more readily acquire programming skills.

Surprisingly, a universally-accepted principle of good teaching and good learning has not been taken seriously enough in designing programming environments – *learning by example*. A good teacher presents examples of how to solve problems, and points out what is important about the examples. The student generalizes from the examples to learn principles and techniques. This paper describes a programming environment called *Tinker*, in which a beginning programmer presents examples to the machine, distinguishing accidental and essential aspects of the examples. The programmer demonstrates how to handle the specific examples, and the machine formulates a procedure for handling the general case. Because people are much better at thinking about concrete examples than they are at thinking about abstractions, and because examples provide immediate feedback, Tinker is a more congenial environment for a beginner than conventional programming systems.

1.0 AI AND EDUCATION SHARE CONCERNS ABOUT HOW TO COMMUNICATE EXPERTISE

A major enterprise in artificial intelligence is discovering how to communicate problem-solving skill from a programmer to a machine. Education is the enterprise of communicating problem solving skill from a teacher to a student. Research in both AI and education is concerned with the question of what expertise is and how it can be communicated.

[1] Major support for the work described in this paper was provided by Wang Laboratories and by the System Development Foundation. Other related work at the MIT Artificial Intelligence Laboratory was supported in part by the Defense Advanced Projects Agency under Office of Naval Research Contract N00014-80-C-0505.

One way that education can benefit from AI is that progress in AI can lead to putting more powerful computing in the hands of less sophisticated users. The more intelligent a machine becomes, the easier it can be to program, and ease of programming is the primary criterion for judging systems intended for beginners. Also, the study of machine learning can elucidate principles of learning and learning strategies which can then be applied to teaching.

Not only is work in AI useful for education, but AI has much to learn from the education community as well. Programming and knowledge acquisition are processes that involve transfer of expertise from a person to a computer, and this activity can benefit from what we know about the process of communicating procedures from one person to another. This paper reports an experiment in trying to apply a principle of good teaching and good learning to the problem of trying to teach a computer how to do something. The result is a programming system which is especially well-adapted to the needs of beginning programmers, who require a system that is both easy to learn and easy to teach.

2.0   LEARNING BY EXAMPLE IS THE MOST EFFECTIVE LEARNING STRATEGY

Teachers and students alike agree that one of the best kinds of learning is *learning by example*. The best teachers do not present mere facts and directions to students, but motivate their presentations by supplying illustrative examples for each concept to be learned.

A poor teacher will simply make the student memorize facts or memorize the steps of some problem-solving procedure. Besides being boring for the students, rote-learning is ineffective. Students who are spoon-fed complex sets of rules for integrating formulas without practice in concrete examples will tend to forget the rules or misapply them.

In some ways, the need for examples is a paradox, because the examples don't add any more information from a strictly logical viewpoint. If the rules are precise and complete, memorizing them "should" be enough. But people need examples to help *visualize* the operation of procedures. Students can check their understanding of each step of the procedure as it proceeds. Mistakes in understanding rules become apparent as their effect on examples is noticed. It is simply an indisputable fact about human learning that people are much better at learning procedures by abstracting from concrete examples than by trying to learn abstract general procedures and specialize them to specific cases. Lawler (Lawler, 1985) a compelling case of the superiority of example based learning. A child who was unable to reliably perform addition with numbers written on paper (where numbers were abstractions) was nevertheless quite competent in adding the value of coins when she needed to buy something!

3.0   TEACHING BY EXAMPLE HAS ADVANTAGES LIKE LEARNING BY EXAMPLE

Not only is learning by example better for the student, but *teaching by example* is easier on the teacher than teaching by presenting abstract principles alone. The use of concrete examples make it easier for the teacher to articulate expertise. Using specific examples to aid visualization, the teacher can make sure that the statement of principles has the intended effect in particular cases, guarding against giving the students incomplete or contradictory information.

Sometimes, general procedures will be so complex that the knowledge can't be conveyed at all except by example. An English teacher trying to get students to improve their grammar would find it hopeless to try to give the students complete rules for parsing the entire English language. Instead, the teacher presents examples of both grammatical and common ungrammatical sentences in the hopes that the students will learn to generalize the concepts of grammaticality to the sentences they write in their papers.

Teaching is also a learning experience for the teacher. Teachers often remark that the process of teaching a subject leads to deepening their own understanding of that subject. "I thought I understood the material before, but after teaching it, now I feel I *really* understand it!" a teacher will often say. This understanding often develops in the process of elaborating examples for the benefit of students. Part of good teaching requires teachers to *put themselves in the student's shoes* while teaching, to verify to themselves that each lesson is succeeding in conveying the intended information. Checking the connection between abstract knowledge and concrete examples helps the teacher to empathize with the students' viewpoint.

Aside from its intrinsic utility, one of the reasons learning programming is educationally valuable is that, in the process of teaching the machine how to perform a procedure, programmers improve their own understanding of the subject matter. Because the computer is such a dumb student, procedures must be spelled out in considerable detail, forcing students to clarify their thinking.

If examples play such an important role in teaching, the analogy between teaching and programming leads us to ask, *Why can't examples play a more important role in programming?*

4.0 LEARNING BY EXAMPLE LEADS TO PROGRAMMING BY EXAMPLE

Unfortunately, programming as we know it today is very much like a rote-learning situation. Programming is more like making the machine memorize a sequence of abstract rules than having the machine learn a procedure from examples. Although the machine doesn't have the problem of forgetting what a programmer tells it, the absence of examples makes the programmer's role as teacher very difficult.

This suggests that we might try to develop a new kind of programming, where a procedure is communicated to the machine by presenting examples, and demonstrating the steps of the procedure on those examples, using the principles of good teaching. *Tinker* is an experimental programming environment I have implemented to test the hypothesis that using examples in programming will yield the same kind of benefits as using examples in teaching.

Figure 1: Tinker Learns Programs From Examples Like a Student Learns Examples From a Teacher.

Tinker behaves like a (very dull) student, starting out by merely remembering the examples shown, and the steps which the teacher performs. Since Tinker doesn't have a human student's capacity to automatically decide what features of one example may be relevant for future examples, the programmer must *tell* Tinker which features of the examples are important, and which can be ignored in general. Once this is done, though, Tinker can generalize a procedure from watching its operation in specific examples. Furthermore, like a good student, Tinker can build up its knowledge little by little. A sequence of examples can be shown, starting with simple examples illustrating common cases and leading up to complicated procedures for exceptional cases. At each step, Tinker always shows its teacher what it has learned so far, both in the effect of what it has been told on particular examples, and in the form of a Lisp program. The programmer can then correct any misconceptions on Tinker's part before proceeding to the next step, so that testing a program happens *while* the program is written, rather than afterward.

5.0 FROM AN "INSTANT TURTLE" TO AN "INSTANT PROGRAMMING LANGUAGE"

Before getting to the details of Tinker, I would like to introduce the approach by relating how my interest in example-oriented environments for beginning programmers grew out of my earlier work with Seymour Papert's group at the MIT Artificial Intelligence Laboratory. This group developed the educational language Logo, derived from the AI language Lisp, and now available on most microcomputers. Despite Logo's initial success in teaching children techniques of learning and problem-solving, we found that teachers experienced some difficulty introducing Logo to younger children.

The kids had little difficulty learning about the *turtle*, a graphics cursor they could use to draw pictures on the screen by moving it with commands like [Forward 100] and [Right 90]. Teachers would introduce Logo to students by having them type these commands to the computer and watch the responses of the turtle. Often, the biggest hurdle was that the children were very slow at typing on a keyboard.

The following sequence of turtle commands could draw a triangle.

```
Forward 100 Right 120 Forward 100 Right 120
        Forward 100 Right 120
```

But trouble came when the teachers tried to introduce the notion of procedures. The simplest notion of a procedure is introducing a name for a group of turtle commands, using the Logo command To. To make a procedure that draws a Triangle, the student must say

```
To Triangle Repeat 3 (Forward 100 Right 120)
```

But when the student types Forward 100 this time, the turtle doesn't move! Why not?! Was something wrong with the computer, the student wondered?

The teacher then had to patiently explain that the computer was just *remembering* that it was supposed to do the Forward 100 as part of the Triangle procedure, and you couldn't actually get it do anything until you finished the procedure (with End) and called it by typing Triangle. But this explanation seemed very abstract to a beginner, who was just trying to learn the concept of a procedure.

Furthermore, it seemed to require that you type everything twice! Once you performed the turtle commands that drew a triangle on the screen, why did you have to type those commands all over again just to have the computer remember them to make a Triangle procedure?

The teachers came up with a very ingenious solution to this. Because typing long words is an obstacle for young children, they wrote a "one finger" Logo called *Instant Turtle* that let a child move the turtle by typing F for Forward, B for Back, etc. Typing numbers would set default values for commands. Though this was before mice were commonly found on computer systems, today we would recognize this as a *menu-driven* interface.

After the student learned how to move the turtle, the teachers wanted to introduce the notion of a procedure as a remembered set of turtle commands. They decided that whenever the student typed a turtle command, it would *always* be remembered in a list. A new command, Teach, would take the current list of turtle commands, and make a procedure out of it, asking the student for a name. This new procedure was then available as another command.

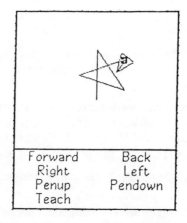

Figure 2:   Instant Turtle is a Menu-driven Interface for Logo.

This turned out to be an enormous success. A student could issue the turtle commands for drawing a triangle, and get the immediate feedback of seeing the triangle appear on the screen. The student could then simply do Teach Triangle to make a triangle procedure, without retyping the Forward and Right commands.

This is a very simple kind of "programming by example," since the triangle drawn on the screen serves as an example of what the Triangle procedure will do. Even if the procedure did not have arguments, a triangle drawn the next time the procedure was called still might be different, appearing at a different place on the screen or in a different orientation. Showing the computer how to draw an example triangle could be used to teach the machine how to draw triangles in general, just as showing a person an example of how to perform a procedure can help them learn that procedure.

But Instant Turtle was very limited in its expressive power, and as soon as a child gained mastery of basic turtle manipulation and the concept of a procedure, it was time to move on to full Logo. After all, Instant Turtle couldn't define procedures with input arguments, procedures that called other procedures or called themselves recursively, or that contained conditionals. But moving from Instant Turtle to full Logo loses the immediacy of defining procedures from remembered sets of interactively executed actions. Is it possible to create a programming environment as friendly as Instant Turtle, but for a language as powerful as Lisp? Could procedures be defined by demonstrating them on concrete examples, always giving the user immediate feedback, without sacrificing expressive power? This is the motivation that led to my work on an experimental programming environment, *Tinker*.

6.0   THE SIMPLEST KIND OF PROCEDURE IS REMEMBERING A SET OF COMMANDS

When a beginner sits down for the first time at a computer, the first thing that he or she learns is that the computer is a machine that *responds to commands*, either typed or chosen from menus. Starting with the "login", "loading" or "booting" incantantion, the beginner learns that the machine is capable of doing any one of a fixed repertoire of things, each accessed through a name. Much of a first session is devoted simply to getting used to the idea of invoking commands. Logo, especially Instant Turtle, provides a nice "microworld" for experimenting with commands, since each command has immediate, visible effect and the beginner can see how using different arguments affects the behavior of commands.

From there, an environment like Instant Turtle smoothly introduces the idea of a procedure. The computer can remember a set of commands, give a name to refer to the whole set, and subsequently, whenever the name is given, the computer performs the whole set of commands.

Frequently, another learning path to learning the concept of a procedure involves a beginner learning to use an "applications" program such as a text editor or spreadsheet. The most advanced applications of this kind permit *keyboard macros* (Stallman, 1981; Lotus Corp., 1983) A keyboard macro records keystrokes or mouse selections for subsequent playback, in a manner similar to Instant Turtle. Unlike Instant Turtle, a "recording mode" must usually be turned on. However, like Instant Turtle, a program recorded in this manner can only repeat the exact same action each time it is invoked.

7.0 PROCEDURES WITH ARGUMENTS CAN DO SOMETHING DIFFERENT EACH TIME

Tinker takes the concept of a procedure as a remembered set of actions and generalizes this to more complicated kinds of procedures. The next step is to define a procedure which can be given *arguments*, enabling the remembered sequence of steps to do something different each time it is invoked. This involves introducing the concept of a *variable*, a name used to denote an object which can be different each time the procedure is used.

In Tinker, a procedure which takes arguments is defined by presenting an example of the procedure, with a specific value for each of the arguments. Tinker creates a new variable for each argument. The user then demonstrates to Tinker how to use the arguments to perform the procedure.

In the figure below, we see how Tinker can be used to define a procedure to draw a square, with one argument saying how big each side of the square should be. The operation New Example from the menu at the upper left was selected for the code (Square 200). Tinker generated an argument variable, which the user named side using Give something a Name, and is displayed showing both its name and current value. For each Forward command, the user pointed to the side variable, having the effect of making the turtle go 200 steps immediately. But Tinker remembers that the Square procedure should use whatever the current value of the side variable is in the Forward command. Thus, we *generalize* the example of a square of size 200 to a procedure that can draw squares of any size.

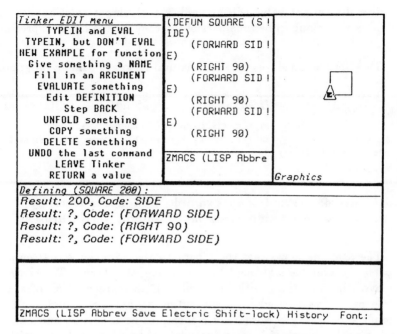

Figure 3:   Drawing a Square of Size 200 Serves as an
             Example for Squares of Any Size.

8.0   THE RESULT OF ONE ACTION CAN BE USED AS PART OF ANOTHER ACTION

Instant Turtle and its kin are only suitable for *imperative* domains like graphics, where each command is performed for its side effect. In *functional* languages like Lisp and Logo, expressions return *values*, and a value returned by one expression can be used as an argument to another function. How does this concept fit in to a programming-by-example system?

The idea of a procedure as a remembered set of actions is generalized in Tinker from a simple linear list as in Instant Turtle and simple keyboard macros, to the tree structure necessary for building expressions in a functional language. The key idea is that the result or *value* produced by a set of actions can be used as input to subsequent actions.

In the center window of a Tinker display, each line displays an expression. Every time an expression is evaluated, it shows two parts, the Value in the current environment, and the Code which gave rise to that value. Using the menu operation Fill in an Argument, the user can *point* to some expression appearing on the display to feed it as an argument to a function. Its current value will be used in the computation, but its code will be carried along to become part of the code for the larger expression.

This illustration shows part of a natural language parsing program.

```
Defining (PARSE-SENTENCE (QUOTE (* THIS CAT ATE THAT RAT)))
Result: (*), Code: S
Result: (NP (ART THIS) (NOUN CAT)), Code: (NOUN-PHRASE S)
Result: (VP (VERB ATE) (NP (ART THAT) (NOUN RAT))), Code: (VERB-PHRASE
Code: (LIST (QUOTE S))
```

Figure 4:   Parsing an Example Sentence is Done by
              Parsing Example Noun and Verb Phrases.

The title line shows that the program Parse-Sentence is attempting to parse the example sentence "This cat ate that rat". The third line displays a list beginning with the symbol NP, a representation of a noun phrase parse tree created by a subroutine Noun-Phrase applied to this example sentence. The word This is identified as an article, and cat as a noun. Similarly, on the following line, Verb-Phrase returned a list with the verb ate. and the noun-phrase that rat, in this particular example. The desired parse tree for The cat ate that rat, is a list whose first element is S, indicating "sentence", and whose remaining elements are the parse tree for the noun phrase The cat and the verb phrase ate that rat. The last line shows code for constructing this list in formation.

The next step, illustrated below creates that list. The code for generating each element of the list appears as part of the code for constructing the whole list. (Stars indicate elements too big to fit on the screen.)

```
Defining (PARSE-SENTENCE (QUOTE (* THIS CAT ATE THAT RAT)))
Result: (*), Code: S
Result: (S (NP ** **) (VP ** **)), Code: (LIST (QUOTE S) (NOUN-PHRASE S) (
```

Figure 5:   Combining the Parsed Phrases Results in a
              Parse Tree for the Entire Sentence.

Beginners typically have difficulty programming complex expressions involving nested function calls. They find it hard to keep in their heads what the effect of each subexpression will be. Tinker relieves this problem by allowing a beginning programmer to build up a complicated expression incrementally, examining the result of each piece in a representative case before using it as part of some larger expression.

9.0   A GROUP OF SEVERAL EXAMPLES SHOW HOW A PROCEDURE CAN MAKE A DECISION

If we don't want a remembered procedure to do the same thing every time it is called, it must have some way to make a *decision* among alternative courses of action. To demonstrate this to Tinker we must show several examples for the same procedure, each illustrating what happens in case each of the alternatives is chosen.

If a teacher shows a student several examples for the same concept that receive different treatment, the bright student will raise his or her hand and ask the teacher "How did you decide which alternative to use?" The teacher is being asked to provide decision criteria by which a new example could be classified as being like one of the alternative examples already presented. The teacher who is trying to teach a procedure involving decision-making should show students at least one example in which the decision turns out to be each of the possible alternatives. This is analogous to the programmer's truism that a program containing a conditional must be tested with at least one example for each of the conditional branches.

When more than one example is provided for a function, Tinker acts like that bright student. For each new example, it asks the user to provide a test which can distinguish the most recent example from others it already knows.

In the figure below, a menu-driven command system with commands Insert and Delete is being defined. The programmer gives two examples for the command loop of the system one showing how to implement the insert command, another showing how to implement the delete command. Each example is presented after choosing one of the menu items with the mouse.

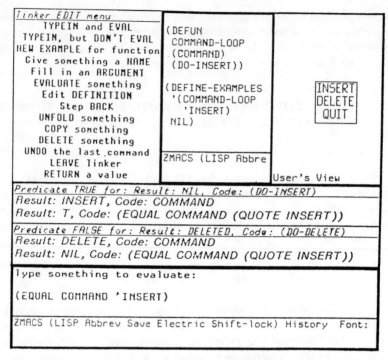

Figure 6:   Two Examples Implementing Different
Menu Commands are Distinguished.

The center window is split into two halves, each showing the situation
in different examples simultaneously. The programmer provides a *predicate*,
which should evaluate to *true* in one case, *false* in the other, distinguishing
the examples. The resulting program constructed by Tinker will contain
a *conditional* test, which generalizes the procedures which handled each
example separately.

10.0   SHOWING HOW ONE EXAMPLE REDUCES TO ANOTHER DEFINES RECURSIVE PROCEDURES

Teaching *recursive* procedures involves several examples as well. The teacher
can either first show the *base* case, the simplest and most trivial example,
and then show a *recursive* example, where the procedure for handling an
example depends on the knowledge of how to deal with simpler examples.
This is a *bottom-up* style.

Alternatively, the teacher can start with a complex example, and show
how it can be reduced to simpler examples, then simpler ones still, until
finally a trivial example has a trivial solution. This is a *top-down* style. Fi-

nally, in either style, a test for recognizing the base case must be presented, to show how to determine when to stop the recursion.

Tinker supports both the top-down and bottom-up methods of building recursive functions from examples. A bottom-up style starts with defining an "incorrect" procedure which handles the base case only. An example for the recursive case makes use of the already-defined base case procedure, and having two examples leads to constructing a test which distinguishes them. Starting with the recursive case, computation "whittles down" the procedure to simpler cases. When the base case is reached, the New example operation can be invoked from *within* the definition of the non-trivial case.

```
Defining (FRINGE (QUOTE ((A) B))):
Result: ((A) B), Code: TREE
Result: (A), Code: (FRINGE (CAR TREE))
Result: (B), Code: (FRINGE (CDR TREE))
```

Figure 7:   The Fringe of ((A) B) is Defined in Terms of the Fringes of (A) and (B).

In the figure, we are defining the fringe of the list ((A) B), flattening the tree structure to a linear list of atoms. Breaking the list into its Car and Cdr, namely (A) and (B), generates recursively smaller Fringe problems. We can use the New example operation recursively on the problem (Fringe '(A)), showing Tinker how to take the fringe of a one-element list. The knowledge can then be applied automatically to computing the Fringe of the list (B). The next step would be to call Append on the fringes generated by the recursive subproblems.

11.0   PROGRAMMING A VIDEO GAME BY EXAMPLE SHOWS HOW MORE COMPLEX PROGRAMS WORK

We will now show how Tinker can be used to program a more complex and realistic task – the simple video game *Pong* (Lieberman, 1984). This task involves coordinating several procedures, but the basic example-oriented methodology remains the same.

We assume that we already have a set of predefined objects representing common components of video games: balls and paddles which can move, scoreboards which can display scores. Tinker is used to program the dynamics of the game in a manner similar to the way in which one person might teach another the "rules of the game": through examples which illustrate important situations that can occur in the game. We set up each situation graphically, using the mouse to position the ball and the paddles, then write code which performs the action appropriate to that situation. The graphical effect of each instruction is displayed immediately. When all the examples are presented, the game is ready to play!

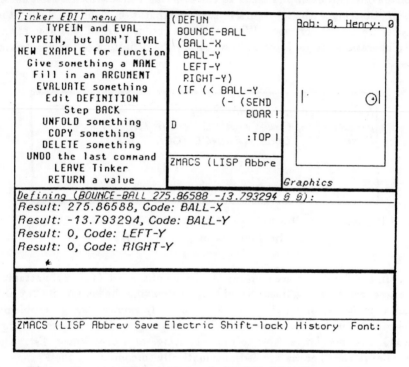

**Figure 8:   A Video Game is Defined by Examples
Illustrating Situations that Occur in
the Game.**

The Pong game could be described by procedures to move the paddles in response to user input, procedures to move the ball and procedures to check for collisions and manage scoring. To control the paddles, three examples are needed: one in which no input is given, one example in which input from the joysticks should move the left paddle, and another for the right paddle.

We start defining the procedure to check for collisions by showing an example situation in which the ball is not touching anything. Then, an example is shown where the ball hits the top wall. In this case, the ball is directed to bounce off the wall by changing its heading.

Having two examples for the collision-detection procedure, Tinker asks us to provide some criterion by which the two examples can be distinguished. Telling Tinker to check for the ball's proximity to the wall synthesizes a procedure containing a conditional, and capable of handling both classes of situations.

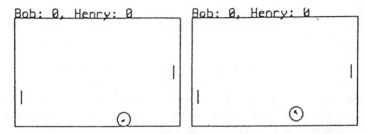

Figure 9:   Going Between These Frames Shows Tinker
              How a Ball Bounces Off a Wall.

A third example illustrates the case where the ball touches a paddle. Here, too, the ball bounces, and proximity to the paddle is the distinguishing feature of the situation.

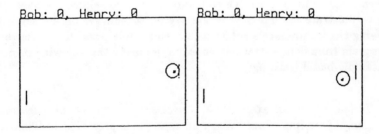

Figure 10:   This Example Shows Tinker How to Bounce
              a Ball Off a Paddle.

Yet another example shows the ball hitting a side wall. But this case is different from hitting the top wall – here one of the players has scored a point!

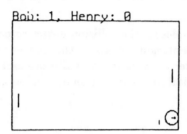

Figure 11:   In this Example, the Paddle Missing the Ball
Causes One Player to Score.

We tell the scoreboard object to increment the score of the appropriate
player and start a new round of the game. This example is distinguished
from the rest, so that when Tinker encounters a new situation – one with
positions for the ball and paddles it has not seen before – it can select one
of the procedures it already knows from previous examples.

12.0   THE ART OF CHOOSING GOOD EXAMPLES IS AN IMPORTANT PROBLEM-SOLVING SKILL

Teaching successfully depends, to a large extent, on the art of choosing good
examples to present to students. Programming, too, depends on the art of
choosing good examples, to an extent which is not sufficiently appreciated in
conventional computer science education. Good examples are ones which
clearly illustrate the ideas they are trying to convey, in the sense that
knowing the idea makes a solution to the example possible. Tinker builds
a program from demonstrations on examples using the following principles
of example-based learning:

*To learn from an example, it is necessary to know which features of
the example are important.* When an example is presented to Tinker, the
programmer indicates which constants in the example are to be generalized
when Tinker constructs a function definition. Although Tinker lacks the
capability of *automatically* figuring out what is important in an example
the way a human student would, keeping a close correspondence between a
concrete example and a general procedure ensures that the programmer's
intentions are faithfully captured.

*Examples which show the similarities and differences between one idea
and related ideas help clarify principles.* Tinker constructs conditional code
by presenting one example for each important case in the resulting program.

Because conditional procedures are developed in this way, no untested code can arise in the final program.

A sequence of examples should start with simple examples and build to more complex examples and exceptional cases. Recursive and conditional procedures can be developed incrementally by starting with simple, "incorrect" definitions, and later adding more examples to handle more complicated and special-purpose situations.

I hope that the examples of programming in Tinker shown above illustrate how Tinker gives students practice in the art of example selection by rewarding appropriate choices of examples. Since examples play such a crucial role in teaching and learning, an example-based programming environment like Tinker should be a superior vehicle for learning and utilizing programming skills.

ACKNOWLEDGMENTS

I would like to thank Bob Lawler for the encouragement that led to writing this paper.

REFERENCES

Finzer, W., & Gould, L. (1984). Programming by rehearsal, *Byte*, June.

Lawler, R. (1985). *Computer Experience and Cognitive Development*. New York: John Wiley & Sons.

Lieberman, H. (1984). Video games by example. *SigGraph Video Review (videotape)*, *12, 1*.

Lieberman, H. (1984). Seeing what your programs are doing. *International Journal of Man-Machine Studies, 21, 4*, October.

Lieberman, H. (1982). Constructing graphical user interfaces by example. *Proceedings of the Graphics Interface Conference*, Toronto, Canada, May.

Lieberman, H. (1982). Designing interactive systems from the user's viewpoint. In P. Degano & E. Sandewall, (Eds.), *Integrated Interactive Computer Systems*, North Holland.

Lotus Documentation Dept. (1983). *Lotus 1-2-3 Manual*, Lotus Development Corporation.

Papert, S. (1980). *Mindstorms: Children, Computers and Powerful Ideas*. New York: Basic Books.

Stallman, R.M. (1981). Emacs: the extensible, customizable, Self-documenting display text editor. *Proceedings of the ACM SigOA Conference on Text Manipulation*.

8 OBJECT-ORIENTED LOGO

Gary L. Drescher

Massachusetts Institute of Technology
Cambridge, MA

ABSTRACT

In object-oriented programming, one constructs entities, called objects, each with its own *state* and *behavior*. A new object is constructed either from scratch, or as a *specialization* of another object (or objects); a specialized object *inherits* the attributes of the object it's based on, but can be given additional (or alternative) attributes of its own.

ObjectLogo is a new dialect of Logo(Papert, 1980), designed to facilitate object-oriented programming. In ObjectLogo, an object is simply an entity that has its own versions of certain functions and variables. One communicates with an object by telling it to execute some ordinary Logo expression. The expression is run inside the object; while inside, each function or variable name refers to the object's own version (if any; else to the usual, global version). The traditional object-oriented mechanism of *message passing* is not needed; objects' local versions of functions serve the same purpose.

ObjectLogo also departs from tradition by refusing to enforce a distinction between *class* and *instance*. Rather, the distinction, when desired, is made by convention: a "class" object is given its own function definitions to establish the behavior of instances of that class; an "instance" object is a specialization of a class that inherits its behavior (function bindings) from the class, and is given its own variable bindings to describe its individual attributes. Thus, a uniform, simple paradigm – specialization, realized by the primitive kindof – is used to make all objects, including instances, and specialized classes. And because the class-instance distinction is optional, beginners (and experts building objects on the fly) are free to ignore it, building a "class" object and using it directly as a prototype instance. Objects' function and variable bindings can be added (or deleted) incrementally and interactively, rather than having to be declared in advance.

ObjectLogo is useful when one builds a system with related, interacting objects. In addition, using ObjectLogo promotes learning about modular design, since organizing things into functional modules, subject to specialized redefinition, is at the heart of ObjectLogo programming.

1.0 OBJECTS AND NAMES

It is useful to give things names. One reason is *conciseness*: it is less cumbersome to recite a name than to spell out the details of its definition. A deeper reason concerns *variability*: often what is meant by a name changes from time to time or situation to situation. A tract formulated in terms of things' names adapts automatically; a tract expressed in terms of detailed definitions instead of names would need to be changed whenever the details of the referents were altered.

These considerations apply to naming in computer programs as well as in natural language, principally in the form of function and variable names. When a program is expressed in terms of variables rather than constant values, its behavior is automatically adapted to a parameterized family of situations, depending on the variables' current values. Even better, when some pattern of activity is defined as a function, and invoked by its name, you can:

- Use the function without having to know *how it works*, just *what it does* (and what it's named).

- Change how it works without affecting how it is used; extant invocations needn't be changed.

- Amend what it does, perhaps adding an auxiliary side-effect, or altering its behavior for some special inputs. Again, the changes propagate automatically to extant and future invocations.

Sometimes, the meaning of a name, the definition of a function, varies according to context, rather than just changing serially with successive re-definitions. If simultaneously I tell a driver and a bicycle rider to "brake", the bicyclist responds with a hand motion, while the driver uses her foot. Similarly, if I have a number of graphic icons on my computer screen, I'd like to be able to tell each to vanish, or to move to certain coordinates. Different icons' responses to the same command should be within the general meaning of the command, but should be allowed individual idiosyncracies;[1] for example, a particular icon might make a sound whenever it moves. Varying a function's meaning according to context is characteristic of *object-oriented* programming. In this way, object-oriented programming amplifies the power of naming.

---

[1] I am only concerned here with related variants of a name's meaning, not with a name that has *unrelated* meanings in different situations, so that the duplication of the same name is just an accident.

2.0 OBJECTS AS ENVIRONMENTS

Logo pedagogy emphasizes the importance of giving names to functions and variables. ObjectLogo is a dialect of Logo that extends the power of naming by promoting object-oriented programming. In keeping with Logo's "no threshold, no ceiling" slogan, ObjectLogo is an ample basis for sophisticated object-oriented programming, but is designed to be very accessible to novices.

This section introduces ObjectLogo's concept of objects. Section 4 analyzes the basic differences between ObjectLogo and traditional object-oriented languages. Section 5 addresses some pedagogic issues.

2.1 An Object has Variables and Functions of its Own

In ObjectLogo, an object is simply an entity that has its own versions of certain variables (each with its own value) and certain functions (each with its own definition). An ordinary Logo expression, such as fd 100 rt 90, can be run *inside* some object, e.g., by saying tell :turtle4 [fd 100 rt 90].[2] Inside an object, the object's own versions of variables and functions are in effect – meaning, for example, that if an object has its own definition of fd, then that definition is invoked whenever fd is called from inside that object (and similarly for variables).

- An object is created and output by the primitive function something; so, for example, make "talker something saves a new object as the value of talker.

- The primitive have gives the current object – the one we're currently inside – its own version of some variable, with some value; for example, tell :talker [have "name "gertrude] gives :talker its own version of name, with value gertrude.

- The primitive howto is used to define functions, and to give the current object its own definition of a function. For example, this:
    ```
    tell :talker [howto say :msg
                  print (sentence :name "says :msg)]
    ```

gives :talker its own definition of say.[3]

---

[2] I am imagining here that Logo's traditional turtle has been reimplemented as an ObjectLogo object, and that there are several turtle objects, e.g., :turtle4.

[3] The name howto is used, instead of Logo's traditional to, to avoid the strong English connotation of an imperative if to were used in an expression like the preceding.

Typing tell :talker [say "hi] invokes :talker's definition of say,
causing Logo to print GERTRUDE SAYS HI. gertrude, of course, comes
from :talker's value of the variable :name; but notice that the reference
to the variable name does not appear textually inside the tell expression
we typed. Nevertheless, the reference happens *during* that tell, while we
are inside :talker; thus, it is :talker's binding that is in effect.

2.2 One Object Can be Based on Another

The primitive kindof creates an object that is a *specialization* of another
object (also said to be *based on* that object). For example, make "shouter
kindof :talker builds a specialization of :talker, the object :shouter.
A specialized object, too, can be given its own variables and functions. In
addition, it *inherits* the variables and functions of the object(s) it's based
on. An exception occurs only when the new object is given its own version
of a variable or function that it would otherwise have inherited; an object's
own version always *replaces* the version that would have been inherited.

Suppose we give :shouter its own definition of say, replacing the one
it would otherwise inherit from :talker:

```
tell :shouter [howto say :msg
               type "hey!
               usual.say :msg]
```

If we type tell :shouter [say "hello], Logo responds with HEY! GER-
TRUDE SAYS HELLO. We've added an idosyncracy – typing HEY! at the beginning of the message – to say's "usual" definition, the definition that
would have been inherited by :shouter from :talker, had not :shouter's
own version replaced it. Within a definition of function-name, the name
usual.function-name, is used to access the version that this definition
replaces. Thus, the "usual" definition of a function can be incorporated
wholesale into an idiosyncratic replacement. This has the customary importance of referring to something by name: one need not know how the
definition is implemented, and one's reference adapts automatically to any
changes to the definition. One consequence of this is that a student can specialize an extant object without having to know how it works; for example,
if prefabricated turtle objects are provided, a student can easily specialize
a certain turtle to beep whenever it goes forward (see Section 5.2).

2.3 An Object Can be Based on Several Others

It is possible to make a specialization of several objects combined (this is
called *multiple inheritance*. For instance, here we create an object :whis-
perer, and then an object :combination that inherits from both :shouter
and :whisperer:

```
make "whisperer kindof :talker
tell :whisperer [howto say :msg
                 type "shhh...
                 usual.say :msg]
tell :whisperer [say "howdy]
```

Logo prints SHHH... GERTRUDE SAYS HOWDY.

```
make "combination(kindof :shouter :whisperer)
tell :combination[say "howdy]
```

Logo prints HEY! SHHH... GERTRUDE SAYS HOWDY.

:combination has been given no variables or functions of its own; it has only what it inherits from :shouter and :whisperer. Each of those two objects has a version of say that contributes an idiosyncracy to :talker's commonly inherited version. :combination's version automatically combines say's inherited idiosyncracies with its common "usual" behavior.

More precisely, when :shouter and :whisperer were passed to kindof, kindof noticed that they are specializations of a common object, :talker. kindof built the new object as though the two specializations had been made successively – as though :shouter were based on :whisperer, in turn based on :talker. Inside :combination, say therefore refers to :shouter's definition, which types HEY! and then calls usual.say. Here, usual.say refers to :whisperer's version, which types SHHH... and then calls usual.say. *This*, finally, refers to :talker's definition, which prints the rest of the message. The order of the idiosyncracies (shouting, then whispering) is explained by the order of the specializations. Often, though, the order of idiosyncracies doesn't matter; then, one can settle for the less elaborate explanation in the preceding paragraph.

Technically, an object is a dynamically-scoped environment with bindings of values and functions. A specialized object is a nested environment, which inherits the bindings of its superior, except for bindings that it shadows. I avoided this terminology in the foregoing discussion in order to offer not only a specification of ObjectLogo objects, but also a sketch of how this specification might be introduced to students (more on this in Section 5).

3.0 CLASSES AND INSTANCES

You may have noticed something odd about the examples so far. Ordinarily
in object-oriented programming, we distinguish *classes* from *instances*; a
class specifies the behavior of an entire collection of things; instances are the
individual elements of a class. The objects :talker,:shouter,:whisperer,
and :combination were built as though they were class objects – they were
given, or else inherited, function definitions (for say) that determined the
behavior of those objects. On the other hand, each of these objects was also
used as though it were an instance – each was gotten to say something, to
exhibit the behavior characteristic of members of its class.

In fact, ObjectLogo does not enforce any distinction between class
and instance – an object is just an object. Often, though, the distinction
needs to be made. For example, suppose we wish to make several different
talkers and shouters. Each should have, say, its own name and address, but
otherwise its attributes should just be those of a general talker (or shouter).

```
make "tk1 kindof :talker tell :tk1 [ have "name "chris
                                     have "address "boston"]
make "tk2 kindof :talker tell :tk2 [ have "name "kim
                                     have "address "cambridge]
make "sh1 kindof :shouter tell :sh1 [have "name "fred
                                     have "address "exeter]
tell :tk1 [speak sentence [i live in]:address]
```

Logo prints: CHRIS SAYS I LIVE IN BOSTON.

```
        tell :sh1 [speak sentence [i live in] :address]
```

Logo prints: HEY! FRED SAYS I LIVE IN EXETER.

The object :tk1 (for example) is intended as an instance of :talker,
which is now thought of as a class. Notice that the familiar relation of
specialization, realized by kindof, is used here. This is appropriate, since
an instance should indeed inherit the attributes of the class it's based on,
except for those attributes that distinguish one individual from another;
each instance needs its own version of those (replacing any version that
might otherwise have been inherited from the class). That is accomplished
here by giving each of the three new instances its own versions of the
variables name and address.

The construction of new instances can be institutionalized by defining functions to aid in setting up the instances' variables, rather than doing it manually each time.

```
tell :talker [howto exist :myname :myaddress
              have "name :myname
              have "address :myaddress]
make "wh1 kindof :whisperer
tell :wh1 [exist "anonymous "earth]
tell :wh1 [sayaddress]
```

Logo prints: SHHH... ANONYMOUS SAYS EARTH].

Here, the instance is given its individual attributes by the function exist (which :wh1 inherits from :whisperer, which inherits it from :talker). The attributes' values are input to the exist function. A specialized class object might be given an exist function that adds some attribute peculiar to that specialization, then calls usual.exist to set up whatever attributes are needed by the class that the new one based on.

Despite the importance of distinguishing classes from instances, it is important that the user not be *forced* to do so. An undifferentiated object – serving at once as class and instance – can be made and used (as in the previous section's examples) by someone who does not yet understand about classes and instances, though this will be inadquate when several instances are needed. But this intermediate object can serve as a steppingstone to fuller understanding – especially since, as we have just seen, the intermediate object becomes a *component* of the more complicated class-instance structure; the intermediate object serves as the class that gets instantiated. Furthermore, even for advanced users, creating a new class, or class hierarchy, on the fly is easier if the classes under construction can also be tried out as prototype instances.[4]

---

[4] A class serving as prototype instance is a bit reminiscent of Piagetian *transduction*, where a child's early concept of a generality is conflated with particular examples (e.g., a child might explain that a table's shadow "comes from under the maple tree," merging the general concept of a shadow's source with a particular and a prototypical example). Using kindof at times to make a subclass of a class, at other times to instantiate a class, is more like Plato's theory of universals: classes are distinguished from instances, but classes, as well as instances, are perfectly real, concrete objects.

4.0 OBJECTS AND MESSAGES

4.1 Functions are More Convenient Than Messages

Traditionally, object-oriented languages rely on *message passing* to distinguish the behavior of one object from another.[5] If ObjectLogo used message passing, tell :turtle4 [fd 100] would instead be written (send :turtle4 "fd 100), where send expects an object, followed by a message word, followed by any arguments associated with the message. send looks up the message word in a table built into the object, finding the object's method for responding to that message.

Judging from this example, there would seem to be just a trivial typographic difference between the message passing approach and ObjectLogo's function calling approach. In fact, however, the difference runs deeper.

- Although tell :turtle4 [fd 100] translates smoothly into message syntax,

```
tell :turtle4 [if visible?
               [setheading towards :turtle2]]
```

fares poorly. It becomes:

```
(if (send :turtle4 "visible?)
    [(send :turtle4 "setheading
     (send :turtle "towards :turtle2)])
```

It is easy to compose function calls, one call providing an input to another; it becomes awkward when a function is treated as a message, because the message recipient has to be specified.

- Often the current "message recipient" needs to be implicit. Consider:

```
howto square :n
repeat 4 [fd :n rt 90]
tell :turtle4 [square 50]
```

---

[5] Major examples include Smalltalk (Goldberg & Robson, 1983) and Lisp Flavors (Moon, Stallman, & Weinreb, 1983).

square calls fd and rt inside :turtle4, referring to :turtle4's versions of those functions. A message passing translation would look like this:

```
howto square :n
repeat 4 [(send :self "fd :n) (send :self "rt 90)]
(send :turtle4 "square 50)
```

Here, we've had to introduce a variable self, whose value is always the recipient of the currently-running message. self is like ObjectLogo's current object; but in ObjectLogo, *all* function and variable references are *implicitly* "messages" to "self". Unless a message-passing language uses messages to the complete exclusion of function calls, it requires us, when writing square, to *anticipate* (or else go back and change the definition) that fd and rt will need to be shadowed inside some objects, hence need to be messages. In ObjectLogo, an ordinary global function call is shadowed whenever we're inside an object that has a special definition for that function.

• Often there is no reasonable "message recipient" for a particular function call: for example, (list "a "b "c) or (sum :x :y :z). Message-passing purists insist that (sum :x :y :z) really means:

```
(send :x "add-self-to (send :y "add-self-to :z))
```

But in addition to the syntactic contortion (which can be remedied by a macro that simulates function calling), passing each argument to the next one seems like a less natural way to think of a multi-argument function call than the traditional image of arguments going into a box, a value coming out.

Some systems (e.g., Lisp Flavors) elude this last problem by adopting a hybrid approach, using function calling most of the time, but relying on message passing to elicit object-specific behavior. But this leads to the second problem above. And in any case, since all message-passing expressions can be reasonably translated into function-calling form (though not vice versa, as the above examples illustrate), there is no need to have both paradigms. Function calling suffices.

4.2   Function-Variable Symmetry Promotes Class-Instance Uniformity

The idea of nested environments, with inherited and shadowed bindings, is an elegant one, and quite familiar in Logo and its parent language Lisp.

It is desirable, if possible, to ground a new programming paradigm in such a basic idea. The possibility of construing objects as environments was first elaborated by Sussman (see Abelson & Sussman, 1985). Sussman only uses environments to bind instances' variables; he still has message passing instead of classes' function bindings.[6]

Once messages are transformed into functions, they become symmetrical to variables. Since classes typically define functions while instances typically have their own variables, the symmetry of function and variable bindings leads in turn to the possibility of uniform classes and instances – treating both simply as objects that can inherit bindings from other objects. This has several advantages:

- The same basic, elegant mechanism – nested-environment inheritance – is used to construct both specialized classes, and instances of classes. This makes specialization and instantiation more easily comprehensible.

- As discussed above, class and instance are partly interchangible, a class serving as prototype instance. Conversely, an instance can be customized as a prototype specialized class; see Item 4 in Section 5.2.

- While usually it is instances that bind variables and classes that bind functions, the reverse is also possible, and sometimes useful (Item 4, Section 5.2 again). Though message passing systems could provide an equivalent capability, the asymmetry between messages and variables leads most such systems to neglect instance functions or class variables, or both.

- Bindings can be created (or deleted) incrementally and interactively. Other object oriented-systems require separate, advance declaration of objects' variables (this, again, is not an intrinsic problem, but is promoted by function-variable asymmetry). But for the beginner (and

---

[6] This is actually forced by Sussman's implementation of objects as *lexically scoped* environment. Lexical scoping is appropriate for function parameters, but it has the wrong semantics for objects' function bindings. The problem is that one function's reference to another – such as square's reference to fd, above – must get shadowed if the first function is called from inside an environment that binds the second function. Lexical scoping prohibits such shadowing, unless it is has already happened where the first function is *defined*. Sussman circumvents the problem with his message lookup mechanism, which is really manually-implemented dynamic scoping. Dynamic scoping provides the right kind of shadowing for implementing objects.

for the expert working on the fly), it is important not to be forced to anticipate everything, to be free instead to add pieces one at a time.

5.0 OBJECTS AND STUDENTS

5.1 Using Objects Teaches Modular Design

One reason to encourage object-oriented programming is that it lends itself to building any system where a number of related objects or structures interact with one another, taking actions and changing state. Simulations, games, and many system utilities (e.g., graphics systems) are familiar examples. But object-oriented programming has another, less obvious, specifically pedagogic virtue. This concerns modularity.

At the start of this paper, I mentioned the importance of *naming*: when details are organized into a module that is invoked by its name, changes inside the module need not affect how it is used. This is a central theme of good programming; in fact, it is central to the engineering of *any* complicated system.

The virtue of modular design is subtle, however, and it is often missed by beginners. One reason is that the chief purpose of modularity is to facilitate revision. The beginner has had little experience with revising programs; and for most beginning projects, the expectation of later revision is unrealistic, hence unmotivating. But an object-oriented program exhibits revision with a vengeance. When a piece of code is run in several kinds of objects successively, it is as though there are successive redefinitions of all functions bound by those objects. Revising a function's definition becomes a common, concrete, runtime event, not just a matter of hypothetical future editing of a program. Lessons learned in this environment about organizing systems into coherent modules are applicable to modular design in general.

5.2 Acquaintance with Objects Can be Gradual

Just as Logo can be used by students far too young to understand the explicit rules of evaluation, a student should be able to use ObjectLogo long before she or he has an explicit understanding of nested environments and the like. This section recommends a sequence of ways to use ObjectLogo starting with minimal prerequisite knowledge, and building up to a sophisticated understanding. Regrettably, ObjectLogo has yet to be used by children, so this recommendation is only speculative. Still, the logical progression of the ideas involved reasonably suggests this sequence as a point of departure.

1. Start with simple Logo expressions (e.g., turtle commands) without using objects at all. An object evaluates Logo expressions inside itself, so evaluating Logo expressions should be familiar first.

2. Use a number of prefabricated objects. Multiple turtles are an obvious example. It is best to start using talkto instead of tell. talkto takes just one input, an object, and places us inside the object *permanently* (or until a subsequent talkto); all subsequent expressions are evaluated inside the object. Thus, the student needn't wrestle with the limited duration of a tell, or with the syntax of passing an expression to tell. When the student begins to switch frequently from one object to another, tell should be useful and comprehensible.

3. Make and use instances of an existing class. If a :turtle class object is provided, new turtle instances can be made from it to augment the supplied menagerie.

4. Customize existing instances. For example, a particular turtle might be given its own definition of fd, causing it to beep whenever it goes forward:

```
tell :turtle4 [howto fd :distance
               beep
               usual.fd :distance]
```

This introduces the idea of giving an object its own version of a function.

5. Build an object from scratch, giving it its own functions and variables, as in the :talker example above.

6. Make specializations of one's own objects, as in the :shouter and :whisperer examples.

7. Home-made objects can be treated as classes and instantiated, as prefabricated objects were instantiated earlier. At first, establishing instance variables can be done manually; when this becomes tedious, the idea of defining an exist function will proved helpful.

8. Multiple inheritance – basing an object on more than one other object – is one of the most advanced aspects of object-oriented programming. My emphasis in this paper is on the threshold side of ObjectLogo, so I have not dwelt on uses of multiple inheritance.

Explicit models of environments, nesting, inheritance, and shadowing (as discussed in Sections 2 and 3 can be presented in parallel with the above practical sequence. I do not know at which point (if any) in the sequence such explicit understanding becomes indispensible; I expect that the point (and extent) that explicit modelling becomes helpful will vary from person to person.

6.0 SUMMARY

Object-oriented programming is useful for systems with related, interacting objects, and promotes understanding of modular design. ObjectLogo makes object-oriented programming especially accessible, in that:

- An object is invoked by telling it to run an ordinary Logo expression.

- An object can be given its own variables and functions, interactively and incrementally.

- The distinction between class and instance is not required, but is easy to establish. For beginners, this means that the (rather subtle) distinction can be *ignored*. And for advanced users, a uniform paradigm of specialization is used to make all objects, including instances and specialized classes.

Despite its accessibility to beginners, ObjectLogo includes advanced features such as multiple inheritance, making its power competitive with much more complicated systems.

REFERENCES

Abelson, H., Sussman, G., & Sussman, J. (1985). *Structure and Interpretation of Computer Programs*. Cambridge: MIT Press.
Moon, D., Stallman, R., & Weinreb, D. (1983). *LISP Machine Manual, Fifth Edition*. Cambridge: MIT Artificial Intelligence Laboratory.
Papert, S. (1980). *Mindstorms: Children, Computers, and Powerful Ideas*. New York: Basic Books.
Goldberg, A., & Robson, D. (1983). *Smalltalk-80: The Language and its Implementation*. Reading, MA: Addison-Wesley.

9 DESIGN AND USE OF A CONSTRAINT-BASED LABORATORY IN LEARNING DESIGN

Mark D. Gross

Design Theory and Methods Group
School of Architecture and Urban Studies
Massachusetts Institute of Technology
Cambridge, MA 02139

ABSTRACT

This paper reports on current work in MIT's school of architecture and urban planning. Our group is developing a computer-based environment for doing design and for learning to design. This environment, in the form of a constraint-based programming language, provides the means to convey design knowledge and expertise operationally. It enables novice designers to work explicitly, encourages methodical and systematic ways of working, and supports the construction of an explicit understanding of how to design.

1.0 INTRODUCTION

Our concern is the design of the built environment, which includes urban and site planning, architecture, and to some degree the graphic arts. These fields are concerned with decisions about the identity, positions, and dimension of material and space elements in making buildings and places. Traditionally in these domains, students learn to design by apprenticing with a master. In contrast to engineering design disciplines where principles are more explicit, design expertise in these areas is largely tacit or implicit. Journals in environmental and architectural design record examples, unlike journals of engineering, which record principles. We are building a programming language for designers to capture and convey their design knowledge and expertise based on our understanding of design as exploring constraints. We seek to account for design method, strategy and heuristics. We seek especially to codify those aspects of design expertise involving reasoning, inference and argument. We believe such codification is useful to the novice as well as to the expert designer. The programming language provides a laboratory for design experiments in which the novice

This paper is based on work reported in the author's doctoral dissertation, "Design as the Exploration of Constraints," MIT 1986).

designer can explore different sets of design constraints, as well as alternative design solutions within one set of constraints. It provides a powerful and explicit means and medium to study and to practice designing.

Our approach to computers and learning – the idea that it is valuable for novices to express, examine and refine their understanding of what they know through the medium of a programming language – is by no means new. Papert's "Teaching Children to be Mathematicians" (Papert, 1972) proposed the use of a computer as a laboratory for learning mathematics. The computer supports a simulated mathematics world: it "speaks" the language of mathematics. By writing, debugging and observing the performance of algorithms to guide the Logo turtle, the student participates directly in doing experimental mathematics. Carrying Papert's work further, Abelson and diSessa's lovely book *Turtle Geometry* presents an advanced high-school/first year college mathematics curriculum organized around the same computational device, the turtle (Abelson & diSessa, 1981). The work of Papert and of Abelson and diSessa shows how, coupled with an interesting agenda of research topics to explore, the computer can be a fascinating and stimulating way to study mathematics. To explain a complex task or problem by programming a computer demands of the student rigorous and precise articulation; it requires careful thinking and reflection on method and it facilitates experimentation and exploration that would otherwise be tedious, if not also technically difficult. Given that a programming language can support mathematics learning, might not the same approach work for learning to design? In this spirit we have designed and are developing a laboratory in the form of a programming language for experiments in design, and we are beginning to compile a curriculum – a collection of topics in design – to explore with this laboratory.

The first section of this report presents our understanding of designing as a process of describing and exploring constraints. Constraints derive from a variety of sources: some are physical laws, some are conventional ways of working, some are related to the particular problem at hand. A building, for example, must stand up; it must be buildable by available methods using available materials; and it must respond to specific conditions of its site. Constraints describe relations between attributes or variables of the design; therefore fixing values to some variables can determine the values of others. For example, "square" is a simple constraint on the surface area and dimensions of a polygon. Fixing the area of a square determines the dimension of its side and vice versa.

A set of constraints bounds a space of design alternatives. For most design problems this space is large, thus there are many satisfactory solutions. Designing involves exploring this constraint-bounded space for good alternatives, determined by various design goals or objectives. Exploration proceeds by fixing values to variables within a prescribed set of constraints as well as by adding to and changing the constraints themselves. In exploring, the designer tries to find alternatives that best achieve the objectives. Since design problems seldom involve only one objective and because objectives may conflict, the concept of a single best solution is often inappropriate. In addition, as designs typically involve large numbers of sparsely connected variables, it is often helpful to decompose the problem into relatively independent parts and work each part separately. Then local optimization of different objectives in the different parts may be useful.

The second section of this report describes the computer language we are developing as an environment for learning and for doing design, structured around constraint descriptions, and based on our understanding of the design process as outlined above. We think that a constraint language better matches the ambiance of designing than do traditional procedural and applicative programming languages. The design of our language follows closely that of other languages for programming with constraints. The final section discusses the use of a constraint-based laboratory as an environment for teaching and learning design. The specific constraints from a typical site-planning problem – road-design – are presented along with a brief scenario of their application.

2.0 OUR UNDERSTANDING OF THE DESIGN PROCESS

We have arrived at a provisional understanding of the design process that guides our efforts at constructing a computer-based learning environment. This understanding seems to match our experience with designing and follows the proposition advanced by Simon in *Sciences of the Artificial*, that design problems can be viewed as search in a space bounded by constraints (Simon, 1969). Our understanding, however, emphasizes the changing of constraints and objectives throughout the design process, and the presence of multiple objectives.

Let us suppose that we can describe any design alternative we are interested in by using a finite set of attributes, or variables. Variables describe measurable properties of the designs. The variables in architectural design, for example, are the positions and dimensions of elements, as well as spatial and other qualities such as privacy, outlook and daylight. Values of variables are more or less linked through relations or constraints. Constraints play many roles: they describe physical laws, working conventions, and stylistic agreements. For example, one constraint relates the daylight entering a room at a given time to the position and dimensions of the window openings and the orientation of the room. Another constraint requires a certain minimum level of daylighting. Another constraint governs the position of the window as an element in the facade.

In these terms, a design "problem" is a set of constraints on a set of variables. A complete solution to the problem is a set of variable values meeting all constraints. For example, a solution to the window-location problem described above specifies a position for the window in the wall such that it meets the requirements of the facade and admits sufficient light. A partial solution is one where the values of some variables are as yet undetermined. For example, a partial solution to the window-location might determine the window's vertical position in the wall but leave its horizontal position free to vary. Note, however, that if a set of constraints has one solution then it will likely have many alternative solutions. Thus, each set of constraints bounds a large region – or space – of design alternatives. Within the constraints adopted, adapted and invented, the designer works towards achieving certain goals or objectives, for example: "minimize cost," "maximize privacy," "maximize public open space." Objectives provide a means to compare alternatives and to judge progress in designing.

This framework of constraints, variables and objectives is useful in accounting for various kinds of expertise involved in designing. One kind of design expertise involves defining the problem – identifying the variables to consider, the constraints on and relations between the variables and the objectives to strive for in the design. A second kind of design expertise involves strategies or heuristics for searching or exploring this constraint-bounded space for good alternatives where "good" is measured according to various objectives. Because designing usually involves more than one objective and because objectives may conflict, global optimization is seldom a useful technique. However, local optimization of different objectives in different parts of the design may be useful. Therefore a third kind of design expertise involves recognizing parts of the design that hardly interact and can therefore be worked relatively independently.

Although we have distinguished three kinds of expertise in designing – identifying variables, constraints and objectives; exploring constraint-bounded-spaces; decomposing large sets of constraints into independently workable parts – there is no predetermined order for applying them. All three kinds of expertise are exercised throughout the design process. Designers constantly redefine the problem, change the objectives. New constraints and objectives emerge in the course of designing. Constraints and objectives deemed important earlier in the design may later be discarded or downgraded in importance. Neither the set of constraints that bound the exploration for good alternatives nor the objectives that measure progress are fixed at the outset of designing.

Formally, we can describe designing as an activity involving a set of variables $X = \{x[1], \ldots x[m]\}$ co-constrained by a set of relations (constraints) $R = \{R[1], \ldots R[n]\}$. Each variable $x[i]$ in X has a domain $d[i]$ that may be specified by one or more of the relations in R. Each variable $x[i]$ may have a value $v[i]$. A (alternative) solution is a set of values V for all variables X that satisfies all relations R. A set of objectives $O = O[1], \ldots O[k]$ measures the performance of design alternatives according to various goals. Stated most generally then, designing consists in specifying a set of relations R on variables X, and finding a set or sets of values V for variables X that satisfy relations R and are good, as measured by objectives O.

Having given a general framework in which to understand design processes, let us immediately caution against two frequently made simplifications of these ideas. These simplifications are (1) design is solving a linear programming problem, and (2) design is constraint-satisfaction. Let us consider these two matters in some detail.

Simon uses linear programming to illustrate the idea of design as choosing values of variables to satisfy constraints with objectives (Simon, 1969). Linear programming is a restricted version of the general design problem just described. In a linear programming problem, the variable values are all numbers and the relations are all linear inequality constraints. There is only one objective, which is also a linear function of the variables, and therefore there is one solution to the design problem: the set of variable values that maximizes the objective function. Linear programming problems can always be solved, though some methods are more efficient than others. Linear programming shows how mathematical methods can apply to design and it illustrates the concepts of constraints, variables, and objectives. Real design problems, however, are usually more complex than linear programming problems. Many real-world constraints are not linear inequalities, nor can we expect all variables to represent numbers. The outstanding simplification in linear programming as a model of designing, however, is that it considers only one objective. As mentioned above, we seldom have but one objective to consider, therefore, seldom can we conceive of a single best design.

Another simplification is one that models design as a problem in satisfying constraints. The motivation for this simplification derives from observing that an optimum solution may be far more costly to compute than a satisfactory solution, disproportionate to the difference in the quality of the two solutions (Simon, 1969). Our real problem, however, is not that optimization is costly, but that (as noted above) in the face of multiple and possibly conflicting objectives, optimization – at least global optimization – is simply inappropriate. There are two versions of the constraint-satisfaction problem, a simple version and a complete version. The simple version of the constraint-satisfaction problem is to find one set of values V for the variables X that meet all the constraints in R. The complete version of the constraint-satisfaction problem is to find all such solutions. Note that the simple version is easier to solve than the general design problem outlined above, for constraint-satisfaction knows no objectives; the problem is only to find any solution. Algorithms have been devised for finding a solution to a set of constraints. However, unless either the constraints truly describe exactly what the designer wants, or else the designer can accurately adjust the satisfaction mechanism, an algorithm that delivers but one design alternative is of little interest. Likewise, a solution to the complete constraint-satisfaction problem is also unhelpful, for in an interesting design problem there are far too many solutions to consider them all. Simply seeing design as a constraint-satisfaction problem begs an important question of design expertise: preference among alternatives. It neglects the differences among alternative solutions, implying that all solutions are equally good.

In summary, our understanding frames designing as an activity of exploring sets of values for attribute variables subject to a set of constraints that describe design rules, natural laws, and stylistic conventions, and objectives by which alternatives can be judged and compared. As design problems usually involve more than one objective, global optimization is inappropriate, though local optimization of different objectives in different parts of a design may be a good thing to do. The design problem is not predetermined at the outset of designing; rather, constraints and objectives emerge and change constantly throughout the design process, as the designer explores. Thus, designing is a process of defining and redefining the constraints and searching within the constraints for good solutions. As design problems may be complex, involving many design constraints and many objectives, design expertise also involves partitioning large problems into relatively independent pieces.

3.0 CONSTRAINT-BASED PROGRAMMING LANGUAGES

Having established our goals and theoretical framework we turn now to more practical matters: the specification of a computing environment to support the designing activities discussed in the previous section. Our outlook on the design process strongly suggests adopting a particular kind of declarative programming environment that has recently received much attention: a constraint language. This section discusses the principal features of constraint languages in general and some special features of the language we are developing. We are currently implementing in Objectlisp (see Drescher, this volume), but we are also planning a Scheme implementation shortly.

The first constraint-based programming language was Sutherland's remarkable program, Sketchpad (Sutherland, 1963). Though Sutherland described Sketchpad as a "man-machine graphical communication system," it was in fact much more than that. Among other innovations, Sketchpad introduced the idea of describing a computer program as a connected network of constraints. Because it presented the program as an editable network diagram, it also enabled the programmer literally to see the program as a connected network of constraints. Sketchpad maintained geometric constraints – for example perpendicularity and proportionate dimensions – on graphics objects such as line segments, arcs and circles, simulating the dynamic behavior of complex objects. Sketchpad's built-in satisfaction mechanisms worked to enforce constraints as the user fixed and changed properties of the graphics objects. Sketchpad's applications included simulating stresses in loaded truss structures and simulating the behavior of mechanical linkages with moving parts. Sutherland, in discussing the relevance of his program to design, suggested that "the ability of Sketchpad *to satisfy the geometric constraints applied to the parts of a drawing* models the ability of a good designer to satisfy all the design conditions imposed by the limitations of his materials, cost, etc." (Sutherland, 1963, p. 8). Many of the ideas originally expressed in Sutherland's program have been developed, extended and applied by others (Borning, 1977; Sussman & Steele, 1980; Steele, 1980; Gosling, 1983; Levitt, 1985; Gross, 1986).

A constraint language is a programming environment that simulates the behavior of a complex system described by the programmer as a set of relations, or constraints, on a set of variables. It is convenient to think of the constraint language as an interpreter, managing this system of constraints and variables. The interpreter calculates the consequences of fixes to variable values and changes to constraints, flags inconsistencies when it can detect them and keeps track of changes to the state of the system. Unlike programs in procedural programming languages (Lisp, C, etc.) that consist of a sequence of operations to be performed, a constraint language program defines a system of relations without determining a-priori the sequence of computation and direction of data-flow. For example, a program might contain the relation" X is immediately to the left of Y." This relation may be interpreted in either of two ways, depending on whether X or Y is positioned first. If, at run-time, X is positioned first, then the relation determines Y's position; if Y is positioned first, then the relation determines X's position. The interpreter computes variable values whenever the system contains or receives enough information to do so. Thus no distinction is made between dependent and independent variables; every variable may play the role of either argument or returned value, depending on the sequence of run-time fixes.

By aggregating built-in primitives, users can define higher-level variables and constraints, thereby extending the language. Any such collection of constraints and variables is called an "object." For example, we might define an object called "rectangle," as a collection of variables describing coordinates of its corner points as well as constraints on these variables to ensure that the rectangle has the correct shape. Once an object definition has been given, the object may be instantiated and replicated. We can use the definition for rectangle to make many rectangles all with different positions and dimensions, but all subject to the basic rectangularity constraints given in the definition. We might also define spatial relations that apply betweeen rectangle objects, such as "to the left of," "inside," "aligned along top edges," "above," by composing primitive constraints on the variables that describe the coordinates of the two objects. Both rectangles and spatial relations would be defined as objects, collections of already defined constraints and variables.

In addition to providing the means to extend the language by aggregating constraints and variables, objects can also be arranged into a hierarchy of inheritance. Objects lower in the hierarchy inherit – by default – both variables and constraints defined in their superiors. Inheritance is masked (inhibited) by the most local, or lowest, definition in the hierarchy. Masking provides a convenient way to handle both defaults and exceptions. The inheritance mechanisms enable the programmer to describe new constraint and variable objects simply by describing their differences with previously defined objects. For example, if rectangle objects have been previously defined, a square could be defined simply as "a kind of rectangle whose width equals its height." Likewise, if the spatial relation "above" has been defined, the relation "resting-on" might be described as "a kind of above relation where the distance between objects is zero."

Our interpreter design consists of four modules sharing a database that contains the constraints and variables in the system. This shared database represents the developing state of the design. The four modules operating on the design database are called the solver, the packager, the secretary of state and the graphical interface. Each module operates independently of the others and is driven either by changes in the design or by direct commands from the designer. We can thus work on each module separately as we refine and develop our implementation. The remainder of this section discusses the functions of each module. Because the solver is the most vital of the four modules we shall consider it in greatest detail. The solver therefore seems a logical place to begin.

The solver's job is to calculate, or infer the consequences of adding new constraints and fixing values to variables. The solver is the "inference engine" of the constraint language; it occupies as central a role in the operation of the language as does the evaluator in Lisp or unification in Prolog. It consists of a collection of symbolic and numeric mathematics routines. The choice of solver routines determines what constraints the language can handle. The primitive constraint types currently in our solver are the usual arithmetic and boolean relations, though we are planning to add set-membership relations as well. Our solver is implemented as a combination of procedural and production-rule programming. It is data-driven (energetic), making inferences as antecedents are asserted in the database. Alternatively, we could have made our solver demand-driven (lazy), attempting to calculate values for variables only when asked.

The simplest means of solving and one that suffices in a great many instances is the propagation of values. Propagation is essentially the calculation of the value of a variable that is functionally related to one or more other variables when the values of the other variables are known. For example, consider the constraint $A + B + C = 100$. If values for A and B are fixed, then the value of C can be calculated. Propagation is essentially substituting values for bound variables and then, when possible, using these to compute the values of unbound variables. In the above example, C's newly computed value then propagates to other relations, for example, yielding a value for D in the constraint $C * D = 4$. Thus the effect of fixing a variable propagates through the constraints, determining the values of other variables in the system.

Though propagation works well for simple cases, there are inferences about a system of constraints and variables propagation can not make. Propagation is essentially a local, "arithmetic" technique; it cannot make inferences that require a global or "algebraic" viewpoint. For example, propagation will not solve quadratic equations. Even if we restrict constraints to linear equations (and we would rather not!), still propagation cannot determine values when two or more contraints are simultaneous. Thus a robust constraint language must include ways to infer values for variables in cases where propagation fails. For example, many simple problems may require solving systems of simultaneous linear (and also higher-order) equations, also quadratic, trigonometric and other such specific methods. When none of the solver's methods apply, a derivative-finding algorithm constructs linear approximations for nonlinear functions over limited domains, enabling the solver to apply linear solving methods. As constraints may be given in any form, the solver must also have procedures to simplify expressions and to isolate variables. For example, given the constraint $a * a - 9 = 0$, the solver must be able to reformulate this as $a^2 = 9$, then compute that $a = \sqrt{9}$, and finally determine that $a = \pm 3$.

Though some constraints in design can be expressed as equations, most cannot be so expressed. Therefore, in addition to handling systems of equations, the abilities of an equation-based solver must be extended to handle inequality constraints by introducing a special numerical datatype: the interval number. Interval numbers enable us to treat inequality relations as equations so that the solver can operate on them. An interval number is a pair of rational numbers representing lower and upper bounds. The usual arithmetic relations can be easily extended to work for interval numbers; with a few restrictions algebraic techniques that work on real numbers work also on interval numbers (Moore, 1966). In addition to interval numbers, the arithmetic and algebraic routines of our solver also operate on sets of values. For example, the ± 3 mentioned above is returned by the solver as a set with members 3 and -3.

We now consider another module of the interpreter, the packager. The constraints and variables in a design problem will likely describe a large but sparsely connected system. It is useful to break the system into parts and work the parts independently. Based on the system's inherent structure (connectedness), the packager decomposes (partitions) the system of constraints. It identifies groups of constraints and variables that interact closely. Though the groupings of constraints and variables entered by the programmer, as objects, may represent a natural way for the designer to structure the design, other groupings may be more effective for solving and working the constraints. The solver, for example, need not work the entire constraint system at once, but may rely on the packager to identify clusters of closely related constraints. Groupings of the constraints and variables, whether they are grouped a-priori – as objects defined by the programmer – or a-posteriori – as identified by the packager – do not, of course, change the underlying system of constraints and variables.

Different algorithms for grouping the constraints will usually involve different notions of togetherness, thereby identifying different parts. A great deal of work has been done on graph-partitioning and block-structuring and there are many ways to decompose a system of constraints. Fortunately, we do not need to decide on only one. Our current design for the packager includes Tarjan's algorithm for recognizing strongly-connected components of graphs (Tarjan, 1972), Kernighan and Lin's algorithm for graph-partitioning (Kernighan & Lin, 1970), and a simple algorithm that we have devised for identifying sets of simultaneous constraints. Several partitionings (or partial partitionings) of a system of constraints may be in effect at one time. This allows the designer to see a design simultaneously from several viewpoints, to break the design into parts in different ways.

The secretary of state module is responsible for recording changes to the state of the constraints and variables; that is, for maintaining design history. It is insufficient merely to recall the previous values of variables in previous states; one also wants to remember what constraints (and objectives) were in effect at that time. The state of the entire system at any time – all constraints, variables, and values – represents the current context of the design. This context changes constantly as the designer works. The secretary of state provides the designer with a facility to reconstruct previously reached states of a design, to simultaneously maintain several active contexts and also to construct new contexts by combining pieces from different designs.

In our constraint language design, history is kept locally. Following Steele (Steele, 1980), dependency information is stored along with each constraint and variable in the design. Constraints and variable values that are inferred by the solver record the antecedents of the inference. For example, if the value of variable C was calculated using the constraint $A + B + C = 100$, then C's antecedent information would point to variables A and B and to the constraint $A + B + C = 100$. Storing this dependency information enables the secretary to support non-chronological (e.g., dependency directed) backtracking. That is, if A, B, or the constraint are subsequently retracted, then the value computed for C is no longer justified. The secretary presides over a dependency network that describes the origins of every constraint and variable value in the design.

Finally let us consider the graphical interface module of our language. In our domain, architectural and environmental design, graphics is the primary medium for communication. We distinguish two roles for graphics in a constraint language. In the first role, graphics is used for display; we might call this role "constraint driven graphics." In this role, graphics displays the values of constrained variables. In the second role graphics is used as a means of defining constraint language programs; we might call this role "visual programming," in which the programmer defines, edits and debugs a system of constraints and variables by using graphic representations of the system, for example a network diagram.

Traditionally, designs are presented in the form of a set of drawings that document the set of design decisions made. When drawings are made for the purpose of illustrating a design rule, they typically serve as examples, to be used with a precise verbal description. Thus graphics are primarily used for display of decisions (as in Role 1), not for conveying systems of design rules or constraints. In preparing graphics for display, graphic editors are gaining acceptance among design professionals and students demand instruction in their use. At present these graphic editors assist only with the mechanics of constructing a drawing; they do not understand or enforce any design rules or constraints.

Just as advanced text editors (emacs for example) contain macro-definition and storage register capabilites that enable advanced users to construct special purpose editing functions from primitives, we are embedding our constraint language within a graphic editor. The purpose is to ease the designer's transition from using a drafting tool to working with explicit representations of design expertise and inferences. Novice users can use our constraint language as an ordinary graphic editor, constructing and viewing a three-dimensional representation of a design. More sophisticated users can also inspect and modify definitions of elements and configurations in the representation. These definitions describe constraints on properties of elements in the design. Embedding a constraint language within a graphic editor allows the designer to think of programming simply as annotating a drawing with specifications of the relations between elements to be maintained.

The visual programming role of graphics (Role 2) has always been associated with constraint-based programming. Sketchpad introduced the idea of using network diagrams to put in, edit and view systems of constraints. To this day the typical constraint-language user-interface follows Sketchpad closely, displaying a system of constraints and variables as a graph where nodes represent constraints and links represent variables. The function of each constraint is indicated on its node; the value of each variable (if determined) is labelled along each link. The user edits the system of constraints graphically, using a network editor. The user defines new constraints by constructing and encapsulating networks of existing constraint; the new, aggregate constraint then appears as a simple node in the network but it can be opened up (e.g., for editing) on request, revealing its definition.

The network is a powerful way to represent a system of constraints visually; it also reminds us that graph-theory methods may be useful in working with systems of constraints. But the visual representation of the constraints as a network, however compelling, is not essential to our conception of a constraint language. We suggest that representing systems of constraints in ways other than as network diagrams may be at least as effective. For the experienced programmer, expressing the constraints textually as code, may well be a more straightforward way to work. We are interested in developing other graphical and diagrammatic ways to express and edit systems of constraints that may be more appropriate for architects and environmental designers than network diagrams. For example, designers often communicate spatial relations by giving a series of examples; how might we support this mode of constraint definition? We expect to continue to think about these and other questions regarding the graphical user-interface of our constraint language.

4.0 THE USE OF A CONSTRAINT-BASED LABORATORY IN LEARNING DESIGN

We are developing the constraint-based programming language described in the previous section in order to use it as a learning laboratory in architectural and environmental design workshops at MIT The constraint language comprises the laboratory. Each workshop will engage students in using the laboratory to work several design problems involving, for example: floorplan and facade layout, simple solar building design and road design. For each problem we will furnish the laboratory with a basic set of predefined elements and relations. In facade design, for example, the laboratory kit will contain a variety of windows, doors and other panels, as well as some generally useful positioning relations, all described as collections of constraints and variables. We will ask students to use the given elements and relations in their designs and to work towards certain goals. Students are not limited to the elements and relations we provide, rather, we hope that they will modify the given elements and rules and invent their own as well. The problems we set will be sufficiently open as to allow a variety of good alternative design solutions. Therefore, to limit alternatives to a manageable number, students will need to invent and apply additional constraints and objectives. We will also ask students to study existing coherent built environments and to try to identify the constraints that structure them. For example, we will ask students to articulate the positioning rules on elements in facades of Amsterdam canal-houses, then to test the design rules they describe by using them to design. The laboratory provides the means for student/designers to design by constructing explicit representations of design constraints and objectives and applying them to their designs.

Road design is a typical first-year site-planning subject. There are three main sets of constraints. The first set of constraints describes the basic properties of roads in plan and in cross-section. A road is broken into a sequence (or list) of road-elements. Each road-element is in plan either a straight segment or an arc; connections between consecutive road-elements must be continuous. That is, a road is a linear connected population of straight line segments and curves. There is also a maximum curvature (related to the maximum safe velocity of travel). These simple constraints suffice to describe the properties of all roads in plan. In cross-section each road-element is also either straight or a segment of a parabola. In section as in plan, consecutive road elements must be continuous where they join. The maximum allowable slope of each road-element is also constrained by climate and safety considerations. This first set of constraints is defined in the road-design kit given to students. The second set of constraints on the design of the road is given when the site-planner draws a "traverse," a connected sequence of line-segments on the topographic site map, deciding the approximate course of the desired road. The traverse is an approximation of the road to be designed; the road is essentially a smoothed traverse. Straight segments of the road lie along the segments of the traverse; turns fall within the angle between segments. In transforming a traverse to a road, the angle between each two traverse segments is replaced by an arc, thus each segment is shortened by arcs on both ends. The third set of constraints is imposed by the site's topography – in general the road must lie more or less on the surface of the earth; special circumstances dictate local minimum or maximum elevations. Minor adjustments to fit the slope of the road to a straight line or parabola are made by cut-and-fill roadworks operations that adjust the topography locally.

There will likely be many road designs that meet these three sets of constraints. The set of possible roads falls within a region near the given traverse. The laboratory displays this region on the topographic map as soon as the traverse is given. To refine the solutions, therefore, the site-planner applies other constraints and objectives to the design. For example, a limit might be placed on the total amount of cut-and-fill work, the total length of the road or the proximity of the road to other site features. Each of these constraints might also be applied as an objective: minimize cut-and-fill; select the shortest road design; select the road design that comes closest to point X. The road might be required to pass through certain points on the map. Objectives and constraints may be applied to the road as a whole or they may be applied to individual road elements. Different objectives may be applied to different road-elements. For example, the student may choose to maximize curvature of certain road-elements (hairpin turns), while maximizing the elevation of others (scenic lookouts). Additional complications and constraints arise when dealing with a system of roads: intersections must meet specified criteria and a hierarchy of road sizes and construction methods may be imposed. Finally, the entry sequence, lines of sight and the view from the road may also be considered.

The curious site-planner will try out different sets of constraints and apply different objectives to see how the road comes out. When a solution pleases, the site-planner can obtain a record not only of the road itself, but also of the particular configuration of constraints and objectives used to design it. In addition to saving complete road-designs, the site-planner will also be able to store partial solutions and use these as starting points for developing alternatives.

We are asking students to perform their designing in an environment that records and thus allows them to later re-examine the moves they make throughout a design process. We want students to think explicitly about what they are doing. We want them to gain experience with and an explicit understanding of the effects of applying various constraints and objectives at various times in the design process. That is essentially what we teach in design studios without the laboratory, however, the process of documenting and analyzing each alternative by hand is sufficiently tedious that students seldom have time or energy to explore more than one or two alternatives. By reducing the time and effort needed to specify and evaluate each alternative we hope to encourage students to explore a larger number of solutions. In addition to providing an environment for exploring design problems, we also hope to interest our students in our attempts at explicitly codifying design expertise.

ACKNOWLEDGEMENTS

The author would like to thank James Anderson, Navin Chandra, Stephen Ervin and Aaron Fleisher for stimulating and useful discussions.

REFERENCES

Abelson, H., & diSessa, A. (1981). *Turtle Geometry,* Cambridge: MIT Press.

Borning, A. (1977). Thinglab – An object-oriented system for building simulations using constraints. In *Proceedings IJCAI 81,* 497.

Gosling, J. (1983). Algebraic constraints. Ph.D. Dissertation, Carnegie-Mellon University (CMU-CS-83-132).

Gross, M.D. (1986). Design as the exploration of constraints. Ph.D. Dissertation, MIT.

Kernighan, B.W., & Lin, S. (1970). An efficient procedure for partitioning graphs. *Bell Sys. Tech. J.,* (February).

Papert, S. (1972). Teaching children to be mathematicians versus teaching about mathematics. *Int. J. Educ. Sci. Technol. 3,* 249.

Levitt, D. (1985). A representation for musical dialects. Ph.D. Dissertation, MIT.

Moore, R. (1966). *Interval Analysis,* Englewood Cliffs, New Jersey: Prentice-Hall.

Simon, H. (1969). *Sciences of the Artificial,* Cambridge: MIT Press.

Steele, G.L. (1980). The definition and implementation of a programming language based on constraints. Ph.D. Dissertation, MIT (AI TR-595).

Steele, G.L., & Sussman, G.J. (1980). CONSTRAINTS – A language for expressing almost-hierarchical descriptions. *Artificial Intelligence 14,* 1.

Sutherland, I.E. (1963). Sketchpad, a man-machine graphical communication system. Ph.D. Thesis, MIT, Cambridge (Lincoln Laboratory TR-296).

Tarjan, R.E. (1972). Depth first search and linear graph algorithms. *SIAM J. Computing 1:2,* 146.

10 INTELLIGENT TUTORING SYSTEMS: AN OVERVIEW

Masoud Yazdani

Department of Computer Science
University of Exeter
Exeter, United Kingdom

ABSTRACT

In this paper we look at the evolutionary development of Computer Assisted Instruction from the early days of linear programs up to the use of "expert systems" in education and training. We present the basic principles of Intelligent Tutoring Systems (ITS), which are capable of rich interaction with the student, which know how to teach, and know who and what they are teaching. We point out the need for knowledge representation formalisms which can support ITS and present one such formalism (production systems). In the framework presented we describe systems developed for the teaching of modern languages, electronic trouble-shooting and computer programming. Finally, we point out the shortcomings of ITS and identify areas where a consensus of opinion does not exist.

1.0 COMPUTER ASSISTED INSTRUCTION

Computer Assisted Instruction (CAI for short) has followed an evolutionary path since it was started in the 1950s with simple "linear programs". The development of such programs were influenced by the prevailing behaviorist psychological theories (Skinner, 1958) and the programmed learning machines of the previous century. It was believed that if the occurrence of an operant is followed by the presentation of a reinforcing stimulus, the strength is increased. To this end, a computer program will output a frame of text which will take the student one small step towards the desired behavior. The student then makes some kind of response based on what he already knows, or by trial and error! Finally, the program informs the student whether he is correct. A stream of such steps form what is known as a "linear program". The student may work through the material at his own pace and his correct replies are rewarded immediately.

In the 1960s it was felt that one could use the student's response to control the material that the student would be shown next. In this way students learn more thoroughly as they attempt problems of an appropriate

Reprinted from *Expert Systems*, Vol. 3, No. 3 with permission of Learned Information Ltd., 1986.

difficulty, rather than wading their way through some systematic exploration. The "branching programs" therefore offered corrective feedback as
well as adapted their teaching to students' responses. However, the task of
the design of the teaching materials for such systems was impossibly large.
This led to the birth of "author languages", specific languages suitable for
the development of CAI material.

In the 1970s a new level of sophistication was discovered in the design
of CAI systems where, in some domains such as arithmetic, it was possible
to generate the teaching material itself by the computer. A random number
generator could produce two numbers to be added together by the student,
and then the result of the computer's solution of the addition would be
compared with that of the student's, in order to generate a response. Such
systems need only, therefore, to be given general teaching strategies and
they will produce a tree of possible interaction with infinitely large numbers
of branches. Such "generative" systems could answer some of the questions
from the students, as well as incorporate some sort of measure of difficulty
of the task.

By looking at the development of algorithms for CAI developed over
the last 30 years, we see that they have improved on the richness of feedback
and the degree of individualization they offer the students. CAI systems
seem to have improved beyond expectation in computational sophistication from their humble beginnings of replacing the programmed learning
machines. However, they fall far short of being any match for human teachers. The main problem is the impoverishment of knowledge which they
contain. In generative systems there is a mismatch between the program's
internal processes (Boolean arithmetic) and those of the student's cognitive processes (rules and tables). None of these systems have human-like
knowledge of the domain they are teaching, nor can they answer serious
questions of the students as to "why" and "how" the task is performed.

2.0 THE BASICS OF INTELLIGENT TUTORING SYSTEMS

Intelligent Tutoring Systems (ITS for short) started as an enterprise attempting to deal with shortcomings of generative systems and can be seen
as Intelligent CAI of the 1980s. This enterprise has benefitted from the
work of researchers in the field of Artificial Intelligence (AI for short) who
have had a long standing preoccupation with the problem of how best to
represent knowledge within an intelligent system. Various techniques have
been tried within AI with varying degrees of success. One of these methods
seems to be well suited to the domain of tutoring (Anderson, 1985) where it
can be claimed that people seem to show some indications in the structure
of their behavior to support the feasibility of using "production systems"
as a way of modelling their behavior. "Production systems" have been

used extensively within the psychological experimentation for the analysis of peoples' behavior, in addition to being used as a method of representing knowledge within computer based "expert systems". A production system is a particular method of organizing knowledge into three different categories:

1. Facts: Factual (declarative) knowledge about a particular case. (This animal has feathers.)

2. Rules: Procedural knowledge on how to reason in a domain expertise. (If it has feathers then it is a bird.)

3. Inference: Control knowledge of how to carry out reasoning from a set of given facts and rules to come up with a conclusion.

Most tutoring systems focus on communicating expertise at the second level above. Such production rules can be written as:

IF precondition1....precondition2

THEN conclusion.

Such a simple structure can then encode a variety of forms of knowledge. (See Anderson, 1985 for a detailed exposition of this). At one end it encodes general notions such as the use of analogy.

IF the goal is to write a solution to a problem and there is an example of a solution to a similar problem

THEN set a goal to map the [already known] template to the current case.

At the other end it could be used to represent specific knowledge of the domain at hand. For example, in Anderson's (Anderson & Reiser, 1985) LISP tutor, the above rule is complemented with another which is a representation of some part of LISP:

IF the goal is to get the first element of LIST1

THEN write (CAR LIST1)

The student is expected to be able to use knowledge structures such as those above, plus example LISP code given to him in books, such as one to define a function which translates Farenheit degrees to Centigrade:

(DEFUN F-T-C(TEMP)

```
(QUOTIENT (DIFFERENCE TEMP 32)1.8))
```

as well as the text book explanation of function definition in LISP

```
(DEFUN ⟨function name⟩

    (⟨parameter1⟩⟨parameter2⟩...)

    ⟨process description⟩)
```

in order to write the answer to the exercise "Write a function which returns the first element of a list".

The correct solution is:

```
(DEFUN FIRST(LIST1)(CAR LIST1))
```

If the student comes up with a wrong answer, the tutoring program would attempt to simulate the student's behavior and see how he could have gone wrong and offer advice, which is to some extent the result of a reasoning process similar to that of the student's.

The notion that the tutoring program itself can solve the problem which it is setting for the student and in a way similar to that of the student, is the basis of a large number of ITSs (Sleeman & Brown, 1982).

3.0 EXPERT SYSTEMS FOR TUTORING

"Expert systems are such knowledge based systems which use inference to apply knowledge to perform a task. Such systems are currently being built to handle knowledge in many areas of human thought and activity from medical diagnosis to complex engineering design, from oil technology to agriculture, military strategy to citizens' advice" (Alvey, 1982). It has been claimed that these systems can not only be useful for automating some part of human decision-making, but also they could be used for imparting knowledge from an expert in a field to a large number of trainees (O'Shea & Self, 1983). After an expert system has been built by extracting the knowledge of the domain expert and embodying it into the computer system, trainees can then observe the knowledge and the line of reasoning of the program. Trainee doctors could be asked to look over the shoulder of a program such as MYCIN (Shortliffe, 1976), devised for the diagnosis of infectious blood diseases. MYCIN's representation of medical knowledge is, in fact, a form of production system. Furthermore, when all the necessary support levels are added to it to make it useful as a training tool, MYCIN looks very similar to any other intelligent tutoring system developed from scratch specifically with tutoring in mind.

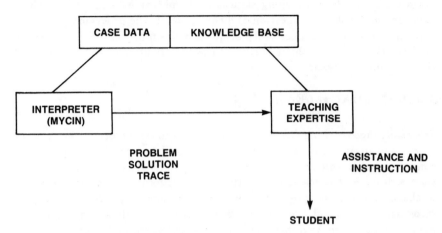

Figure 1. The Overall Structure of GUIDON

GUIDON (Clancey, 1979) is a system which uses MYCIN for tutoring. It includes an independent module containing the teaching expertise as well as a limited amount of competence to carry out a coherent dialogue with the student. GUIDON attempts to transfer expertise to the students exclusively through case dialogues where a sick patient (the "case") is described to the student in general terms. The student is asked to play the role of a physician and ask for information which he thinks might be relevant to this case. GUIDON compares the student's questions to those which MYCIN would have asked and critiques him on this basis. GUIDON uses a "closed world" model where all objects, attributes and values that are relevant to a case are determined before the tutorial session begins.

GUIDON can therefore provide at any point:

1. A list of all data relevant at that point.

2. Sub-tasks to be performed.

3. Hints on how to go about a problem.

4. A summary of all evidence already discussed.

5. Exposition of a task.

6. Completion of a diagnosis if the student gives up.

Clancey's work on GUIDON shows a great deal of promise for the use of expert systems in the next generation of CAI systems. In frame oriented CAI systems for a similar domain, the medical and teaching expertise is "compiled" into the branching structure of the frames while in GUIDON these are available for inspection and change while the program is running. This also provides the possibility of quick and simple modifications to be made to the system without needing to worry about the fixed structure of the dialogue in advance.

4.0 LANGUAGE LEARNING

Most language teaching CAI systems rely on a massive store of correct sentences and derivations from them. Despite the large number of legitimate constructs with which they can deal, the programs are really nothing more than a dumb – if effective – pattern matcher, linking unintelligible orders of characters to those pre-stored. As a consequence, the programs cannot recognize or comment upon errors encountered, even if the errors are frequent, unless these have been individually and specifically anticipated by the programmer. Therefore, the standard of accuracy required (coupled with the time for preparation of exercises) seems very high indeed.

Instead, systems such as FROG (Imlah & du Boulay, 1985) and the French Grammar Analyser (FGA for short, Barchan, Woodmansee, & Yazdani, 1986), which use a general purpose language parser, can cope with an indefinite number of possibilities without being programmed in advance to anticipate all the possibilities. These systems are also more flexible as, unlike GUIDON, they are not designed with all objects and their relationships known in advance.

The FGA program began as an attempt at a rational reconstruction of FROG. However, in order to ease the task of future extensions, we decided to produce FGA in a highly modular form. The dictionary, grammar and error reporting routines are all kept as distinguishable data structures which are clearly intelligible by anybody without intimate knowledge of the system and they can be modified with ease. Like FROG, FGA anticipates grammatically incorrect input and the need to successfully parse such to its best degree, rather than simply giving up.

FGA, unlike other attempted natural language parsers, is based on only a small subset of the complete French grammar and dictionary. Limitations of time, speed and space, as well as the (current) impossibility of defining a full natural language grammar, dictate the need for subsets. As the result of the admission of the fact that FGA's own knowledge of the language is incomplete, there is therefore a need to handle grammatically correct but unanticipated structures, as well as those which are definitely wrong. When a seemingly erroneous lexeme, word group or structure is encoutered there are, effectively, two different explanations: if we take the case of an individual word, it may appear in the dictionary but be incorrect in its context (misspelling, bad ending, incorrect agreement, wrong position/function in the sentence), or it may be potentially quite correct but not present in the subset dictionary. The same holds for structures and the grammar. We are particularly aware of this latter danger when attempting to cope with unknown words, resorting to intelligent guesses dependent upon position and spelling to identify their most probable identity and attributes and also informing the user of the assumptions made.

The fact that FGA's grammar is a restricted subset is considered by us to be one of the values of our system as we feel that systems which tend to be somewhat over ambitious in the extent of the attempted coverage of the language lose the generality, clarity and modularity which we consider so essential when the work is basically a research oriented one. We therefore have subscribed to a sort of "equation" which reads like:

$$\text{Subset} + \text{Modularity} \rightarrow \text{Clear and General Principles.}$$

These features of our system have provided a variety of applications within our University's French Department. One Lecturer presents his students with English passages which students are then asked to translate into French. The student submits the French text to FGA for analysis before handing in the program's comments to the lecturer for grading. The grammar and the dictionary of our system has had to be extended continuously in order to cope with the variety of constructions used by advanced students.

We have found a new and unexpected way of using our system as the result of its current limitation of grammar. We have allowed some advanced students to play with different versions of the program, each incorporating a different grammar. The students try various sentences on these systems and try to discover the grammar used by each version. Some of us feel this rather devious use of FGA may be educationally more beneficial than the former one.

This exercise has helped to clarify our intentions. We now clearly know that we are producing an aid for the teacher and not replacing him. Hoping to build complete computational tutoring systems seems to us to be a premature exercise. Teaching is such a complex task that we should first attempt to build computational tools for practicing teachers who could customize the systems to fit in with their own individual way of teaching. The situation in which teaching happens would involve students, the teacher and the computational system.

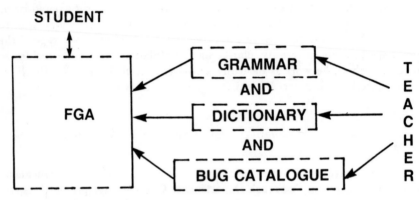

Figure 2. The Overall Structure of FGA.

5.0 ELECTRONIC TROUBLE-SHOOTING

Most ITSs (see Sleeman & Brown) have been designed and remain as protoypes. There are some notable exceptions; SOPHIE (Brown, Burton, & de Kleer, 1982) is the oldest and most well known one. SOPHIE, sponsored by the US Department of Defence (AFHRL, ARPA, Tri Services), which, after limited use for on-site job training over the ARPA network for two years, is no longer maintained.

The three stages of development of SOPHIE (I to III) incorporate the most intensive attempt at building a complete ITS. The American Air Forces interest was in using computers in their onboard trouble-shooting, particularly in a laboratory setting. The intention of the researchers in development of the system has been to explore an interactive learning environment that encourages explicit development of hypotheses by the student carrying out problem solving which is then communicated to the machine so they may be critiqued.

SOPHIE uses a general-purpose electronic simular (Nagel & Pederson, 1973) in order to provide a simulation of the domain both for the student and itself. The key idea is to construct and "run" an experiment in order to "see" what happens, as opposed to the logical deduction of an answer. This is achieved by SOPHIE containing an articulated expert trouble shooter which it can use. It enables the student to insert arbitrary faults in the circuit and watch the expert system locate them. In order to see how SOPHIE works we shall look at each stage of its development separately.

I. In the first instance SOPHIE is created out of a simulation of the chosen electronic device (the IP-28 regulated power supply) which is capable of being faulted, a simple language interface and a database of knowledge about the electronic device. In addition, it contains the basics of an automated laboratory instructor which is itself capable of a limited amount of reasoning. Most of SOPHIE's intelligence resides in a collection of routines which are selected, set up and run important experiments on the circuit simulator. In this way SOPHIE evaluates students' hypotheses, engages in question answering, checks redundancy and accordingly provides useful helpful to the student.

II. The major addition in the second stage has been to add a "canned" articulate expert trouble shooter. This expert is not a general-purpose one but is constructed by observation of the expert's way of trouble shooting the electronic device on a defined set of problems. In return for the limited number of problems that the expert can solve, it is capable of explanation of both its tactics for choosing measurements of voltages etc. and, more importantly, explanation of its high level strategies for attacking the problem.

The expert trouble shooter creates a long explanation for each measurement it makes explaining "why" it was made and "what" logically follows from the value obtained. The educational aspect of this stage is that the student chooses the fault (out of a reasonably large but nevertheless limited set) and watches the tactical reasoning processes of an expert in finding the fault chosen.

At this stage SOPHIE still has a limited automatic laboratory instructor and coach. Most of the educational benefits of thhe system are result of providing some laboratory based games as well as acting as an interactive book where written material describing a particular piece of equipment can be printed as and when it is relevant to the student's task.

III. The final stage attempts to become a complete tutor where the emphasis moves away from the use of simulation to more powerful and human-like reasoning capability for the system and addition of coaching strategies and student modelling. Figure 3 presents the overall structure of the full SOPHIE system.

The most interesting underlying philsophy of SOPHIE is its "best of both worlds" approach. The old fashioned dichotomy of a "teacher centered" versus "student centered" view of education has shown its counterpart in computer based learning systems too.

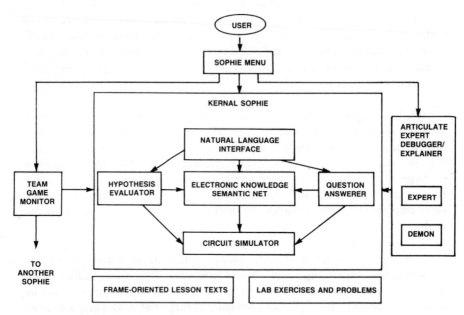

Figure 3. Extended SOPHIE System

AI applications in education mostly seem to fall at the two ends of a spectrum. At one end we can see open ended problem solving environments (Papert, 1980; Yazdani, 1984) and, at the other end, we see directed individualistic tutoring systems (Sleeman & Brown, 1982; Ohlsson, in this volume). Both these approaches have their own shortcomings; in the former the unstructured exploration is inefficient use of time, especially when one of the purposes of computer based education is efficiency. Further, when (as occurs frequently), the student gets lost as the system cannot offer the necessary support. I have discussed some of these issues elsewhere (Yazdani, in press). The latter system's directed approaches do not allow the student to explore topics of interest to the student who is denied control of the interaction.

In order to produce the "best of both worlds" SOPHIE's use is part of a general training course. A typical SOPHIE mini-course consists of four parts:

A. The first two-hour period is used to give a brief introduction of the SOPHIE system itself, an intensive study of an instructional booklet on electrics and detailed explanation of the device question (the IP-28 regulated power supply).

B. The second period covers the use of SOPHIE's expert trouble-shooter and the student doing the trouble-shooting himself in the simulated laboratory.

C. The third period consists of two activities. One is concerned with finding faults which are propogated to blow out specific components. The second takes the form of a game where the students are asked to play against one another, diagnosing each other's chosen faults on the system.

D. The final part brings the two-person teams to play against each other where members of each team attempt to cooperatively diagnose the faults chosen by other teams. The course concludes with a trouble-shooting test for each individual on the course.

6.0 COMPUTER PROGRAMMING

If computer technology is so powerful, why shouldn't it be used to help people to learn computer programming? There is a growing need for training of personnel to use computers and any form of automated support system for novice programmers can speed up this process. Further, the domain of computer programming, being a very structured one, makes it the most suitable testbed for ITS development. It is not surprising that the only two ITSs which are currently offered for sale are both in this area, one for LISP (Anderson & Reiser, 1985) and the other for Pascal (Johnson & Soloway, 1985).

Finding syntactic errors in computer programs is a reasonable straightforward job. The reporting of these errors in a form which will make it possible for the novice to learn more about the structure of the language is not that straightforward. Nevertheless, it is clearly an accepted part of mainstream computer science. Computer scientists are primarily concerned with the analysis of what the program actually does rather than with what the user intended it to do.

Dealing with non-syntactic errors of novice programmers, especially in programming languages such as Pascal and LISP (which are popular teaching languages at universities), has attracted a good deal of attention (see du Boulay, in this volume) in AI research in general and its applications to education in particular.

PROUST (Program Understanding for Students) is an intelligent tutoring system which finds errors ("bugs") in Pascal programs written by novice programmers. It is not confined to a narrow class of error, but designed to find "every" bug in most beginner's programs. It is claimed (Johnson & Soloway, 1985) that PROUST can currently identify 70 percent of all the bugs in the programs that students write for moderately complex programming assignments. Having identified the bug, PROUST determines how the bug can be corrected and suggests why the bug arose in the first place. PROUST, therefore, is part of a wider system which assigns exercises to students, analyzes their work and gives them helpful suggestions.

The teaching of computer programming requires a great deal of individualization. A class of 100 students write 100 different programs, each different in design and with different bugs for the same programming exercise. Bugs in programming arise from a number of different sources: accidental ommissions (missing variable declaration or initialization), failure to work out how all the different procedures hang together (each piece of the program appears correct, but the program does not run properly), and misconceptions about the language (the program does not do what is expected of it).

If an automatic tutor is to cope with variations and with types of student errors, it must understand what the programmer is trying to do. PROUST achieves its level of competence by being provided in advance with a description of the problems set for the students. Each of the problems which is handed out to students is also coded in a frame-based problem-description language and added to PROUST's library. Furthermore, PROUST has a further knowledge base of common bugs in Pascal programs. Therefore, as long as it knows what problem the student is trying to solve, and what possible mistakes are possible in the language, it can identify them in the student's various programs.

PROUST synthesizes each program, looking up the corresponding problem description in the library and making a hypothesis about the methods by which programmers may solve each part of the problem. If one of these hypothesis fits the student's code, then PROUST concludes that the student is correct. If not, it checks its library of common bugs to see if any of them fits the code.

PROUST has been tested on a large number of Yale University undergraduates. It has also been used on a bank of recordings of student programs submitted to the Pascal compiler. PROUST has managed to score well over 70 percent in the tests in identifying all the bugs in Pascal programs. However, "17 percent of programs are analyzed partially ... four percent of the programs, deviated from PROUST's expectations so drastically, it could not analyse them at all" (Johnson & Soloway, 1985). A major problem with PROUST is that when it fails to understand a program completely, its ability to recognize bugs deteroriates dramatically. This indicates the sensitive role of a complete problem-description library.

PROUST has been developed at a cost of half-million dollars over a four-year period at Yale University with two programming assistants. It consists of 15,000 lines of LISP code (four megabytes of memory) running on a DEC VAX750. It takes three to five minutes but correctly identifies over 70 bugs in novices' Pascal programs. Micro-PROUST is a version of the system running on an IBM PC (512K) in Golden Common LISP. It is claimed to have taken one programmer two months to produce and only has one-fifth of the bug catalogue of PROUST, taking only 90 seconds to run but with an unknown rate of success.

7.0 ITS ARCHITECTURE

As the result of the experimental nature of work in the area of ITS, no clear general architecture for such systems can be identified as yet. However, the work of the Carnegie-Mellon University psychologist John Anderson and his colleagues, on the LISP tutor (Anderson & Reiser, 1985) and the geometry tutor (Anderson, Boyle, & Yost, 1985) are offering a strong hint of a breakthrough. The underlying structure of Advanced Computer Tutoring (Anderson, Boyle, & Reiser, 1985) principles used in system for such diverse applications as LISP and Geometry, seems capable of supporting other subjects, too. At the same time, Anderson's earlier work (1982) on Adaptive Control of Thought Theory gives this approach a psychological plausibility.

There are four components to ACT's ITS architecture:

1. Domain expert: this module is capable of actually solving problems in the domain. This is sometimes also referred to as the "ideal student" model.

2. Bug catalogue: this is an extensive library of common misconceptions and errors in a domain.

3. Tutoring knowledge: this module contains the strategies used to teach the domain knowledge.

4. User interface: this is the module which administers interaction between the tutor and student.

The "ideal student model", or the domain expert, enables the tutor to solve for itself the problem on which the student is working. Rules of LISP programming are represented as production rules of a Goal-Restricted Production System (GRAPES). These differ from a general-purpose production system in that the conditions of a rule include a specific goal, i.e.,

IF the goal is to multiply

NUMBER1 by NUMBER2

THEN use the function TIMES and set as subgoal to code

NUMBER1 and NUMBER2

IF the goal is to code a recursive function, FUNCTION with integer argument INTEGER

THEN use a conditional structure and set as subgoals

1) to code the terminating case when INTEGER is 0 and

2) to code the recursive case in terms of FUNCTION (INTEGER-1)

The same formalism is used to code the "buggy" rules representing misconceptions novice programmers often develop. The ACT theory does not claim that these productions exist in the student's head, but rather that the student's behavior could be modelled with these productions.

In contrast to the richness of student modelling of some other ITSs, the ACT tutors seem to incorporate a very dogmatic and authoritarian approach to education. The main driving force behind these tutoring systems is the derivation from the ideal student model. Whenever the student makes a planning or coding error, the tutor guides the student back to the correct path. This obviously has some dangers, especially when the student is following a correct path but one which differs from the path that the system is following. Nevertheless, the LISP tutor seems to be able to turn problem solving episodes into learning experiences which they would otherwise not have been.

The student's interface presents itself as a smart screen editor. As long as the student does not make an error, the tutor remains quiet and therefore is seen as no more than an editor. If the student exhibits an error in his program, the system diagnoses the error and provides feedback in the form of a hint.

The LISP tutor contains approximately 325 production rules about planning and coding LISP programs and 475 buggy versions of those rules. It is claimed to be effective in diagnosing and responding to between 45 and 80 students' errors (Anderson & Reiser, 1985). It can be run under VMS or UNIX operating systems on DEC VAXs. A single workstation with two megabytes of memory could support one user with three to four megabytes on the VAX730, it can support two users and with six to eight megabytes it could be used as a time-sharing program. The LISP tutor is commercially available from Advanced Computer Tutoring, Inc.

8.0 THE ROLE OF STUDENT MODELLING

It is possible to argue that the architecture of ITS presented in the previous section is consistent with other proposals (Hartley & Sleeman, 1973; O'Shea et al., 1984). However, this is only on a superficial level, as there seems to be major differences between the competing proposals in a number of issues, most importantly on the role of student modelling. Hartley and Sleeman (1973) have suggested that ITS should normally have four distinct knowledge bases.

1. Knowledge of the task domain.

2. A model/history of the student's behavior.

3. A list of possible teaching operations.

4. Mean-ends guidance rules which relate teaching decisions to conditions in the student model.

This proposal differs from Anderson's (1985) inasmuch as it does not give the representation of misconceptions in the domain (the bug cata-logue) primary importance, but instead introduces the student model as a primary component which is created for each individual user. Further, this proposal subsumes the user interface in a more tutoring-oriented module which includes guidance rules on how to carry out an interaction with the user.

What then are the counterparts for the "student model" and "guid-ance rules" in Anderson's tutoring systems? A simple answer would be that within Anderson's overall tutoring philosophy, these two features are not necessary. The role of the student model is not as important as in its place we have two knowledge bases of ideal and buggy representations of the knowledge of the domain. Immediately, a behavior is exhibited which indicates a bug, we nudge the user to follow the correct version by presenting that ideal version. There is, therefore, also a simple guidance rule to discover deviations from the norm and correct them.

The five ring model presented by O'Shea et al. (1984) which bears some similarity to Hartley and Sleeman (1973) shows how the difference of emphasis on student modelling and teaching strategies leads to an architecture which is radically different from Anderson's. This includes

1. Student history.

2. Student model.

3. Teaching strategy.

4. Teaching generator.

5. Teaching administrator.

In this proposal the role of an explicit representation of the knowledge in the domain (ideal model) or the common misconceptions in the domain (the bug catalogue) are undermined in favor of emphasis on the importance of various teaching skills.

I believe that these three proposals can be viewed as points on a spectrum where at one end Anderson's proposal is closer to the more open-ended exploratory learning environments of Papert (1980) and Yazdani (1984). At the other end of the spectrum O'Shea et al.'s (1984) proposals are closer to the traditional CAI systems which sacrificed a rich representation of the knowledge domain in favor of emphasis on general purpose teaching skills.

←──→

| Learning environments | Anderson's proposal | Hartley and Sleeman's proposal | O'Shea et al.'s proposal | Traditional CAI |

The choice of a position on the above spectrum is not simply a matter of convictions of the individual researchers, but is influenced by the nature of the expertise which is to be taught. Exceptionally, abstract and general concepts such as model building, use of analogy, etc., can be better taught within an exploratory learning environment through the construction of an appropriate computer-based microworld (Lawler, 1984). The teaching of skills which are basically problem solving in a specific domain can be best achieved via problem solving monitors such as Anderson's. As the tasks become more concrete and specific, the proposals of Hartley and Sleeman, O'Shea et al. and those of traditional CAI become more appealing.

There is, however, one major drawback of this diversity of methods for the design of ITS. While the development of traditional CAI systems is greatly facilitated by the use of author languages, construction of an ITS still seems to be a one of process. O'Shea et al., due to the closeness to traditional CAI, have the most concrete proposal for a tool kit for ITS while any form of a counterpart for author langauges in ITS seems a long way away. What is clear, however, is that ITS needs powerful knowledge representation formalisms and production systems, but those used in Anderson's work seem to be as good as any other while offering a degree of psychological plausibility.

9.0 CONCLUDING REMARKS

While CAI can be considered a mature technology, ITS are currently at a pre-technology phase. However, with the arrival of the first commercial fruits of research in this area (so far primarily producing prototypes), we can expect the beginning of a new phase of development where consideration of architectures and tool kits for the development of ITS will play a major role. Following the footsteps of CAI, ITS needs a counterpart for author languages where it is estimated that an hour of CAI would require 100 hours of an experienced programmer's time to produce. With future toolkits, ITS development could possibly take twice as long but, in the current state of the art, it is estimated to be in the order of magnitude higher than CAI.

In the absence of any tool kits for ITS development, any serious attempt at construction of an ITS should be based around the 'know how' of tutor construction. Some attempts are currently being made to build tutoring prototype frameworks where the system could easily be changed from application in one domain to another similar domain. Davies et al. (1985) presents one such framework which, although designed in the first place to teach the highway code, is now used for teaching flight safety regulations to air traffic controllers.

Our own work on the teaching of French grammar (Barchan, Woodmansee, & Yazdani, 1986) is currently being extended (Barchan, in preparation) to other Western European languages. Our approach has been to build a Language Independent Grammatical Error Reporter (LINGER) where the system acts as a general purpose shell which, when supplied with the databases specific to a language, would teach that language. The motivation behind the project lies in the duplication of effort and code involved in separate development of tutoring systems for languages which show so many common features.

The progression from the FGA to LINGER can be seen as increasing movement from constructing tutoring systems for specific tasks towards tools for even greater generality. The object is to produce flexible systems which possess knowledge of their domain and which can be put to a wide variety of potential uses according to the imagination of a human tutor or the learner himself. In this respect the focus of our work is in finding an approach even closer to exploratory microworlds than that of Anderson's on a spectrum which has CAI at its other end.

ACKNOWLEDGEMENTS

This paper is partly based upon a presentation to the Italian National Council for Research, and partly on a presentation to ITT Europe Engineering Support Centre. The author gratefully acknowledges their support.

REFERENCES

Alvey, P. (1982). A programme for advanced information technology. *Her Majesty's Stationary Office*, London.

Anderson, J.R. (1982). Acquisition of cognitive skills. *Psychological Review 89*, 369-406.

Anderson, J.R. (1985). *Skill acquisition: compilation of weak method problem solution.* Pittsburgh: Carnegie-Mellon University.

Anderson, J.R., Boyle, C.F., & Yost, G. (1985). The geometry tutor. *Proceedings of the 1985 International Joint Conference on Artificial Intelligence.* Los Angeles, CA.

Anderson, J.R. & Reiser, B.J. (1985). The LISP tutor. *Byte, 10*(4).

Anderson, J.R., Boyle, C.F., & Reiser, B.J. (1985). Intelligent tutoring systems. *Science 228*, 456-462.

Barchan, J. (in preparation). *Language independent grammatical error reporter.* Master's thesis, University of Exeter, Exeter, United Kingdom.

Barchan, J., Woodmansee, B.J., & Yazdani, M. (1986). A prolog-base tool for french grammar analyses. *Instructional Science, 15.*

Brown, J.S., Burton, R.R., & de Kleer, J. (1982). Pedagogical, natural language and knowledge engineering techniques. In D.H. Sleeman and J.S. Brown (Eds.) *SOPHIE I, II and III.*

Burton, R.R. (1982). DEBUGGY: diagnosis of errors in basic mathematical skills. In D.H. Sleeman and J.S. Brown (Eds.). *Intelligent Tutoring Systems.* Academic Press.

Burton, R.R. & Brown, J.S. (1982). An investigation of computer coaching for informal learning act. In D.H. Sleeman and J.S. Brown (Eds.). *Intelligent Tutoring Systems.* Academic Press.

du Boulay, B., & Sothcott, C. (in this volume). Computers teaching programming.

Clancey, W.J. (1979). Tutoring rules for guiding a case method dialogue. *Int. J. of Man-Machine Studies, 11*, 9.

Davies, N. G., Dickens, S.L., & Ford, L. (1985). TUTOR – A prototype ICAI system. In Bramer M. (ed.), *Research and Development in Expert Systems*. Cambridge University Press.

Hartley, J.R. & Sleeman, D.H. (1973). Towards intelligent teaching systems. *Int. J. of Man-Machine Studies, 15*, 2.

Imlah, W. & du Boulay, B. (1986). Robust natural language parsing in computer assisted language instruction. *System, 13*, 2.

Johnson, W.L. & Soloway, E. (1985). PROUST. *Byte 10*(4).

Lawler, R. (1984). Designing Computer-based Microworlds. In Yazdani (Ed.), *New Horizons in Educational Computing*. Ellis Horwood/John Wiley.

Nagel, L.W. & Pedersen, D.O. (1973). Simulation program with integrated circuit emphasis. *Proceedings of the 6th Midwest Symposium Circuit Theory*, Waterloo, Ontario, Canada.

Ohlsson, S. (in this volume). Some principles of intelligent tutoring.

O'Shea, T. & Self, J. (1983). *Learning and Teaching with Computers*. Harvester Press.

O'Shea, T., Bornat, R., du Boulay, B., Eisenstad, M., & Page, I. (1984). Tools for creating intelligent computer tutors. In Elithor and Banerjii (eds.), *Human and Artificial Intelligence*. North Holland.

Papert, S. (1980). *Mindstorms, Children, Computers and Powerful Ideas*. Harvester Press/Basic Books.

Shortcliffe, E.H. (1976). *Computer-based Medical Consultations: MYCIN*. American Elsevier.

Skinner, B.F. (1958). Teaching machines. *Science, 128*.

Sleeman, D.H., & Brown, J.S. (Eds.) (1982). *Intelligent Tutoring Systems*. Academic Press.

Winograd, T. (1972). *Understanding Natural Language*. Edinburgh University Press.

Yazdani, M. (Ed.) (1984). *New Horizons in Educational Computing*. Ellis Horwood/John Wiley.

Yazdani, M. (in press). Artificial Intelligence, powerful ideas and childrens' learning. In J. Rutkowska & C. Crook (Eds.), *Computers and Child Development*. John Wiley & Sons.

11   SOME PRINCIPLES OF INTELLIGENT TUTORING

Stellan Ohlsson

Learning Research and Development Center
University of Pittsburgh
Pittsburgh, PA 15260

ABSTRACT

Research on intelligent tutoring systems is discussed from the point of view of providing moment-by-moment adaptation of both content and form of instruction to the changing cognitive needs of the individual learner. The implications of this goal for *cognitive diagnosis, subject-matter analysis, teaching tactics,* and *teaching strategies* are analyzed. The results of the analyses are stated in the form of principles about intelligent tutoring. A major conclusion is that a computer tutor, in order to provide adaptive instruction, must have a strategy which translates its tutorial goals into teaching actions, and that, as a consequence, research on teaching strategies is central to the construction of intelligent tutoring systems.

1.0 INTRODUCTION

Proponents of individualized instruction, or, as it is sometimes called, adaptive education (Glaser, 1976; Wang & Walberg, 1985), have sought to tailor instruction to such characteristics of the student as initial competence, educational goal, learning style, and, most often, learning rate, in recognition of the fact that interindividual differences in cognition implies that different learners need different instruction. Neither the history (Grinder & Nelsen, 1985) nor the current state (Bangert, Kulik, & Kulik, 1983) of such efforts are encouraging.

The birth of the computer tutor alters this situation drastically. The computer offers the potential for adapting instruction to the student at a finer-grain level than the one which concerned earlier generations of educational researchers. First, instead of adapting to global traits such as learning style, the computer tutor can, in principle, be programmed to adapt to the student *dynamically,* during ongoing instruction, at each moment in time providing the kind of instruction that will be most beneficial to the student at that time. Said differently, the computer tutor takes a longitudinal – rather than cross-sectional – perspective, focussing on the fluctuating cognitive needs of a single learner over time, rather than on stable interindividual differences. Second, and even more important, instead of adapting to content-free characteristics of the learner, such as learning rate, the computer can, in principle, be programmed to adapt both the *content* and the *form* of instruction to the student's understanding of the subject matter. The computer can be programmed, or so we hope, to generate exactly that question, explanation, example, counter-example, practice problem, illustration, activity, or demonstration which will be most helpful to the learner. It is the task of providing dynamic adaptation of content and form which is the challange and the promise of computerized instruction.[1]

When we envisage computer tutors helping out in the classroom, it is easy to be trapped into thinking in terms of particular tutors. If we want good tutoring in, say, arithmetic, what more is needed, we might ask, than a good arithmetic tutor? This perspective forgets, in the concretion of the vision, that the task of tutoring is forever changing. School systems undergo reforms, student populations follow the rhythms of the surrounding society, topics are added to (or deleted from) the curriculum, courses are moved from one age-level to another, and course contents vary from textbook to textbook, from classroom to classroom. What we need, then, are not particular, quickly outdated, computer tutors but the know-how of tutor construction. As everyone knows who have written a large computer program, it is possible to proceed by accumulating tricks and patches, ending up with a system that is so irregular that, in a sense, one cannot say why it works. But even a pedagogically successful tutor has limited interest if it leaves system designers without any information about how to design the *next* system. The output of research into computer tutoring should consist, not of particular systems, but of principles which allow specifications – in terms of course content and student characteristics – to be turned into effective tutors. The main points of the present article will be formulated as informal principles of intelligent tutoring; some of these principles summarize beliefs which are commonly held in the field, others indicate new directions.

In summary, the main promise of computer tutors, I claim, lies in their potential for moment-by-moment adaptation of instructional content and form to the changing cognitive needs of the individual learner, and our task, as I see it, is to find principles which can guide the construction of tutors which fulfill that promise. My main goal in the following is to clarify the implications of this view for intelligent tutoring research. I break the discussion into four sections, dealing with *cognitive diagnosis, subject matter analysis, teaching tactics,* and *teaching strategies,* respectively. In each section, I propose one or more principles which, I argue, constitute minimal criteria of adequacy for a tutor which is to provide dynamically adaptive

---

[1] In this article, the terms "teaching," "tutoring," and "instruction" will be used as synonyms.

instruction. My secondary goal is to point out some often-overlooked relations between different strands of research relevant to the construction of tutoring systems. I end with a summary of the main argument.

2.0 COGNITIVE DIAGNOSIS

If the purpose of intelligent tutoring systems, their *raison etre*, is to provide adaptive instruction, then such a system must know something about the cognitive state of the student, what he knows and how he thinks, and preferably how he learns. I will call the process of inferring a person's cognitive state from his performance for *cognitive diagnosis*.[2] To the extent that the major failure of current educational practices is the failure to provide adaptive instruction, then the limits on the sensitivity and resolving power of our diagnostic procedures are also the limits on the amount of pedagogical progress attainable through intelligent tutoring systems.[3] Therefore, we should look carefully at current methods for cognitive diagnosis.

Research on cognitive diagnosis has been conducted from several viewpoints. Educators have developed tests for what they call assessment or normative diagnosis (Ginsburg, 1983; Nitko, in press), and there are materials available for diagnostic teaching, materials which emphasize the diagnosis of particular kinds of errors (e.g., Hill, 1980). The problem of describing the mental state of single individuals has also been addressed by psychologists, most notably developmental psychologists (e.g., Smedslund, 1969), even though the mainstream of academic psychology has been more interested in finding regularities across individuals. Information-processing psychology has contributed new methods for inferring the mental states and processes of single individuals, as well as a new formal rigor (Newell & Simon, 1972; Williams & Hollan, 1981). Research on cognitive diagnosis from the point of view of intelligent tutoring systems goes one step further in that it aims for computer implemented diagnostic methods (e.g., Burton, 1982). This exciting development, originating – somewhat paradoxically – from within computer science, adds potential to this methodological tradition, which so far has not held center stage in psychological research.

What kind of diagnostics do we need in a computer tutor which is to provide adaptive education? In order to approach this question, we need

---

[2] In research on tutoring systems, the term "student modelling" is often used, but I will avoid it, since it is unnecessarily restrictive. Students are not the only human beings who can be diagnosed, and a model is not the only possible kind of diagnosis.

[3] An immediate corollary is that commercially available educational software which, as a rule, do not have any diagnostic capabilities, will not, in fact, produce more learning than traditional teaching materials.

a framework within which various types of diagnosis can be compared. In the next section, I review some types of diagnostic methods. I propose to discuss them in terms of (a) the kinds of *empirical observations* they operate upon, as well as the kinds of *knowledge structures* they need to carry out the diagnosis (i.e., their "inputs"), (b) the *procedures* by which they infer the cognitive state of the student, and (c) the *types of descriptions* they generate (i.e., their "outputs"). In addition, we ought to consider (d) the *theoretical commitments* of the various methods, and (e) the *teaching actions* they are intended to support. Of these four categories, the type of description generated by the diagnostic system is the more fundamental. There are characteristic ways of deriving each type of description, as well as typical ways of using it in instruction. Also, the theoretical commitments of a diagnostic method usually reside in the type of description it generates (rather than, say, in the procedure by which it is generated). The review in the next section has four parts, corresponding to four types of diagnostic descriptions: performance measures, overlays, error descriptions, and simulations. In a later section, I describe a new perspective on diagnosis which, I believe, is more relevant for instruction.

Before getting started, we need to be clear about terminology. In the following, "error" is used as a generic term for misconceptions, false beliefs, procedural bugs, etc. An error resides in the head, as it were. The observable expression of the error is referred to as an "incorrect answer," or "incorrect performance."

2.1 Varieties of Cognitive Diagnosis

2.1.1 Performance Measures

The simplest way to describe a person in relation to an area of knowledge is to measure how successfully he solves problems in that area. Performance measures appear in educational contexts under a variety of labels, such as "test scores", "examination results", "assessment levels", etc. Computation of such a measure requires nothing but the student's answers – a type of data which is readily available in most contexts – and some statistical aggregation procedure. It may seem as if a performance level, being an observational construct, is blessed with theoretical innocence. However, use of the performance level as a basis for instruction assumes that we need not know *what* knowledge a student has acquired in order to tutor him effectively, only *how much*. Since such a measure is a global representation of the student, it can only support global actions on the part of the tutor. For instance, a tutor can upgrade or downgrade the difficulty of practice items, it can speed up or slow down a presentation, it can provide either terse or full explanations, etc. But performance measures do not, as one authority agrees (Glaser, in press), provide the level of detail necessary to decide what *this* student needs *right now* in order to learn *that* concept, procedure, fact, or principle.[4]

2.1.2 Overlays

To provide dynamic adaptation of the content of instruction, we must move from a concern with how much knowledge a student has to a concern with what he knows. Given an analysis of the subject matter to be acquired, we can represent a student by the set of subject-matter units he has mastered, for instance, the geometric theorems which he knows how to apply. Such a description is called an *overlay model* in the literature on intelligent tutoring systems (Carr & Goldstein, 1977). The student is represented as a network of tick-marks which, as it were, is laid over the representation of the subject matter to show which parts of it he already knows. From the overlay point of view, the student knows a subset of what a domain expert knows. Learning is the process of acquiring a progressively more-complete subset of the expert's knowledge units, but different learners can acquire those units in different orders, so that two learners who have roughly the same amount of knowledge can, nevertheless, know very different things.

Overlays are particularly natural models of students when the subject matter to be learned is represented as a *prerequisite hierarchy*. In such hierarchies, which have great intuitive appeal in mathematics and other problem-solving domains, each knowledge unit is broken down into its components or prerequisites, e.g., addition and subtraction are prerequisites for long division. Prerequisite hierarchies have been investigated by educators and psychologists (e.g., Gagne, 1962; Resnick, 1973; Resnick, Wang, & Kaplan, 1973) and have been re-invented by computer scientists. They are used quite frequently in intelligent tutoring systems, without the kind of empirical verification which educational researchers regard as necessary (Resnick & Wang, 1969).

The typical procedure for inferring an overlay works by relating the student's performance to the prerequisite structure of the subject matter. If a student reliably succeeds on a particular type of task, then he can be inferred to have acquired whatever knowledge items are prerequisites for succeeding on that task. If he fails reliably, at least one of the prerequisites can be assumed to be missing from his competence. Since the various knowledge items are needed in different combinations for different problem types, one can puzzle out which items a student has mastered by a judicial

---

[4] Some educators are thinking hard about how to use recent research results from cognitive psychology to construct more informative educational tests (Glaser, in press; Nitko, in press), but such tests still belong to the future.

choice of problems. Sandra Marshall (1980; 1981) has worked out a precise theory for how to compute an overlay model for a prerequisite hierarchy. The essence of her diagnostic procedure is to compute a probability distribution over the set of possible diagnoses, to revise that distribution after each response from the student on the basis of Baysian decision theory, and to use statistical information theory for choosing maximally informative problems to present. This kind of diagnosis is widely used in intelligent tutoring systems, usually without the mathematical sophistication introduced by Marshall.

Like the performance level, the overlay at first seems to be innocent of theoretical commitments. In fact, overlays make two assumptions which limit their usefulness for instruction. A prerequisite hierarchy – or any other type of analysis – views the subject matter in a particular way, from a particular vantage point. Since the overlay representation of the student is parasitic on the representation of the subject matter, the overlay shows how far the student has progressed in acquiring a *particular view of the subject matter*. However, rarely – if ever – is there only one possible view, and, unfortunately, if the view used by the tutor is not the view which the student is trying to attain, as it were, then the overlay might be useless as a basis for instruction.

The second detrimental property of an overlay is that it assumes that a student is a subset of an expert. The learner is seen as knowing the same things as an expert, only fewer of them. This perspective ignores the possibility of *distorted knowledge*. However, recent research into arithmetic, algebra, and physics has revealed that different learners do not just differ in which subset of the subject matter they have acquired, but also in how they misunderstand that part of the subject-matter which they have not yet mastered (see below). There are no resources within the overlay to represent this fact.

An overlay model, particularly when coupled with a prerequisite analysis of the knowledge domain, can guide the decision of what topic to tutor next: In general, the next topic should be chosen from those subject-matter units which are not yet mastered, but which have all their prerequisites ticked off as known. Thus, an overlay allows a tutor to solve the traditional pedagogical problem of sequencing the subject matter, and, moreover, to solve it *adaptively*, for each student, and *dynamically*, while instruction is happening.

2.1.3 Error Descriptions

The empirical evidence is now overwhelming that learners do not only fail to acquire the content presented to them during instruction, they also *mis-*

represent it. Students acquire erroneous procedures, false principles, and incorrect facts, both inside and outside school (e.g., Gentner & Stevens, 1983; VanLehn, 1983). The most spectacular progress in cognitive diagnosis in the past years is the appearance of computerized diagnostic methods for identifying the errors of individual learners. Such methods have so far been successful in a small number of knowledge domains, most notably arithmetic (e.g., Burton, 1982), algebra (e.g., Sleeman, 1982), and elementary programming (Johnson & Soloway, 1983; 1984; Soloway, Rubin, Woolf, Bonar, & Johnson, 1982).

These diagnostic systems usually work with performance data, i.e., the pattern of correct and incorrect answers on a set of problems, or, in the case of programming, a single answer. The inferential procedure which is used in this type of diagnosis is based on an *error library*, i.e., a list of possible errors. Given a particular student, it is possible to compute which error (or combination of errors) best account for the incorrect answers of that student. The basic difficulties in constructing such systems are (a) to establish the error library, which is a labor-intensive empirical undertaking, and (b) to invent methods which can compute the best-fitting error combination efficiently enough to deliver a diagnosis in a reasonable time.

The basic idea of error identification through an error library has been significantly extended in the PROUST system by Johnson and Soloway (1983; 1984), which takes a programming problem, i.e., a specification of a program, and a (typically incorrect) program as inputs, and tries to understand the incorrect program. PROUST has several different knowledge structures to draw upon, including an error library, a library of programming plans, knowledge of programmers' goals, etc. Its inferential procedure attempts to develop a goal structure for the problem which accounts for all the parts of the code in the observed program, using both correct, and, if necessary, incorrect programming plans as bridges between a particular goal decomposition and the faulty code. PROUST delivers a hypothesis about the programmer's intentions, and about how he tried to realize them, i.e., it generates an account of how the faulty program was *created.* Besides the programmer's intentions in writing the program (the goal hierarchy), the account also includes the domain-specific knowledge the programmer used (the correct programming plans), and the mistakes he did (the errors that must be posited to make the account complete). PROUST has been successful in diagnosing incorrect programs by novice programmers.

The theoretical commitments of error-identification systems hide in their descriptions of errors. An error library reifies the errors, as it were, by making a decision as to what is a primitive error and what is a compound error. Furthermore, since errors are unavoidably described as deviations from correct knowledge, error descriptions presuppose a particular representation of the subject matter. Different analyses of the subject matter may result in different error libraries, and so in different diagnoses of particular students.

The pedagogical promise of an error description is that it might enable *remedial instruction*. Given knowledge of which particular error a student is suffering from, we should be able to help him overcome it. However, deciding on the best remedy for a particular error is not a trivial matter, and, in fact, error descriptions have not been used in many tutoring systems. The approach taken by Attisha and Yazdani (1983; 1984) is to have the tutoring system type out a prestored natural language description of an error. The same idea has been used in the tutors constructed by John Anderson and his co-workers (Anderson, Boyle, & Reiser, 1985; Anderson, Boyle, & Yost, 1985; Reiser, Anderson, & Farrell, 1985), with the extension that they link specific errors with natural language *templates* containing variables which are filled with situation-specific information at the time they are output to the student. Reaching for the next level of flexibility, Woolf and McDonald (1984) are designing a system to do remedial teaching through a didactic dialogue. As we shall see in the section on teaching tactics, talking to a student about his error is not the only kind of remedial teaching.

2.1.4 Simulations

A description of a student's cognitive state can consist of a simulation model which performs like him in the relevant knowledge domain. The main characteristic of such a representation is that it is *runnable*, i.e., that it will generate behavior when applied to a task. The behavior is a prediction of what the simulated person would do, if he solved the same task. With this kind of representation, we can explain the student's steps towards his answer to a problem, as well as the answer itself.

The first systematic method for constructing simulation models was proposed by Newell and Simon (1972). Their method takes think-aloud protocols as input, and the inference from data to simulation model proceeds in three steps. First, the protocol is scanned for evidence concerning the student's[5] mental encoding of the task, as well as for the cognitive operations he is applying to it. An encoding of a task and a set of operators together define a *problem space*; consequently, we call this the problem space approach to diagnosis (Ohlsson & Langley, in press; 1985). Second, the sequential information in the protocol is used to construct the student's path to solution. Third, problem-solving rules are invented which

---

[5] The method was conceived in the context of basic research on human problem-solving, but in keeping with the terminology in the rest of this article, I will write about "students" rather than "subjects".

can generate the solution path. The rule set is a model for the student's performance on the relevant task. This is a very labor-intensive diagnostic method. Early efforts to computerize it were not successful (Waterman & Newell, 1972), because, one might guess, of the need for such a system to understand the utterances in the think-aloud protocol, a task that was beyond the natural language capabilities of computers at the time.

Pat Langley and I have recently collaborated on a different effort to computerize the problem space approach to cognitive diagnosis (Langley, Ohlsson, & Sage, 1984; Ohlsson & Langley, in press; 1985). We constructed a computer program which takes an answer as input, rather than a think-aloud protocol, plus a problem space. The system searches the given problem space for a path which leads to the observed (possibly incorrect) answer, chosing between alternative paths on the basis of psychological criteria. Like the PROUST system discussed in the previous subsection, our program creates an account of how the incorrect answer was *created*. However, our type of account – a solution path – is much simpler than the type of generated by account used by PROUST. Once a path has been found, so-called machine learning methods can be applied to it in order to generate problem-solving rules which will reproduce the observed answer. Our program has successfully diagnosed a small set of subtraction errors.

The output from the problem space approach to diagnosis does not, in a sense, *describe* the errors of the diagnosed student. Rather, the method generates a procedure which performs the relevant tasks in the same way as the student. Whether that procedure is to be classified as correct or incorrect cannot be determined with reference to the way in which it was generated. The diagnostic method does not make use of the concept of "correctness", nor of an error library. Errors are *implicitly* described in the way in which the rules are stated, rather than explicitly described, as in the error identification methods described previously.[6]

It is interesting to contrast our diagnostic method with the *model-tracing* method used by John Anderson and his co-workers (Anderson, Boyle, & Yoost, 1985; Reiser, Anderson, & Farrell, 1985). The model-tracing method operates in the context of intelligent tutoring systems which monitor students' problem-solving activity. In that context, the diagnostic component need not compute the student's solution path, because it can

---

[6] The explicit description of the error can be recovered by comparing the rules generated by the diagnostic procedure with the rules for correct performance. However, this would introduce a difficulty which is now familiar: *which* representation of correct performance should the student's rules be compared to? Different representations of the correct procedure will lead to different characterizations of the differences.

observe what the student does, step by step. Also, the diagnostic system has a knowledge base consisting of several hundred problem-solving rules which encode both correct knowledge about the domain and typical errors. The system builds a model of the student by locating, for each problem-solving step he takes, which rule (or rules) corresponds to that step. By operating in a context where the solution path is observable and by having a large rule library, model-tracing diagnosis essentially *side-steps* the diagnostic problem that the problem space approach tries to solve. There is a lesson to be learned here with respect to intelligent tutoring which will be spelled out in detail in the next section.

The product of a model-tracing diagnosis is similar to an overlay, in that it consists of a selection of knowledge units from a pre-established set. However, since the rule base can include incorrect as well as correct rules, the model-tracing diagnosis can represent both the student's knowledge and his errors. Also, since the rule base can contain alternative versions of the correct problem-solving rules, model-tracing diagnosis can model a learner with respect to several alternative versions of the correct problem-solving skill. Finally, since the knowledge units are executable rules, the rule set which represents the student is, in principle,[7] a runnable model.

The theoretical commitments of simulations are more visible than the commitments of the other types of descriptions discussed. A simulation pre-supposes a performance theory. It must specify the mental representation of both declarative and procedural knowledge, it must assume something about memory stores and their properties, it must take a stand on whether human cognition is goal driven or not, and, if so, how goals are managed, it must run under some particular cognitive architecture, etc. The problem space approach to diagnosis is based on the theory that thinking consists of heuristic search through a problem space (Newell & Simon, 1972). The model-tracing methodology is strongly influenced by the general idea of heuristic search, but builds in its specifics on the ACT* theory (Anderson, 1983). Other performance theories might lead to yet other diagnostic methods.

A simulation model is a powerful description. Intuitively, we would expect such a description to buy us dramatic advantages in instruction, particularly with respect to individualized instruction. It is, therefore, surprising to realize that it is not clear what one can do with a simulation of the student that one cannot do without it. Planning and designing instruction which is maximally useful for a student is not a simple task, even with the help of a powerful description of that student.

---

[7] Anderson and co-workers do not make any strong claims about the runnability of their student models.

2.2 Improving Cognitive Diagnosis

The different types of cognitive diagnosis discussed in the previous section form a regular progression towards more and more powerful descriptions of the student. A performance measure indicates the proportion of the subject matter which the student has mastered; an overlay model specifies *which* portion, and thereby – indirectly – which knowledge units the student still needs to learn. Error descriptions add information about what we might call negative subject matter, i.e., the distorted and twisted knowledge units which the student needs to *unlearn*. Finally, simulations enable us to run the representation of the student, and thereby to make detailed predictions about his performance.

Although they differ with respect to completeness of description, all the diagnostic systems reviewed in the last section, with the exception of the model-tracing method, share a common perspective. They are based on a view of diagnosis as "research in miniature", to use Ginsburg's (1983) happy phrase. The task of diagnosis is, according to this perspective, to explain, or account for, a set of observations (performances). These methods (again, with the exception of model tracing) do not take into account how the diagnosis they produce is going to be *used*. But we need to know what the purpose of diagnosis is in order to decide how powerful a diagnostic method we should incorporate into our tutoring systems.

Let us consider the decision situation of a tutor, and what role the diagnostic component can play in it. A computer tutor is usually able to present practice problems and to provide feed-back; it might be able to demonstrate correct solutions, to provide explanations, give hints, ask questions, etc. But no matter how sophisticated and versatile the tutoring system is, it will only have a finite number of actions to choose from, and its only task, one might claim, is to select one of those actions as the next thing to do. (This is a fair description of how some tutoring systems work.) The tutor's only use of the diagnosis, it seems, is to help select that next action. This perspective tempts us to view the diagnostic component of the tutor as a mechanism for mapping tutorial situations onto instructional actions, i.e., as imposing an equivalence-classification on the set of tutorial situations, one class containing all situations in which action A (e.g., explaining) is pedagogically superior, another class containing all situations in which action B (e.g., demonstrating), is superior, etc. This kind of diagnosis seems ripe and ready to be attacked with the well-established methodology of expert systems (e.g., Waterman, 1986).

Before falling for the temptation to develop this perspective further, we should remember that intelligent teaching does not consist of sequences of unrelated actions. A tutoring effort is structured; it coordinates the individual teaching actions, subsumes them under a plan for how to transmit the relevant knowledge. The moment-to-moment behavior of the tutor originate in the execution of that plan, rather than in successive decisions about what to do next. If the student model is to be useful, it has to contribute in some way to the construction and execution of instructional plans. This perspective is sufficiently different from the idea of "research in miniature" to be stated as a principle:

> The Principle of Pragmatic Diagnosis. The purpose of the diagnostic component of an intelligent tutoring system is to support the execution of its instructional plan.

Considering diagnosis from this point of view, we are lead to ask what function cognitive diagnosis could have in the construction and execution of instructional plans. The crucial link between an instructional plan and a student model is, I propose, that instructional plans contain (implicit) *expectations* about what the student will do in response to the tutor's actions. For instance, consider the following simple, two-step plan for teaching the solution to problem Y: "first review problem X (e.g., addition of proper fractions), then introduce problem Y (e.g., addition of mixed fractions), and then show how the solution to X can be applied to Y as well." This plan implicitly presupposes that the student knows how to solve problem X correctly, so that X can be used as a pedagogical resource or lever in the teaching of Y. If this expectation is violated – the student fails to solve X – then the plan becomes irrelevant and has to be revised. Every instructional plan, I believe, contains implicit expectations about the student, expectations which, if violated, render the plan irrelevant.

This observation suggests that one function of cognitive diagnosis in tutoring is to test the viability of the expectations underlying the tutor's instructional plan.

> The Principle of Expectation Testing. The function of the diagnostic component of an intelligent tutoring system is to test whether the expectations presupposed by the tutor's current plan are consistent with its current model of the student.

One procedure for making such a test is to predict, from the current model of the student, how he will respond to the tutor's actions, and then compare the predictions with the expectations. If they diverge, then the plan is not viable *vis-a-vis* current knowledge of the student. The plan should then be revised, and the expectations of the new plan tested, etc., until a viable plan is found. If it turns out that the *actual* (as opposed to the predicted) behavior of the student does not conform to the expectations/predictions, then, of course, both the instructional plan and the student model have to be revised. This argument speaks strongly in favor of runnable student models.

In summary, a number of diagnostic methods exist which generate more or less powerful representations of the cognitive state of the student. They typically perform the task of diagnosis independently of the pragmatics of teaching. By changing the diagnostic question from "What goes on in the head of the student?" to "What does the tutor need to know in order to teach?" we turn our attention to the nature of teaching strategies. A crucial property of such strategies is that they contain implicit expectations about student behavior, which, in turn, suggests that one important function for cognitive diagnosis in instruction is to help decide whether those expectations are viable or not.

3.0 SUBJECT-MATTER ANALYSIS

Teaching, as Wenger (1985) reminds us, is an act of knowledge communication, even when it is carried out by an artifact. Its goal is to transmit a particular subject matter to the student. We need to ask what the implications of computer tutoring and adaptive instruction are for representations of subject-matter. I will argue (a) that subject-matter analysis is important because an adaptive computer tutor needs to make a distinction between the subject matter itself and its surface manifestations, and (b) that a central obstacle to intelligent tutoring is the fact that different learners may acquire different representations of the target knowledge.

In our discussion of cognitive diagnosis, we noticed that three different communities of scholars have been involved in research on diagnosis, namely educators, psychologists, and computer scientists. With respect to subject-matter analysis, we would have to mention those three, and then add that domain experts often engage in such analyses as well, particularly in areas like mathematics and physics. But commonalities in goals, methods, and results are often obscured by differences in terminology. What is known as "subject-matter analysis" among educators often goes under the name "task analysis" among psychologists (e.g., Gardner, 1985); a mathematician might prefer the term "didactic analysis" (e.g., Steiner, 1969), while a computer scientist is certain to use "knowledge representation" (e.g., Brachman & Levesque, 1985). The term "subject-matter analysis" is used here without any ulterior motive; either term could have served equally well.

3.1 Why is Subject-Matter Analysis Important?

The traditional educational task of finding the right representation of the subject matter has been taken up with a vengeance by the community of scholars involved in intelligent tutoring systems research. A glance at recent research (e.g., Sleeman & Brown, 1982) shows cognitive scientists hard at work giving their artificial tutors explicit representations of the relevant subject matter. Indeed, Wenger (1985), in his comprehensive review, argues that the major research questions addressed in intelligent tutoring research are issues of knowledge representation, and even draws the line between the prehistory and the history of intelligent tutoring systems at the moment when the tutors began to acquire an internal representation of the subject matter.

From the point of view of individualized instruction, the importance of subject-matter analysis is not immediately obvious. The knowledge to be taught is that which remains the same across students. Like gasoline, a substance which can drive many different kinds of vehicles without adapting itself to them, the content of a course may drive the learning of many different students, while remaining the same course content. If so, how does subject-matter analysis contribute to individualized instruction, if at all?

We can approach this question through a distinction between a knowledge item, a piece of subject matter, and the *form* in which it is presented to the student. For instance, consider a mathematical theorem, such as the familiar Cancellation Law for fractions:

$$\frac{a \times N}{b \times N} = \frac{a}{b}$$

This piece of knowledge can be presented in at least the following formats: (a) as a principle (e.g., "A fraction in which the numerator and the denominator share a factor ....."); (b) as a mathematical formula (e.g., the one above); (c) as an algorithm (e.g., "First find the factors of the numerator, then ....."); (d) as a demonstration of how to execute the algorithm on a particular problem; (e) as a demonstration of the algorithm with respect to some illustrative materials (e.g., Dienes blocks); (f) as a collection of solved examples in which the algorithm has been applied; and (g) as a proof that the theorem is correct. The range of possible presentation formats is no more restricted for other types of knowledge units.

A student struggling to learn the Cancellation Law may benefit most from one or the other of these presentations, depending upon the nature of the obstacle to his learning. A justification may enhance memory for the theorem; a demonstration might facilitate its application. It follows that a tutor, to be maximally helpful, must generate the presentation of the theorem on the spur of the moment, in response to the cognitive needs of the student at that moment. This implies, in turn, that the tutor must possess a core representation of the theorem, a deep structure – as it were – which is independent of the different presentation formats, but from which the specific presentations – the surface structures – can be derived. There is thus a strong connection between individualized instruction, on the one hand, and the separation between content and form, between subject matter and its tutorial shape, on the other.

The Principle of Generative Interfaces. In order to provide adaptive instruction, a tutor must distinguish between the subject matter and the formats in which it can be presented, and be able to generate different presentations of each subject-matter unit as needed, at each moment in time choosing the form which is most beneficial for the learner at that moment.

The above principle spells out the essential difference between intelligent tutoring systems and other types of teaching materials. The printed page, the audiotape, and the movie are all equally incapable, in principle, of separating content from form. Older, so-called frame-based CAI systems also failed to separate the two, and so constituted a very limited advance upon traditional teaching materials, if any at all.[8] However, the computer has the potential to teach the way a good human tutor would teach, adapting the form of his presentation to the individual student by applying generative procedures, guided by diagnostic information, to a deep representation of the subject matter.

We can now understand why designers of intelligent tutoring systems pay so much attention to subject-matter analysis. Implementing a presentation-neutral representation of domain knowledge, plus the generative mechanism which is to produce the surface presentations of it, usually requires considerable clarification and extension of existing representations of the subject matter. The reader is referred to the retrospective report by Brown, Burton, & DeKleer, 1982 (particularly pp. 244–279), on the SOPHIE trouble-shooting tutor for an illustration of just how much thinking may be needed to implement a so-called domain expert. In short, the Principle of Generative Interfaces is not a new insight; instead, it explains why the field of intelligent tutoring concerns itself almost exclusively with

---

[8] It is worth noticing that most commercial educational software is of the frame-based variety.

intelligence, but hardly at all with tutoring: The need for a deep representation of the subject matter puts the issue of knowledge representation at the top of the tutoring agenda, and the difficulty of that issue ensures that it stays there.

3.2 The Problem of Alternative Learning Targets

A computer tutor typically embodies a representation of the subject matter, a domain expert. The target knowledge has only one representation inside the tutoring system. Considering the effort required to implement even a single domain expert, this is not surprising.

But there are no canonical representations of knowledge. Any knowledge domain can be seen from several different points of view, each view showing a different structure, a different set of parts, differently related. This claim, however broad and blunt – almost impolite – it may appear when laid out in print, is, I believe, uncontroversial. In fact, the evidence for it is so plentiful that we do not notice it, like the fish in the sea who never thinks about water. For instance, empirical studies of expertise regularly show that human experts differ in their problem solutions (e.g., Prietula & Marchak, 1985); at the other end of the scale, studies of young children tend to show that they invent a variety of strategies even for simple tasks, (e.g., Svenson & Hedenborg, 1980; Young, 1976). As a second instance, consider rational analyses of thoroughly codified knowledge domains, such as the arithmetic of rational numbers. The traditional mathematical treatment by Thurstone (1956) is hard to relate to the didactic analysis by Steiner (1969), which, in turn, does not seem to have much in common with the informal, but probing, analyses by Kieren (1976; 1980) – and yet, they are all experts trying to express the meaning of, for instance, "two-thirds." In short, the process of acquiring a particular subject matter does not converge on a particular representation of that subject matter. This fact has such important implications for instruction that it should be stated as a principle.

The Principle of Non-Equifinality of Learning. The state of knowing the subject matter does not correspond to a single, well-defined cognitive state. The target knowledge can always be represented in different ways, from different perspectives; hence, the process of acquiring the subject matter have many different, equally valid, end states.

The non-equifinality of learning causes severe difficulties for intelligent tutoring, some of which have been discussed by Burton, 1982; (see in particular pp. 94–95) in connection with the WEST tutor. As discussed in the section on diagnosis, if the representation of the student is parasitic on the representation of the subject matter, as in the case of overlay models, then the diagnosis interprets the student in terms of how far he has developed toward acquiring a particular view of the subject matter, which may or may not be a useful representation of him. The corresponding problem occurs on the output side of the tutor: Which analysis of the subject matter should be used in deciding which topic to tutor next? Which breakdown of the subject matter into topics is relevant for the particular student?

One partial solution to the non-equifinality problem is to implement more than one representation of the subject matter, and allow the tutor to use all of them both when trying to understand the student and when making instructional decisions. This solution might work in domains where a small number of different representations of the target knowledge cover a large proportion of students. For instance, in the domain of subtraction, there might be only a small number of psychologically plausible encodings of the correct skill, and a computer tutor could try to judge which of these encodings a particular student is *en route* toward, and base its instruction on that hypothesis. The solution to implement more than one representation of the domain knowledge might also work well in domains where the knowledge can be expressed in very modular units, e.g., production rules. The representation of the domain could, in this case, consist of a highly *redundant* rule set, with several different versions of each correct rule. A particular representation of the subject matter can then be created on-line, as it were, by selecting a subset of rules. This is the solution used in the tutoring systems by John Anderson and his co-workers (Anderson, Boyle, & Yost, 1985; Reiser, Anderson, & Farrell, 1985). Its success depends upon the procedure used for selecting the right subset of rules.

An entirely different approach to the obstacles caused by non-equifinalty in learning is to try to minimize the effects of the subject-matter representation on the tutoring effort, an idea which goes at right angles to the current direction of the field of computer tutoring, where most researchers seem intent on getting as much out of their domain experts as possible, once implemented. It is unclear to what extent a tutor can be made independent of its representation of the subject matter. It seems possible to design a diagnostic method which is not parasitic on the subject matter by using data-driven techniques. But it does not seem possible to design a tutoring strategy which can choose which topic to teach next without accessing a representation of the subject matter; indeed, such an idea seems self-contradictory.

However, one might imagine that we could program a general notion of *improvement of knowledge*. Such a notion would make it possible to construct a tutor which dispenses with a representation of the *target* knowledge, but bases its tutoring on a represenation of the student's *initial* knowledge instead. Such a tutor would try to make the student improve his knowledge, in any direction, applying its general criterion of improvement to guide the student's learning, not caring, as it were, where the student is going, as long as he is going somewhere. Whether it is possible to define a notion of knowledge improvement which is content-free enough to support such tutoring we do not know.

In short, the non-equifinality of learning poses serious problems in the construction of intelligent tutoring systems. It affects central aspects like diagnosis of the student and pedagogical decision making. No principled solution to this problem has been proposed yet.

4.0 TEACHING TACTICS

Consider a pianist playing a complicated piece, score spread out in from of him. In a sense, the player is trying to *follow* the score. He has a number of actions to choose from – all the key-presses, with the appropriate variations – and for each symbol in the score, each note, there is one action, one key-press, which is the right one; that single note is played in the context of the key, the tempo, and the adjacent notes. Consider how much more difficult it would be to play the piano, if the player were guided by a screen, on which the notes were projected one at a time, at the rate at which the piece should be played. The situation of the one-on-one tutor is similar. The tutor is following the learner, trying to respond to each action or performance or utterance with the right tutorial action.

Pushing the analogy one step further, consider what would happen if we deprived the piano player of the lower and the upper octaves, and perhaps of every other key in between as well. With such a narrow range of keys the player could not always follow the score. There would be many pieces of music that he could not play on such a mutilated instrument. As with playing the piano, so with one-on-one tutoring. If the tutor has a limited range of actions to choose from, it cannot adapt its teaching to the cognitive needs of the student. Where one student needs a definition, another needs an explanation, while a third student might learn better from a practice problem. This idea is simple but important, and so is expressed in the following principle.

> The Principle of Versatile Output. In order to provide adaptive instruction, a tutor must have a wide range of instructional actions to choose from.

An obvious source of information about useful instructional actions is the performance of teachers, in particular, expert teachers. (The computer tutor is not limited to the actions used by human teachers, but neither is there any reason to believe that it can make do with a *narrower* range of actions.) Inspired by Leinhardt and Greeno's (in press) careful analysis of the skill of teaching, let us think through the major types of teaching tactics needed for adaptive instruction.

In order to keep the following remarks within reasonable bounds, I will only consider tactics for teaching cognitive skills, like those involved in elementary mathematics.[9] The procedure to be taught will be referred to as the *target procedure.* I will define six classes of tactics and give some examples of each class. For the teaching of facts and principles, we have to imagine yet other tactics.

Category 1: Tactics for Presenting the Target

The actions in this category have to do with ways of presenting the target procedure. Obvious actions of this sort are to *define terms* needed to talk about the procedure, to *describe* the procedure, and to *prompt recall* of the procedure. A procedure can also be *demonstrated,* i.e., executed. In fact, there are several different kinds of demonstrations, such as *annotated* demonstrations, where the tutor explains and justifies each step as it is being executed, and *interactive* demonstrations, where the the student specifies the steps to be taken, but the tutor executes them. A procedure can also be *applied,* i.e., executed on a concrete example (e.g., the standard procedure for subtraction can be applied to, say, Dienes blocks). A procedure can also be *practiced,* of course, and there are many different types of practice: *guided* practice, in which the tutor specifies the steps one at a time, but the student executes them; *annotated* practice, in which either the tutor or the student justifies the steps as they are being executed; *corrected* practice, in which the tutor immediately corrects any incorrect step on the part of the student; practice in which the tutor *hints* at the correct steps; and sheer *drill,* in which the tutor does not intervene unless the student asks for help.

Category 2: Tactics for Presenting Precursors

A precursor to a target procedure is a skill that the learner is expected to have mastered before he attempts to learn the procedure. A precursor is usually, but not always, a prerequisite, i.e., a skill which constitutes a component of the target skill. The multiplication of integers is a precursor to the multiplication of fractions; it is also a prerequisite. But the multiplication of fractions is, in most schools, a precursor to the multiplication of

---

[9] No stand is implied on the old issue of whether mathematics should be taught through understanding or through drill.

decimals, but it is not a prerequisite. Actions in this category include the following: *priming*, in which the tutor reminds the student of the precursor by naming it or by locating it (e.g., "remember the theorem we learned last time"); *reviewing* the precursor; and *marking* those steps in a presentation which should be familiar, and distinguish them from those steps which are expected to be unfamiliar.

Category 3: Tactics for Presenting Purposes

The actions in this category serve to explain what the target procedure is *for*, what it is supposed to achieve. The tutor can describe the purpose of a new procedure by *giving a goal*, i.e., describing a desired result, and then introducing the target procedure as a method for achieving that result. Other tactics include to *criticize* the precursors by showing a problem for which they are insufficient, but which the target procedure can solve; to describe the target as a *generalization*, or, more generally, *replacement*, of the precursor (e.g., the arithmetic of decimals is, in a sense, a replacement for the arithmetic of fractions).

Category 4: Tactics for Presenting Justifications

The tutor can justify a procedure by *annotating* it, i.e., by relating each step in its execution to some principle. Another way is to *give transparent cases*, i.e., the tutor executes the target procedure on problems in which the steps taken are intuitively obvious (e.g., using unit fractions to show how multiplication of a fraction with an integer works). Yet another way is to relate the target procedure to some *equivalent procedure*, which already is justified; the target procedure then inherits the justification. The various ways of *verifying* the results of executing the target procedure constitute a useful subcategory. One can verify the outcome of a procedure by computing it with an *alternative* procedure, in some cases by applying the *inverse* procedure, or by making an *empirical* test of it.

Category 5: Tactics Related to Errors

The programming term "bug" is often used in the literature on intelligent tutoring systems to refer to systematic procedural errors. A tutor can *reveal* a bug in a procedure by applying the procedure on a problem where it will generate an obviously incorrect, absurd, or impossible result, or he can explicitly *mark* the buggy step as it is generated in execution. The tutor can also choose to *explain* a bug, i.e., to show which principle is being violated by the bug.

Category 6: Tactics Related to Student's Solutions

The most common tactics in this category are to *give feedback* and to *locate* the error. But a tutor can also *prompt a self-check* on the part of the student, *prompt a self-review* in which the student tries to describe a sequence of steps he has taken, or *prompt self-annotation*, i.e., exhort the student to justify his own steps.

The six categories of teaching tactics presented above is only an initial attempt to list the various actions an intelligent tutor needs in its behavioral repertoire in order to provide adaptive instruction in the acquisition of procedural knowledge. Further reflections and more detailed observations of expert teachers will no doubt lead to extensions of the list. Even as it stands, however, the above list is an order of magnitude richer than the behavioral repertoire of any existing intelligent tutoring system.

There are several reasons why current computer tutors tend to have limited output repertoires. First, many computer tutors are restricted in their *pedagogical scope*. For instance, some tutors do not teach or tutor in the ordinary sense of the word. Instead, they monitor practice, i.e., they generate practice problems and give feedback. Second, the richness of tutorial actions derives to a large extent from the variety of ways in which a particular knowledge unit can be presented. Unless the tutor can present its subject matter in more than one way, this richness will not be reflected in its action repertoire. Third, many tutorial systems have a narrow behavioral repertoire because they have a primitive diagnostic component. Unless the tutor can distinguish between many different cognitive states of the learner, it does not need a rich output repertoire. Fourth, many tutoring systems have a narrow behavioral repertoire because they have a simplistic teaching strategy. Unless the system designer knows how to make use of a particular teaching tactic – when, under what circumstances, to evoke it – then there is little purpose in implementing it.

> **The Principle of Strategic Repertoires.** The range of teaching tactics in a tutoring system is ultimately limited by the conditionality of the teaching strategy of the system; unless the strategy can identify circumstances under which a particular tactic is to be evoked, the tactic will not increase the power of the system.

Like the diagnostic component, the behavioral repertoire of an intelligent tutoring system is logically secondary to its teaching strategy.

5.0 STRATEGIES FOR TEACHING

Cognitive diagnosis and subject-matter analysis generate the "inputs" to a tutoring system, the information which forms the basis for its tutorial decisions. The teaching tactics discussed in the previous section, on the other hand, represent its "output," i.e., its behavior *vis-a-vis* the student. However, so far I have said nothing about *how to teach*, about how to generate a sequence of teaching tactics which will successfully transmit the subject matter to a particular student.

In spite of the fact that millions of teachers spend millions of hours every year teaching millions of students, nobody seems to know how to teach. There is no *Handbook of Pedagogical Methods* which we can take down from the shelf and from which we can read off the correct teaching strategy for some important part of the curriculum, such as arithmetic. Educators often invent interesting strategies for specific topics (e.g., Beede, 1985), but they have not made it part of their professional commitments either to empirically validate their proposals, or to explain, through theoretical analyses, why we should expect those proposals to be effective.

Psychologists are, of course, concerned with empirical verification, but, as a recent review reminds us (Bell, Costello, & Kuchemann, 1983, Chap. 7), they have chosen to work with global ideologies of teaching, rather than with specific teaching strategies. The section headings of Bell, Costello, and Kuchmeann (1983, Chap. 7) reads like so many old friends: exposition vs. discovery, meaningful vs. rote learning, learning hierarchies, advance organizers, etc., until, at the end, we reach the Grand Daddy of all topics in experimental educational research, the spacing of repetitions. Even if this research was in the habit of generating strong conclusions, such high-level ideas would only go part of the way towards the construction of specific teaching strategies. Cognitive scientists could have made it their business to analyze teaching, but, as we have seen, they believe that the greatest profits are to be found in the area of knowledge representation. In short, none of the three communities of scholars who are involved in research on education have made it their primary task to study teaching strategies.

The question to be asked here is how the goal of providing dynamically adaptive instruction constrains the method of teaching. What teaching strategies are compatible with this goal and which are not? I approach this question, first, by presenting an example of teaching methods invented by teachers, and, second, by analyzing the teaching strategies used in the most successful current computer tutors, primarily the tutors designed by John Anderson and his co-workers. In a third section, I outline a view of teaching which, I claim, is powerful enough to support adaptive instruction.

5.1 Plans in the Classroom

The classroom is an obvious source of inspiration when thinking about strategies for instruction. The methods being employed in classrooms have passed a stringent field test of sufficiency, since most school children do learn what they are supposed to learn. Leinhardt (1985) observed one expert teacher using the following plan for teaching multicolumn subtraction with regrouping:

1. Mix subtraction problems for which borrowing is necessary with the nonborrowing problems, and make the student observe and recognize them before he knows how to solve them, indeed, even before he has completely mastered nonborrowing subtraction.

2. Once subtraction without borrowing is understood, i.e., set the goal of learning how to solve the borrowing problems.

3. Leave the subtraction context, and teach the regrouping procedure in isolation. Prove its validity by presenting cases in which the learner can check that it works, i.e., that the value of the regrouped number is not changed by the procedure. Use concrete illustrations as well as numerical examples. Provide a large number of cases.

4. Move back to the context of subtraction, and show how the regrouping procedure can be applied to borrowing problems, i.e., to the class of problems that was set aside previously.

This plan emphasizes the fact that intelligent instruction does not consist of sequences of *unrelated* actions, but, on the contrary, coordinates several actions in the service of a particular pedagogical goal, in this case the goal of overcoming the common difficulties with the borrowing operation. The justification for a plan consists of means-ends relations, e.g., the plan above seems to be based on the idea that distinguishing between borrowing and nonborrowing problems from the beginning of instruction in subtraction helps the child learn the correct conditions for when to apply the regrouping operation. Such relations are not explicitly stated in the plan, but implicitly expressed in the way it orders the teaching tactics.

The means-ends structure of the plan is important, because some of the actions the teacher performs while executing the plan would serve no purpose, have no meaning, in isolation from the other actions. For instance, making the learner recognize and acknowledge borrowing problems before they can solve them has no meaning within the task of mastering nonborrowing subtraction. It is purposeful within the plan because it prepares the learner for the following step of learning how to borrow. As a second instance, the action of proving that the regrouping operation does not change the value of the regrouped number serves a purpose in the above plan only because the regrouping operation is later to be executed within the context of subtraction; outside that context, who cares whether the value of the number remains constant or not? In short, the teaching tactics in a plan are meaningful because of their means-ends relations to other parts of the plan.

The above plan has a number of other noteworthy properties. First, it extends over several lessons, coordinating a large number of what is known as *activity segments* (Leinhardt & Greeno, in press). Second, in all likelihood, the teacher proceeds according to the above plan every time she teaches subtraction with regrouping. The plan can be stored and used over and over again. Third, the plan presupposes a particular view of the subject matter, involving a cut between nonborrowing subtraction and borrowing subtraction and the identification of the regrouping operation as an educationally crucial subskill. This view is likely to be based on experience, rather than on rational analysis of the domain. Fourth, the plan seems to be based on some hypothesis about learning, although it is unclear how to state it. By way of illustration, we might conjecture that the teacher's hypothesis is that *integrating a subskill into its superskill is facilitated if both the subskill and the superskill are mastered before the integration occurs.*

As a second example, let us consider the following low-level plan, which applies when the teacher has discovered that a learner who has been taught the arithmetic of fractions nevertheless does not know how to multiply them correctly. The plan is taken from the teaching materials by (Hill, 1980).

1. Give the student graph paper that is twelve squares wide, and have him cut a strip that is twelve squares long and one square wide.

2. Review the definition of multiplication of whole numbers, explain the meaning of multiplication of fractions, and point out the similarities.

3. Demonstrate the meaning of 1/3 times 3/4 with the help of the strips. This is done as follows:

   (a) Take a twelve-squares long strip, and apply 3/4 to it, i.e., cut it to make a strip nine squares long.

   (b) Apply 1/3 to the nine-squares long strip, making a strip three squares long.

   (c) Count the number of squares in the remaining strip, thus establishing that 1/3 times 3/4 is 3/12.

4. Next, let the student solve the problems 5/6 times 1/2 and 1/4 times 1/3 in the same way.

5. Let the student generate verbal descriptions of these three problems and their solutions.

6. Help the student induce the following rule for multiplying fractions from their own descriptions: "To multiply two fractions, multiply the numerators and then multiply the denominators."

The basic properties of the previous plan are exemplified here as well: the means-ends structure and the existence of steps which would not be meaningful in isolation. But in contrast to the first example, this plan should only take a few minutes to execute. It is worth noticing that the actions in it are specified in detail, including the exact digits used in the examples.

Could we construct an intelligent tutoring system by storing teaching plans in the machine? We can readily imagine a library of such plans culled from observations of what teachers do, from recommendations of what they ought to be doing, and from our own imagination. For each teaching situation, the tutor could retrieve the appropriate plan and execute it.

From the point of view of individualized instruction, the disadvantage of a teaching plan is obvious. Because it consists of a pre-assembled list of actions, the plan has no capacity to adapt itself to the learner. Perhaps some learners acquire the regrouping procedure easier and with more understanding if it is taught in the context of solving subtraction problems. Clearly, what we want to do is to teach regrouping either within the context of subtraction or in isolation, depending upon our beliefs about the student. What is the teacher who uses the second of the above plans supposed to do with the student who, at Step 3(b) in the plan, produces a strip 6 squares long? Clearly, the rest of the plan then becomes irrelevant with respect to that student, but there is no information in the plan about what to do instead. There are no resources within a plan for accommodating changes.

The linear nature of the plan is both its beauty and its flaw. The sequential relations between the actions can encode complicated means-ends relations and so free the tutor from the need of computing those relations at run-time, as it were; but, exactly because they are not computed at run-time, those relations cannot be adapted to the changing cognitive needs of a particular learner. But the idea of a teaching plan should not be abandoned. The advantages of having a coordinating structure which maps out what tactics should be used in the service of a tutorial goal is very powerful. The idea of a plan is not faulty, only incomplete. Teachers do not execute their plans slavishly or without flexibility; they do not need to go on blindly to the plan's bitter end, if there is evidence that the student(s) are not benefiting from it. The idea of a teaching plan should be augmented with the knowledge teachers bring to the execution of their plans, so that the computer tutor can use its plans with the same flexibility.

The question of what is needed in order to use plans flexibly will be taken up again in a later section. The next section deals with the teaching strategies in current computer tutors.

5.2 Rules in the Machine

A second obvious source of inspiration with respect to teaching is the strategies which have been implemented in existing tutoring systems. For instance, the tutors constructed by John Anderson and his co-workers (Anderson, Boyle, & Reiser, 1985; Anderson, Boyle, & Yoost, 1985; Reiser, Anderson, & Farrell, 1985) are successfully implemented, state-of-the-art designs for teaching complicated subject matters like mathematics and programming; they are based on a theory of learning, empirically tested and – it is almost overwhelming – found to produce learning in ecologically valid settings. How do these tutors go about the task of teaching?

In brief, the strategy of the Anderson tutors is to watch the student closely and intervene when he makes an error. Let us see in some detail how this is done in, for instance, the Lisp tutor (Reiser, Anderson, & Farrell, 1985). The activity of the student while interacting with the Lisp tutor is to build a Lisp program (function), i.e., to write and combine calls to other programs (functions) according to the rules of Lisp. At the top level, the interaction between the tutor and the student consists of two parts: The tutor poses a programming task, and the student responds by typing in his solution, i.e., his code. The Lisp tutor has a knowledge base consisting of several hundred problem-solving rules which can solve the Lisp programming task, and several hundred more incorrect rules, representing typical novice programming errors. Every time the student takes a step towards completing his Lisp function, i.e., every time he types in a new part of his code, the tutor tries to map that step onto one of its rules. If the matching rule is a correct rule, the tutor does not intervene; if the matching rule is incorrect, the tutor explains the error. If the student nevertheless cannot continue on the correct solution, the tutor can show what the correct step is, or invoke a planning mode, in which the tutor demonstrates the algorithm to be programmed.

The geometry tutor (Anderson, Boyle, & Yoost, 1985) is built on the same basic design as the Lisp tutor. The student's activity in that case is to construct a geometry proof by successively applying geometric theorems, and the tutor compares his steps to a large knowledge base consisting of both correct and incorrect problem-solving rules. The tutor intervenes when the student applies an incorrect rule, i.e., makes illegal or useless moves in the space of possible inferences.

The teaching task performed by the Anderson tutors might be characterized as *the intelligent monitoring of student activity*. The student is struggling with an intellectual construction, and the tutor helps him complete it. To what extent is the help provided by the tutor adapted to the individual student, and how is this adaptability achieved? With respect to moment-by-moment flexibility, these tutors are hard to beat. The grain-size of the tutor's behavior is determined by the grain-size of the student's activity. For instance, the Lisp tutor can react to each Lisp atom as it is typed in; the geometry tutor can react to the selection of a theorem, or the application of it. Since the tutor decides whether to intervene, and, if so, how to intervene, after each action on the part of a the student, the flexibility of the tutor could not be greater without becoming irrelevant, as their designers point out (Reiser, Anderson, & Farrell, 1985, p. 12).

The question of whether the *content* of instruction is adapted to the cognitive needs of the learner is more complicated to answer. Recall that the tutor responds to each action on the part of the learner by mapping his action onto a problem-solving rule, and then retrieving the appropriate tutorial action connected with that rule. (For the sake of uniformity, I regard "doing nothing" as a kind of action.) This means that the student draws out of the tutor, as it were, a particular sequence of tutorial messages by generating a particular sequence of rule applications. Since the tutor knows several hundred different rules, the number of distinct lessons it is capable of delivering is astronomical. At *the level of the lesson*, then, the adaptation to the student is impressive.

However, this adaptivity is achieved with the help of predefined units. Each incorrect problem-solving rule is paired with a particular tutorial action, typically a stored message.[10] Any student who takes a step which matches a particular incorrect rule receives the message associated with that rule. For instance, a geometry student who applies a congruence theorem incorrectly for the first time receives the same instruction as a student who makes the same error, but who have also made a large number of other errors in applying congruency theorems. There is no on-line design of a tutorial message on the basis of the entire model of that student, i.e., on the entire set of rules he has used, rather than on a single rule. At *the level of the single tutorial action*, then, there is no adaptation to the current cognitive state of the learner other than the classification of his last step as an instance of a particular type of error.

It is instructive to consider how the Anderson architecture could be extended to allow tutors to base their tutorial decisions on more information about the student than his last step. The obvious solution is to write

---

[10] The messages contain variables which can be bound to the objects in the particular situation in which they apply. Strictly speaking, then, what is prestored is not the surface form of the message, but its tutorial gist.

tutorial rules which test for a *sequence* of steps on the part of the student,
e.g., "if the student has applied rules x, y, and z, then given him message
A," "if x, y, w, then message B," etc. The fallacy in this solution becomes
apparent when we consider the fact that the tutor knows many hundreds of
rules. A set of, say, 400 rules implies 1600 two-rule sequences, 640,000 three-
rule sequences, etc. The number of tutorial rules quickly grows beyond
practical limits. The more radical solution is to dissolve the prestored links
between the step-classifications, the rules, and the tutorial actions, the
messages, and replace them with intelligent agents which compute what
the appropriate tutorial message is, given a particular error by a particular
student in a particular problem-solving situation. However, this solution
is equally fallacious, because the term "intelligent agents" hides within it
all the problems of intelligent tutoring. If we knew how to design such
agents, we would construct one to *replace* the tutors John Anderson and
his co-workers have constructed. These two fallacious extensions illustrate,
I think, the boundaries of the Anderson tutoring architecture.

In summary, the Anderson tutoring architecture is geared towards
the intelligent monitoring of practice, and it is build around performance-
instruction pairs, where the performance part consists of a mechanism for
classifying a student's problem-solving steps as instances of particular errors and the instruction part consists of prestored tutorial messages relevant
to those errors. Given a large data base of such performance-instruction
pairs, a tutor delivers a lesson by responding to each error on the part of the
student as it occurs in the problem-solving context. The question of how
well these tutors adapt to the student receives different answers, depending
upon the level at which the question is asked. At the level of a particular
(incorrect) problem- solving step, each student receives the same tutorial
message; at the level of an entire problem-solving attempt, each student
receives a unique sequence of tutorial messages, as a function of his own
activity.

Other projects in the field of intelligent tutoring research have proposed
strategic rules for instruction as well. For example, the tutoring rules of
the GUIDON system (Clancey, 1982; 1983) are different in character from
performance-instruction pairs, because many of them, rather than recommend specific tutorial actions, revise the quantitative parameters of the
system, which, presumably, has global effects on how GUIDON carries out
its tutorial dialogue. The author's statement of the "set of tutoring principles that appear implicitly in the tutoring rules" (Clancey, 1983, p. 6)
does not explicitly treat the question of how to adapt the content of the
instruction to the individual. His principles deal with global aspects – attitudes, as it were – of the tutor. As an example, consider the principle,
"provide orientation to new tasks by top-down refinement." Such a principle does not tell us what to do with students who do not benefit from

top-down refinement. In short, the adaptability of the GUIDON system seems to be of the same nature as the adaptability of the Anderson tutors: Each student gets a unique lesson by drawing out a unique sequence of locally determined responses from the tutor. As a second example, consider the eleven pedagogic principles which Burton (1982, pp. 90–92) propose in connection with the WEST tutoring system. They, too deal with global aspects, attitudes, on the part of the tutor, e.g., "Do not intervene on two consequetive problem-solving steps, no matter what" (Principle 5). The rule which comes closest to have something interesting to say about how to shape the instruction is Principle 2: "If the student made a bad problem-solving step, the tutor should present an alternative step only if there exists an alternative step which is dramatically superior to the step the student took." In general, these rules seem rather far removed from the teaching plans we discussed in the previous subsection.

5.3 Teaching as Problem Solving

The notion of a teaching plan and the notion of a local performance-instruction unit are equally unsatisfactory as a basis for teaching. The reason for this is that neither notion helps us understand how a teaching goal (e.g., "explain borrowing") becomes translated into a sequence of teaching tactics designed to satisfy that goal (e.g., "mark borrowing problems," "prove invaliance under regrouping," etc.). Neither construct makes explicit the means-ends relations which connect what a teacher does with what he wants to achieve.

But understanding the connection between goals and actions is a prerequisite for the construction of artificial teachers capable of delivering adaptive instruction. As a conjecture, I propose that an intelligent tutor must have the following capabilities. First, it must be able to decompose its goals into subgoals. Second, it must be able to access descriptions of the student and of the subject matter and on their basis generate a plan for how to satisfy the tutoring goal. Third, it must be able to execute such a plan. Fourth, it must be able to detect mismatches between a student and a plan. As mentioned in the discussion of diagnosis, a teaching plan contains implicit expectations about what the student will do. When these expectations are violated, the plan is not quite right for that student. Finally, a tutor must be able to revise a plan, or generate a completely new plan for a particular tutoring goal. In summary, we should think of tutoring, I suggest, as proceeding through cycles, each cycle consisting of plan generation, plan execution, and plan revision. According to this view, the coordination of tutoring stems from a tutor's ability to follow a plan; the flexibility of tutoring stems from its ability to revise a plan.

The Principle of Teaching Plans. A tutor needs to be able to generate a teaching plan on the basis of its representation of the student, its knowledge of the subject matter, and its current tutorial goal; furthermore, it should be able revise its plan if it discovers that the plan does not fit the student.

This principle is not a teaching strategy, but it describes the kind of strategies I suggest we should be trying to incorporate into computer tutors. Whether tutors with such capabilities produce more learning than other kinds of tutors is not known. The above principle is only a *design hypothesis.*

Of course, the kind of system I have outlined in the above design hypothesis is entirely familiar: it is a *problem solver.* The topics of subgoaling, of plan generation, and plan revision are all familiar items in the discussion of problem solving. Thus, my suggestion could be restated by saying that a teacher needs a strategy for how to solve the problem of bringing the student from a state of ignorance to a state where he has acquired the subject matter. What research is relevant to the construction of such strategies?

The literature on formal analyses of problem-solving strategies in general is of course extensive (e.g., Pearl, 1984). But with respect to teaching strategies, in particular, the pioneering work of Gaea Leinhardt is the only available analysis. Leinhardt and Greeno (in press) present a general analysis at the skill of teaching. Leinhardt and Smith (1985) have applied the notion of a planning net (VanLehn & Brown, 1980) to the phenomenon of teaching, showing how one can generate a particular teaching plan from a structure of goals and a set of teaching tactics. This is the kind of generative mechanism that an intelligent tutoring system needs.

The theoretical analysis of teaching strategies presuppose detailed empirical studies of the strategies used by teachers. The studies by Leinhardt (1985), Leinhardt and Smith (1985), and Leinhardt and Greeno (in press) have already been mentioned. As a second instance of the kind of empirical work we need, let me mention the study by Collins and Stevens (1982) of rules for guiding Socratic dialogues in geography. These rules make recommendations about what kind of case the tutor should present and what kind of question to ask in response to particular properties of the current dialogue situation, e.g., "if one or more factors (such as heavy rainfalls) have been identified with respect to a particular value of the dependent variable (such as amount of rice grown), then ask if those factors are necessary conditions for that value or not." These strategies were identified in detailed studies of expert teachers.

In summary, I suggest that we view a one-on-one tutor as a problem solver who is trying to execute a teaching plan which will help the student to progress in his learning, constantly updating the plan on the basis of the student's performance. The theoretical research needed to implement this view of tutoring systems is to invent and formalize problem-solving strategies which can connect tutoring goals with teaching tactics. Such analyses, in turn, would be much helped if we had available, as a source of inspiration, a large collection of field-tested teaching plans. The empirical research needed to progress towards intelligent tutoring systems consists of detailed studies of expert teachers.

6.0 CONCLUSION

The present discussion opened with the claim that the promise and the challenge of computer tutors lie in their potential for providing instruction which is dynamically adapted to the learner. What kind of tutor is capable of delivering such instruction? Let us recapitulate the main course of the argument.

A tutoring system must have an internal representation of the student, in order to adapt its teaching to him. However, a student can be described in many ways. The only way to decide what kind of description is needed is to consider the function of the description within the tutoring system. The idea was advanced that the function of diagnosis is to test the viability of expectations implicit in teaching plans, which implies that the design of a diagnostic component depends upon the teaching strategy of the system.

A tutoring system must also have an internal representation of the subject matter, because in order to adapt its teaching to the individual learner, it must be able to generate the particular presentation of the subject matter which suits the learner best. The main difficulty in the representation of subject matter is that the learner can acquire many different internal representations of the subject matter, all equally satisfactory from an educational point of view. This ambiguity in where the learner is going causes difficulties for both the diagnosis of the student and the representation of the subject matter. There is no principled solution to this problem yet.

A tutoring system must, in order to be able to adapt its teaching to the individual learner have a large number of teaching tactics available, so that it can choose, at any one moment, that tactic which will benefit the learner most. Thus, in principle, the richer the behavioral repertoire of the tutoring system, the more adaptive it becomes.

Finally, in order to adapt its instruction to the individual learner, a tutor must be able to compute means-ends relations between its goals and its actions, and to make those relations dependent upon its representation of the student. From this perspective, a tutor is a problem solver, a point of view which has been most clearly expressed by Leinhardt and Greeno (in press). Like other artificial problem solvers, a tutoring system should be build around its strategy. Precise teaching strategies can be defined by applying formal analyses to detailed observations of expert teachers. The ultimate conclusion of the present analysis is that in order to construct artificial teachers, we must first discover how to teach.

ACKNOWLEDGEMENTS

To appear in *Instructional Science.*

Preparation of this manuscript was supported in part by NSF grant MDR-8470339, and in part by funds from the National Institute of Education (NIE), United States Department of Education. The opinions expressed do not necessarily reflect the position of NIE, and no official endorsement should be inferred. I thank my colleagues Jeff Bonar, Glynda Hull, and Gaea Leinhardt for useful comments on both content and style.

REFERENCES

Anderson, J.R. (1983). *The Architecture of Cognition.* Cambridge, MA: Harvard University Press.

Anderson, J.R., Boyle, D.F., & Reiser, B.J. (1985). Intelligent tutoring systems. *Science, 228*, 456–462.

Anderson, J.R., Boyle, C.F., & Yost, G. (1985, August). The geometry tutor. *Proceedings of the Ninth International Joint Conference on Artificial Intelligence*, 1–7.

Attisha, M., & Yazdani, M. (1983). A micro–computer based tutor for teaching arithmetic skills. *Instructional Science, 12*, 333–342.

Attisha, M., & Yazdani, M. (1984). An expert system for diagnosing children's multiplication errors. *Instructional Science, 13*, 79–92.

Bangert, R.L., Kulik, J.A., & Kulik, Chen–Lin, C. (1983). Individualized systems of instruction in secondary schools. *Review of Educational Research, 53*, 143–158.

Beede, R.B. (1985, October). Dot method for renaming fractions. *Arithmetic Teacher*, 44–45.

Bell, A.W., Costello, J., & Kuchemann, D.E. (1983). *A Review of Research in Mathematical Education. Part A. Research on Learning and Teaching.* Berks, U.K.: NFER – Nelson.

Brachman, R.J., & Levesque, H.J. (Eds.) (1985). *Readings in Knowledge Representation.* Los Angeles: Morgan Kaufmann.

Brown, J.S., & Burton, R.R. (1978). Diagnostic models for procedural bugs in basic mathematical skills. *Cognitive Science, 2*, 155–192.

Brown, J.S., Burton, R., & DeKleer, J. (1982). Pedagogical, natural language and knowledge engineering techniques in SOPHIE I, II, and III. In D. Sleeman & J.S. Brown (Eds.), *Intelligent Tutoring Systems*, 227–282. London: Academic Press.

Burton, R. (1982). Diagnosing bugs in a simple procedural skill. In D. Sleeman & J.S. Brown (Eds.), *Intelligent Tutoring Systems*, 157–183. London: Academic Press.

Carr, B., & Goldstein, I. (1977). Overlays: a theory of modeling for computer–aided instruction. (Tech. Rep. A.I. Memo 406). Cambridge: MIT.

Clancey, W.J. (1982). Tutoring rules for guiding a case method dialogue. In D. Sleeman & J.S. Brown (Eds.), *Intelligent Tutoring Systems*, 201–225. London: Academic

Press.

Clancey, W.J. (1983). Guidon. *Journal of Computer–Based Instruction, 10*, 8–15.

Collins, A., & Stevens, A.L. (1982). Goals and strategies of inquiry teachers. In R. Glaser (Ed.), *Advances in Instructional Psychology*, (Vol. 2, 65–119). Hillsdale, NJ: Erlbaum.

Gagne, R.M. (1962). The acquisition of knowledge. *Psychological Review, 69*, 355–365.

Gardner, M.K. (1985). Cognitive psychological approaches to instructional task analysis. In E.W. Gordon (Ed.), *Review of Research in Education*, (Vol. 12, 157–195). Washington, DC: American Educational Research Association.

Genter, D. & Stevens, A.L. (1983). *Mental models.* Hillsdale, NJ: Erlbaum.

Ginsburg, H.P. (1983). Cognitive diagnosis of children's arithmetic. *Issues in Cognition: Proceedings of a Joint Conference in Psychology*, 287–300. Washington, DC: National Academy of Sciences and American Psychological Association.

Glaser, R. (1976). The processes of intelligence and education. In L.B. Resnick (Ed.), *The Nature of Intelligence*, 341–352. Hillsdale, NJ: Erlbaum.

Glaser, R. (in press). The integration of testing and teaching. In *The Redesign of Testing for the 21st Century. The Proceedings of the 1985 ETS Invitational Conference.* Princeton, NJ: Educational Testing Service.

Grinder, R.E., & Nelsen, E.A. (1985). Individualized instruction in American pedagogy: the saga of an educational ideology and a practice in the making. In M.C. Wang & H.J. Walberg (Eds.), *Adapting Instruction to Individual Differences*, 24–43. Berkeley, CA: McCutchen.

Hill, M. (1980). *Diagnosis. An Instructional Aid.* Chicago: Science Research Association.

Johnson, W.L., & Soloway, E. (1983, August). *PROUST: Knowledge-based Program Understanding.* (Report No. Yale U/CSD/RD#285). New Haven, CT: Yale University, Dept. of Computer Science.

Johnson, W.L., & Soloway, E. (1984). Intention–based diagnosis of programming errors. *Proceedings of the AAAI Conference*, 162–168.

Kieren, T.E. (1976). On the mathematical, cognitive, and instructional foundations of rational numbers. In R.A. Lesh (Ed.), *Number and Measurement*, 101–145. Columbus, OH: ERIC Clearinghouse for Science, Mathematics, and Environmental Education.

Kieren, T.E. (1980). The rational number construct – its elements and mechanisms. In T.E. Kieren (Ed.), *Recent Research on Number Learning*, 125–149. Columbus, OH: ERIC Clearinghouse for Science, Mathematics, and Environmental Education.

Langley, P., Ohlsson, S., & Sage, S. (1984). *A Machine Learning Approach to Student Modeling*, (Tech. Rep. CMU-RI-TR-84-7). Pittsburgh: Carnegie-Mellon University, The Robotics Institute.

Leinhardt, G. (1985, March). *The Development of an Expert Explanation: An analysis of a Sequence of Subtraction Lessons.* Paper presented at the meeting of the American Educational Research Association, Chicago.

Leinhardt, G., & Greeno, J.G. (in press). The cognitive skill of teaching. *Journal of Educational Psychology.*

Leinhardt, G., & Smith, D.A. (1985). Expertise in mathematics instruction: Subject-matter knowledge. *Journal of Educational Psychology, 77*, 247–271.

Marshall, S.P. (1980). Procedural networks and production systems in adaptive diagnosis. *Instructional Science, 9*, 129–143.

Marshall, S.P. (1981). Sequential item selection: Optimal and heuristic policies. *Journal of Mathematical Psychology, 23(2)*, 134–152.

Newell, A., & Simon, H.A. (1972). *Human Problem Solving.* Englewood Cliffs, NJ: Prentice-Hall.

Nitko, A.J. (in press). Designing tests that are integrated with instruction. In R.L. Linn

(Ed.), *Educational Measurement*, (3rd ed.).

Ohlsson, S., & Langley, P. (in press). Psychological evaluation of path hypothesis in cognitive diagnosis. In H. Mandl & A. Lesgold (Eds.), *Learning Issues for Intelligent Tutoring*. New York: Springer Verlag.

Ohlsson, S., & Langley, P. (1985). Identifying solution paths in cognitive diagnosis. (Tech. Rep. CMU-RI-TR-85-2). Pittsburgh: Carnegie-Mellon University, The Robotics Institute.

Pearl, J. (1984). *Heuristics. Intelligent Search Strategies for Computer Problem Solving*. Reading, MA: Addison-Wesley.

Prietula, M., & Marchak, F. (1985, August). Expert variance: Differences in solving a dynamic engineering problem. *Proceedings of the Seventh Annual Conference of the Cognitive Science Society*, 335–340.

Reiser, A.J., Anderson, J. R., & Farrell, R.G. (1985, August). Dynamic student modelling in an intelligent tutor for Lisp programming. *Proceedings of the Ninth International Joint Conference on Artificial Intelligence*, 8–14.

Resnick, L.B. (1973). Hierarchies in children's learning: A symposium. *Instructional Science, 2*, 311–362.

Resnick, L.B., & Wang, M.C. (1969, June). Approaches to the validation of learning hierarchies. *Proceedings from the Eighteenth Annual Western Regional Conference on Testing Problems*. San Francisco.

Resnick, L.B., Wang, M.C., & Kaplan, J. (1973). Task analysis in curriculum design: A hierarchically sequenced introductory mathematics curriculum. *Journal of Applied Behavior Analysis, 6*, 679–710.

Sleeman, D. (1982). Assessing aspects of competence in basic algebra. In D. Sleeman & J.S. Brown (Eds.), *Intelligent Tutoring Systems*, 185–199. London: Academic Press.

Sleeman, D., & Brown, J.S. (Eds.). (1982). *Intelligent Tutoring Systems*. London: Academic Press.

Smedslund, J. (1969). Psychological diagnostics. *Psychological Bulletin, 71*, 237–248.

Soloway, E., Rubin, E., Woolf, B., Bonar, J., & Johnson, W.L. (1982, December). Meno-II: An AI based programming tutor. (Research Rep. #258). New Haven, CT: Yale University, Computer Science Dept.

Steiner, H.G. (1969). Magnitudes and rational numbers: A didactic analysis. *Educational Studies in Mathematics, 2*, 371–392.

Svenson, O., & Hedenborg, M.–L. (1980). Strategies for solving simple subtractions as reflected by children's verbal reports. *Scandinavian Journal of Educational Research, 24*, 157–172.

Thurstone, H.A. (Ed.). (1956). *The Number System*. New York: Dover Publications.

VanLehn, K. (1983). Felicity Conditions for Human Skill Acquisition: Validating an AI–based theory. (Tech. Rep. No. CIS–21). Palo Alto, CA: Xerox PARC.

VanLehn, K., & Brown, J.S. (1980). Planning nets: A representation for formalizing analogies and semantic models of procedural skills. In R.E. Snow, P.-A. Frederico, & W.E. Montague (Eds.), *Aptitude, Learning and Instruction: Vol 2. Cognitive Process Analysis and Problem Solving*, 95–137. Hillsdale, NJ: Erlbaum.

Wang, M.C., & Walberg, H.J. (Eds.) (1985). *Adapting Instruction to Individual Differences*. Berkeley, CA: McCutchan.

Waterman, D.A. (1986). *A Guide to Expert Systems*. Reading, MA: Addison-Wesley.

Waterman, D.A., & Newell, A. (1972). Preliminary results with a system for automatic protocol analysis. (CIP Rep. No. 211). Pittsburgh: Carnegie-Mellon University, Department of Psychology.

Wenger, E. (1985). AI and the communication of knowledge: An overview of intelligent tutoring systems. Irvine: University of California, Irvine Computational Intelligence Project, Department of Information and Computer Science.

Williams, M.D., & Hollan, J.D. (1981). The process of retrieval from very–long term memory. *Cognitive Science, 5*, 87–119.

Woolf, B., & McDonald, D.D. (1984, August). Context-dependent transitions in tutorial diaglogues. *Proceedings of the National Conference on Artificial Intelligence,* 355–361. University of Texas at Austin.

Young, R.M. (1976). *Seriation in Children. An Artificial Intelligence Analysis.* Basel, West Germany: Birkhauser Verlag.

Sleeman, D., & Brown, J. S. (Eds.). (1982). *Intelligent tutoring systems*. New York: Academic Press.

Wenger, E. (1987). *Artificial intelligence and tutoring systems*. Los Altos, CA: Morgan Kaufmann.

12 PIXIE: A SHELL FOR DEVELOPING INTELLIGENT TUTORING SYSTEMS

D. Sleeman

School of Education and
Knowledge Systems Laboratory*
Stanford University
Stanford, CA 94305

ABSTRACT

This paper reviews the inherent difficulties in producing highly adaptive CAI material. It points out the necessity of using AI techniques, and goes on to review recent research activities in ITSs (Intelligent Tutoring Systems). Student modelling is identified as an important capability for an Intelligent Tutoring System. The bulk of the paper describes an ITS Shell, PIXIE, which has that capability. (A shell is a system which is data-driven, and so can cope with different domains; specific knowledge of the domain is contained in the domain data-base). PIXIE's recent extension to include a remedial sub-system is also discussed. The paper concludes with a discussion of possible extensions to PIXIE.

1.0 INTRODUCTION

The early practitioners of CAI (Computer Aided Instruction) hoped that this technology would produce instructional materials that could adapt to the needs of the individual student (Alpert & Bitzer, 1970; Suppes & Morningstar, 1969). Although much good educational material has been produced using this approach, see for instance Bork (1979), I believe that the technology has fundamental limitations. Most author language-based systems, now, as two decades ago, are organized as a series of frames in which each frame has the following form:

- Name of the frame;

- Material (text and audio/visual) to be displayed to the student;

- List of answers anticipated by the teacher and associated destination node/actions.

---

*Current Address: Department of Computing Science, King's College, University of Aberdeen, AB9 2UB, Scotland, UK.

The set of responses that can be matched is predetermined by the instructional designer, and, consequently, answers from students who have difficulties or misunderstandings not anticipated by the teacher, or students who suggest a unique or different response, cannot be accommodated. The principal objection, then, is not that these programs do not make good decisions, rather these decisions and their rationale are buried in the text and are not accessible for analysis by the "delivery" system.

Several workers (e.g., Carbonell, 1970) believed that this form of adaption would be achieved only by using AI (Artificial Intelligence) techniques. Subsequently, Hartley and Sleeman (1973) proposed that ITSs (Intelligent Tutoring Systems) should make all their essential knowledge accessible, and further suggested that ITSs would normally contain the following databases:

- Knowledge of domain

- Student model/history

- List of teaching operations

- List of means-ends guidance (or tutorial) rules that correlate teaching operations with conditions in the student model.

These databases can, in principle, be accessed by *any* part of the ITS. Such an architecture should make for flexible designs, in that databases could be used in ways other than those for which they were initially intended.

During the 1970s, a series of ITSs were implemented. In reviewing the state of the art around 1980, Sleeman and Brown (1982) noted four major shortcomings in the field, namely:

"The instructional sequence produced in response to a student's query or mistake is often at the wrong level, as the system assumes too much or too little student knowledge.

The system assumes a particular conceptualization of the domain, thereby coercing a student's performance into its own conceptual framework. None of these systems can discover, and work within, the student's own (idiosyncratic) conceptualization to diagnose his "mind bugs" within that framework.

The tutoring and critiquing strategies used by these systems are excessively ad hoc, reflecting *unprincipled* intuitions about how to control their behavior. Discovering consistent principles would be facilitated by constructing better theories of learning and mislearning – a task requiring detailed psychological theories of knowledge representation and belief revision.

User interaction is still too restrictive, limiting the student's expressiveness and thereby limiting the ability of the tutor's diagnostic mechanisms." (p. 3).

Section 2 of this paper addresses some of the interdisciplinary research which is currently being undertaken to help address the issues listed above. Section 3 discusses a particular shell, PIXIE, for implementing ITSs, which creates detailed student models; current research aims to base effective remedial dialogues on these models.

2.0   A REVIEW OF CURRENT ACTIVITIES IN ITSs RESEARCH

By its very nature, research in Intelligent Tutoring Systems is an interdisciplinary activity which includes the fields of cognitive science, artificial intelligence, human-computer interface design, educational evaluation, etc. The principal current activities are reviewed below:

2.1 Cognitive Science and ITSs

At this time, there are two major activities, namely collecting empirical data about students' (mis)learning and about teaching processes, and, secondly, the formulation and testing of psychological theories, or heuristics.

2.1.1 Empirical Studies

In my view, empirical studies continue to be an important precursor to building an ITS – if one does not have a good knowledge of students' misunderstandings in a domain, it is not possible to produce an effective ITS (or CAI system, for that matter). ITS workers involved in collecting such data from empirical studies include Sleeman (1982a, 1985a) and Soloway et al., (1982); data collected by cognitive scientists not directly involved with ITS research are also useful (e.g., Davis, 1984; Gentner & Stevens, 1983). Similarly, if one wishes ITSs to emulate aspects of how a teacher tutors or remediates, one must study these activities (e.g., Clancey, 1985; Collins, Warnock, & Passafiume, 1974; Kelly & Sleeman, 1985).

2.1.2   Formulation and Testing of Psychological/Educational "Theories"

The field of ITSs – being part of expert systems research – is committed to codifying expertise, translating, as it were, "art into science". For example, the "art" of medical diagnosis (Shortliffe, 1976), and the "art" of designing synthesis paths for complex chemical molecules (Wipke et al., 1977)

have been shown to be reducable to systematic algorithms. A major aim of
the ITS field is to do precisely that for the "art" of instruction. Given that
there are no broad-based theories available to predict how students learn
different subject areas, it is thus entirely appropriate that this knowledge
should be captured as a series of ad hoc heuristics. So far, only one group
of ITS workers, those at Carnegie-Mellon University, have claimed there is
a tight coupling between a psychological theory, ACT* (Anderson, 1983),
and the design and implementation of their ITSs (Anderson et al., 1984).
The ACT* theory is concerned with understanding how practice effects the
learning of topics for which there is a well-articulated algorithm.

Further, although the aim of systematically encoding teaching/tutor-
ing/instructional knowledge is a laudable one, if one takes seriously the
findings of the ATI (Aptitude Treatment Interaction) work of Cronbach
and Snow (1977), it would appear that there is little likelihood of producing
instruction that is uniquely individualized. ATI results indicate that it is
merely possible to say that Treatment A worked on Topic T on Day D with
Teacher P, and that it is *not* possible to infer any generalizations to other
situations. For example, Treatment A has been shown *not* to work with the
same student on what appears to be a highly related topic with the same
teacher. Cronbach and Snow (1977) argue:

"No Aptitude X Treatment interactions are so well confirmed that they
can be used directly as guides to instruction." (p. 492)

The proposers of theories of human learning *assume* that their theories
have *universal* applicability. The ATI work suggests that these workers,
including Anderson, should specify the range of conditions under which
their psychological theory is applicable.

The Carnegie group claims that their tutors conform to and incorporate eight psychological principles (Anderson et al., 1984). I would like
to raise two issues – the first questions whether all of their practices are
consistent with these principles, and the second questions whether the principles are themselves sufficient for all instruction. Firstly, I note that the
ITSs produced by the group give targetted remediation to some errors, but
merely state what should be done in response to other sorts of errors. Is
this dual treatment of errors the result of some theoretical insight or does
it follow from the pragmatic (ad hoc) knowledge of frequently occurring
errors? Namely, the knowledge that good human tutors and workers in the
fields of CAI and ITS have been using for decades? Secondly, I question
whether keeping students on the "straight and narrow" – the correct – instructional path is optimal under all conditions. Programmed instruction
and early "linear" CAI were found to be boring and ineffective. More recent work on metacognition (Brown, 1975) suggests that allowing students

to explore their environment and to introspect on the process can be highly effective. Sleeman and Brown (1982) note:

> "Some floundering can be vitally important. The crucial meta-skill of knowing when one's floundering is useless can only be discovered by trial and error. The subtlety of separating potentially productive exploration from useless wanderings only points to the challenges of constructing sensitive and well-motivated tutorial principles." (p.2)

2.2 Educational Evaluation of ITSs

The ITS field is beginning to undertake detailed evaluations both *before* and *after* the introduction of innovation. John Anderson has recently demonstrated that students using the CMU LISP tutor performed better than students in a standard classroom and nearly as well as students with personal tutors (Anderson & Reiser, 1985). Sleeman (1982a) reported that his diagnostic modelling system, LMS, gave essentially the same detailed diagnosis for an individual student as that of three experienced mathematics educators (whereas, it should be noted that most hard-pressed teachers would only have recorded that the students' answers were right or wrong, thereby missing a great deal of valuable diagnostic information).

2.3 ITS and AI Research

The activities reviewed here include the issues of student modelling and the inference of plans from student programs. Indeed, these are related activities.

2.3.1 Student Modelling

Sleeman and Brown (1982) identified student-modelling as being a major thrust in their review. Considerable work continues on user- and student-modelling: for a recent overview of this work see Sleeman et al. (1985) and Sleeman (1985b). In particular, we have been addressing the challenging problem of inferring previously unencountered mal-rules from protocols, given additional knowledge about the domain (Sleeman, 1982b; Hirsh & Sleeman, 1985). This is intrinsically a very open-ended problem, as student responses are essentially unbounded and frequently very noisy, i.e., students make "random" errors.

2.3.2 Inference of Plans for Student Programs

This is analogous to student modelling. Genesereth (1982) implemented a system that was able to infer the plan of a user of MACSYMA, an algebraic manipulation package. More recently, Soloway and his co-workers have implemented PROUST, which is able to infer plans from a student's PASCAL program (Johnson & Soloway, 1983). The latter argue that it is necessary to have such a plan to be able to comment meaningfully on the errors made by the student programmer.

2.4 AI Technology

The two topics to be reviewed here are the design of tutorial dialogues and the implementation of shells as aids for the building of Intelligent Tutoring Systems. I have chosen to classify these issues as technology and not research per se, as I believe that no principles have so far evolved for the design of dialogues, and that each instance needs to be hand-crafted. On the other hand, I believe we do understand at some level the principles behind model building, and the building of shells is an attempt to make these techniques more readily accessible so that knowledge bases can be created for several domains.

2.4.1 Engineering Tutorial Dialogues

Even if one had a precise model for a student, decisions would still need to be made about *when* the remediation should take place, and the form of that remedial dialogue (whether it should be example- or rule-based, etc.). Generally, we need to engineer the dialogue so that it flows nicely from one topic to the next, bearing in mind comments made earlier in the dialogue. (Exactly what Weizenbaum's ELIZA program was *unable* to achieve (Weizenbaum, 1966). ELIZA was generally able to deal effectively with the latest input, but had no "memory". So having been told early in a dialogue that the patient's father had died, it was quite capable of asking subsequently what the patient's father thought about a topic.) I have classified as "engineering" the several techniques for controlling such dialogues, because they appear to be a series of ad hoc heuristics, which do not provide any deep insights into how humans control dialogues. (A model that gave insights as to how humans controlled dialogues would be considered to be a contribution to cognitive *science*.) The explanation work of the Guidon project (Hasling et al., 1984) and the work of the University of Massachusetts' group (Woolf & McDonald, 1984) both have this flavour.

2.4.2 ITS Shells as Aids for System Building

Following Shortliffe's pioneering work with MYCIN (Shortliffe, 1976), there has been considerable interest in making a separation between the inference engine and its knowledge base (vanMelle, 1980). Users of shells such as EMYCIN have only to implement a knowledge base for a new domain and *not* a complete system. In the area of Intelligent Tutoring

Systems, several shells have been implemented to date; these include shells with somewhat differing characteristics:

- BIP (Wescourt et al., 1977): a system that uses a curriculum script (and a set of topics to be instructed) to control the task selection process.

- BYTE (Bonar, 1985): an instructional system driven by a curriculum network, which includes detailed descriptions of the knowledge to be communicated.

- Micro-SEARCH (Sleeman, in press): A system that allows students to explore solution-spaces produced by non-deterministic tasks.

- LMS/PIXIE (Sleeman, 1982a): A data-driven diagnostic/remedial system, which will be described in greater detail in the next section.

The next section gives a detailed description of PIXIE.

3.0 PIXIE AS AN ITS SHELL

3.1 Introduction to PIXIE and Its Databases

PIXIE is an Intelligent Tutoring System that attempts to identify student errors in a particular domain; it is essentially a diagnostic modelling system; recent research has been aimed at implementing a remedial sub-system which is based on the inferred diagnostic models. This sub-system has again been implemented in a domain-independent way, and thus requires additional information to be provided in the knowledge-base. PIXIE gives a student a range of tasks, interprets his/her answers and determines individual problem-solving strategies and consistent bugs. If the appropriate option is selected, it will attempt to remediate the student if this is necessary. The overall structure of the several programs that constitute the PIXIE system is given in Figure 1.

In order to give a fast response, PIXIE compares the student's answer with solutions and *models* that have been created previously in an "offline" phase. These models incorporate typical bugs, predetermined through paper tests and one-to-one interviews. Therefore, during the on-line phase, PIXIE is able to detect only previously-encountered bugs. (Getting a program to detect such bugs is a research topic that we are currently pursuing (Sleeman, 1982b; Hirsh & Sleeman, 1985).) For the moment, unanticipated answers that are not matched can currently be reprocessed during the post-interaction analysis phase. If these bugs are consistent, it is possible to add them to the existing database.

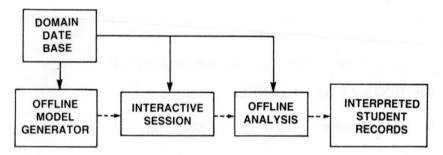

Figure 1: The PIXIE Modelling System

The complete PIXIE modelling system has been developed so that it can be used with numerous subject areas. Each domain is represented by components called "task sets", "good rules", and "mal-rules" ("buggy" rules), which – together with other parameters – form a database, or knowledge base.

3.2 Developing a Domain

In order for a diagnosis to be specific, it is frequently necessary for the domain of a database to be narrow, so that the bugs and strategies one wishes to uncover are unambiguous. For example, an arithmetic database that includes addition, subtraction, multiplication, division of integers and fractions, and order of operations would be much too broad. On the other hand, analyzing arithmetic operations with small negative integers is feasible and important since students find this task difficult (Ashlock, 1982). In the rest of this sub-section, the principal components of the PIXIE databases will be introduced in a non-technical way (technical detail will be provided in Section 3.3).

3.2.1 Rules and Mal-rules

One must decide on a complete and consistent set of concepts and operations in the domain, and then determine possible difficulties that students have. In the negative numbers domain, sample tests could include adding and subtracting negative numbers. Some students replace addition with subtraction (and vice versa); they also lose or add a minus sign. Therefore, for a task like $5 - 7$, the valid operation produces the answer -2, while "buggy" procedures give the answers 2, 12, and -12. In the PIXIE system, the "good" procedure is represented by a "rule", and incorrect, "buggy" methods by distinct "mal-rules".

3.2.2 Tasks Sets

During an interactive session, a student is presented with several "task sets", each of which tests a particular construct and contains a variable and implementer-determined number of tasks. The tasks in a particular task-set should be of similar form. For example, while a mathematically literate person would see the task $-7 + 5$ as "equal" to the above example $(5 - 7)$, a learner may not. Therefore, in the negative number database, one task-set should contain tasks of the form $A - B$ and another set of the form $-B + A$.

3.2.3 Template Models

In the database, each task-set has a corresponding "template model" that contains the set of rules that, when "fired", will solve correctly all the tasks in a particular task-set. The rule order in a model is significant, because the modeller executes the first rule whose conditions are satisfied. This provision is a convenient mechanism for replicating precedence requirements, which are important in many domains. For example, to correctly solve the expression $4 + 5 \times 3$ the multiplication operation must be used first, and this is simulated by a multiplication rule preceding an addition rule in the template. A "buggy" model can be created (to demonstrate a precedence problem) by switching these rules. The offline part of the PIXIE modelling system generates good models, and generates incorrect models by substituting mal-rules into the templates, and further produces all significant orderings of rules and mal-rules.

3.3 Creating a Simple Database

A version of the PIXIE system (and its databases) has been written in many dialects of LISP, including IQ-LISP for the IBM-PC micro-computer. (A Common LISP version will be available shortly).

3.3.1 Database Contents

Every database used by the PIXIE modelling system must contain:

1. PRINT & PACKAGING – Package and file heading (required by IQ-LISP).

2. EGS – A list of all task sets.

3. GBRLS – A list of all rule names and associated mal-rules.

4. RULES – A list of all rule definitions.

5. TM – A list of template models corresponding in order to the task sets.

6. IDEAL – A list of rules that will solve any problem.

7. SINTLS – A list of interaction rules; the first sub-list corresponds to the interaction at the first level, etc.

8. PRULELST – A list of mal-parsing rules.

9. BASICRLS – A list of completion rules.

10. SUBLS – A list of rules that subsume each other.

11. G2 – The grammar syntax for the database; all student input is parsed against this grammar.

12. TRM1 – A list of terminating symbols for the grammar.

13. PROMPT1 – The initial student prompt during a session.

14. PROMPT2 – A second prompt used when a student must evaluate his answer further.

15. INTLIST – A list of comments for interacting rules.

16. A-COMMENTS – A list of comments relating to each rule for use in remediation. (Imperative form).

17. A-COMMENTS-DONE – A list of comments relating to each rule for use in remediation. (Reports action done).

18. Predicate definitions.

Variables that are not used within a particular database may be omitted, as the system will give them a default value. The following is a simple database that contains only *correct* rules for the domain of negative integers. Various mal-rules will be added in later examples.

3.3.2 The "Correct" Version of the NEGNUM (Negative Number) Database

A database that is capable of correctly solving negative integer tasks is given in Figure 2. (See Appendix A for an explanation of rule syntax.)

3.3.3 Explanation for the Execution of a Production Rule

The template (or ideal) model for level 1 is (SUBNEG FIN) and the first task for this task-set is $(5 - 7)$. Below, I give the trace of PIXIE's production system handler as it solves the task with that model; the left-hand column gives the name of the rule that fired and the right-hand column gives the value of the state:

	(SHD 5 − 7)
SUBNEG	(SHD −2)
FIN	(SHD −2)

(Note: SHD is an abbreviation for "String Head" and is an artifact to help reduce the complexity of domain rules. The global variable, STATE, initially contains the task to be solved, and subsequently contains the intermediary values.)

Below, I explain the structure of a rule, how it matches against the original task and how it returns a value (which becomes the next value for the state). Each rule has a *condition* and an *action* part. For the SUBNEG rule, the condition part is:

$$(!L \; (*R >M \; POSNUM) - (*R >N \; GTNUM) \; !R)$$

and the action part is:

$$(NAPPEND \; L \; (LIST \; (- M \; N)) \; R)$$

Matching the condition part of a rule can be a non-deterministic process as strings such as !L and !R are able to match against either none or many tokens in the state. Clauses of the form $(*OR >OP + - \times)$ specify that the condition element can be satisfied only if the state contains one of the literals $+$, $-$ or $\times$.

Figure 2:   NEGNUM Database: Version 1 –
                       Only "Correct" Rules

~
~ NEGNUM
~

```
(PRINT 'NEGNUM)
(PACKAGE NEGNUM                        PACKAGE list includes all
  (SETQ EGS GBRLS RULES TM IDEAL       values and functions which
SINTLS PRULELST BASICRLS SUBLS)        must be defined in a
  (SETQ G2 TRM1 PROMPT1 PROMPT2)       database
  (SETQ INTLIST A-COMMENTS
A-COMMENTS-DONE)
  (DEF NEGNUM POSNUM GTNUM))
(SETQ EGS                              EGS is the list of problems
  '(((5 - 7)(3 - 8)(6 - 10)            in the task sets for the
    (2 - 12))                          NEGNUM database.  Note
   ((-8 - 4)(-4 - 8)(-12 - 3)          that there are nine task
    (-1 - 4))                          sets each of which includes
   ((-4 + 3)(-9 + 12)(-5 + 5)          four examples.
    (-6 + 10))
   ((-6 * 4)(-5 * 7)(-3 * 3)
    (-2 * 8))
   ((-3 * -5)(-1 * -4)(-4 * -4)
    (-6 * -3))
   ((4 * -5)(1 * -8)(3 * -3)
    (8 * -5))
   ((-8 / 2)(-15 / 3)(-5 / 5)
    (-20 / 4))
   ((-35 / -7)(-8 / -2)(-10 / -10)
    (-24 / -6))
   ((30 / -5)(40 / -4)(9 / -9)
    (18 / -3))))
(SETQ GBRLS                            GBRLS are the good and bad
  '((FIN (FIN))(SUBNEG (SUBNEG))       rules that apply to a given
    (SUBNEG2 (SUBNEG2))                rule.  In this database
    (SUBNEG3 (SUBNEG3))                there are only good rules,
    (MULNEG (MULNEG))                  otherwise the sublists
    (DIVNEG (DIVNEG))))                would contain mal-rules
                                       also.

(SETQ RULES                            RULES defines the structure and
  '((FIN ((SHD (*R >M NUMBERP))        actions of each rule:
    (LIST (QUOTE FIN) M)))             FIN is the final rule.
   (SUBNEG ((!L (*R >M POSNUM)         SUBNEG evaluates "M-N" where
    - (*R >N GTNUM) !R)                M is positive and N is
    (NAPPEND L (LIST (- M N)) R)))     greater than M.
   (SUBNEG2 ((!L (*R >M NEGNUM)-       SUBNEG2 evaluates "M-N" when
    (*R >N NUMBERP) !R)                M is negative.
    (NAPPEND L (LIST (- M N)) R)))
   (SUBNEG3 ((!L (*R >M NEGNUM) +      SUBNEG3 evaluates "M+N" if
```

```
  (*R >N NUMBERP) !R)                     M is negative.
  (NAPPEND L (LIST (+ M N)) R)))
(MULNEG ((!L (*R >M NUMBERP) *           MULNEG evaluates "M*N".
  (*R >N NUMBERP) !R)
  (NAPPEND L (LIST (* M N)) R)))
(DIVNEG ((!L (*R >M NUMBERP) /           DIVNEG evaluates "M/N".
  (*R >N NUMBERP) !R)
  (NAPPEND L (LIST (/ M N)) R))) ))
(SETQ TM                                 TM is the list of template
  '((SUBNEG FIN)(SUBNEG2 FIN)            models.  These are the models
   (SUBNEG3 FIN)(MULNEG FIN)             that will answer the task sets
  (MULNEG FIN)(MULNEG FIN)               correctly.  Notice that each
    (DIVNEG FIN)(DIVNEG FIN)             template in this list
     (DIVNEG FIN)))                      sequentially corresponds to
                                         a task set, i.e., there are
                                         9 task sets and 9 template
                                         models in NEGNUM.

(SETQ IDEAL                              IDEAL represents a model
  '(DIVNEG MULNEG SUBNEG                 that will answer any problem
   SUBNEG2 SUBNEG3 FIN))                 in this domain correctly.
(SETQ SINTLS                             SINTLS is the interaction list
  '(NIL NIL NIL NIL NIL NIL              and will be explained later.
   NIL NIL NIL))
(SETQ PRULELST                           PRULELST is the Mal-Parsing
  'NIL)                                  rule list.  Note that even
                                         though it is not used in the
                                         NEGNUM database, it is
                                         defined to NIL.

(SETQ BASICRLS                           BASICRLS is the completion
  '(NIL))                                rule list.
(SETQ SUBLS                              SUBLST is a list of rules which
  '((DUMMY (DUMMY))))                    subsume each other.  In this
                                         database it is not used, but if
                                         by invoking one rule another
                                         is unable to fire (i.e., it is
                                         subsumed), then the rules are
                                         listed here with the subsumed
                                         rule in the sublist.

(SETQ G2                                 G2 defines the syntactic grammer
  '((G (OR (AND *SHD *QUIT)              for tasks in NEGNUM.
(AND RHS)))(RHS (AND *SHD
EXPR))
(EXPR (OR (AND *OP TERM *OP EXPR)
(AND TERM *OP EXPR) TERM))
(TERM (OR BRAEXP REMEXP DECEXP
*NUM))
(BRAEXP (AND *OB EXPR *CB))
(REMEXP (AND *NUM REM *NUM))
(DECEXP (AND *NUM *SEPARATOR *NUM))
(REM (OR *REM *REMAINDER))))
(SETQ TRM1                               TRM1 is a list of terminal symbols.
  '((*QUIT (Q))(*OP(+ - * /))
```

```
(*OB ((QUOTE OB)))(*CB((QUOTE CB)))
(*SHD(SHD))(*REM (REM))
(*REMAINDER (REMAINDER))
(*SEPARATOR (DEC))))
```

```
(SETQ PROMPT1
  "Solve")
```
PROMPT1 is shown at the beginning
of every problem.

```
(SETQ PROMPT2
  "Simplify")
```
PROMPT2 is used when a student must
evaluate his answer further.

```
(SETQ INTLIST 'NIL)
```
INTLIST
is a list of comments for
interacting rules.

```
(SETQ A-COMMENTS
  '((FIN("FINISH"))
    (SUBNEG("Subtract"))
    (SUBNEG2("Subtract"))
    (SUBNEG3("Subtract"))
    (MULNEG ("Multiply"))
    (DIVNEG ("Divide")) ))
```
A-COMMENTS is the explanations
of rules and mal-rules and is used
for remediation and analysis.
(Comments are imperatives.)

```
(SETQ A-COMMENTS-DONE
  '((FIN ("FINISHED"))
    (SUBNEG ("Subtracted))
    (SUBNEG2 ("Subtracted"))
    (SUBNEG3 ("Subtracted"))
    (MULNEG ("Multiplied"))
    (DIVNEG ("Divided")) ))
```
A-COMMENTS-DONE is the
explanation of rules and mal-rules
and is used for remediation and
analysis. (Comments are past
tense.)

```
(DEF 'NEGNUM
  '[LAMBDA (N)
  (COND
    [(AND (NUMBERP N)
      (MINUSP N))
    T]
    [T
    NIL])])
```
NEGNUM is a predicate which
returns T for a negative integer
and NIL otherwise.

```
(DEF 'POSNUM
  '[LAMBDA (N)
  (COND
    [(AND (NUMBERP N)
      (NOT (MINUSP N)))
    T]
    [T
    NIL])])
```
POSNUM is a predicate that
returns T if the parameter is a
positve integer and NIL
otherwise (i.e., negative).

```
(DEF 'GTNUM
  '[LAMBDA (NN)
  (COND
    [(AND (NUMBERP NN)
      GT NN M))
    T]
    [T
    NIL])])
```
GTNUM is a function that returns
T if the parameter is greater
that the defined
value for the variable "M".

Clauses of the form (*R >M POSNUM) are satisfied only if the next literal in the state satisfies the predicate that tests if the literal is a positive integer (in this case the implementor-defined predicate POSNUM). Similarly GTNUM is a user-defined predicate to check if the next item is a number greater than the integer bound to the global variable, M. (Literals can also form part of the condition-list). If all the conditions in a condition-list are satisfied, the match succeeds; otherwise it fails and no variables are bound.

Consequently, in this case, the rule SUBNEG results in the following bindings:

L is bound to (SHD), M to 5, N to 7 and R to NIL.

Appendix A.1 discusses the syntax of the possible condition elements, and Appendix A.2 explains how rules return values.

Note that if a rule does *not* successfully match, the production-rule handler tries to match the *next* rule against the state. If *no* rule is satisfied, an error is reported. After a rule has successfully matched, the match-process starts again with the *first* rule in the model, in this case SUBNEG. In this example, SUBNEG fails on the second cycle when the state is (SHD −2); however, FIN succeeds and returns a state that indicates to the production-system interpreter that the evaluation cycle has successfully completed.

3.3.4 Generating Models

The offline model generator uses each template model defined in the database to produce a complete set of "models" in which all meaningful orders of rules are proposed. Additionally, it substitutes the appropriate mal-rules for each good rule in each of the "models". The resulting models are then applied to the corresponding task-set to produce all correct and "buggy" answers. However, in the above version of the NEGNUM database (the Negative Number database) there are no mal-rules, so the model generator only creates ideal models, i.e., the templates provided. (For more details of the generation process, see below.) If a student used PIXIE with this database and answered any question incorrectly, his behavior could not be matched by PIXIE.

3.3.5 Negative Number Database with Some Mal-rules

What follows is an updated version of NEGNUM, that includes some mal-rules. These new rules will demonstrate various errors, or mal-rules, which we have noted with this student population. Below, I give only the parts that *differ* from the earlier database.

Figure 3:   NEGNUM Database, Version 2 – Mal-Rules
(Differences only from Figure 2)

```
(SETQ GBRLS
 '((FIN (FIN))(FIN2 (FIN2))
  (SUBNEG (SUBNEG M1SUBNEG
 M2SUBNEG M3SUBNEG))
  (SUBNEG2 (SUBNEG2 M1SUBNEG2
 M2SUBNEG2 M3SUBNEG2))
  (SUBNEG3 (SUBNEG3 M1SUBNEG3
 M2SUBNEG3 M3SUBNEG3))
  (MULNEG (MULNEG M1MULNEG
 M2MULNEG))(DIVNEG (DIVNEG
 M1DIVNEG M2DIVNEG)) ))
```

GBRLS now contains sets of good and bad rules for each rule type.

```
(SETQ RULES
 '((FIN ((SHD (*R >M NUMBERP))
  (LIST (QUOTE FIN) M)))
  (FIN2 ((SHD (*R >M NUMBERP) /
  (*R >N NUMBERP))
  (LIST (QUOTE FIN) (LIST M N))))
  (SUBNEG ((!L (*R >M POSNUM) -
  (*R >N GTNUM) !R)
  (NAPPEND L (LIST (- M N)) R)))
  (M1SUBNEG ((!L (*R >M POSNUM) -
  (*R >N GTNUM) !R)
  (NAPPEND L (LIST (- M N)) R)))
  (M2SUBNEG ((!L (*R >M POSNUM) -
  (*R >N GTNUM) !R)
  (NAPPEND L (LIST (+ M N)) R)))
  (M3SUBNEG ((!L (*R >M POSNUM) -
  (*R >N GTNUM) !R)
  (NAPPEND L (LIST (- (MINUS M)
 N)) R)))
  (SUBNEG2 ((!L (*R >M NEGNUM) -
  (*R >N NUMBERP) !R)
  (NAPPEND L (LIST (- M N)) R)))
  (M1SUBNEG ((!L (*R >M NEGNUM) -
  (*R >N NUMBERP) !R)
  (NAPPEND L (LIST (- (MINUS M)
 N)) R)))
  (M2SUBNEG2 ((!L (*R >M NEGNUM)SPACE-
  (*R >N NUMBERP) !R)
  (NAPPEND L (LIST (MINUS (- M N)))
 R)))
  (M3SUBNEG2 ((!L (*R >M NEGNUM)SPACE-
  (*R >N NUMBERP) !R)
  (NAPPEND L (LIST (+ M N)) R)))
  (SUBNEG3 ((!L (*R >M NEGNUM) +
  (*R >N NUMBERP) !R)
  (NAPPEND L (LIST (+ M N)) R)))
```

RULES now contains the definitions of the mal-rules:

FIN2 is a final rule which handles fractional answers.

SUBNEG evaluates "M-N" correctly.

M1SUBNEG evaluates "M-N" incorrectly as "N-M".

M2SUBNEG evaluates "M-N" as "M+N".

M33SUBNEG evaluates "M-N" incorrectly as "-M-N".

SUBNEG2 evaluates "M-N" when M is negative.

M1SUBNEG2 evaluates "M-N" as "-M-N".

M2SUBNEG2 evaluates "M-N" improperly as "-(M-N)".

M3SUBNEG2 evaluates "M-N" incorrectly as "M+N".

SUBNEG3 evaluates "M+N" if M is negative.

```
(M1SUBNEG3 ((!L (*R >M NEGNUM)SPACE+
(*R >N NUMBERP) !R)
(NAPPEND L (LIST (MINUS (+ M N)))
R)))
```
M1SUBNEG3 evaluates "M+N" incorrectly
as "-M+N".

```
(M2SUBNEG3 ((!L (*R >M NEGNUM) +
(*R >N NUMBERP) !R)
(NAPPEND L (LIST (+ (MINUS M)
N)) R)))
```
M3SUBNEG3 evaluates "M+N" as
"-M+N".

```
(M3SUBNEG3 ((!L (*R >M NEGNUM)+
(*R >N NUMBERP) !R)
(NAPPEND L (LIST (+ M (MINUS N)))
R)))
```
M3SUBNEG3 evaluates "M+N" as
"M+(-N)".

```
(MULNEG ((!L (*R >M NUMBERP) *
(*R >N NUMBERP) !R)
(NAPPEND L (LIST (* M N)) R)))
```
MULNEG evaluates "M*N".

```
(M1MULNEG ((!L (*R >M NUMBERP) *
(*R >N NUMBERP) !R)
(NAPPEND L (LIST (MINUS (* M N)))
R)))
```
M1MULNEG evaluates "M*N"
improperly as "-(M*N)".

```
(M2MULNEG ((!L (*R >M NUMBERP) *
(*R >N NUMBERP) !R) (COND
((ZEROP (% M N))
(NAPPEND L (LIST (/ M N)) R))
(T (NAPPEND L (LIST (/ M (GCD MN))
(QUOTE /)(/ N (GCD M N))) R)))))
```
M2MULNEG evaluates "M*N" as
"M/N" and takes into
consideration the possibility
of a fractional answer. It is
in this case that FIN2 is used.

```
(DIVNEG ((!L (*R >M NUMBERP) /
(*R >N NUMBERP) !R)
(NAPPEND L (LIST (/ N M)) R)))
```
DIVNEG evaluates "M/N".

```
(M1DIVNEG ((!L (*R >M NUMBERP) /
(*R >N NUMBERP) !R)
(NAPPEND L (LIST (MINUS (/ M N)))
R)))
```
M1DIVNEG evaluates "M/N"
incorrectly as "-(M/N)".

```
(M2DIVNEG ((!L (*R >M NUMBERP) /
(*R >N NUMBERP) !R)
(NAPPEND L (LIST (* M N)) R))) ))
```
M2DIVNEG evaluates "M/N" as
"M*N".

3.3.6 Generating Models for NEGNUM

The mal-rules added to the above version of NEGNUM handle common
and simple errors that youngsters are known to make with negative numbers
(Ashlock, 1982). These include losing or adding a minus sign, doing division
instead of addition (or vice versa), and similar mistakes with multiplication
and division.

When this database is used by the offline model generator (see Sleeman
& Berger (1985) for details), it will evaluate all the tasks in the task-sets
using all models generated with the database. For instance, it generates
the models (SUBNEG FIN), (M1SUBNEG FIN), (M2SUBNEG FIN), and
(M3SUBNEG FIN) from the template model (SUBNEG FIN). The generator also points out any ambiguous examples – tasks for which more than one

model has the same answer. For example, the third task of the third task-set $(-5+5)$ is numerically degenerate. The correct model (SUBNEG3 FIN) evaluates M+N when M is equal to −N and produces 0, yet the incorrect model, (M1SUBNEG3 FIN) also evaluates to 0, i.e., −(M+N). Therefore, it is necessary to replace this task, with one which is more discriminatory.

The effect of precedence can be illustrated by the template model:

$$\text{(PMULT PADD FIN)}$$

In this model PMULT and PADD are rules that match patterns of the form M×N and P+Q, where M, N, P and Q are all positive integers. M1PMULT is a mal-rule that captures a student *applying* the + operator instead of the × operator. Then, because PMULT and PADD are order sensitive and because of the mal-rule, M1PMULT, the algorithm will generate four models:

(PMULT PADD FIN)

(PADD PMULT FIN)

(M1PMULT PADD FIN)

(PADD M1PMULT FIN)

The first is the original template – the *correct* model; in the second, the two rules have been interchanged; in the third and fourth, the rule, PMULT, has been replaced by its mal-rule in the former two models. This process is performed exhaustively, i.e., for all order-sensitive pairs and for all mal-rules. (See Sleeman (1983) for a more detailed discussion of this algorithm.)

3.3.7 Mal-Parsing Rules Versus Mal-Rules

The mal-rules included in the above version of NEGNUM demonstrated errors in evaluation. For example, the mal-rule M2SUBNEG solves the task $6 - 8$ incorrectly (by adding +6 and +8 to get the answer 14 instead of −2). However, another type of erroneous rule, called a mal-parsing rule, functions differently from "regular" mal-rules. Moreover, mal-parsing rules were inspired by a need to explain a different class of behavior. For instance, in the algebra domain, some students change the equation

$$3x + 5x = 19$$
$$\text{to}$$
$$x + x = 19 - 3 - 5.$$

Figure 4: NEGNUM Database, Version 3 – Mal-Parsing Rules (Additional Changes Only)

```
(SETQ GBRLS
  '((FIN (FIN)) (FIN2 (FIN2))
    (SUBNEG (SUBNEG M1SUBNEG
    M2SUBNEG M3SUBNEG))
    (SUBNEG2 (SUBNEG2 M1SUBNEG2
    M2SUBNEG2 M3SUBNEG2))
    (SUBNEG3 (SUBNEG3 M1SUBNEG3
    M2SUBNEG3 M3SUBNEG3))
    (MULNEG (MULNEG M1MULNEG
    M2MULNEG))(DIVNEG (DIVNEG
    M1DIVNEG M2DIVNEG))
    (ADDSUB (ADDSUB M1ADDSUB))))
```
GBRLS now also includes ADDSUB and its mal-rules.

```
(SETQ RULES
  '((FIN ((SHD (*R >M NUMBERP))
    (LIST (QUOTE FIN) M)))
    (FIN2 ((SHD (*R >M NUMBERP) /
    (*R >N NUMBERP))
    (LIST (QUOTE FIN) (LIST M N))))
    (ADDSUB ((!L (*R >M NUMBERP)
    (*OR >OP + -)(*R >N
    NUMBERP) !R)
    (NAPPEND L (LIST (OP M N)) R)))
    (M1ADDSUB ((!L (*R >M NUMBERP)
    (*OR >OP + -) (*R >N

    NUMBERP) !R) (NAPPEND L (LIST
    (MINUS (OP M N))) R)))

    (SUBNEG ((!L (*R >M POSNUM) -
    (*R >N GTNUM) !R)
    (NAPPEND L (LIST (- M N)) R)))
    (M1SUBNEG ((!L (*R >M POSNUM) -
    (*R >N GTNUM) !R)
    (NAPPEND L (LIST (- N M)) R)))
    (M2SUBNEG ((!L (*R >M POSNUM) -
    (*R >N GTNUM) !R)
    (NAPPEND L (LIST (+ M N)) R)))
    (M3SUBNEG ((!L (*R >M POSNUM) -
    (*R >N GTNUM) !R)
    (NAPPEND L (LIST (- M (MINUS M)
    N)) R)))

    (SUBNEG2 ((!L (*R >M NEGNUM) -
    (*R >N NUMBERP) !R)
    (NAPPEND L (LIST (- M N)) R)))
    (M1SUBNEG ((!L (*R >M NEGNUM) -
    (*R >N NUMBERP) !R)
    (NAPPEND L (LIST (- (MINUS M)
```

RULES now includes the definitions for the completion and mal-parsing rules:

ADDSUB evaluates "M+N" or "M-N" correctly.

M1ADDSUB incorrectly solves" "M+N or "M-N" by negating the answer.

```
N)) R)))
(M2SUBNEG2 ((!L (*R >M NEGNUM) -
(*R >M NUMBERP) !R)
(NAPPEND L (LIST (MINUS (- M N)))
R)))
(M3SUBNEG2 ((!L (*R >M NEGNUM) -
(*R >N NUMBERP) !R)
(NAPPEND L (LIST (+ M N)) R)))
(SUBNEG3 ((!L (*R >M NEGNUM) +
(*R >N NUMBERP) !R)
(NAPPEND L (LIST (+ M N)) R)))
(M1SUBNEG3 ((!L (*R >M NEGNUM) +
(*R >N NUMBERP) !R)
(NAPPEND L (LIST (MINUS (+ M N)))
R)))
(M2SUBNEG3 ((!L (*R >M NEGNUM) +
(*R >N NUMBERP) !R)
(NAPPEND L (LIST (+ (MINUS M)
N)) R)))
(M3SUBNEG3 ((!L (*R >M NEGNUM) +
(*R >N NUMBERP) !R)
(NAPPEND L (LIST (+ M (MINUS N))) R)))
(MULNEG ((!L (*R >M NUMBERP) *
(*R >N NUMBERP) !R)
(NAPPEND L (LIST (* M N)) R)))
(M1MULNEG ((!L (*R >M NUMBERP) *
(*R >N NUMBERP) !R)
(NAPPEND L (LIST (MINUS (* M N)))
R)))
(M2MULNEG ((!L (*R >M NUMBERP) *
(*R >N NUMBERP) !R) (COND
((ZEROP (% M N))
(NAPPEND L (LIST (/ M N)) R))
(T (NAPPEND L (LIST (/ M (GCD M N))
(QUOTE /)(/ N (GCD M N))) R)))))
(MP1MULNEG ((MPARSE !L (*R >M NUMBERP)
* (*R >N NUMBERP) !R)
(NAPPEND (LIST (QUOTE SHD)) L (LIST
M (QUOTE +) N) R)))
(MP2MULNEG ((MPARSE !L (*R >M NUMBERP)
* (*R >N NUMBERP) !R) (NAPPEND (LIST
QUOTE SHD)) L (LIST M (QUOTE -) N) R)))
(DIVNEG ((!L (*R >M NUMBERP) /
(*R >N NUMBERP) !R)
(NAPPEND L (LIST (/ M N)) R)))
(M1DIVNEG ((!L (*R >M NUMBERP) /
(*R >N NUMBERP) !R)
(NAPPEND L (LIST (MINUS
(/ M N))) R)))
(M2DIVNEG ((!L (*R >M NUMBERP) /
(*R >N NUMBERP) !R)
(NAPPEND L (LIST (* M N)) R)))
(MP1DIVNEG ((MPARSE !L (*R >M NUMBERP)
```

MP1MULNEG mal parses "M*N"
to M+N".

MP2MULEG turns "M*N" into
"M-N".

MP1DIVNEG incorrectly

```
/ (*R >N NUMBERP) !R) (NAPPEND (LIST        parses "M/N" to be
(QUOTE SHD)) L (LIST M (QUOTE +)            "M+N".
N) R)))
(MP2DIVNEG ((MPARSE !L (*R >M NUMBERP)       MP2DIVNEG turns "M/N"
/ (*R >N NUMBERP) !R)(NAPPEND (LIST          into "M-N".
(QUOTE SHD)) L (LIST M (QUOTE -)
N) R)))))
```

I believe that such students do not consider using a correct form of a rule, but rather a radically different one, which I term a "mal-parsing" rule. Such an error should not be handled by a variant on the good rule, but by a different type of rule. Experience has also shown that these parsing errors usually occur only once in a task, e.g., after changing

$$3x + 5x = 19 \text{ to } x + x = 19 - 3 - 5$$

and then reducing it to

$$2x = 11$$

the student did NOT repeat the parsing error to get

$$x = 11 - 2$$

Therefore, PIXIE allows the mal-parsing rules to fire only once per task. Figure 4 gives examples of mal-parsing rules for this domain.

3.4 The Remedial System

We have observed teachers using the models inferred from PIXIE to remediate their students, and have based the design of the prototype remedial system on these protocols. Currently, the sub-system does the following:

1. Demonstrates that the student has incorrectly solved the task.

2. Displays the particular error(s) that PIXIE believes the student has made.

3. Gives an explanation for the incorrect transformation.

4. Shows the working of the *correct* rule.

5. Shows the complete correct TRACE.

Sub-steps 2 to 4 are executed for each error noted by PIXIE.

Below, we give a protocol for the system, albeit with the introductory algebra database, which illustrates these features. The student's responses are preceeded by the > character; the rest of the protocol is produced by RPIXIE.

```
Solve (f = Finished, q = Quit early)

3x = 7
>x + 3 = 7
>x = 7-3
>x = 4
>f

Thank you,
but you didn't get that one right.
We will now look at that task again.
Press C and RETURN:
>

Here we are considering the task 3x = 7

Did you work the task something like this?:

3x = 7
x + 3 = 7
x = 7 - 3
x = 4
Please type YES or NO; >y

It seems that you changed 3x=7 to something like x + 3 = 7

This is WRONG.
Do NOT separate a coefficient from the x-term.
You should divide both sides of the equation by the
coefficient to change 3x = 7 to x = 7/3

Press C and RETURN:
>

Now let me show you how you SHOULD have worked the
whole task.

x = 7/3     Divide both sides of the equation by
                the coefficient
x = 7/3     Finished
```

3.5 Further Work with the PIXIE System

1. Build further databases. Currently, we have data-bases for linear algebra, negative integers and precedence in arithmetic expressions. A fractions database is being produced.

2. Test the effect of the remedial subsystem. Compare the effect of targeted remediation versus simply reteaching.

3. Build a remedial subsystem that will attempt to tailor the explanation of errors provided to suit the individual's learning style. (This may well involve building a natural-language interface to enable PIXIE to probe the student about steps in his/her solution path.)

4. Increase PIXIE's diagnostic abilities. Create larger sets of mal-rules and model sets, and incorporate the results of on-going research to infer previously unknown mal-rules from protocols.

5. Modify PIXIE so that it is able to tutor in several domains during a single session. For example, if a student has difficulties with precedence in algebra expressions, it would be useful to determine whether the student has difficulties with precedence in arithmetic. Similarly, if a student has difficulties with algebra tasks whose answers were mixed fractions, it would be desirable to investigate (arithmetic) fractions. (Such a facility would make PIXIE more like a human tutor!)

6. Produce a "friendlier" authoring interface, both for the input of new rules and parameters, and to edit existing knowledge bases.

7. Create a variant of PIXIE, TPIXIE, to give teachers practice with diagnosing prototypical errors; determine whether this is effective in enhancing teachers' diagnostic abilities. A running version of TPIXIE is now being tested.

4.0 CONCLUSION

Several important themes in current ITS research were identified in the introduction, including the ability to infer student models. Section 3 discussed in some detail the data-driven PIXIE system, which can infer student models and can carry out remedial dialogues based on these models. Thus, the PIXIE shell has made it possible to create relatively easily several working diagnostic ITSs, and as such it must be considered to be a successful piece of engineering.

ACKNOWLEDGEMENTS

Numerous co-workers have helped shape this project. In particular, Daniel Berger was very involved in the writing of the PIXIE database manual, and so indirectly contributed to this paper. The IBM corporation and ARI/ONR Grant Number 903-84-K-0279 provided support for part of this work. The author acknowledges the helpful comments made on an earlier draft of this paper by Anthony E. Kelly and Masoud Yazdani.

REFERENCES

Alpert, D., & Bitzer, D.L. (1970). Advances in computer-based education. *Science*, *166*.

Anderson, J.R. (1983). *The Architecture of Cognition*. Cambridge, MA: Harvard.

Anderson, J.R., Boyle, C.F., Farrell, R., & Reiser, B. (1984). Cognitive principles in the design of computer tutors. *Proceedings of the 6th Annual Conference of the Cognitive Science Society*.

Anderson, J.R., & Reiser, B.J. (1985). The LISP tutor. *Byte, 10*, (4), 159–179.

Ashlock, R.B. (1982). *Error Patterns in Computation*. Third Edition. Columbus, Ohio: Merrill.

Bonar, J. (1985). Bite-sized intelligent tutoring. LRDC Working Document.

Bork, A.M. (1979). Interactive learning. *Am. J. Physics, 47*, 5–10.

Brown, A.L. (1975). The development of memory: knowing, knowing about knowing, and knowing how to know. In H.W. Reese (ed.), *Advances in Child Development and Behavior, Vol. 10,* New York: Academic Press.

Carbonell, J.R. (1970). AI in CAI: an artificial intelligence approach to computer-aided instruction. *IEEE Transactions on Man-Machine Systems, 11*, 190–202.

Clancey, W.J. (1985). Acquiring, representing, and evaluating a competence model of diagnostic strategy. Tech. Memo CS-85-1067, Dept. of Computer Science, Stanford University.

Collins, A., Warnock, E.H., & Passafiume, J.J. (1974). Analysis and synthesis of tutorial dialogues. BBN Report 2789, Bolt, Beranek & Newman, Inc., Cambridge, MA.

Cronbach, L.J., & Snow, R.E. (1977). *Aptitudes and Instructional Methods*. New York: Irvington.

Davis, R. (1984). *Learning Mathematics: A Cognitive Science Approach*. London: Croom Helms.

Genesereth, M.R. (1982). The role of plans in intelligence teaching systems. In D. Sleeman & J.S. Brown (Eds.). *Intelligent Tutoring Systems*, 137–155, London: Academic Press.

Gentner, D., & Stevens, A. (1983). *Mental Models*. New Jersey: LEA.

Hartley, J.R., & Sleeman, D.H. (1973). Toward intelligent teaching systems. *Int. J. of Man-Machine Studies, 5*, 215–236.

Hasling, D.W., Clancey, W.J., & Rennels, G.R. (1984). Strategic explanations for a diagnostic consultation system. *Int. J. of Man-Machine Studies, 20*, 3–19.

Hirsh, H.B., & Sleeman, D. (1985). Inference of incorrect operators. *Proceedings of the 3rd Int. Workshop on Machine Learning*. Skytop, PA.

Johnson, W.L., & Soloway, E. (1983). PROUST: knowledge-based program understanding. *Proceedings of the 7th Int. Conference on Software Engineering*. IEEE: Orlando, FL.

Kelly, A.E., & Sleeman, D. (1985). A study of diagnostic and remedial techniques used by master algebra teachers. Occasional Paper, School of Education, Stanford University.

Shortliffe, E.H. (1976). *Computer-based Medical Consultations: MYCIN*. New York: American Elsevier.

Sleeman, D.H., & Brown, J.S. (1982). Intelligent tutoring systems: an overview. In D.H. Sleeman & J.S. Brown (Eds.), *Intelligent Tutoring Systems*, 1–11. London: Academic Press.

Sleeman, D.H. (1982a). Assessing competence in basic algebra. In D.H. Sleeman & J.S. Brown (Eds.), *Intelligent Tutoring Systems*, 185–199. London: Academic Press.

Sleeman, D.H. (1982b). Inferring (mal)rules from pupil's protocols. In the *Proceedings of the 1982 European AI Conference*, 160–164. (Republished in *Proceedings of the International Machine Learning Workshop*, Illinois, June 1983.)

Sleeman, D.H. (1983). A rule directed modelling system. In R. Michalski, J. Carbonell, and T. Mitchell (Eds.), *Machine Learning*, 483–510, Tioga: Palo Alto.

Sleeman, D., Appelt, D., Konolige, K., Rich, E., Sridharan, N.S., & Swartout, W. (1985). User modelling. *IJCAI–85, Conference Proceedings*. 1298–1302.

Sleeman, D.H. (1985a). Basic algebra revisted: a study with 14-year-olds. *Int. J. of Man-Machine Studies*, 127–149.

Sleeman, D. (1985b). A user modelling front end subsystem. *Int. J. of Man-Machine Studies, 23*, 71–88.

Sleeman, D.H., & Berger, D. (1985). Creating databases for the PIXIE modelling system. Technical Manual, School of Education, Stanford.

Sleeman, D. (in press). Micro-SEARCH. In G. Kearsley (Ed.), *Artificial Intelligence and Instruction*. Reading, MA: Addison-Wesley.

Soloway, E., Ehrlich, K., Bonar, K., & Greenspan, J. (1982). What do novices know about programming? In A. Badre & B. Schneiderman (Eds.), *Directions in Human-Computer Interactions*, 27–54, Norwood, NJ: Ablex.

Suppes, P., & Morningstar, M. (1969). Computer-assisted instruction. *Science, 166*, 343–350.

VanMelle, W. (1980). A domain independent system that aids in constructing consultation programs. Tech. Report. STAN-ES-80-820, Computer Science Department, Stanford University.

Weizenbaum, J. (1966). ELIZA – a computer program for the study of natural language communication between man and machine. *CACM, 9* 36–45.

Wescourt, K.T., Beard, M., Gould, L., & Barr, A. (1977). Knowledge-based CAI:CINS for individualized curriculum sequencing. Tech. Report 290: Institute for Mathematical Studies in Social Sciences, Stanford University.

Wipke, W.T., Braun, H., Smith, G., Choplin, F., & Sieber, W. (1977). SECS-simulation and evaluation of chemical synthesis: strategy and planning. In W.T. Wipke & W.J. House (Eds.), *Computer-assisted Organic Synthesis*, 97–127, American Chemical Society.

Woolf, B., & McDonald, D.D. (1984). Building a computer tutor: design issues. *IEEE: Computer*, 61–73.

APPENDIX A. Syntax of PIXIE Rules

I hope that non-LISP programmers will not find the LISP syntax too intrusive. I suggest that the reader carefully study the form of the rules given in the sample databases; hopefully this will help you formulate other databases by analogy.

Every rule definition in a PIXIE database contains two parts: a condition and an action part. The action is carried out when the requirements stated in the condition are satisfied. Appendix A.1 discusses the conditions of PIXIE rules; Appendix A.2 discusses the action parts.

A.1 The CONDITION Half of a Rule Definition

There are four types of elements that can occur in the condition part of a rule:

1. Literal atoms (e.g., $X, +, -, \times$, etc.).

2. !STRING (e.g., !LHS or !RHS) None or many tokens can be assigned to the variable. Also note that a *list* will be returned.

3. (*OR >VARIABLE t1, t2...tn) will be satisfied only if the next token in the string being parsed is either t1, t2...or tn. The matched element is then assigned to the VARIABLE. For instance, the requirement (*OR >OP $\times \div$) would be satisfied if the next token was either $\times$ or $\div$ and would then be assigned to the variable OP.

4. (*R >VARIABLE PREDICATE) is similar to the *OR element described above. This requirement will be satisfied only if the next token in the input string satisfies the PREDICATE. The PREDICATE can be either a standard LISP predicate (like NUMBERP) or one defined by the designer of the database; examples of user-defined predicates in the NEGNUM database include POSNUM, and GTNUM. Example: (*R >M NUMBERP). If the next token in the string being parsed is a number, this requirement is satisfied, and M will be assigned the integer.

NOTE: All variables assigned in these condition parts have global scope. The whole condition will not be satisfied if any of the requirements fail to match the input string. However, since the !STRING variables can match none or many tokens, the process is non-deterministic, i.e., a search is often required.

A.2 The ACTION Part of a PIXIE Rule Definition

The action part of a rule determines the value that the rule returns, and in this production-system interpreter, the action replaces the entire state. The value is created using the LISP function NAPPEND, which takes any number of lists and returns a "concatenated list." For instance, in the case of the SUBNEG rule defined in the NEGNUM database:

CONDITION: (!L (*R >M POSNUM) − (*R >N GTNUM) !R)

ACTION: (NAPPEND L (LIST (− M N)) R),

it could parse the string: (SHD 5 − 7) and !L would be assigned (SHD), M the integer 5, N the integer 7, and R would have the value NIL, the null string. The ACTION part of the rule would return the value:

(SHD −2),

Evaluated as:

(NAPPEND (SHD) (LIST (− 5 7)) NIL)

> (NAPPEND (SHD) (−2) NIL)

> (SHD -2)

13 THE APPLICATION OF MACHINE LEARNING TO STUDENT MODELLING

John Self

Department of Computing
University of Lancaster
United Kingdom

ABSTRACT

This paper considers the prospects for applying machine-learning techniques to the problem of maintaining the dynamic student models needed for intelligent tutoring. We imagine a learner endeavoring to understand a climate classification scheme through exploring a database guided by a tutorial system which does not itself know the classification rules. We consider the possible use of the focussing algorithm for concept-learning as a basis for such a tutorial system. Several difficulties with this approach to "guided discovery-learning" are discussed.

1.0 INTRODUCTION

Two contemporary developments in computing suggest that a different style of computer tutor may be contemplated. First, the availability of large databases will enable learners to explore factual domains much more flexibly than is possible with conventional reference books and encyclopedia. Moreover, this exploration will be largely self-motivated and not driven by explicit learning goals. Secondly, the development of machine-learning techniques suggests ways in which a conceptual structuring of such databases may be built. By applying such techniques to monitor a learner's exploration it may be possible to design computer tutors able to intercede to make such explorations more fruitful.

In this paper a concept-learning task of this kind is first defined, and then the possibility of applying existing machine concept-learning techniques to it is considered. Various difficulties are described, leading to a comparison of machine concept-learning with theories of human concept-learning. Finally, a design for a guided discovery learning system for tutoring concepts is proposed.

2.0 LEARNING CONCEPTS BY EXPLORATION

Imagine that a learner has access to a database containing details of the climatic data at many weather stations, e.g., the 1500 stations listed in Rudloff (1981), a typical entry of which is shown in Figure 1.

Latitude 33.20n				Longitude 44.24e				Height 34m				
BWil 038-5	Jan	Feb	Mar	Apr	May	Jun	Jul	Aug	Sep	Oct	Nov	Dec	Year
tx	20	23	29	34	40	44	47	47	44	39	30	22	48
t	10	12	16	22	28	33	35	34	31	25	17	11	23
tn	−2	1	4	10	14	21	23	22	17	12	4	1	−3
clothing	n	n	n	s	t	t	t	t	t	t	s	n	--
stress				o	*f*	*ff*	*ff*	*ff*	*f*	*f*	o		--
p	25	25	29	16	7	0	0	0	0	3	22	26	156
dp	4	4	4	3	1	0	0	0	0	1	3	4	23
sunshine	192	204	246	256	300	348	348	354	316	273	213	194	3241
%	61	66	66	66	70	81	79	85	85	77	8	63	73

Figure 1. A Typical Entry from Rudloff (1981).

Let us assume that he knows the meaning of the symbols in the entry, i.e., that "p" means precipitation, that "tx" means maximum temperature, and, in particular, that the two characters in the top left ("BW" in this case) denote the class of climate. Let us now imagine that our learner decides to explore the database in an attempt to discover the conditions under which an entry is assigned to the BW class, and similarly for the other classes, of which there happen to be 15. (This particular problem is, of course, only put forward to make the following discussion more concrete: it has no more intrinsic interest or importance than a whole series of similar problems involving the exploration of large databases.)

3.0 THE ROLE OF A COMPUTER TUTOR

There are two extreme strategies which could be adopted by a computer tutor intended to aid such an exploration. At one extreme, it could simply answer the questions posed by the learner, without considering their appropriateness or what might be learned from their answers. This is the approach of conventional database systems such as QUEST or DBASEII, which are already being used in the classroom (Freeman & Tagg, 1985). The limitation of this approach is clear: much time may be "wasted" by learners following fruitless paths or not interpreting the data correctly. To be successful, this strategy must be buttressed with detailed curriculum-related worksheets and with a teacher monitoring the use of the database.

At the other extreme, we have tutoring systems which in some sense "know" the concepts to be learned and endeavor to guide the learner explicitly towards those concepts. For example, CLIMATE is a simple drill program which can answer a small set of questions about climate types but is limited by not being able to use this knowledge in any other way (Self, 1985a). Expert system-based tutorial systems such as GUIDON (Clancey, 1983) are better able to explain their own knowledge, but their focus on expert knowledge makes it difficult for them to understand a learner's activities (Clancey, 1984). In short, both extreme strategies have limitations in fostering self-directed enquiry learning.

To constructively guide a learner's use of a database, a computer tutor must have some understanding of what the learner is trying to do and of what the learner could reasonably be expected to have learned at any stage. The computer tutor must try to maintain a student model which learns in tandem with the learner. This implies that the tutor should make use of appropriate machine-learning techniques. In order to concentrate on the role of machine-learning in the following, we will assume that the tutor does not itself know what the learner is trying to learn. This is, of course, an expository device: it is well-known that the most powerful strategy for teaching someone a specific concept is to first define the concept (Tennyson & Park, 1980). Similarly, an ideal computer tutor would know what is to be learned.

4.0 CONCEPT-LEARNING BY FOCUSSING

Several programs have been developed which attempt to learn concepts, that is, to construct a method for distinguishing members of a concept from non-members, which is what our illustrative problem involves. Holte (1985) gives a good overview of these programs. We might hope that they will provide the basis for the dynamic student models we need.

Holte and Bundy, Silver and Plummer (1984) consider the focussing algorithm of Young, Plotkin and Linz (1977) to provide the most powerful framework for discussing concept-learning programs. For completeness, a brief summary of the focussing algorithm now follows.

The concept being learned is represented by a set of trees, each tree describing the structure of one dimension of the instance. For example,

Figure 2 shows a possible set of trees for the "BW concept". Each tree is marked with two lines, L and U, so that any node above U is outside the concept and so is any node below L. So, with the L and U marks shown in Figure 2, we could say (loosely) that all BW stations have a maximum temperature greater than 17 but that it is not yet determined whether the rainfall has to be heavy. The set of nodes within the L-U marks constitute the "version space".

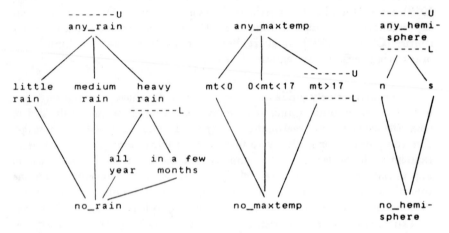

Figure 2. A Description Space for Focussing on Climates.

Concepts are learned by moving the L and U marks respectively up and down the trees, as follows.

First, each instance is described by a set of nodes, one from each tree (call these the instance-nodes).

For positive instances:

- for each tree, move L to be above or coincident with the instance-node.

For negative instances,

- select a tree in which U is above the instance-node,

- move U towards L to a node above or coincident with L which is not above the instance-node

- (if there is more than one way to do this, create a set of version spaces to explore in parallel).

If the desired operation is not possible, discard that version space.

The concept is learned when the L-U marks enclose a single node in each tree.

The power of the focussing algorithm lies in its concise description of large version spaces and in the ease with which the version spaces may be updated. The suggestion, then, is that we use this description and the focussing algorithm as the basis for our student model. The basic idea is to have an "internal learner" using focussing to work out what *it* would learn from the instances seen by the learner. The tutor would then use this internal description to provide guidance, as necessary, for the learner. Some such scheme is necessary for any tutoring system which makes a serious attempt to monitor an open-ended concept-learning activity.

5.0 NECESSARY EXTENSIONS OF FOCUSSING

While the outline of such a system is fairly clear, it is even more clear that there are considerable design and pedagogic problems. First, however, we must consider whether focussing (or any other concept-learning technique) is up to the role proposed.

5.1 Disjunction

Most concept-learning techniques, including focussing, are acknowledged to have problems with disjunctive concepts. The above algorithm is appropriate only for conjunctive concepts, such as "heavy rain *and* maxtemp > 17", although there is, of course, an implied exclusive-or within the trees, e.g., "heavy rain" is "rain throughout year *or* heavy rain in a few months". Focussing could not learn "heavy rain *or* maxtemp > 17", at least, not without remembering all instances seen and then rebuilding the trees when an inconsistency is detected, a process which, according to Bundy, Silver and Plummer (1984), "appears to be a requirement for all systems that learn disjunctive concepts".

This seems an odd conclusion to draw. For one thing, we know from de Morgan that conjunctions can be turned into disjunctions – the negations so introduced not being fundamentally significant, since it is often an arbitrary choice as to whether a feature should be considered "p" or "not-p" in the first place. Anyway, the steps of the focussing algorithm only make sense for conjunctive concepts: it is to be expected that they will fail for disjunctive concepts. What is needed is a different algorithm, one appropriate for disjunctive concepts.

A version of such an algorithm follows (using the same style as conjunctive-focussing above):

For negative instances:

- for each tree, move U to be below or coincident with the instance-node.

For positive instances:

- select a tree in which L is below the instance-node.

- move L towards U to a node below or coincident with U which is not below the instance-node

- (if there is more than one way to do this, create a set of version spaces to explore in parallel).

Further details are given in Self (1985b), but it would be a digression to consider them further here. Such a disjunctive-focussing algorithm is only the first step, for we need also to be able to handle combinations of conjunctions and disjunctions, such as "wettest month is in [June, July, August] and northern hemisphere or wettest month is [December, January, February] and southern hemisphere", for the concept "rains most in summer". But the main point is that more research needs to be done on the technical aspects of concept-learning techniques – they cannot be easily applied as they stand for our purposes.

5.2 Learning of Formulas

It turns out that (according to Rudloff, 1981) one of the conditions for a climate to be classified as BW is that the annual rainfall R satisfies

$$R < 10(t - 10) + 300 \times Rs \div R$$

where t is the mean annual temperature and Rs is the mean summer rainfall. Informally, this means that BW climates have low "useful" rainfall, allowing for evaporation, i.e., taking into account temperature and when the rain falls. Our problem is simply that focussing (and other concept-learning techniques) cannot discover such formulas in any obvious way. The machine-learning work that comes closest to tackling this is that on the BACON series (Langley, Zytkow, Simon, & Bradshaw, 1984). Clearly, any effort to model the learning of such concepts must involve similar techniques.

5.3 Probabilistic Concepts

One way of side-stepping the problem of learning formal, mathematical definitions such as the above is to be content for the learner to develop informal, imprecise concepts, e.g., that BW climates usually have "very low rainfall". A guess at a value for "very low", say 100mm, may enable us correctly to identify perhaps 95% of BW climates, but no such guess will correspond to the correct concept definition. But obviously something useful has been learned, and a tutor should be able to recognize this. Focussing, however, has no notion of "partially correct" concepts: learned concepts identify positive or negative instances, but nothing in between. Machine concept-learning work has concentrated on formal concepts, assumed to have precise definitions to be discovered. This is unsatisfactory as a basis for computer tutoring because many concepts are not formally defined, and those that are (e.g., climates) are learned through the progressive refinement of informal definitions.

5.4 Description Space

Focussing assumes that the description space, the set of trees, is given. Minor dynamic changes to the trees are possible, for example, to modify the boundary of "very low" rainfall or to introduce extra disjunctions, but the overall content and structure of the trees is assumed given and unchangeable. It is unreasonable, however, to assume that all learners start off with the same structuring of the space. Even though the difficult problem of determining potentially relevant features has been pre-empted by what has been included in the database, it is still not obvious what should be treated as independent features and so represented as separate trees. For example, from the temperature figures, should we focus on maximum temperature, minimum temperature, temperature range, average temperature, month of highest temperature, average summer temperature, or what? To model a learner's investigation of the database in the way suggested, our tutor needs to be able to create a description space appropriate to that learner.

5.5 Background Knowledge

The difficulty with the description space is only one aspect of the wider problem of background knowledge. Focussing and similar techniques assume that the only background knowledge needed is that represented by the description space. This idealization is reasonable only for very artificial learning situations. Even for our simple climate problem, learners (and our programs should) use considerably more knowledge than is contained within the description space. Some of this is general knowledge, such as "given an array of figures, don't treat them as independent but look at their distribution, the maximum and minimum, and so on". Some is specific to the domain, for example, "it makes more sense to add rainfall figures than temperature figures". And some is actually to do with the concepts to be learned, such as "deserts are very dry", and a learner might proceed by trying to see if, for example, BW corresponds to his informal concept of "desert". We might also suspect that the classes BW and BS have something in common. The research on machine-learning by analogy (Carbonell, 1983; Burstein, 1983) should be relevant here.

The problems of background knowledge cannot be ignored for the proposed monitoring of self-directed enquiry learning. No learner will embark on a "self-directed" exercise without the background knowledge to motivate it.

6.0 HUMAN CONCEPT-LEARNING

Some of the problems discussed above are limitations of the machine-learning technique of focussing (and similar algorithms), but some concern its inadequacies as a model of human learning. It is, of course, unfair to criticise machine-learning techniques for their psychological implausibility when they have been designed only to perform a task. But if such techniques are to have a role within student models, then comparison with human learning processes will have to be made.

Research on human concept-learning has undergone something of a revolution in the last ten years. The two major changes concern (a) what is considered to be an acceptable "concept" to study and (b) the mode of description of concept-learning theories. Earlier work studied the learning of artificial concepts, such as "blue triangles", in laboratory experiments. Today, the emphasis is more on "natural" concepts, that is, concepts that occur in the real world, such as "chair" or "bird", and how they are learned during normal life experiences.

With the artificial concepts having exact definitions, it was possible to develop fairly precise theories to explain the experimental results. Most of these theories took the form of "hypothesis-testing" models, which assumed that learners formed one or more hypotheses about the concept and then adopted an information-seeking strategy to test those hypotheses. The focussing and scanning strategies described by Bruner, Goodnow and Austin (1956) were perhaps the first such models. Detailed variations of the models were developed, culminating in the theory of Levine (1975).

This view of concept-learning, then, is that one abstracts some kind of rule for determining class membership which can be applied to test instances. Various criticisms of this view can be made (Medin & Smith, 1984) but it is sufficient for us to note that the view is inappropriate if there is, in fact, no such rule to be learned. This appears to be the case for many, if not most, natural concepts, i.e., ones that are not given formal, mathematical or scientific definitions. For most people and most purposes, climate classes are natural concepts (that is, concepts without precise boundaries) and it is only when a formal definition is imposed that a precise rule exists. Anybody learning climate classifications would probably learn the informal concepts first, and so our proposed tutor ought to be able to deal with them.

The newer view of concept-learning derives mainly from the work of Rosch (1978) on "prototypes". The prototype of a category is the central tendency of the set of instances of that category. The description by Smith and Medin (1981) of this view as "probabilistic" captures the most significant difference. No longer do we expect a concept to be represented by a rule, giving a set of necessary and sufficient conditions, but a concept is described by a summary representation in terms of feature values that are related probabilistically to concept membership. The details of this relation do, of course, remain to be worked out.

But if we compare this view of concept-learning with that adopted in machine-learning research (as surveyed by Holte, 1985), then it is striking that most of the latter is more compatible with the earlier hypothesis-testing models of human concept-learning. It is natural to prefer algorithms which are guaranteed to provide clear-cut decisions ("this instance is definitely a desert"), and it may be believed that such decision algorithms need to be developed first before we should tackle probabilistic algorithms. But it may be that no such decision algorithms are attainable for concepts worth learning, and that the search for them may prevent us developing serviceable probabilistic algorithms.

If human concept-learning is, in fact, a process of refining probabilities, then a computer tutor to aid the learning of concepts needs to be able to represent this process. Unfortunately, the newer views of human concept-learning are not yet sufficiently precise to form the basis of a computer implementation. Fried and Holyoak (1984) present a promising model based on probability distributions, taking account of global assumptions about the shape of those distributions. Easterlin and Langley (1985) propose a concept-learning scheme which incrementally adjusts weights attached to features, an approach related to that of "conceptual clustering" (Michalski, 1983). Alternative computational representations do not appear to help psychologists much: fuzzy set theory is considered unable to account for many phenomena involving concept-learning, and complex structures such as frames and scripts are too ill-defined to be explicitly commented upon in the psychological literature.

7.0 COLLABORATIVE CONCEPT-LEARNING

Where does this leave the proposed design of a tutor to monitor self-directed concept-learning? We have machine-learning procedures which are fairly simple, with well-understood formal properties but lacking psychological plausibility. We have more complex procedures which may in practice be more powerful, but we cannot analyze them formally nor determine their psychological validity. We have a large volume of experimental data on human concept-learning and a range of theories to account for them, but none are well-developed or expressed computationally. The safest course may be to adopt a formal procedure, like focussing (which was, after all, originally proposed as a psychological model), and attempt to relax it to cater for probabilities (by perhaps regarding L and U as vague rather than rigid boundaries) and background knowledge so as to better correspond to human concept-learning, and to extend it to handle more complex concepts, including disjunctions and formulae. At least this way, we may retain some formal understanding of the properties of the systems we build.

Let us assume now that we have an adequate model of human concept-learning and a description of the learner's current understanding of the concept, perhaps expressed as a version space, as above. The basic operation of the tutor would then be as shown in Figure 3.

Clearly, if the tutor never interfered with this loop we would have a conventional database system. Figure 4 indicates some possible augmentations of this loop.

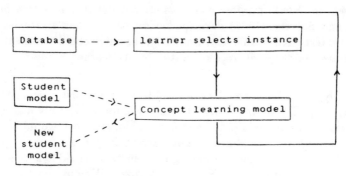

Figure 3. Basic Operation of Tutor

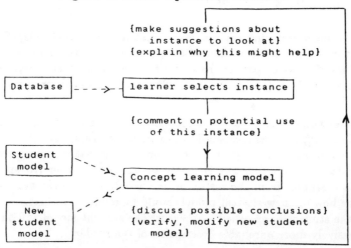

Figure 4. Augmented Operation of Tutor

We assume that the learner is not simply taking instances as they come, i.e., following the "reception procedure" typical of many psychological experiments and machine-learning algorithms (including focussing, in fact), for which the order of instances does not matter. For humans, the order of instances does matter – Tennyson and Park (1981) discuss in general terms the properties of a good sequence of instances. The learner is to select instances which he thinks will be useful, e.g., by asking "which BW has the lowest maximum temperature?" (He may in fact simply ask questions: "do all BWs have maximum temperatures greater than 17?")

The tutor may, if asked or if it decides to do so, suggest an instance to look at. It would do this by considering which instances would enable the student model to be refined. Several existing programs show how this might be done: Mitchell (1982) and Lenat (1982) developed techniques by which their programs could propose problems for independent investigation, and Collins and Stevens (1982) developed a set of teaching strategies which could be interpreted in this way. Similarly, the tutor could comment on the appropriateness of an instance requested by the learner.

Ideally, this advice would be derived from an explicit concept-learning strategy, e.g., "Try to find a negative instance for which only a single tree in the version space needs to be modified". If so, the tutor would be able to justify specific advice in general terms, and so help the learner to develop concept-learning strategies. Learning such meta-level skills is much more important than learning specific concepts (like BW) but computer tutors rarely say anything about them.

The suggestion that concept-learning skills are to be developed during the tutorial implies (notwithstanding Figure 4) that the concept-learning model should also be part of the student model, since it is idiosyncratic to the learner and needs to be dynamically updated as skills are developed.

After the instance has been presented and the tutor has determined the effect that the instance would have on its internal student model, the tutor may discuss with the learner the conclusions that may be drawn from this instance. This dialogue is partly to help the learner (to appreciate what is learnable from the instance) and partly to help the tutor (to determine how the new student model should be modified to better represent what the student has learned – otherwise the student model will become a progressively more unreliable description of the student).

In Figure 4, the tutor activities are shown in brackets to indicate that they are optional. Clearly, it would be a non-trivial task to determine how these activities could be made effective. For one thing, it is difficult to predict how students would react to a tutoring situation in which the tutor genuinely does not know the "answer".

8.0 CONCLUSIONS

Good tutoring is based upon a theory (usually implicit) of a student's learning processes. This paper has considered the possibility of developing a computer tutor around an explicit concept-learning theory, derived from machine-learning techniques. Some problems with using the focussing algorithm (and similar algorithms) in this role were discussed, and some possible solutions, or approaches to solutions, developed. In particular, the need to relate such algorithms to what is known about human concept-learning was emphasised. Finally, we speculated on the design of a tutor which might guide a student to discover concepts.

REFERENCES

Bruner, J.S., Goodnow, J.J., & Austin, G.A. (1956). *A Study of Thinking*. New York: John Wiley.

Bundy, A., Silver, B., & Plummer, D. (1984). An analytical comparison of some rule learning programs. Research Paper 215, Department of Artificial Intelligence, University of Edinburgh.

Burstein, M.H. (1983). Concept formation by incremental analogical reasoning and debugging. *Proc. Int. Machine Learning Workshop*, Illinois.

Carbonell, J.G. (1983). Derivational analogy in problem solving and knowledge acquisition. *Proc. Int. Machine Learning Workshop*, Illinois.

Clancey, W.J. (1983). GUIDON. *J. Computer-Based Instruction*, 10, 8-15.

Clancey, W.J. (1984). Methodology for building an intelligent tutoring system. In W. Kintsch (Ed.), *Methods and Tactics in Cognitive Science*. Hillsdale, NJ: Lawrence Erlbaum.

Collins, A., & Stevens, A.L. (1982). Goals and strategies of inquiry teachers. In R. Glaser (Ed.), *Advances in Instructional Psychology, Vol 2*. Hillsdale, NJ: Lawrence Erlbaum.

Easterlin, J.D., & Langley, P. (1985). A framework for concept formation. *Proc. 7th Ann. Conf. of Cognitive Science Society*, Irvine, CA.

Freeman, D., & Tagg, W. (1985). Databases in the classroom. *J. Computer-Assisted Learning*, 1, 2-11.

Fried, L.S., & Holyoak, K.J. (1984). Induction of category distribution: a framework for classification learning. *J. Exp. Psychol.: Learning, Memory and Cognition*.

Holte, R.C. (1985). Artificial intelligence approaches to concept learning. In I. Aleksander (ed.), *Advanced Digital Information Systems*. London: Prentice-Hall.

Langley, P., Zytkow, J., Simon, H.A., & Bradshaw, G.L. (1984). The search for regularity: four aspects of scientific discovery. Report CMU-RI-TR-84-20, The Robotics Institute, Carnegie-Mellon University, Pittsburgh, PA.

Lenat, D.B. (1982). *The Role of Heuristics in Learning by Discovery*. Palo Alto: Tioga.

Levine, M. (1975). *A Cognitive Theory of Learning: Research on Hypothesis Testing*. Hillsdale, NJ: Erlbaum.

Medin, D.L., & Smith, E.E. (1984). Concepts and concept formation. *Ann. Rev. Psychol.*, 35, 113-38.

Michalski, R.S. (1983). A theory and methodology of inductive learning. *Artificial Intelligence*, 20, 111-161.

Mitchell, T.M. (1982). Generalization as search. *Artificial Intelligence*, 18, 203-226.

Rosch, E. (1978). Principles of categorization. In E. Rosch & B.B. Lloyd (Eds.), *Cognition and Categorization*. Hillsdale, NJ: Erlbaum.

Rudloff, W. (1981). *World-Climates*. Stuttgart: Wissenschaftliche Verlagsgesellschaft.

Self, J.A. (1985a). *Microcomputers in Education: a Critical Appraisal of Educational Software*. Brighton: Harvester Press.

Self, J.A. (1985b). Learning disjunctions by focussing. Internal report, Department of Computing, University of Lancaster.

Smith, E.E., & Medin, D.L. (1981). *Categories and Concepts*. Cambridge, MA: Harvard Univ. Press.

Tennyson, R.D., & Park, O-C. (1980). The teaching of concepts: a review of instructional design research literature. *Rev. Educ. Research*, 50, 55-70.

Young, R.M., Plotkin, G.D., & Linz, R.F. (1977). Analysis of an extended concept learning task. *IJCAI-77 Proceedings*. Los Altos, CA: Morgan Kaufmann, Inc.

14 QUALITATIVE MODELS AND INTELLIGENT LEARNING ENVIRONMENTS

Barbara Y. White and John R. Frederiksen

BBN Laboratories
10 Moulton Street
Cambridge, MA 02238

ABSTRACT

One promising educational application of computers derives from their ability to dynamically simulate physical phenomena. Such microworlds permit students to explore, for instance, electrical circuit behavior or particle dynamics. In the past, these simulations have been based upon quantitative models. However, recent work in artificial intelligence has created techniques for basing such microworlds on qualitative reasoning. Qualitative models not only simulate the phenomena of the domain, but also can generate explanations for the behavior under study. Sequences of such models, that attempt to capture a progression from novice to expert reasoning, permit microworlds to incorporate features of intelligent tutoring systems. The learning environment can embody the model progression by making available to students (1) microworlds of increasing complexity, (2) problems classified by the level of model required for their correct solution, and (3) explanations focused on the differences between models and their predecessors. Students can then utilize these microworlds, problem sets and explanations to aid them in developing an understanding of the domain.

1.0 INTRODUCTION

Studies of problem solving have shown that experts make use of multiple conceptualizations in reasoning about a complex domain such as that of electrical circuits. For example, they rely initially on qualitative reasoning and, if the problem requires it, employ quantitative models after they have analyzed the problem in conceptual, qualitative terms (Chi et al., 1981; Larkin et al., 1980). In spite of these characteristics of experts' reasoning, electrical theory is usually taught by first introducing equations for particular circuit conditions (e.g., Ohm's law, formulas for the resistance of resistors in series and in parallel, Kirchhoff's voltage and current laws), and then teaching strategies for applying these equations in the solution of circuit problems. The circuit problems to be solved are largely quantitative, and the mathematical relationships among circuit variables are treated as "laws" that explain circuit function. Yet, there are some fundamental peculiarities in using such "laws" as causal explanations of circuit behavior: (1) they are algebraic rather than causal; (2) their exclusive use implies that scientific understanding and explanation must inevitably be in the form of quantitative relations; and (3) there is a single, "correct" such model for students to learn and apply.

In our research, we have focused on an alternative view of scientific explanation (modelling) and its use in instruction: that scientific theories need not at all times be algebraic and quantitative, that when qualitative explanations are constructed, they can be causally explicit and consistent, and that multiple conceptualizations of circuit behavior can be built that answer different questions about circuit behavior, while remaining conceptually consistent with one another. This mutual consistency allows such multiple models to be used together in reasoning about circuit behavior and in solving problems such as troubleshooting.

In developing this theoretical framework, our research has focused on

1. modelling possible evolutions in students' reasoning about electrical circuits as they come to understand more and more about circuit behavior, and on

2. using these model progressions as the basis for an intelligent learning environment that helps students learn

   a. to predict and explain circuit behavior, and

   b. to troubleshoot by locating opens and shorts to ground in series-parallel circuits.

We have found that, even for the simplest circuit, there are different kinds of questions that you can ask about the behavior of the circuit that require different kinds of reasoning. For example, consider the elementary circuit illustrated in Figure 1, containing a battery, a switch, a light bulb and a variable resistor. One could start by asking, "Is the light in this circuit on or off?" One could then go on to ask, "What happens to the light as I open and close the switch?" This type of question can be answered by a simple form of qualitative reasoning, which we call "zero order" (because it employs no derivatives). Zero order models reason (1) about whether or not devices have voltages applied to them based upon the conductivity and resistance of other devices within the circuit, and (2) about how dramatic changes in conductivity, such as closing a switch, can affect the behavior of the circuit.

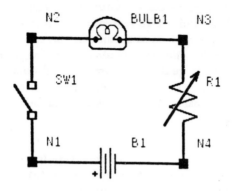

Figure 1

However, asking whether the light is on or off is not the only type of question that one could ask about the behavior of the circuit illustrated in Figure 1. One could also ask, for instance, "What happens to the light as I increase the resistance of the variable resistor? Does the light get brighter or dimmer?" Answering this type of question requires a more sophisticated form of qualitative reasoning, which we call "first order." First order models reason about how increasing the resistance in a branch of a circuit increases and decreases voltages within the circuit. The qualitative model is thus no longer simply reasoning about whether or not there is a voltage applied to a device, rather, it is determining whether the voltage is changing and is, therefore, utilizing qualitative derivatives. This type of analysis is crucial when analyzing, for instance, the occurrence of feedback within a circuit.

Finally one can ask still more precise questions about the behavior of the circuit shown in Figure 1. For example, one could ask, "When I close the switch, how bright will the light be?" Similarly, one could ask, "When I alter the variable resistor, how much brighter or dimmer will the light get?" To answer such questions requires a quantitative analysis of the circuit. Purely qualitative models are no longer sufficient to capture the reasoning necessary to answer this type of question.

We argue that in instruction, one should start by helping students to acquire a progression of increasingly sophisticated, zero order, qualitative models that enable students to reason about gross aspects of circuit behavior. This class of models can help students to develop basic circuit concepts such as resistance, conductivity, and voltage drop. It can also introduce students to fundamental circuit principles such as Kirchhoff's voltage law and help them to understand how changes in one part of the circuit can cause changes in other parts of the circuit. Once these fundamental aspects of circuit behavior have been mastered in qualitative terms, we argue that one should then introduce students to reasoning about more subtle aspects of circuit behavior by helping them to acquire first order, qualitative models of circuit behavior. Finally, only after students can reason about and understand circuit behavior in qualitative terms, should quantitative reasoning be introduced. Further, the form of quantitative circuit analysis taught should be a logical extension of the qualitative reasoning that the students have already mastered.

This approach represents a radical departure from how physical theories are typically taught. Traditionally, only quantitative analysis is taught and students are left to develop their own qualitative methods, which they rarely do until long after they become experts at quantitative analysis (Larkin et al., 1980; Chi et al., 1981; Cohen et al., 1983).

In this paper, we will argue for the instructional necessity of starting with zero order, qualitative models. We will then go on to describe an instructional environment that we have implemented and tried out with high school students.

1.1 The Instructional Need for Zero Order Models

The pioneering work of deKleer (1979) and others (Bobrow, 1985) has shown how models can be developed that enable a computer to reason qualitatively about a physical domain. Further, these researchers have demonstrated that such models can be adequate to solve a large class of problems (e.g., deKleer in Bobrow, 1985). Our work on the design of qualitative models for instructional purposes has focused on creating models that (1) enable decompositions of sophisticated models into simpler models that can, nonetheless, accurately simulate the behavior of some class of circuits, and (2) enable the causality of circuit behaviors for the simpler models to be clear and compatible with that for more sophisticated models.

DeKleer (1985, p. 208) argues that: "Most circuits are designed to deal with changing inputs or loads. For example, ...digital circuits must switch their internal states as applied signals change.... The purpose of these kinds of circuits is best understood by examining how they respond to change." DeKleer's behavioral circuit model reasons in terms of qualitative derivatives obtained from qualitative versions of the constraint equations ("confluences") used in quantitative circuit analysis. These enable it to analyze the effects of changing inputs on circuit behavior.

The difficulty with utilizing such a model – at least at the initial stage of instruction – is that novices typically do not have a concept of voltage or resistance, let alone a conception of changes in voltages or resistance (Collins, 1985; Cohen et al., 1983). For example, as part of a trial of our instructional system, we interviewed seven high school students who had studied physics as part of a middle school science course, but who had not taken a high school physics course. They all initially exhibited serious misconceptions about circuit behaviors. For example, when asked to describe the behavior of the light in the circuit shown in Figure 2 as the switches are opened and closed, only one of the seven students had a concept of a circuit. The other students predicted that the bulb would light if only one of the switches were closed. The following was a typical remark, "If one of the switches on the left is closed, the light will light. It does not matter whether the switches on the right are open or closed. Further, if you close both switches on the left, the light will be twice as bright as if you close only one of them." In addition to this lack of a basic circuit concept, all seven of the students predicted that when you close the switch in Figure 3, the light would still light – the statement that the switch was not resistive when closed did not matter. In fact, five of the students stated that they did not know what was meant by the term "not resistive." They thus had no conception of how a non-resistive path in a circuit could affect circuit behavior.

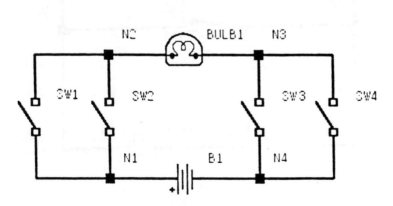

Figure 2

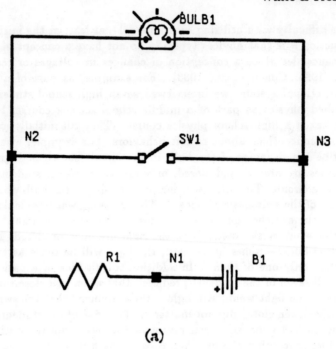

(a)

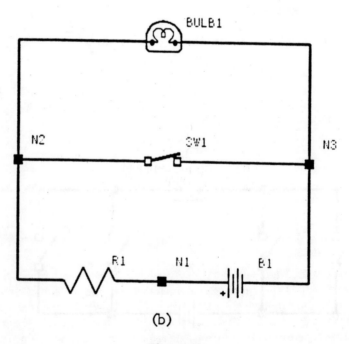

(b)

Figure 3

Novices such as these, who do not have accurate models of when a voltage is applied to a device in a circuit, could not possibly understand what is meant by a change in voltage across a device. Thus, we argue that students should initially be taught a progression of zero order, qualitative models that reason about gross aspects of circuit behavior. This type of model can accurately simulate the behavior of a large class of circuits, and can be utilized to introduce fundamental ideas about circuit behavior.

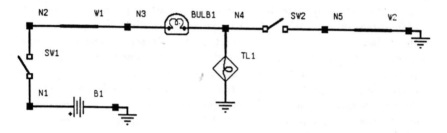

Figure 4

The knowledge embedded in the zero order models has been shown to be the type of knowledge that even college physics students lack (Cohen et al., 1983), and is also crucial knowledge for successful troubleshooting. For example, consider an elementary form of troubleshooting such as trying to locate an open in the circuit shown in Figure 4. Imagine that a test light is inserted into the middle of the circuit as shown in the figure. In order to make an inference about whether the open is in the part of the circuit in series with the test light or the part in parallel with it, one needs to know that if switch #1 were open, the light would *not* be on even if the circuit had no fault. Similarly, one needs to understand that if switch #2 were closed, the test light would *not* be on even if the circuit were unfaulted. Thus, even for performing the most elementary type of electrical troubleshooting, one needs a "zero order understanding" of circuit behavior.

2.0 AN OVERVIEW OF THE INSTRUCTIONAL SYSTEM

The learning environment we have constructed lets students solve problems, hear explanations and perform experiments, all in the context of interacting with a dynamic simulation of circuit behavior. However, unlike most simulations, the underlying model is qualitative, not quantitative. Further, the simulation is performed not by a single model, but rather by the progression of zero order models that increases in sophistication in concordance with

the evolution of the students' understanding of the domain. Learning thus
is regarded as a process of model evolution: students attempt to formulate
a series of partial models, each of which is adequate for solving some subset
of problems within the domain.

Viewing instruction as producing in the student a progression of models permits a tutoring system architecture with elegant properties. Within
our system, the student model, the tutor and the domain simulation are
incorporated within the single model that is active at any point in learning.
This model is used to simulate the domain phenomena, is capable of generating explanations by articulating its behavior, and furnishes a model of the
students' reasoning at that particular stage in learning. The progression of
models also enables the system to select problems and generate explanations that are appropriate for the student at any point in the instructional
sequence. In order to motivate students to transform their models into new
models, they are given problems that the desired model can handle but
their present models cannot. This evolution of models also enables the system to focus its explanations on the difference between the present model
and the desired model.

Such a system architecture also permits a variety of pedagogical strategies to be explored within a single instructional system. Since the system
can turn a problem into an example by solving it for the student, the students' learning can be motivated by problems or by examples. That is,
students can be presented with problems and only see examples if they run
into difficulty; alternatively, they can see examples first and then be given
problems to solve. Also, by working within the simulation environment,
students can construct their own problems and thus explore the domain in
a more open ended fashion. Further, the learning process can be managed
either by the system or by the student. For example, students can be given
a map of the problem space and can decide for themselves what class of
problems to pursue next or even what pedagogical strategy they want to
employ.

In order to support this variety of pedagogical strategies, the system
must be capable of generating runnable qualitative models for any circuit
that the student or instructional designer might create. Thus, students
can – for example –use a circuit editor to create circuits and experiment
with them by changing the states of devices, inserting faults and adding or
deleting components.

3.0 THE ZERO ORDER MODELS

The progression of zero order behavioral models incorporate knowledge of the topological structure of the circuit, the behavior of the devices within the circuit and basic electrical principles relating to the distribution of voltages within the circuit. These principles enable the model to reason about the effects of changes in the conductivity of circuit components. The instructional system also includes a progression of general troubleshooting algorithms for localizing faults within a circuit. These algorithms utilize the behavioral models as part of their problem solving process. Both the behavioral models and troubleshooting algorithms can articulate their thinking – both visually and verbally – when simulating the behavior of a given circuit or when troubleshooting.

3.1 Circuit Topology

The topology of the circuit is represented by the set of devices included in the circuit, together with the set of interconnections between designated ports of those devices. Thus, each instantiation of a device type within a circuit includes a table containing, for each of its ports, the electrical node to which it is connected.

3.2 Device Models

The behavioral models contain device models for devices typically found in circuits. The devices modelled are batteries, switches, resistors, bulbs, diodes, fuses, capacitors, transistors, test lights, and wires (wires are explicitly introduced as devices). Device models include rules for determining a device's *state*, based upon the circuit environment of the device. For example, if there is a voltage drop across the two ports of a light bulb, the light bulb will be in the "on" state; otherwise it is in the "off" state. When a device's state changes, the device model activates additional rules which reevaluate a set of *variables* associated with the device. These variables include (1) the conductivity of the device (is it purely conductive, conductive but resistive, or nonconductive), and (2) whether or not the device is a source of voltage. For example, when a capacitor is in the charged state, it is nonconductive and a source of voltage.

When a particular device, such as a light bulb, is employed within a particular circuit, a data table is created for the specific instantiation of that device in that circuit. This table is used to record (1) the present state of the device, (2) whether it is presently a voltage source, (3) its internal conductivity (what possible internal conductive paths exist among its ports and whether they are presently purely conductive, resistive, or nonconductive), and (4) the device polarity, as well as (5) its connections to other devices in the circuit.

3.3 Circuit Principles

When simulating a particular circuit, the only information that the qualitative simulation requires is information about the structure of the circuit, that is, the devices and their interconnections. All of the information about circuit behavior, as represented by a sequence of changes in device states, is inferred by the qualitative simulation as it reasons about the circuit. To reason about device polarity and state, the device models utilize general qualitative methods for circuit analysis. For instance, when attempting to evaluate their states, device models can call upon procedures to establish voltages within the circuit. In the case of the zero order models, these procedures determine, based upon the circuit topology and the states of devices, whether or not a device has a voltage applied to it.[1] The most sophisticated zero order voltage rule is based on the concept that, for a device to have a voltage applied to it, it must occur in a circuit (loop) containing a voltage source and must not have any non-resistive paths in parallel with it within that circuit. More formally, the zero order voltage rule can be stated as:

> If there is at least one conductive path to the negative side of a voltage source from one port of the device (a return path), and if there is a conductive path from another port of the device to the positive side of that voltage source (a feed path), with no nonresistive path branching from any point on that "feed" path to any point on any "return" path, then the device has a voltage applied to that pair of ports.[2]

Changes in a circuit – such as closing a switch – can alter in a dramatic way the conductivity of the circuit, and thereby produce changes in whether or not a device has a voltage applied to it. To illustrate, when the switch is open in the circuit shown in Figure 3(a), the device model for the light bulb

---

[1] In the case of the first order models, these procedures reason about whether the voltage drop across a device is increasing or decreasing as a result of changes in its resistance and the resistance of other devices in the circuit.

[2] By "voltage applied to a device," we mean the qualitative version of the open circuit (or Thevenin) voltage, that is, the voltage the device sees as it looks into the circuit. In the case of the zero order voltage rule, this is simply the presence or absence of voltage.

calls upon procedures for evaluating voltages in order to determine whether the light's state is on or off. The procedure finds a good feed path and a good return path and thus the light bulb will be on. When the switch is closed, as shown in Figure 3(b), the procedure finds a short from the feed to the return path and thus the light bulb will be off.

3.4 Causal Explanations

Simply having the model articulate that when the switch is closed, the light will be off because there is a non-resitive path across it, is not a sufficient causal explanation for students who have no understanding of (1) what is meant by non-resistive, or (2) what affect such a path can have on circuit behavior. First of all, students need definitions for concepts such as voltage, resistance, current, device state, internal conductivity, series circuit, and parallel circuit. Further, they need a "deeper" causal explanation of the circuit's behavior. For instance, Brown and deKleer (in Bobrow, 1985) point out that there are two alternate perspectives on the causality of circuit behavior: a current flow perspective and a voltage drop perspective. To illustrate, the following are explanations that (1) a current flow model, and (2) a voltage drop model could give as to why the light is off when the switch is closed for the circuit shown in Figure 3.

1. The current flow model could state:

> In order for the bulb to light, current must flow through it. There is a device in parallel with the bulb, the switch. In parallel paths, the current is divided among the paths. More current flows through the path with the least resistance. If one of the paths has no resistance, all of the current will flow through it. Since the bulb has resistance and the switch does not, all of the current will flow through the switch. Since there is no current flow through the bulb, it will be off.

2. Whereas, the voltage drop model could state:

> In order for the bulb to light, there must be a voltage drop across it. There is a device in parallel with the bulb, the switch. Two devices in parallel have the same voltage drop across them. Voltage drop is directly proportional to resistance: If there is no resistance, there can be no voltage drop. Since the switch has no resistance, there is no voltage drop across the switch. Thus, there is no voltage drop across the light, so the light will be off.

One could be given even "deeper" accounts of the physics underlying circuit causality. For instance, the system could present physical models that attempt to explain why current flow and voltage drop are affected by resistance in terms of electrical fields and their propagation. However, for our present purposes, the system presents a causal account to the depth illustrated by the preceding model.

In explaining the behavior of the light in the preceding example, one could utilize either the voltage drop explanation or the current flow explanation, or both. Our view is that giving students both types of explanations, at least in the initial stages of learning about circuits, would be unnecessary and confusing. It would require students to construct two models for circuit behavior, and this would create a potential for them to become confused about circuit causality.

We therefore selected only one of the causal models. We chose the voltage drop explanation because current flows as a result of an electromotive force being applied to a circuit; because troubleshooting tasks typically are based upon reasoning about voltages and testing for them; and because research has shown that this is an important way of conceptualizing circuit behavior that even sophisticated students lack, as illustrated by the following quotation from Cohen, Eylon, and Ganiel (1983):

> "Current is the primary concept used by students, whereas potential difference is regarded as a consequence of current flow, and not as its cause. Consequently, students often use $V = IR$ incorrectly. A battery is regarded as a source of constant current. The concepts of emf and internal resistance are not well understood. Students have difficulties in analyzing the effect which a change in one component has on the rest of the circuit."

In addition, reasoning about how circuits divide voltage is a major component of our first order models. These models reason about changes in resistances and voltages within a circuit, using a qualitative form of Kirchhoff's voltage law. Thus, getting students to reason in terms of voltages is compatible with the type of reasoning that will be required later on in the evolution of the students' models.

3.5 Topological Search

The rules that embody circuit principles, such as the zero order voltage rule, utilize topological search processes that are needed, for example, to determine whether a device has a conductive path to a source of voltage. The search processes utilize the information maintained by the device data tables concerning the devices' circuit connections, polarity, internal conductivity, and whether or not they serve as voltage sources. The topological search processes can locate conductive paths within the circuit. For example, they can find all conductive paths from one port of a device to another port of the same device or to a port of another device. They can also check to see if the paths are resistive or non-resistive.

3.6 Establishing Device Polarities

The topological search processes are guided by polarities assigned to the ports of each device in the circuit. For example, when the light bulb in the circuit shown in Figure 5 is attempting to evaluate its state, it calls upon the voltage rule which invokes a search for – amongst other things – a conductive path to the positive side of the battery. This search immediately reaches a potential branching point: it could pursue the path starting with resistor R_3 and/or it could pursue the path starting with resistor R_2. However, the search is reduced to only following the path starting with resistor R_2, because the polarities of the connecting ports for the light bulb and resistor R_3 are both positive, and therefore, this path through resistor R_3 cannot lead to the positive side of the voltage source. The device polarities can thus be used to prune the topological searches.

Device polarities are established by a general qualitative circuit orientation algorithm that reorients the circuit whenever a topological change in the circuit occurs or whenever a device alters its status as a source of voltage. The algorithm begins by identifying all electrical nodes[3] in the circuit, and labelling them. Then it recursively recognizes and removes all series and parallel subcircuits. Two components that are connected together at both ends are recognized as a parallel subcircuit and are treated as a unit. Two components that are connected only to each other at one end are recognized as a series subcircuit and are also treated as a unit. The algorithm first brackets all parallel subcircuits as units and then, working with what are currently the highest level bracketed units, all series subcircuits. This process of alternately removing parallel and series subcircuits continues until there are no such subcircuits remaining. The algorithm constructs the innermost groupings first and proceeds in this way until the final grouping is reached, namely one that encompasses the entire circuit. The result is a hierarchical parsing of the circuit. The units are then assigned polarities in relation to the voltage source, starting at the outermost grouping and moving inwards. The side of a unit connected to the positive terminal of

---

[3] Electrical nodes are points of connection between two or more resistive devices. Any non-resistive devices present are collapsed into a single electrical node.

the battery is assigned a plus, and the other side a minus. Units contained within larger units are assigned the same polarities as those of the larger units which contain them.[4]

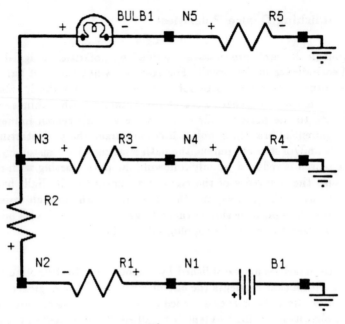

Figure 5

This circuit orientation algorithm was designed to be easy for students to learn and execute. However, in the initial progression of models, the complexity of circuits that students are exposed to is not sufficient to require teaching the algorithm. Determining the orientation of devices within the circuit is straightforward. Thus, we assume that students can identify device orientations within the initial progression of circuits, and therefore, the algorithm does not articulate its behavior and is not explicitly taught.

---

[4] This algorithm can identify indeterminacies in the assignment of polarities to a unit. For instance, if a unit has *both* feed and return paths from each of its ports then its orientation may not be determined. If all of these paths lead to the same voltage source, it is a bridge element in the circuit. If the paths lead to different voltage sources having different polarities, the orientation of the unit is also indeterminant.

3.7 Control Structure

The simulation of circuit operation is driven by changes in the states of the devices in the circuit. These changes are produced by (1) changes in states of other devices, such as a battery becoming discharged causing a light to go out; (2) external interventions, such as a person closing a switch or a fault being introduced into the circuit; and (3) increments in time, such as a capacitor becoming discharged. Whenever a device changes state, its status as a voltage source is redetermined by the device model, along with its internal conductivity/resistance. Whenever any device's internal conductivity or status as a voltage source changes, then time stops incrementing within the simulation and all of the other devices in the circuit reevaluate their states. This allows any changes in conductivity or presence of voltage sources within the circuit to propagate their effects to the states of other devices. The circuit information used for this reevaluation is the set of device data tables existing at the initiation of the reevaluation (not those that are being created in the current reevaluation cycle). This is to avoid unwanted sequential dependencies in determining device states. If in the course of this reevaluation some additional devices change state, then the reevaluation process is repeated. This series of propagation cycles continues until the behavior of the circuit stabilizes and no further changes in device states have occurred. Time is then allowed to increment and the simulation continues. When any further changes in device states occur, due either to the passage of time or to external intervention, time is again frozen and the propagation of state changes is allowed to commence once again.

3.8 A Sample Zero Order Circuit Simulation

As an illustration of how a zero order model reasons, consider a simulation of the behavior of the circuit illustrated in Figure 6. Initially suppose that both switches are open, the light bulb is off, and the capacitor is discharged. Then, suppose that someone closes switch #1. This change in the internal conductivity of a device causes the other devices in the circuit to reevaluate their states. The capacitor remains discharged because switch #2 being open prevents it from having a good return path. The light bulb has good feed and return paths, so its state becomes on. Since, in the course of this reevaluation no device changed its conductivity, the reevaluation process terminates. Note that even though the light bulb changed state, its internal conductity is always the same, so its change of state can have no effect on circuit behavior and thus does not trigger the reevaluation process.

Now, imagine that someone closes switch #2. This change in state produces a change in the conductity of the switch and triggers the reevaluation process. The light bulb attempts to reevaluate its state and finds that its feed path is shorted out by the capacitor (which is purely-conductive because it is in the discharged state) and switch #2 (which is also purely-conductive because its state is closed), so its state becomes off. The capacitor attempts to reevaluate its state and finds that it has a good feed and return path, so its state becomes charged. This change in state causes it to reevaluate its internal conductivity, and to reevaluate whether it is a source of voltage. As a result of the capacitor becoming charged, it becomes non-conductive, and a source of voltage. This change in the internal conductivity of the capacitor causes the reevaluation process to trigger again. The light bulb reevaluates its state and finds that it has a good feed and return path (it is no longer shorted out by the capacitor because the capacitor is now charged and therefore non-conductive) and its state becomes on. This change in the light bulb's state has no effect on the light bulb's internal conductivity so the reevaluation process terminates.

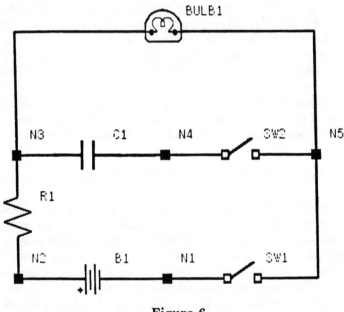

Figure 6

Suppose that someone then opens switch #1. This changes the switches internal conductivity and therefore causes all other devices to reevaluate their states. The light bulb no longer has a good return path with respect to the battery. However, it has a good feed and return path to another source of voltage within the circuit, the capacitor (which is charged and therefore a source of voltage). The state of the light bulb will thus be on. The capacitor no longer has a good return path to a source of voltage and it has a conductive path across it, so its state becomes discharged and it becomes purely-conductive and is not a source of voltage. This change in the capacitors internal conductivity causes the light bulb to reevaluate its state. Since the capacitor is no longer a source of voltage, and since switch #1 is open thereby preventing a good return path to the battery, the light bulb concludes that its state is off. This change in state has no effect on the light bulb's internal conductivity so the reevaluation process terminates.

Notice that this relatively unsophisticated qualitative simulation has been able to simulate and explain some important aspects of this circuit's behavior. It demonstrates how when switch #2 is closed, it initially shorts out the bulb, and then, when the capacitor charges, it no longer shorts out the bulb. Further, it explains how when switch #1 is opened, the capacitor causes the light bulb to light initially, and then, when the capacitor becomes discharged, the light bulb goes out.

3.9 The Troubleshooting Algorithms

The progression of troubleshooting algorithms is based upon a qualitative approach taken by an expert whom we have studied. This expert not only utilizes this approach in actual diagnostic work, but also teaches the technique to students in a technical high school. The method he uses is based upon the fundamental idea of a circuit, and is similar to that of the zero-order models (which was motivated in part by the approach of this expert): For a device to "operate" (e.g., for a test light to light or a capacitor to charge), it must have voltage applied to it. When such an electrical potential exists, a current will flow through the device (provided it is conductive), causing it in some cases to change its state. In order for there to be an electrical potential, there must be a source of voltage. Further, there must be conductive paths leading from each port of the device to, respectively, the positive and negative sides of a voltage source. In a series circuit, one source of faults is the occurrence of opens within either of these paths, which will prevent current from flowing with a resulting effect on the device's state. Another source of faults is the presence of shorts to ground, which introduce non-resistive parallel paths into the circuit. If these shorts occur between the device and the ungrounded side of the voltage source, they will prevent current from flowing through the device. Opens and shorts to ground are types of faults that the troubleshooting algorithm is designed to diagnose.

The goal of the troubleshooting algorithms is to divide the circuit into two parts and then to infer which portion of the circuit contains the fault. The troubleshooting logic is then recursively applied to the faulty segment until the fault has been localized. This is accomplished using the following strategy: first, the circuit is logically divided into two parts by inserting a test light into the circuit between a test point near the center of the circuit and the grounded (negative) side of the voltage source. Second, the circuit simulation is run to determine the correct state of the test light in a circuit that is not faulted. Third, that state is compared with the actual test light behavior, and inferences are made about possible faults that are consistent with the findings. The logic used depends upon whether or not the test light is supposed to be on, given an unfaulted circuit, and upon the actual behavior of the light in the presence of the fault. For instance, if the test light is supposed to be on and is not on, the fault could be in the part of the circuit in series with the test light, or it could be a short to ground in the part of the circuit in parallel with the test light (at a point before any resistance is encountered). Additional troubleshooting operations are then carried out to isolate the fault to either the portion of the circuit in series with the test light, or the one in parallel with the test light. To accomplish this, the expert detaches the latter portion of the circuit from the test point, and observes the effect. If the test light comes on, the fault can be isolated to the portion of the circuit in parallel with the test light. Namely, it was providing a non-resistive path from the feed path of the light to the ground. If the test light remains off, the problem must be an open or a short to ground in the portion of the circuit in series with the test light. When the fault has been isolated to within a portion of the circuit, the expert moves the test light to a new point within the faulty segment of the circuit and reapplies the troubleshooting logic. This process is repeated until the fault is located.

The troubleshooting logic as described here is restricted to series circuits. However, additional principles allow it to be extended to parallel circuits and to series-parallel circuits. In instruction, the troubleshooting algorithm presented to students increases progressively in complexity. The sequence of troubleshooting algorithms is coordinated with the progression of behavioral circuit models that the students acquire.

4.0 MODEL TRANSFORMATIONS

The learning environment, as described previously, is not based upon a single, zero order, qualitative model, but rather, it is based upon a progression of increasingly sophisticated, partial models that correspond to a possible evolution of a learner's model. The system helps students to transform their model by presenting to them problems that can be solved by the transformed model but not by the untransformed model. The students are thus motivated to revise their existing qualitative models in an appropriate direction.

For example, the learning environment can help students who have a rudimentary conception of voltage drop to refine their conception by learning about the effects of non-resistive paths. This particular model transformation can be motivated by giving students problems where they have to predict, for instance, the behavior of the light bulb in the circuit shown in Figure 3 as the switch is opened and closed.

In order to facilitate such a transformation, the system can turn any problem into an example for the student by reasoning out loud while it solves the problem. As models become more sophisticated, they also become more verbose. The mechanism for pruning explanations is to focus the explanations on the difference between the transformed and the untransformed model. Reasoning of the transformed model that was present in the untransformed model either does not articulate itself or, if it is necessary to support the model increment, is presented in summary fashion.

Looking at the difference between the transformed model and the students' current model also helps to define what aspects of the problem solving process should be represented to the students. For instance, if students are learning about determining when there is or is not a voltage applied to a device, the system illustrates paths to voltage sources. However, later in the model progression, when it is assumed that students already know how to determine the presence of an applied voltage, the paths are no longer displayed.

In the present implementation, the path through the space of possible model progressions has been constrained by adopting the instructional goals of (1) teaching circuit concepts and laws needed to enable troubleshooting, and (2) teaching them in an order that would permit students to engage in troubleshooting as early in the progression as possible while still making the principles of circuit behavior clear. The progression of zero order models that we selected, in conjunction with the progression of troubleshooting algorithms, attempts to capture one possible transition from novice to expert status.

The progression thus defines a curriculum for a student. Since the simplest form of troubleshooting is locating an open in a series circuit, the initial sequence in the progression enables the student to construct the concepts and laws needed to support this simplest form of troubleshooting.

4.1 Voltage, Conductivity and the Fundamental Idea of a Circuit

The zero order curriculum we have implemented starts by teaching the fundamental idea of electrical potential and its ability to alter a device's state. In order to understand how an electrical potential can be developed across a device in a circuit, the idea of conductive and non-conductive paths to a voltage source are introduced. Series circuits containing only a battery, wire, light bulb and a switch are utilized. The fault of open is introduced as one means for creating a non-conductive path. The control structure required of the students' mental model is kept simple by asking them to make predictions about the behavior of a single light bulb when a switch is opened and closed, or when a wire is faulted open.

4.2 Reasoning About More Than One Device Changing State

In this model progression, students learn to generalize the concepts related to electrical potential and device states to cases where they must reason about more than one device changing state in the circuit. They learn that when there is a circuit, voltage is applied to all devices within the circuit (this is a zero order version of Kirchhoff's voltage law). Reasoning about the behavior of more than one device increases the complexity of the control structure of the students' model. Since the circuits being presented at this stage contain only devices such as light bulbs and resistors whose internal conductivity never changes, a serial evaluation of device states is all that is necessary. Thus, this model transformation entails only a slight increase in complexity over the control structure of the previous model.

4.3 Alternative Feed and Return Paths

In this transition, students are asked to reason about the behavior of light bulbs in circuits, such as that illustrated in Figure 2, which potentially have multiple feed and return paths. This type of reasoning is necessary for troubleshooting because when a test light in inserted into a circuit, it can introduce multiple feed paths. In this transition, the students' concept of voltage must be refined to incorporate the fact that in a circuit with parallel paths, only one good feed and return path are necessary for a device to have a voltage applied to it.

4.4 Shorts Across a Device

In this model progression, students are exposed to circuits where shorts immediately across a device can exist, and they must expand their circuit principles to account for the effects of such shorts. For example, in the circuit shown in Figure 3, there is a short across the light bulb when the switch is closed. Understanding this type of short is needed when troubleshooting since if there is a purely conductive path in parallel with a test light, the light will be off even if there is no fault in the circuit. In this model progression, students must differentiate their concept of a conductive path into conductive-resistive and purely conductive paths. Thus, their concept of conductivity must be refined and this refinement must be integrated into their voltage rule – the rule must now incorporate the fact that if there is a purely conductive path immediately across a device, then no voltage is applied to that device.

4.5 Purely Conductive Paths in Parallel Circuits

This model progression generalizes the concept of a purely conductive parallel path (a short) from being immediately across a device to being anywhere on the device's feed path to any point on a return path or even immediately to ground (a short to ground). The circuit principles used to infer when voltages are applied must be refined to incorporate the more sophisticated rule presented earlier in our discussion of circuit principles.

4.6 Troubleshooting an Open in a Series Circuit

Students now possess an understanding of circuit behavior that is sufficient to support troubleshooting a series circuit containing a battery, wires, light bulbs, switches and resistors. The simplest troubleshooting algorithm is thus introduced at this point. This subset of troubleshooting logic allows students to learn the basic troubleshooting heuristics of dividing the search space and making inferences about entire portions of the circuit. By limiting the fault to an open, both the conceptual and procedural aspects of troubleshooting are kept simple.

4.7 Troubleshooting Shorts to Ground in a Series Circuit

Students now have a basic knowledge of troubleshooting heuristics and an understanding of circuit behavior sufficient to support locating opens and shorts to ground. Learning how to locate shorts to ground is made easier by considering a short to ground as the only possible fault at this point in the learning sequence. In this transition, students thus generalize the troubleshooting heuristics of dividing the search space and making inferences about entire portions of the circuit to situations in which they must locate shorts to ground in a series circuit.

4.8 Locating Opens or Shorts to Ground in a Series Circuit

Finally, students are given problems to motivate an integration of their troubleshooting model for finding opens with that for finding shorts to ground, since in real troubleshooting situations, they will not know which fault is present in the circuit.

Further model evolutions include (1) increasing the domain of circuits that the student can troubleshoot to include series-parallel circuits, and (2) increasing the repertoire of device models to include capacitors and devices such as diodes and transistors that have polarities associated with them.

On a larger scale, we envision further model evolutions aimed at developing alternative conceptualizations of circuit behavior. These include: (1) first order behavioral models that allow one to reason about *changes* in resistance and voltage and how they propagate within a circuit; (2) extensions of the underlying causal framework of the analysis to include forward reasoning about the effects of voltage and resistance on current, and backward reasoning about how changes in current have been precipitated by changes in voltage; and (3) quantitative circuit analysis based upon the quantitative constraints on voltage, resistance and current that have previously been presented in their qualitative forms.

5.0 LEARNING STRATEGIES

The learning environment consists of an interactive simulation driven by qualitative models. Further, the progression of models defines classes of problems and facilitates explanation generation. This architecture for an intelligent learning environment permits great flexibility in the students' choice of an instructional strategy.

5.1 Open-ended Exploration

Students can construct circuits, explore their behavior (by changing the states of devices, inserting faults and adding or deleting components), and request explanations for the observed behaviors. Students can thus create their own problems and experiment with circuits. The system thereby permits an open-ended exploratory learning strategy.

5.2 Problem-driven Learning

In addition, the progression of models enables the system to present students with a sequence of problem solving situations that motivate the need for developing particular transformations of their models of circuit behavior. In solving new problems, the students attempt to transform their models of circuit behavior in concordance with the evolution of the system's models. The focus is on having students solve problems on their own, without providing them first with explanations for how to solve them. Only when they run into difficulty, do they request explanations of circuit behavior.

5.3 Example-driven Learning

Alternatively, students can be presented with tutorial demonstrations for solving example problems by simply asking the system to reason out loud about a given circuit using its present, qualitative, causal model. Students can thus hear explanations of how to solve each type of problem in the series, followed by opportunities to solve similar problems. Since the focus is on presenting examples together with explanations prior to practice in problem solving, we term this learning strategy "example-driven."

5.4 Student Directed Learning

The classification of problems created by the progression of models provides facilities for students to use in pursuing instructional goals of their own choosing. Problems can be classified on the basis of the concepts and laws required for their solution, and on the instructional purpose served by the problem. This enables students to pursue goals such as acquiring a new concept or differentiating two concepts. The students make their own decisions about what problems to solve and even about what learning strategy to employ.

The system has been tried out with seven high school students. Students were allowed to pursue their own learning strategies with the constraint that use of the circuit editor was restricted to the modification of circuits in the problem sets. Initially, all of the students exhibited serious misconceptions about circuit behavior, and lacked key electrical concepts. Further, none of them had any experience with troubleshooting. After five hours of working with the system on an individual basis, they were all able to make accurate zero order predictions about circuit behavior and could troubleshoot for opens and shorts to ground in series circuits. We found that differences between the students' mental models and those that we were trying to teach were not due to the inevitability of misconceptions, but rather, were due to limitations of the learning environment – a nonoptimality in either the form of the knowledge we were trying to impart, or the progression of models, or the type of problem selected to induce a particular model transformation. Thus, our future research will focus on developing further the theory underlying model forms, model transformations and instructional strategies. Also, we intend to to expand the set of instructional modes and problem types, by – for example – allowing students to design and troubleshoot not only circuits, but also, the qualitative models that perform the circuit simulations.

ACKNOWLEDGEMENTS

This research was supported by the Office of Naval Research and the Army Research Institute, under ONR contract N00014-82-C-0580 with the Personnel and Training Research Program. The work benefited from the perspectives and innumerable contributions of Wallace Feurzeig. The current implementation of the system was programmed by Frank Ritter, who helped with the system design, particularly the circuit orientation scheme. In addition, we would like to thank Allan Collins and Paul Horwitz for their many thought-provoking comments.

This paper incorporates material published in the *Proceedings of the Fifth National Conference on Artificial Intelligence*, (White & Frederiksen, 1986(b)).

REFERENCES

Bobrow, D.G. (Ed.) (1985). *Qualitative Reasoning about Physical Systems*. Cambridge, MA: MIT Press.

Bureau of Naval Personnel (1970). *Basic Electricity*. New York: Dover.

Chi, M.T.H., & Glaser, R. (1980). The measurement of expertise: analysis of the development of knowledge and skill as a basis for assessing achievement. In E.L. Baker & E.S. Quellmalz (Eds.), *Educational Testing Evaluation*. Beverly Hills, CA: Sage Publications.

Chi, M., Feltovich, P., & Glaser, R. (1981). Categorization and representation of physics problems by experts and novices, *Cognitive Science 5*, 121–152.

Cohen, R., Eylon, B., & Ganiel, U. (1983). Potential difference and current in simple electric circuits: a study of students' concepts, *American Journal of Physics 51(5)*, 407-412.

Collins, A. (1985). Component models of physical systems, *Proceedings of the Seventh Annual Conference of the Cognitive Science Society*, University of California, Irvine.

Davis, R. (1983). Reasoning from first principles in electronic troubleshooting, *International Journal of Man-Machine Studies 19*, 403-423.

deKleer, J. (1979). Causal and teleological reasoning in circuit recognition. TR-529, MIT Artificial Intelligence Laboratory, Cambridge, MA.

Forbus, K., & Stevens, A.S. (1981). Using qualitative simulation to generate explanations. BBN Report No. 4490, Cambridge, MA: BBN Laboratories.

Gentner, D., & Stevens, A. L. (1983). *Mental Models*. Hillsdale, NJ: Lawrence Erlbaum Associates.

Gitomer, D. H. (1984). A cognitive analysis of a complex troubleshooting task. Unpublished doctoral dissertation, University of Pittsburgh, Pittsburgh, PA.

Kieras, D. E., & Bovair, S. (1984). The role of a mental model in learning to operate a device. *Cognitive Science 8*, 255-274.

Larkin, J.H., McDermott, J., Simon, D.P., & Simon, H.A. (1980). Expert and novice performance in solving physics problems. *Science 208*, 1335-1342.

Rasmussen, J., & Jensen, A. (1974). Mental procedures in real life tasks: a case study of electronic troubleshooting. *Ergonomics 17*, 193-307.

Riley, M.S. (1984). Structural understanding in performance and learning. Unpublished doctoral dissertation, University of Pittsburgh, Pittsburgh, PA.

Rouse, W.B., & Morris, N.M. (1985). On looking into the black box: prospects and limits in the search for mental models. *Center for Man-Machine Systems Research Report No. 85-2,* Atlanta, GA: Georgia Institute of Technology.

Smith, E.E., & Goodman, L. (1984). Understanding instructions: the role of an explanatory schema. *Cognition and Instruction 1,* 359-396.

Sleeman, D., & Brown, J.S. (1982). *Intelligent Tutoring Systems,* London: Academic Press.

Steinberg, M.S. (1983). Reinventing electricity. *Proceedings of the International Seminar, Misconceptions in Science and Mathematics,* Ithaca, New York.

White, B.Y., & Frederiksen, J.R. (1984). Modeling expertise in troubleshooting and reasoning about simple electric circuits. *Proceedings of the Annual Meeting of the Cognitive Science Society,* Boulder, Colorado.

White, B.Y., & Frederiksen, J.R. (1985). QUEST: qualitative understanding of electrical system troubleshooting. *ACM SIGART Newsletter 93,* 34-37.

White, B.Y., & Frederiksen, J.R. (1986(a)). Progressions of qualitative models as a foundation for intelligent learning environments. Report No. 6277, BBN Laboratories, Cambridge, Massachusetts.

White, B.Y., & Frederiksen, J.R. (1986(b)). Intelligent tutoring systems based upon qualitative model evolutions. *Proceedings of the Fifth National Conference on Artificial Intelligence,* Philadelphia, Pennsylvania.

15 SENSE AND REFERENCE IN THE DESIGN OF INTERACTIVE ILLUSTRATIONS FOR RATIONAL NUMBERS

Stellan Ohlsson

Learning Research and Development Center
University of Pittsburgh
Pittsburgh, PA 15260

ABSTRACT

It is a common tactic in the teaching of arithmetic to provide the learner with pictures and embodiments of various kinds. However, the pedagogy of illustrations is not well understood. Analysis of the concept of meaning in relation to arithmetic shows that full understanding of arithmetic implies intellectual possession of a number of different intellectual constructions, among them a teleological, an analytical, and a referential semantics for arithmetic. It is argued that the primary purpose of illustrations for elementary arithmetic is to clarify the semantics of the language of arithmetic. An informal analytical semantics for rational number concepts is presented, revealing a rather complex system of concepts. Construction of a referential semantics for the concept of ratio leads to the conjecture that illustrations for rational numbers are necessarily incomplete in the sense that they can, in principle, only illustrate some aspects of rational numbers but not others. The results of these analyses are summarized in a prescriptive theory of illustration design.

1.0 INTRODUCTION

Mathematics is the intellectually most straining subject taught in elementary school. The difficulty of mathematics has several sources. However, the intuition of educators tend to single out the *abstractness* of mathematics as the major source of difficulty. The abstract character of mathematics prevents the learner from "seeing" the subject matter clearly, or – to change metaphor – from "grasping" it firmly. As a result, mathematical procedures are not understood, even when they are carried out correctly. The lack of understanding – so the argument continues – causes incorrect application of mathematical concepts and procedures in the solving of novel problems.

The remedy, then, is to concretize mathematics. There are two closely related ways in which teachers, inspired by the two metaphors of "seeing" and "grasping", have tried to achieve this. One way of providing concreteness is to use *pictures*, drawings or diagrams which visually display mathematical objects or operations. In this approach, mathematical objects and operations acquire meaning by becoming visible. Displaying a function by drawing its graph is perhaps the most common use of a picture in mathematics. However, many other mathematical objects, properties, and operations have been pictorially explained in mathematics education, although the pictures do not always have as clear a rationale as in the case of function graphs. Arnheim (1969) and in particular Sawyer (1964) provide interesting collections of examples. As a glance at any textbook in elementary mathematics will show (e.g., Rucker & Dilley, 1981), the use of pictures is a very popular teaching tactic. However, there is little research on how and why and when pictures help learning; recent reviews of research into mathematics education hardly mention the issue (e.g., Davis, 1984; Romberg & Carpenter, 1986).

A related, but distinct approach to concretizing mathematics is to use manipulatives or *embodiments*, physical objects which can be manipulated in ways which are analogous to certain mathematical operations. Embodiments are visible, of course, but their purpose is to be objects of actions. In this approach, mathematical objects become meaningful by becoming touchable. Embodiments are probably used less frequently in teaching than pictures, but there exists a small body of – somewhat discouraging – research on their effectiveness (Bell, Costello, & Kuchermann, 1983, pp. 190-194).

Computer technology and advanced programming techniques make it possible to construct teaching materials which combine the two approaches to concreteness. We can provide the learner with pictures on the computer screen *and* a set of commands for acting upon them, e.g., changing them, moving them about, combining them, etc. I will use the term *interactive illustrations* for graphical displays which are responsive to the learner. Computer graphics allows us to design the visual qualities of an illustration as well as the structure of the actions associated with it so as to optimize its explanatory effect, thus helping the learner to "grasp" the mathematical objects and to "see" the laws which regulate their behavior.

The new possibilities created by computer graphics raises the question of how we can design interactive illustrations for mathematics in a *principled* manner. What are the key features of illustrations? What are the main issues in the design of illustrations? How should one proceed in designing an illustration for a particular mathematical concept? What decisions have to be made, and on what grounds should they be made? This chapter is an attempt to provide the foundation for a discussion of such questions with respect to a particular instructional topic. The main achievement of the present chapter is a prescriptive theory for the design of illustrations for arithmetic.

Since illustrations are intended to increase the understanding of arithmetic, a theory of illustration design has to take into account what it means to understand arithmetic. A secondary achievement of this chapter is a synthesis of different approaches to the concept of understanding with respect to arithmetic. It turns out that "complete" understanding of arithmetic implies intellectual possession of a number of different intellectual constructions. The fundamental issue in the design of an illustration is which of these intellectual constructions the illustration is intended to help the learner achieve.

The theory proposed in this chapter is developed in the context of designing an illustration for the arithmetic of rational numbers. Rational numbers are notoriously difficult to understand for primary and middle school learners. One type of evidence for this is the errors children make (Evertz, 1982; Tatsouka, 1984). A second type of evidence is provided by the curriculum. If we look at the standard school curriculum, we see that rational numbers and related issues take up approximately 20 lessons spread out over 3 or more years. To learn the arithmetic of rational numbers is a major effort. Also, it is an area of arithmetic in which pictures and embodiments are frequently used. The tertiary achievement of the chapter is the design of a novel illustration for this topic.

The chapter is divided into five sections. The first section below locates the use of illustrations within the effort of teaching arithmetic with understanding. I argue that the the main function of an illustration is to provide *referential* meaning, i.e., that illustration design has to begin with semantic, rather than procedural, considerations, a view not generally shared held in the mathematics education community. The second section presents some preliminary results with respect to an analytical semantics for rational number concepts. The main conclusion is that there is a family of such concepts and that the appropriateness of a particular illustration is a function of which concept is employed. Consequently, a particular concept, a sense, has to be selected before a referential semantics – an illustration – can be designed. The third section gives an example of the design of a referential semantics for the ratio concept. Evaluation of the example illustration leads to the conjecture that illustrations for rational numbers are necessarily incomplete in the sense that each illustration can illuminate some aspects of rational numbers but not others. These analyses are brought together in a fourth, theoretical section on the design of interactive illustrations for arithmetic. Finally, the fifth section contains a brief discussion of some issues not treated in the body of the chapter.

2.0 MEANING IN ARITHMETIC

Everyone agrees that instruction should make arithmetic "meaningful". However, the concept of "meaning" is hardly transparent when applied to language, and it becomes even less so when applied to arithmetic. Different perspectives generate different conceptions of what it is to "understand arithmetic". Since illustrations are supposed to help the learner understand arithmetic, principled design of illustrations requires a clear notion of what kind of understanding is involved. I will discuss arithmetic from three perspectives as *theory*, as *activity*, and as *language*.

2.1 Arithmetic as Theory

Mathematical knowledge is organized into theories: the theory of equations, the theory of continuous functions, the theory of matrices, etc. The content of each theory consists of mathematical laws or principles which describe the nature and properties of the mathematical involved. Thinking of arithmetic in this way leads one to locate the meaning of arithmetic in its laws or principles. The basic arithmetic functions of addition, subtraction, multiplication, and division are governed by algebraic laws, such as closure, associativity, commutativity, laws of distribution, laws of identity elements, and of inverse. See Figure 1 for examples. Part of knowing and understanding arithmetic is to know and understand those laws. They constitute a theory of numbers, or, more accurately, a theory of the number system.

However, the hypothesis that understanding of arithmetic consists of knowledge of those laws is implausible. Certainly human beings can perform, say, multi-column subtraction with understanding without being able to state the properties of the number system which are exemplified in Figure 1. Indeed, to most of us, the algebraic laws of the number system seem to *require* explanation (e.g., why is addition commutative, while division is not?), rather than *constitute* an explanation of arithmetic. Laws like those shown in Figure 1 represent the output from the understanding process, not the input into it.

Historically, the discovery of the algebraic structure of the number system came after the discovery of the four basic arithmetic functions and the procedures for computing them. The study of algebraic structures was undertaken in order to construct a systematic development of the number system (see, e.g., Thurston, 1956), an effort that blends into abstract algebra on the one hand and into number theory on the other. Explicit statement of the laws of the number system was an advanced mathematical achievement.

For present purposes, the implication of this is that the *primary* purpose of illustrations for arithmetic cannot be to clarify the laws of the number system. If understanding of arithmetic precedes knowledge of the theory of numbers, then the illustrations used to promote initial understanding must already have done their work – so to speak – when the learner confronts that theory. A closely related purpose of illustrations is to clarify why the arithmetic laws are true, i.e., to give intuitively convincing demonstrations, in lieu of the strict proofs which presumably should take their place when the learner has reached a more mature age. But understanding is not the same as believing. Most young learners are willing to take for granted the truth of the mathematical laws presented to them in schools – very sensibly so. Their difficulties do not reside in the justification of the algebraic laws, but in the content or substance of those laws. These considerations imply that illustrations which provide insights into or justifications for the laws of the number system are not of central importance to initial instruction in arithmetic.

Theorem: *There is just one arithmetic operation* A *such that, for every whole numbers* x *and* y,

$$A(x, 0) = x$$

and

$$A(x, successor(y)) = successor(A(x, y))$$

This operation is known as the sum of x and y, and is usually written "$x + y$".

Theorem: $(x + y) + z = x + (y + z)$ *for every* x, y, *and* z.

Theorem: $x + y = y + x$ *for every* x *and* y.

Theorem: *If* $y + x = z + x$, *then* $y = z$.

Theorem: *If* x *and* y *are any whole numbers, then either* $x = u + y$ *for some* u, *or* $y = v + x$ *for some* v.

Figure 1

In summary, although the algebraic laws of the arithmetic functions from a mathematical point of view constitute the content of arithmetic, intellectual possession of those laws requires understanding of arithmetic, rather than the other way around. Thus, the primary purpose of illustrations in the initial teaching of arithmetic is not to communicate those laws.

2.2 Arithmetic as Activity

Arithmetic is not just the study of the properties of the basic arithmetic functions, but also the study of how they can be computed. The purpose of teaching arithmetic is not only to enable the learner to understand the nature of numbers, but also to enable him/her to find the value of an arithmetic function for any given pair of numbers. (This emphasis on computation is virtually absent from other, higher areas of mathematics, in which the main activity is to conjecture and prove general properties of functions or of classes of functions.) Arithmetic is inherently constructive, in the sense of that term used by intuitionist mathematicians (Calder, 1979),[1] i.e., in arithmetic, mathematical objects (the sums, differences, products, and quotients of pairs of numbers) are produced, rather than just being talked about in the abstract.

What is the relationship between the algebraic laws of the number system, and the computational procedures by which the values of the four basic arithmetic functions are computed? The laws of arithmetic constitute what in computer science is known as an *abstract specification* of the four basic arithmetic functions. *Any* procedure which obeys the algebraic specification of, say, addition is a correct addition procedure; indeed, that is the only precise definition of "correct addition procedure".

However, in pedagogy, the basic arithmetic functions are not introduced as computational procedures which fulfill certain specifications. They are introduced on the bases of the semantics of those functions, e.g., addition is introduced as the mathematical description of actions of joining and combining, division as cutting into parts, etc. Thus, in pedagogy, the intellectual relationship between the algebraic laws of arithmetic and the computational procedures is reversed: Once the procedures are introduced, they can be investigated in order to *discover* that they do, in fact, obey those laws. In this way of proceeding, arithmetic has to be understood before those laws can be discovered, in accordance with the conclusion of the previous section that the laws do not themselves represent understanding of arithmetic. In short, when arithmetic is viewed as activity, understanding arithmetic means understanding its computational procedures, rather than understanding the laws of the number system.

This in turn raises the question of what it means to understand a procedure. What is the difference between blind and insightful execution of a procedure? This question has lead some researchers to look for *the principles which underly the computational procedures* of arithmetic. It is an

---

[1] An area of mathematics which is similar to arithmetic in this respect is the domain of constructions in plane geometry. Construction tasks have the general form "Given a figure F, construct a figure G with properties so-and-so!" where the construction consists of a sequence of actions with a specified set of tools. The reason why geometric constructions never became a central topic in mathematical research is perhaps that the constructions so far have resisted systematization and algorithmization.

interesting and startling fact that the principles which are embodied in the arithmetic procedures are not the principles of arithmetic as mathematicians understand them. The algebraic laws which hold for the arithmetic functions do not suffice for computing the values of those functions (given certain arguments). One can not derive the *value* of, say, $(5 + 6)$ from the knowledge that addition is commutative, obeys the law of associativity, etc. The value has to be constructed with help of some computational procedure and the principles underlying that procedure are not identical to the algebraic laws of the number system.

The one-one principle.

"To follow this principle, a child has to coordinate two component processes, *partitioning* and *tagging*. By partitioning we mean the step-by-step maintenance of two categoriers of items - those that are to be counted ... and those that have already been counted ... . Items must be transferred (either mentally or physically) one at a time from the to-be-tagged category to the already tagged category. Coordinated with this process is a second process that involves summoning up one at a time distinct tags (numerons). ... As an item is transferred from the to-be-counted category to the counted category, a distinct tag must be withdrawn from the set of mental tags. ... In other words, the one-one-principle in counting requires the rhythmic coordination of the partitioning and tagging processes. The two processes must start together, stop together, and stay in phase throughout their use." (Gelman & Gallistel, 1978, pp. 78-79.)

The stable-order principle.

"The tags (numerons) [a child] uses to correspond to items in an array must be arranged or chosen in a stable - that is, a repeatable - order." (Gelman & Gallistel, 1978, pp. 79.)

The cardinal principle.

"The cardinal principle says that the final tag in [a counting series] has a special significance. This tag, unlike any of the preceeding tags, represents a property of the set as a whole." (Gelman & Gallistel, 1978, pp. 79-80.)

The abstraction principle.

"The abstraction principle says that the preceeding principles can be applied to *any* array or collection of entities." (Gelman & Gallistel, 1978, pp. 80.)

The order-irrelevance principle.

"This principle says that the order of enumeration is irrelevant; that the order in which the items are tagged, and hence which item receives which tag, is irrelevant." (Gelman & Gallistel, 1978, pp. 82.)

Figure 2

For instance, the principles underlying our common procedures for counting have been analyzed by Gelman and Gallistel (1978). They are shown in Figure 2. As a second example, Resnick and Omanson (in press) has provided an analysis of the principles underlying multi-column subtraction; they are shown in Figure 3.

What kind of principles are these, and in what sense do they underly the computational algorithms of counting and subtraction, respectively? Inspection of Figures 2 and 3 shows that these principles do not deal with arithmetic *per se*, but with what computer scientists would call the *data-structures* of arithmetic, e.g., place-value notation, and with what computer scientists would call issues of *control*, i.e., decisions about when to do what. The kind of principles uncovered by Gelman and Gallistel (1978) and by Resnick and Omanson (in press) apply to *the activity of computing* rather than to *the mathematical entities* involved in the computation. I will call principles of this kind *operational principles*, to distinguish them from algebraic principles.

Additive composition of quantities.

Any quantity can be expressed as a sum of other quantities, usually in many different ways. A quantity can be "taken apart" into a set of components, and then "put together" again without any change in its value.

Conventions of decimal place value notation.

In a decimal place value notation, each position in a multidigit number represents a successively higher power of ten. The digit in the rightmost position represents the quantity $(1 * d)$, where d is the value of the digit; the digit in the rightmost position but one represents $(10 * d)$; etc.

Calculation through partitioning.

An arithmetic operation of multi-digit numbers can be carried out by decomposing the numbers into components, operating upon the components, and then constructing the answer to the original computation by combining the results of the partial computations. For instance, this is the principle that permits written subtraction to be done column by column.

Recomposition and conservation of the minuend quantity.

According to this principle, it is permitted in a multi-column subtraction problem to decompose the minuend and recompose it again in any way, as long as its value is not changed. Such recomposition of the minuend will not change the answer to the subtraction problem.

Figure 3

Operational principles contribute to the understanding of arithmetic by providing *justification;* the principles just mentioned explain why the computational procedures of counting and subtraction are the way they are. Intellectual possession of these principles allow the learner to *explain* a procedure, why it works, and why it is allowed. The notions of justification and explanation have been given formal expression by VanLehn and Brown (1980) in their study of so-called planning nets. A planning net is a method for deriving a procedure from (a) its goal, (b) the constraints it has to obey, and (c) the elementary operations which can appear in it. This formalism provides a precise definition of what it means for a principle or set of principles to justify a (step in) a procedure. VanLehn and Brown (1980) call this type of analysis *teleological semantics*.

One implication of the planning net analysis is that a test for the understanding of a procedure should reveal whether the procedure can be changed appropriately when the circumstances under which it is executed are changed. This idea has been applied by Greeno, Riley, and Gelman (1984) in a theoretical study of counting procedures. They used the principles of Gelman and Gallistel (1978) in a planning net analysis of the type proposed by VanLehn and Brown (1980). The result is a computer system which can plan a counting procedure, based on the principles of counting, given a specific counting-task. The program is able to act as if it understood the concept of counting.

Should we conceive of illustrations primarily as tools for communicating arithmetic procedures? The discussion of embodiments and pictures in the literature about arithmetic education has often assumed that the purpose of an illustration is to provide meaning for the computational procedures. Seeing the procedures in operation in a medium that is visually richer than the symbolic language of arithmetic is supposed to make them meaningful. This is the essential idea behind, for instance, Dienes blocks, which were intended to provide a concrete version of the procedure for, say, multi-column subtraction.

However, there are several reasons to doubt the pedagogical efficiency of this kind of illustration. First, careful analysis of the specific steps taken when doing multi-column subtraction with numbers and with Dienes blocks reveals that the procedures are not isomorphic. Trading a "tens block" against ten "unit blocks" is not similar to putting a scratch mark over a number and writing the result of subtracting unity from that number above it. The relationship between these two steps is, in fact, obscure enough so that one needs to understand subtraction in order to see the isomorphism, contrary to the pedagogical purpose of producing understanding with the help of the isomorphism. Second, the idea of teaching procedures with the help of embodiments relies on an (usually unstated) assumption that transfer of training will occur from the procedure as practiced to the target procedure. Given the difficulty of transferring solutions from one problem to another even under very favourable conditions, it is unclear why we should expect such transfer to take place. Third, even if the isomorphism could be improved, it is not clear why we should expect a procedure to be easier to learn with respect to concrete objects than with respect to symbols; indeed, if the isomorphism were perfect, i.e., if the procedures were to correspond exactly, then we ought to expect them to be equally difficult to learn. For these reasons, I conjecture that illustrations intended to facilitate procedure acquisition are not useful in elementary mathematics education.

One might object that we should focus on the operational principles, instead of on the procedures themselves. After all, the purpose of an illustration is to facilitate understanding, and the understanding of a procedure, I have just argued, resides in its teleological semantics, i.e ., the operational principles and the connections between those principles and the particular steps in the procedure. However, operational principles refer to the activity of computing, rather than to the objects envolved in the computation. It is unclear what it means to illustrate such principles. One suggestion would be to design a medium in which the (analogues of) the operational principles cannot be violated, so that incorrect procedural steps cannot be taken. One might object to this suggestion, in turn, by asking why such an illustration would teach anyone to avoid incorrect steps in a medium where those steps *can* be taken. Perhaps other, pedagogically useful illustrations ways can be found to illustration operational principles. But at the present time, we lack any compelling examples of such illustrations.

In summary, there is a difference between understanding the number system, and understanding the computational procedures of arithmetic. In both cases, understanding can be thought of as being in intellectual possession of a set of principles. However, the principles involved are different in the two cases. The operational principles which underly the computational procedures are usually not stated explicitly in mathematical works. They resemble the specifications of data-structures and control-structures of computer programs. Understanding a procedure requires some general scheme for relating procedures and operational principles. Such a scheme is known as a teleological semantics. There are several reasons to believe that illustrations which intend to clarify arithmetic procedures and their associated teleological semantics are not of central importance for initial instruction in arithmetic.

2.3 Arithmetic as Language

Arithmetic is carried out in a special-purpose symbolism which allows arithmetic statements to be written succinctly, problems to be stated elegantly, and algorithms to be carried out in a convenient manner. To understand arithmetic is certainly to understand those symbols and the expressions in which they appear. The symbols constitute a part of our language, although a highly refined and specialized part. Arithmetic symbols are linguistic devices for talking about a particular subject matter, namely numbers and quantities. Hogben (1936, Chap. 3) makes the point that numbers act like nouns, the arithmetic operations act like verbs, and equations like statements.

If arithmetic symbolism is a language, then we might clarify the notion of understanding arithmetic by looking at what it means to understand a (natural) language. Studies of the semantics of natural languages have lead to the distinction between *sense* and *reference*. The referent of an expression is the object in the real world which the expression talks about or stands for or asserts something about. The sense of an expression is the idea or concept which lies behind it. (Further discussion of this distinction can be found in linguistic textbooks, e.g., Lyons, 1969, pp. 424-434).

Applying this distinction to arithmetic, we can ask what sense we can assign to the arithmetic symbols and expressions. Some recent research on elementary arithmetic has shown that this question is more complicated than anticipated. The mathematical operations of adding and subtracting can have several different senses, depending upon context (Carpenter & Moser, 1982, 1983; Nesher, 1982; Vergnaud, 1983; Riley, Greeno, & Heller, 1983). For instance, "to add" can have the sense "to join" or "to put together", or, more generally, "to combine". On the other hand, it can also have the sense "to increase", or, more generally, "to change". In the same way, the subtraction symbol can have the sense "to take away" or "to decrease".

Depending upon which sense is being assigned to an arithmetic operation, different senses are appropriate for the numbers involved in the operation. For instance, when using the "change" interpretation of addition, it is natural to assign the first addend the sense of "base" or "measure of interest", while the second addend is assigned the sense of "amount of change". In a "combine" interpretation of addition, it is more natural to assign symmetrical senses to the two addends, e.g., the sense of "parts".

Being able to assign the right sense to the mathematical symbols in the right context is an important part of understanding arithmetic. This aspect of arithmetic is not thoroughly analyzed in the literature on mathematics education. One possible reason for this is that we do not yet have good analyses of the possible senses of various arithmetic concepts. In the next section, I will use some techniques from the study of semantics in order to be begin such an analysis for the concept of rational numbers.

Looking at the other component of the semantics of a language, reference, we can ask what we refer to with the symbols in an arithmetic expression. This question is complicated by the abstract nature of arithmetic. From a mathematical point of view, number symbols refer to *numbers*, ideal objects which have a controversial kind of existence (see Benacerraf & Putnam, 1983). Thus, "8" refers to a mathematical object, namely the number eight. However, in the application of arithmetic to real world situations, we let "8" refer to, say, the length of a rectangle which is 8 units long.

The ability to make such assignments is the basis for using arithmetic in solving, say, engineering problems.

The field of research which concerns itself with referential assignments is usually called "model-theoretic semantics" or "referential semantics". The general approach is the following. Given assignments of referents for the primitive symbols of a language, specify rules of combination such that, for any given well-formed expression constructed out of those primitive symbols, the referent for the complex expression can be identified. In the example mentioned above, the rules of combination would dictate that assigning the length of some object to the primitive symbol "8" and the height of that object to "4" implies that the complex symbol "(8×4)" refers to the area of the side of the object. As the example indicates, the justification for referential assignments are not always obvious.

Natural language is obviously acquired by using it to talk about and describe the world. A natural hypothesis is, then, that the acquisition of the language of arithmetic is facilitated by using it to describe the world, or some part of the world. I want to propose that this is the primary function of illustrations in the initial teaching of arithmetic: to be objects to which the young learner can apply his arithmetic, and thereby facilitate his/her acquisition of the language of arithmetic. Expressed differently, the purpose of an illustration is to provide the learner with a referential semantics for the language of arithmetic.

In summary, knowledge of the various senses of the arithmetic concepts and the ability to decide what arithmetic expressions refer to are components of arithmetic understanding. I propose that the primary function of an illustration in initial arithmetic instruction is to be a world which can easily be described by the language of arithmetic. By facilitating the application of arithmetic, an illustration facilitates the acquisition of the semantics of the arithmetic language.

2.4 Coming to Understand Arithmetic

The picture that emerges from this brief review is that different intellectual traditions have focussed on different aspects of what it means to understand arithmetic. There is no such thing as *the* meaning of arithmetic. Complete understanding of arithmetic presupposes knowledge of at least the following intellectual constructions:

- The algebraic laws of the number system.

- The justifications or proofs of the algebraic laws.

- The arithmetic procedures.

- The teleological semantics of arithmetic procedures, i.e., the principles underlying the procedures, and the connection between the principles and particular procedural steps.

- The language of arithmetic, its vocabulary and syntax.

- The analytical semantics of the senses of the arithmetic concepts.

- The referential semantics of arithmetic expressions.

A complete theory of arithmetic understanding would have to contain the details of how each of these constructions is represented in the human mind, and how it is, or can be, acquired.

The hypothesis advanced here is that *the acquisition of arithmetic understanding proceeds in the opposite direction as compared to the list above.* In other words, arithmetic learning starts with the different senses and the referents of arithmetic symbols and expressions, then proceeds to an understanding of the computational procedures, and ends with an understanding of the number system and its algebraic properties.

The effects of understanding the language of arithmetic is, the hypothesis claims, that procedures and principles become easier to learn and to understand. Indeed, one can ask how it could be otherwise: How can one possibly understand a procedure which manipulates symbolic expressions, before one understands what those expressions mean? How can one understand a principle expressed in certain symbols, before one understands the meaning of those symbols? Understanding the language of arithmetic seems to be a prerequisite for understanding the content of arithmetic, in the same way that understanding natural language is a prerequisite for understanding history and geography.

The conclusion is that in constructing a theory of illustrations for initial instruction in arithmetic, we should focus on the language aspect of arithmetic. An illustration should be conceived of as providing the learner with a referential semantics for the symbolic expressions, a world to which those expressions can be applied. By describing this world with the help of arithmetic symbols, the learner is prompted to induce the mathematical concepts behind those symbols.

In the following two sections, this view of illustrations will be developed in detail with respect to the arithmetic of rational numbers. The first section below distinguishes the many senses of the rational number concept.

In the following section, one of those senses is selected and an illustration is developed for it.

3.0 SENSE

In the teaching of rational numbers, the starting point consists of concepts, here to be called *rational number concepts*, which have everyday origins but for which the arithmetic of rational numbers is the appropriate mathematical expression. Because of their obvious pedagogical importance, several attempts have been made to describe the set of rational number concepts. Two such attempts are summarized in the first subsection below. Each attempt captures a part of the truth, but the analytical methodology used is too weak. Reflection on what questions an analysis of rational number concepts ought to answer points to analytical semantics as the appropriate methodology. A sketch of such a semantics for rational number concepts is presented in the second subsection.

3.1 Rational Number Concepts: Existing Proposals

Kieren (1975, pp. 102-103) lists the following interpretations of rational numbers:

1. "Rational numbers are fractions which can be compared, added, subtracted, etc.

2. Rational numbers are decimal fractions which form a natural extension (via our numeration system) to the whole numbers.

3. Rational numbers are equivalence classes of fractions. Thus, 1/2, 2/4, 3/6, . . . and 2/3, 4/6, 6/9, . . . are rational numbers.

4. Rational numbers are numbers of the form p/q, where p, q are integers and $q/ = 0$. In this form, rational numbers are "ratio" numbers.

5. Rational numbers are multiplicative operators (e.g., stretchers, shrinkers, etc.).

6. Rational numbers are elements of an infinite ordered quotient field. They are numbers of the form $x = p/q$ where x satisfies the equation $qx = p$.

7. Rational numbers are measures or points on a number line."

   In a later article (Kieren, 1980), the list of seven subconstructs is called a "pool" of interpretations, from which five ideas "emerge": part-whole, quotients, measures, ratios, and operators.

Before commenting on this list, let us consider a second list of seven rational number concepts, proposed by Behr, Lesh, Post, and Silver (1983, pp. 99-100), who call them "subconstructs":

- The *fractional measure* subconstruct addresses "the question of how much there is of a quantity relative to a specified unit of that quantity". Behr et. al. (1983) proposes this as a re-formulation of the part-whole interpretation.

- The *ratio* subconstruct.

- The *rate* subconstruct, which defines a new quantity as a relationship between two other quantities. The distinguishing mark, according to Behr et al. (1983), of a rate (as opposed to ratio) is that rates are (frequently) added, while ratios are (usually) not.

- The *quotient* subconstruct, which interprets the rational number as the result of division operation.

- The *linear coordinate* subconstruct, which interprets the rational number as a point on the numberline. This subconstruct emphasizes, according to Behr et al. (1983); that (a) rational numbers is a subset of real numbers, and that (b) "properties associated with the metric topology of the rational number line such as betweenness, density, distance, and (non)completeness" (Behr, et. al., 1983, p. 100).

- The *decimal* subconstruct, which emphasizes "properties associated with the base-ten numeration system" (Behr, et. al., 1983, p. 100).

- The *operator* subconstruct, which interprets a rational number as a transformation.

Comparison with the list by Kieren (1975) shows that only the division, ratio, and operator constructs appear in both lists.

These lists of interpretations can be criticized both for what they contain, and for what they do not contain. For instance, to define rational numbers as equivalence classes of fractions presupposes that fractions can be defined independently of rational numbers, which seems to contradict the idea that fractions *are* rational numbers. This is a surprising move, especially in view of the fact that Kieren at the same time defines rational numbers as fractions. Furthermore, Kieren seems to equate the concept of "measurement" and the concept of "a point on the number line" which seems to me too restrictive a view of the number line. Looking at the list by Behr et al. (1983) we see that it contains the concept of "decimals". However, one could hardly view decimal numbers as a kind of subconstruct of rational numbers, since there are numbers which can be expressed in decimal notation but which cannot be expressed as pairs of integers (i.e., all non-rational real numbers). Also, it does not seem pedagogically useful to regard decimals as a subconstruct to rational numbers. Finally, the meaning of the linear coordinate and fractional measure constructs in the Behr et al. (1983) list escape me.

Looking at these lists from another point of view, there are several concepts which intuitively belong in the set of rational number concepts, but which do not have a place in these lists. First, the idea of a proportion e.g., "the proportion of Americans who live in private homes is close to 80%", is very pervasive in everyday life but it does not appear in either list. Second, the operation of division can be carried out in two distinct ways: by partitioning the numerator into as many equal-sized parts as specified by the denominator and interpreting the answer as the size of one of those parts; or, alternatively, by extracting from the numerator a part of the size specified by the denominator and interpret the answer as the number of such extractions which can be carried out. This distinction fails to appear in either of the lists above.

One possible reaction to these criticisms is to try to provide a better list. However, the problem lies not so much with the content of the particular lists, but with the methodology used. For instance, Kieren (1980) claims that some of the interpretations he has listed are more basic than others, but does not provide any explanation of how one decides whether a particular interpretation is basic or not. (For instance, are rates and ratios fundamentally different, or are rates a kind of ratio?) Also, it is unclear why the lists are not longer: How does one go about finding or constructing additional interpretations? Finally, simply listing a set of concepts does not tell us anything about the relations between the concepts in the list. Proportions and ratios are clearly more alike in meaning than, say, proportions and quotients, an observation which might have pedagogical implications. The list format does not provide such information, nor any systematic way of representing it.

The next subsection begins with a brief look at some analytical devices which have been used to elucidate the meanings of concepts, and then proceeds to lay the foundation for an analytical semantics for rational number concepts.

3.2   Towards an Analytical Semantics for Rational Number Concepts

The proposals by Kieren (1975) and by Behr et al. (1983) reviewed in the previous subsection show that there is a set of interrelated concepts attached to the notion of rational numbers. Using a term taken from psycholinguistics, we can say that the rational number concepts form a *semantic field*. Other examples of semantic fields are color concepts, and concepts of physical motion (Miller & Johnson-Laird, 1976). The concepts in a semantic field are more like each other than they are like concepts outside the field, but within the field they contrast with each other. A theory of a particular semantic field should assign a structure to that field, a structure which explains or brings out the meaning and the semantic relations between the concepts in the field. The problem of how to do this has been approached in different ways by different scholars. For purposes of the present essay, I use the term *analytical semantics* to refer to any such effort.

One technique of analytical semantics is to describe concepts in terms of their *semantic primitives* (or "features" or "components"). Similarity of meaning is then understood in terms of shared primitives. A list of semantic primitives, and the analysis of a set of concepts in terms of them, is usually known as a "decompositional semantics" for that set of concepts. If the semantic components are procedures, so that the meaning of each concept correspond to a complex procedure composed out a set of primitive procedures, then we have an example of a "procedural semantics". See, e.g., Miller & Johnson-Laird, (1976). A much older device for exhibiting the relations between concepts is to organize them in a *taxonomy*, i.e., a tree-like structure that makes explicit which concepts are special cases of other concepts. Similarity of meaning is then understood in terms of distance in the tree. (In Artificial Intelligence research, taxonomies go under the somewhat peculiar name "is a-hierarchies".) Ideally, an analytical semantics should be *generative*, i.e., it should consist of a formal machinery, a set of rules, by which the structure associated with a particular semantic field can be constructed.

In the following, I attempt to describe the structure of the field of rational number concepts. I begin with the mathematical concept of a rational number as an ordered pair of integers. The first step in the analysis is to show that the distinction between quantities and parameters generates three different interpretations of rational numbers, corresponding to the notions of "comparing", "dividing", and "changing", respectively. The hypothesis to be developed is that all rational number concepts can be generated from those three notions by introducing semantic restrictions on the numerators and the denominators.

The mathematical specification of the rational number designated by $< a, b >$ is that number r which satisfies the equation

$$rb = a$$

where a and b are understood to be integers. (The standard terminology is that a is called the "numerator", b the "denominator", and r the "value" of the rational number.) Given this specification, what meaning can we assign to $< a, b >$?

Integers have two basic interpretations: (a) as values or measures of (physical) *quantities*, e.g., the length of a table, and (b) as *parameters* for arithmetic operations, e.g., as the number by which some other number is to be divided. Using this distinction, we can generate three[2] basic conceptions of rational numbers:

- When both the numerator and the denominator are interpreted as quantities, then the rational number is an expression of the idea of *comparison*. One quantity is taken "in relation to" the other quantity. Depending on how the comparison is carried out and on what quantities are being compared, different types of comparisons result, as will be developed in some detail below. In this case, the value of the rational number is to be thought of as a "comparison number".

- If the numerator is taken to be the value of a quantity, while the denominator is taken to be a parameter to the operation of partitioning then the rational number expresses the concept of *division*. In this case, the value of the rational number is known as the quotient of the numerator with respect to the denominator. (Notice that the operation for which the denominator is a parameter operates upon the numerator.)

- If both the numerator and the denominator are taken to be parameters to operations, then the rational number as a whole becomes a composite operator. It expresses the concept of *change*, or, more specifically, the idea of counteracting changes. (Notice that the operations represented by the numerator and the denominator operate on some other quantity, not explicitly mentioned in the rational number itself.)

Thus, there are three basic views of rational numbers: as comparisons between two quantities, as results of dividing a quantity, and as counteracting changes in a quantity. I claim that these three views cannot be reduced to, or derived from, each other; they are semantically independent. Furthermore, I want to propose that all rational number concepts can be derived from these three basic notions by adding semantic constraints on the numerators and the denominators.[3]

---

[2] Strictly speaking, we can generate four combinations. However, so far I have been unable to find any meaning in the combination in which the numerator is a parameter and the denominator is a quantity.

[3] The common interpretation of rational numbers as *fractional parts*

I will distinguish between discrete and continuous quantities. Discrete quantities are represented by sets and can be quantified by counting; the number of persons in a room is a paradigmatic example. Continuous quantities can be quantified by measuring; the length of an object is a paradigmatic example. I will assume that the discrete case is more basic, because the counting operation is more basic than the measuring operation. Indeed, measuring requires knowledge of rational numbers, while counting only requires knowledge of integers.

I will now discuss comparison, division, and change in more detail.

3.2.1 Comparison

Suppose we have two physical quantities P and Q. What are the possible relations between them? In what different ways can they be compared or related to each other? Let us begin with two sets of countable objects, like black and white marbles in an urn, two groups of people, etc.; call them $S1$ and $S2$; call the values of these quantities $P(S1)$ and $P(S2)$, respectively.

We can classify the relation between $P(S1)$ and $P(S2)$ by looking at the relation between $S1$ and $S2$. We find four possible relations: $S1$ is included in $S2$, S_2 is included in $S1$, $< S_1$ is disjoint with $S2$ (i.e., independent of), and $S1$ and $S2$ overlap partially.

Looking first at the situation where $S1$ is a subset of $S2$, i.e., where $S1$ is constrained to be a part of $S2$, we see that $P(S1)/P(S2)$ implies taking the value of the subset and relating it to the value of the superset. In informal language, this concept is expressed by the phrase "x out of y", as in "winning three matches *out* of ten". Clearly, this concept is close to that of *proportion*, as in "the proportion of voters who stayed home in this election was 10%". This concept answers the question "how big is the part compared to the whole?". The intuition that underlies this concept is that, say, 3 out of a hundred, is a smaller amount than, say, 3 out of ten, but that 3 out of a hundred is, in a sense, the same amount as say, 30 out of a thousand. Notice that if we restrict $S1$ and $S2$ to be sets of events, then we generate the concept of *probability*. Thus, a probability is a kind of proportion, which is a kind of comparison between a part and a whole, which in turn is a subspecies of comparisons in general. See Figure 4.

---

may not be covered by this hypothesis. The idea of fractional parts is, I believe, very complex. Its analysis is not included here because it would not contribute to the main purpose of the chapter. A more formal treatment of the analytical semantics of rational number concepts, including the idea of fractional parts, will be presented elsewhere.

Looking next at the situation where $S2$ is a subset of $S1$, we see that $P(S1)/P(S2)$ implies comparing the superset to one of its parts or subsets. This comparison concept answers the question "How many times bigger is $S1$ than $S2$?" This concept does not have a common every day term, but call it "multiplicative comparison".[4] If we restrict $P(S2)$ to be a standard quantity, we generate the idea of measurement. To say that something is, say, 10 meters long is to say that it is 10 times bigger than the 1-meter standard. Thus, measurement is a species of multiplicative comparisons, which is a species of comparison which is a kind of comparison between a whole and as part, which, in terms, is a species of comparisons in general.

Finally, looking at the situation where $S1$ and $S2$ are independent, taking the value of one over the value of the other implies asking "How much of $S1$ there is in relation to $S2$?", or, with discreet quantities, "How many members of $S1$ are there for each member of $S2$?" This is the *ratio* concept, as in "there are two girls for every boy in this class" or in "this rectangle is twice as long as it is wide". If we further restrict the denominator to be a quantity of time, we generate the concept of a *rate*, as in "there are three accidents per weekend". In other words, a rate is a kind of ratio, which is a comparison between wholes, which, in turn, subspecies of comparison in general.

In summary, by considering the possible relations between two quantities, we generate three basic cases, each giving rise to a family of rational number concepts: concepts having to do with comparing a part to a whole, concepts having to with comparing a whole to a part, and comparing two independent quantities. These correspond to the notions of "x out of y", of "x times bigger than y" , and of "$xP : s$ for each $yQ : s$," respectively. (For the case of continuous quantities, the last alternative becomes "x units of P for each y units of Q".)

3.2.2 Division

The comparison concepts presuppose that the two integers which form a rational number are to be interpreted as quantities. However, the notion of *division* stems from a different basic idea, namely that of dividing or partitioning a quantity into equal-sized parts. The numerator is then interpreted as the quantity to be partitioned, and the denominator is interpreted as the parameter to the partitioning operation, i.e., as the specification of the number of parts the quantity is to be partitioned into. The rational number in this case answers the question "How big are the resulting parts?" Whereas the rational number in the previous case was interpreted as a

---

[4] Additive comparison answers the question "How *much* bigger is the x than y?"

"comparison number" which expresses the relationship between two quantities, in this case the value of the rational number is a quantity, namely the size of the part which results from carrying out the partitioning operation. For instance, if a rope 3 meters long is divided by 3, then the length of the part is one meter.

The idea of partitioning separates into two distinct concepts, each appropriate for a different type of quantity. For a discrete quantity, partitioning takes the form of *sorting* the elements in the corresponding set into separate sets. For a continuous quantity, partitioning takes the form of *cutting* the quantity, or the object it is associated with, into parts. The difference between these two operations is that the sorting operation cannot always be performed under the constraint of equal-sized parts, while the cutting operation is always, in principle, possible.

There is a peculiar semantic mismatch between the division concept and the standard arithmetic notation. The value of a rational number in the division interpretation refers to *one* of the parts which result from the partitioning operation. Dividing a rope into three parts gives us three shorter ropes, but the mathematical description of this operation does not express this fact. Semantically speaking, the equation

$$\frac{6}{3} = 2$$

is ill-formed, because from the point of view of the division concept one would read it as saying that "if we have a quantity of 6 and divide it into three parts, we are left with a quantity of 2", which is incorrect or at least incomplete in so far as it fails to mention the fate of the other two parts. From the point of view of division, a more perspicous notation would be

$$\frac{6}{2} = 3 \times 2$$

which has the semantically well-formed reading "a quantity of size 6 divided into 3 parts yields 3 quantities of size 2", but which is inconsistent with the standard interpretation of the arithmetic notation.

One resolution to this anomaly is to re-interpret the concept of division as containing two semantic components, the idea of partitioning and the idea of *selecting*, namely selecting one of the parts which are created by the partitioning operation. The first expression above then has the semantically well-formed reading "if we partition a quantity of size 6 into 3 parts, and *select* one of those parts, then that part has the size 2". The problem with this move is its arbitrariness; we are perfectly capable of carrying out sorting and cutting operations in the real world without at the same time performing selection operations; there is no obvious reason why the two should have to be inextricably joined in the mathematical description.

Another resolution is to re-interpret the division concept as answering the question "How many parts of size x does a quantity of size y contain?". This involves a radical re-interpretation of the rational number. In the new interpretation, the numerator stands for the quantity to be partitioned as before, but the denominator is an expression of the size of the desired part(s), and the value of the rational number stands for the number of such parts. In effect, the denominator and the value of the rational number, i.e., the two parameters to the partitioning operation, have "changed places" as compared to the interpretation discussed above. The concept of division now has become synonymous with the concept of *extraction*, of taking a part and extracting it from a whole until the latter has been "emptied" or "exhausted". The value of the rational number is the number of times the extraction operation can be performed before the whole is exhausted.

The advantage of this concept is that it applies equally well to discrete and to continuous quantities. Also, the standard arithmetic notation now has a semantically well-formed reading: "if we take a quantity of size 6, and repeatedly extract parts of size 3 from it, we will be able to extract 2 such parts before the quantity is exhausted". The need to introduce the idea of selection in order to make the standard notation semantically well-formed has disappeared.

The concept of successive extraction of parts of a given size is rather different from the concept of partitioning, but it is similar to the concept of multiplicative comparison, i.e., of comparing two quantities, one of which is a subset of the first. However, in this case, the concept is an active one rather than just a relational one, and the value of the rational number is interpreted as describing how many times the extraction operation is performed, rather than as a "comparison number" which expresses the relationship between the two quantities.

In summary, the concept of division gives rise to a subset of rational number concepts which have to do with various ways of "taking apart" a quantity. The two notions of cutting and sorting implement the notion of partitioning a given quantity into a given number of equal-sized parts for continuous and discret quantities, respectively, while the notion of extracting a part of a given size is applicable to either. The latter is closely related to the concept of multiplicative comparison.

3.2.3 Change

The final possibility is to let both the numerator and the denominator be parameters of operations. The entire rational number is then conceived of as an operator x/y which corresponds to the composite operation $\text{div}(\text{mult})(x, Q), y)$. Notice that the notion of an operator presupposes an operand, i.e., something for the operator to operate upon. To operate with the entire rational number is to compute what the final result is when both processes operate on the same operand.

Depending upon the interpretation of the multiplication and the division operations, respectively, we get different concepts within this family. Concepts of counteracting processes are rather common in natural science. In an electric circuit, the voltage can be seen as an operator which increases the amount of current through the circuit, and the resistance of the circuit as an operator which decreases the amount of current. Thus, the rational number <voltage> / <resistance> operates upon some constant k in order to give the current:

$$\text{Current} = \text{k Voltage/Resistance}$$

Clearly, formulas of this kind can be interpreted as saying that an increase in one quantity can be offset by an increase in another, such that a third quantity is kept constant. The two processes of "increasing voltage" and "increasing resistance" are counteracting processes in this sense.[5]

3.3 Summary

It is suggested that the different senses of the rational number concept constitute a semantic field in the sense in which this construct is used in the study of semantics of rational numbers. Two previous attempts to describe this semantic field were criticized and an alternative analysis proposed. By starting with the concept of an ordered pair of integers and introducing semantic constraints on the members of the pair, we generated three basic senses for rational numbers, each of which subdivides further into more semantically constrained concepts, etc. The three basic senses are as *comparisons* between quantities, as the result of the *division* of quantities, and as *counteracting changes*. The comparison sense divides further into

---

[5] It is noteworthy that both "voltage" and resistance" are quantities. Thus, we can interpret the rational number <voltage> / <resistance> as a comparison between two quantities as well. It seems plausible that this way of interpreting the rational number is appropriate for stable circuits, while the composite operation interpretation is appropriate for changing circuits.

concepts like proportion, ratio, and multiplicative comparison, depending
upon the relation between the quantities being compared. Further distinctions, such as that between ratio and rate, can be introduced by further
specifying the quantities involved. The division sense comprises the ideas
of partitioning and of extracting; the former splits into cutting and sorting
depending upon the nature of the quantities involved. The change sense
includes many different kinds of change, depending on how the numerator
and the denominator are interpreted, respectively. The semantic distance
between any two senses can be specified in terms of the choices made in
their derivation. See Figure 4.

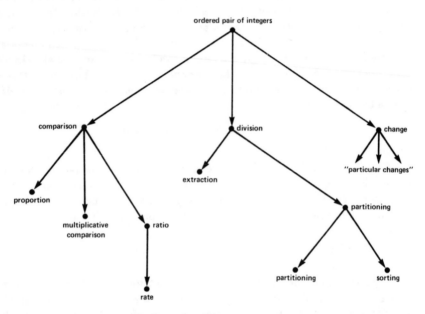

Figure 4

The present analysis only goes part of the way towards the goal of constructing an analytical semantics for the field of rational number concepts.
The treatment is informal and there are a number of questions not answered by the analysis in its current form. For instance, it does not answer
the question of what the boundaries are on this semantic field. Is there an
infinitude of (possible) rational number concepts, or is it a bounded set?
Also, the present treatment does not provide a metric for the semantic
distance between any two concepts in the field.

However, in spite of the informality of the treatment, it supports the
conclusion that a person cannot be said to understand the concept of rational number unless he or she has knowledge of the various senses of that

concept. Thus, in constructing a referential semantics – an illustration – for rational numbers, we must begin by selecting a particular sense to be illustrated. This conclusion will find immediate application in the next section.

4.0 REFERENCE

A concept has many kinds of relations to other concepts, most notably relations of similarity and difference of meaning. Analytical semantics deal with these, as described in the previous section. However, concepts are used to understand the world and so have relations to objects and events in that world, usually called relations of reference. Referential semantics deal with these.

A referential semantics for a language specifies how the expressions in that language refer to the world outside the language, i.e., which object or state of affairs each expression symbolizes. Such a semantics consists of three components. First, there is a vocabulary, a set of primitive symbols. Second, there are rules for which objects or states of affairs the primitive symbols refer to. Finally, there are rules of combination which specify how to compute what the referent for a complex expression is, given the referents for the primitive expressions in it. In short, a referential semantics for a language specifies how that language describes the world.[6]

The purpose of this section is to give an example of a referential semantics for rational numbers. The general method used here is as follows:

- Select a rational number *concept* – a sense – which is to be the basis of the illustration.

- Create a "world" by specifying what kind of objects appear in it and what kind of properties they have, i.e., by specifying its *ontology.*

- Describe the kinds of actions that will be allowed on these objects. We might call this the *action space* of the world.

- Define the *referential mapping* from the primitive symbols in the arithmetic language to the objects and their properties.

- Postulate *rules of combination* which specifies how the referent of a complex expression can be computed, given the referents of the primitive symbols in it.

---

[6] See Anderson (1976), Chap. 7, for a different use of a referential semantics in a psychological context.

The next section carries out these five steps with respect to a novel illustration for the ratio concept.

4.1 A Referential Semantics for the Ratio Concept

Selecting a sense. I have chosen the concept of ratio for the present example. As discussed in the previous section, the concept of ratio is a comparative concept, involving a comparison of the type "how much is there of P for each unit of Q" for some quantities P and Q. In this illustration, we are dealing with a special case of this concept, in which the comparison is carried out between two quantitative properties of one and the same object:

$$\frac{< \text{measure of object O on dimension f} >}{< \text{measure of object O on dimension g} >}$$

In this interpretation the value of the rational number is to be interpreted as an expression of how big the object O is on dimension f in relation to how big it is on dimension g. The particular dimensions used are the height and the width of a rectangle.

An ontology for a rectangle world. In this illustration, there exists:

- A fixed unit of length (which is not named).

- An infinite number of rectangles. Each rectangle is a certain number of length units long and an certain number of length units high. The units are marked off along the base and along the (leftmost) side with what we might call *unit markers*, e.g. little dashes.

- Diagonals, which are straight lines from the lower, left-hand corner of a rectangle to the upper, right-corner.

- Dividers, which are horizontal lines which cut a rectangle into two parts (i.e., into two rectangles); dividers are always aligned with one of the unit markers.

The action space of the rectangle world. In the rectangle world, the following actions are possible:

- An operation which *creates* a rectangle with a specified length and height.

- An operation which *throws away* a rectangle.

- An operation which *moves* a rectangle around.

- An operation which *duplicates* a given rectangle.

- An operation which *cuts* a given rectangle horizontally at the height of any of the left-hand side unit markers by drawing a divider across the rectangle (and thus creates two rectangles).

- An operation which *draws* a diagonal in a rectangle.

- An operation which *superimposes* one rectangle over another.

- An operation which *stacks* one rectangle on top of another.

- An operation which *unstacks* one rectangle from the top of a stack of them, i.e., it takes the top rectangle in the stack and puts it "down" beside the stack.

The set of situations which belong to the Rectangle World can be defined generatively as all rectangle configurations which can be reached by starting with an empty world and applying any sequence of the above actions.

The referential mapping of primitive expressions. The rational number symbols refer to the Rectangle World in the following way:

- A numerator refers to the height of a rectangle, expressed in terms of the unnamed unit of length.

- A denominator refers to the width of a rectangle.

- The value of a rational number (therefore) refers to the diagonal of a rectangle, or, more precisely, to its angle of incline, its steepness.

- An integer refers to a set of rectangles.

See Figure 5 for some examples.

$$\frac{1}{3} \Longrightarrow$$

$$\frac{2}{3} \Longrightarrow$$

$$\frac{3}{1} \Longrightarrow$$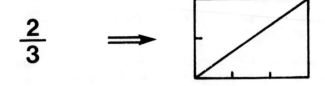

$$\frac{3}{3} \Longrightarrow$$

Figure 5

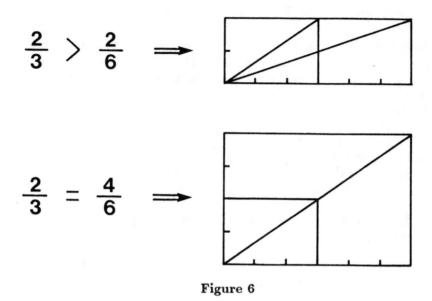

$$\frac{2}{3} > \frac{2}{6} \implies$$

$$\frac{2}{3} = \frac{4}{6} \implies$$

Figure 6

Rules of combination for complex expressions. There are, of course, a very large number of mathematical expressions which one could provide combination rules for. I will only specify rules for expressions of the following two types: a/b and $(x+y)$, where a and b are integers, and x and y are rational numbers, i.e., for the symbols for rational numbers and for the expressions which refer to the sum and difference of two rational numbers.

The rule for constructing the referent of a rational number $< a, b >$ are obvious from the above: Create a rectangle with height a and width b, and draw its diagonal.

The rules for finding the referent of the sum of two rational numbers is as follows: Construct the rectangles corresponding to the two rational numbers, and form a new rectangle by putting one rectangle on top of the other, thereby forming a new rectangle. Draw the diagonal in the new rectangle. (Notice that this presupposes that the bases of the two rectangles are the same, i.e., one can only add rational numbers with equal denominators in this world.)

The procedure for constructing the referent for the difference between two rational numbers is exactly the inverse of the procedure for finding the referent for the sum: Take a rectangle, divide it horizontally into two rectangles, take off the top rectangle, and throw it away. Draw the diagonal in the bottom rectangle.

4.2   Evaluation of the Rectangle Illustration

The referential mapping between rational numbers and the rectangles sets up a correspondence between the two worlds. The instructional value of this correspondance, its pedagogical power, so to speak, is a function of how many ideas and concepts related to rational numbers that it can illustrate. The following properties of the rectangle world are worth noticing (see Figure 7):

- Unlike most illustrations, the Rectangle World provides distinct referents for (a) the numerator, (b) the denominator, and (c) the value of the rational number.

- Some classes of rational numbers have distinct representations in this world.

    o The class of all rational numbers equivalent to some specific rational number is the class of all rectangles with coinciding diagonals.

    o The class of unit-valued rational numbers is the class of squares.

    o Rational numbers with value smaller than unity will be wider than they are high; those with values greater than unity will be higher than they are wide – a very distinct visual difference.

- It is as natural to have numerators larger than the denominator in this illustration as it is to have numerators smaller than the denominator, as should be the case in an illustration for the ratio concept. (Many other illustrations for rational numbers have difficulties with this point.)

- Comparisons between rational numbers reduces to a perceptual comparison between the "steepness" of straight lines. If one diagonal is "steeper" than another, then the corresponding rational number is greater than the other.

However, the rectangle illustration also contains the following conceptual anomaly: Rational numbers with zero numerator are as "impossible" or "illegal" as rational numbers with zero denominator. In both cases, the rectangle "disappears" or is impossible to create, because it will have zero magnitude on either height or width. The dramatic mathematical difference between a zero numerator and a zero denominator has no explanation or representation within the Rectangle World.

Also, there are many types of arithmetic expressions which do not have referents in this world, i.e., no combination rules can be provided for them. They include the sum and the quotient of two rational numbers.[7]

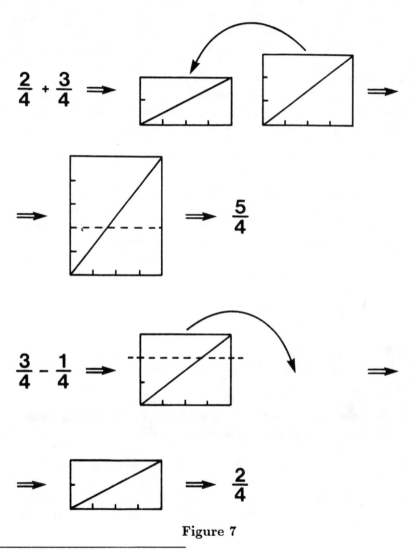

Figure 7

[7] There is no proof that such rules do not exist. My colleague Pearla Nesher has indeed tried to convince me that the Rectangle World *can* illustrate the entire arithmetic of rational numbers, but so far I have been unable to construct natural representations for multiplication and division which are consistent with the referential mapping of this world as I have defined it.

The observations of the proceeding paragraph are, I believe, instances of a more general principle. In designing an illustration, it is tempting to believe that we can illustrate any arbitrary part of arithmetic. However, the analyses I have carried out in connection with the Rectangle World and several other illustration worlds leads me to the conjecture that *there is no illustration which is completely isomorphic with the arithmetic of rational numbers.* One cannot define an ontology and a referential mapping between the arithmetic symbols and that ontology such that one can create combination rules for every type of arithmetic expression consistent with that referential mapping. The structure of rational number arithmetic is such that objects and events in the physical world are inherently incapable of mirroring (all of) that structure. This conclusion, if correct, has important implications for the design of illustrations.

5.0 A THEORY OF ILLUSTRATION DESIGN

It is a commonly held pedagogical goal to teach arithmetic in such a way that learners understand arithmetic concepts, principles, and procedures. The obvious desirability of the goal has obscured the unobvious nature of the goal: What does it mean to understand arithmetic? According to the analysis presented here, arithmetic understanding involves knowledge of at least the following intellectual constructions:

- The language of arithmetic, i.e., the vocabulary of arithmetic symbols and the syntax of arithmetic formulas.

- The analytical semantics of arithmetic, i.e., the different senses which can be expressed by arithmetic symbols and how they relate to each other.

- The referential semantics of arithmetic, i.e., the possible mappings between arithmetical symbols and the world.

- The properties of the mathematical objects involved.

- The computational procedures of arithmetic, i.e., the algorithms for constructing the sum, the difference, the product, or the quotient of various kinds of numbers.

- The teleological semantics of arithmetic, i.e., the principles which shape the computational procedures and the connections between those principles and the steps in the procedures.

- The abstract specification of the computational procedures, i.e., the algebraic laws which define the arithmetic functions.

- Proofs of the algebraic laws, i.e., justifications or reasons for why one should believe in the truth of those laws.

In short, there is no such thing as *the* meaning of arithmetic. Arithmetic is not a well-specified body of knowledge, but involves all of the intellectual constructions mentioned above, each of which can be known and mastered in varying degrees and to varying extents.

The fundamental issue in illustration design is which of the intellectual constructions mentioned above is supposed to be clarified by a particular illustration. I argued that the main task of an illustration for initial instruction in arithmetic should not be conceived of as illustrating the algebraic laws of the number system, because understanding of arithmetic precedes knowledge of those laws. Also, I argued that the main task of an illustration for initial instruction in arithmetic is not to provide an isomorphic procedure to the arithmetic procedure, because (a) isomorphism is hard to achieve, (b) if the isomorphism is imperfect, there is no reason to expect transfer from the illustrative procedure to the target procedure, and (c) is the isomorphism is perfect, there is no reason to expect the illustrative procedure to be easier to learn.

The main hypothesis proposed here is that the primary function of an illustration in the initial teaching of arithmetic is to help the young learner to understand the language of mathematics by providing a referential semantics for it. Having a referential semantics facilitates acquiring the arithmetic concepts in several ways, perhaps primarily by giving the learner something to abstract from. Understanding the language of arithmetic facilitates, in turn, the acquisition of procedures and principles which deal with expressions in that language.

The second hypothesis I want to propose is that an illustration intended to function as a referential semantics for the language of arithmetic should be constructed in the following way:

- Identify the various senses for the mathematical concept to be illustrated. If there are several, select one.

- Construct an illustration world. This involves the following steps:

  o Describe the primitive objects of the world and their properties (the ontology).

  o Describe the possible actions (the action space).

The illustration world is the set of all configurations (situations) which can be generated by applying the actions to the primitive objects.

- Construct a referential mapping between the mathematical notation and the illustration world. This involves two steps:

  o Set up the mapping between primitive symbols and the world.

  o Define combination rules which specifies how the referent for a complex symbol can be computed, given the referents for the primitive symbols.

  The goal is that every configuration in the illustration world should have a meaningful mathematical description, under the particular mapping defined.

- Evaluate the illustration.

  This involves asking the following questions:

  o Which concepts, procedures, and principles have (natural) representations in the illustration world?

  o Which anomalies are there in the illustration? i.e., which incorrect conclusions about arithmetic does the illustration sanction or suggest?

This methodology was applied to the concept of rational number. The analytical semantics presented shows that there is a large set of different interpretations of rational numbers. Selecting the ratio sense, I proceeded to construct a referential semantics for it, namely the Rectangle World. Analysis of the Rectangle World revealed several properties which, I conjecture, are typical of illustrations in general. Some arithmetic concepts turned out to have natural characterizations within the illustration world. For instance "unit-valued rational numbers" correspond to "squares". As a second instance, "equivalent rational numbers" correspond to "rectangles with coinciding diagonals". Also, some rules of rational number arithmetic are explained in a natural way. For instance, the addition of rational numbers (i.e., the stacking of rectangles) requires equal denominators (i.e., rectangles with equal bases).

However, the illustration also contained anomalies and gaps. The referential mapping used in the design of the rectangle illustration implies that rational numbers with zero numerator are as "illegal" or "impossible" as rational numbers with zero denominators. The mathematical difference between them has no explanation or representation in the rectangle illustration. Furthermore, the operations of multiplying and dividing rational numbers have no natural representation in this illustration world. The illustration is radically incomplete.

This prescriptive theory of illustration design is currently being used in the construction of several computer-based instructional systems for a variety of topics in elementary mathematics. If the theory is good, illustrations designed in accordance with it should prove to to be pedagogically powerful. Thus, empirical evaluation of those instructional systems will include an empirical evaluation of the present theory.

6.0 DISCUSSION

The theory of illustration design presented here has been proposed in the context of initial instruction in arithmetic. How useful would the theory be outside this domain? The theory will be useful for designing illustrations in some other domain or topic to the extent that the considerations which lead to it hold in that other domain as well. First, there must be some significant notation introduced which is specific to the topic. Second, understanding of this notation must be crucial to the procedures and principles which belong to the domain. Clearly, many areas of mathematics fulfill these criteria, e.g., calculus[8] However, there are also areas of mathematics in which no new symbolic notations are introduced; instead, well-known symbols are used for new purposes, e.g., trigonometry. In such cases, it is probably not useful to conceive of illustrations as providing the learner with a referential semantics.

The theory of illustration design presented here deal, in principle, with illustrations in general, regardless of the medium in which the illustration is presented. However, the theory was constructed in the context of the design of systems for intelligent computer-aided instruction, and there are some aspects of the theory which favour the computer as the appropriate delivery vehicle. First, the concept of referential mapping is central to the the theory (see previous sections). A computer can be programmed to recognize the referential mapping between the mathematical notation and the illustration world, i.e., to keep track of which number on the screen was introduced as a description of which object. Such reification of the referential mapping has a number of pedagogical uses (see below).

Second, the theory asserts that illustration worlds should be defined generatively (see previous sections). When an illustration world is defined on a computer, the generative character of the definition translates into exploratory freedom for the learner. The learner can literally discover how mathematics describes the world by creating any arbitrary configuration in the illustration world, and then have the computer tell him what the correct mathematical description is.

---

[8] The teaching of calculus has already settled on a very useful illustration world of its own, namely the function graph world.

There are other, less theoretically motivated, advantages of computer-based illustrations as well. Computerized illustrations are more practical in a number of ways than physical embodiments. We can program the computer to do the busy-work connected with the illustration world (e.g. coloring a pie-chart) for the child, instantaneously and correctly, thus eliminating the time otherwise spent in managing activities with little pedagogical value. Also, it is easier to switch back and forth between alternative illustrations on a computer; no time has to be spent packing away the equipment associated with one type of illustration (e.g., bundles of sticks with rubber bands) in order to make room for another (e.g., felt strips).

In short, the computer brings both new principal possibilities to illustration use and increases the practicality of teaching with the help of illustrations. It is noteworthy that these advantages of the computer as a delivery vehicle for pedagogical illustrations are not dependent upon the use of advanced artificial intelligence techniques.

One issue which has not been touched upon in this chapter is how illustrations should be used in teaching. What pedagogical use should we make of them, once they are designed? VanLehn and Brown (1980) suggest that one should present a sequence of illustrations which successively come closer and closer to the content one wants to teach. Resnick (1982) has suggested that one can help the learner generalize by having several illustrations for the same piece of mathematics. Another natural idea is to try to use illustrations to prevent errors and misconceptions from developing or remaining. For instance, one could present an illustration to the learner as an impasse-breaking device: whenever the learner hesitates about what step to take next in a computation, he/she could be encouraged to work out the corresponding problem in an illustration, to see if that helps him understand what he ought to do in the original problem. Another interesting idea is the concept of *yoking* (Resnick and Omansson, in press) which suggests that one should hook one illustration either to another illustration or to the arithmetic symbols in such a manner that whenever the learner changes one of them, the corresponding change in the other occurs automatically. The issue of how to teach with the help of interactive illustrations is unexplored and wide open for experimentation.

The ultimate goal of using illustration in the teaching of rational numbers is, of course, that the learner should come to realize that the mathematics of the various rational concepts is the same, i.e., that the addition of proportions follows exactly the same laws as the addition of quotients, that the multiplication of a ratio with an integer yields exactly the same value as the multiplication of a fraction with an integer, etc. The laws and principles of rational numbers are insensitive to how the user of rational numbers thinks about them. Somewhat paradoxically, then, the ultimate purpose of assigning meaning to arithmetic symbols is to enable the learner to come to understand that the meaning is not important, indeed, that the meaning has to be ignored if the full generality of the mathematical concept of rational number is to be understood. The paradox of arithmetic teaching is that the teacher cannot communicate this directly, cannot simply tell the learner that proportions, ratios, and quotients are added in the same way; if he/she does, then the knowledge is useless. The generalization has to be constructed anew by each generation of learners. The ultimate criterion for a good illustration is one which facilitates this discovery, i.e., one which makes itself unnecessary as soon as possible.

ACKNOWLEDGEMENT

Preparation of this manuscript was supported in part by NSF Grant #MDR-8470339, and in part by the Institutional Grant for the OERI Center for the study of learning, OERI-G-86-0005, United States Office of Education. The opinions expression do not necessarily reflect the position of NSF or OERI, and no official endorsement should be inferred. I thank Gaea Leinhardt, Ralph Putnam, Sharon Lesgold, Pearla Nesher, and Lauren Resnick for helpful discussions concerning the topic of the present chapter.

REFERENCES

Anderson, J.R. (1976). *Language, Memory and Thought*. Hillsdale, NJ: Erlbaum.

Arnheim, R. (1969). *Visual thinking*. Berkeley, CA: University of California Press.

Behr, M.J., Lesh, R., Post, T.R., & Silver, E.A. (1983). Rational-number concepts. In R. Lesh & M. Landau (Eds.), *Acquisition of Mathematics Concepts and Processes*, (pp. 91-126). New York: Academic Press.

Bell, A.W., Costello, J., & Kuchemann, D.E. (1983). *A Review of Research in Mathematical Education. Part A. Research on Learning and Teaching*. Berks, U.K.: NFER – Nelson.

Benacerraf, P., & Putnam, H. (1983). *Philosophy of Mathematics*, (2nd ed.).

Calder, A. (1979). Constructive mathematics. *Scientific American, 241*,(4), 146-171.

Carpenter, T.P., & Moser, J.M. (1982). The development of addition and subtraction problem-solving skills. In T. P. Carpenter, J.M. Moser, & T.A. Romberg (Eds.), *Addition and subtraction. A cognitive perspective*, (pp. 9-24). Hillsdale, NJ: Erlbaum.

Carpenter, T.P., & Moser, J.M. (1983). The acquisition of addition and subtraction concepts. In R. Lesh & M. Landau (Eds.), *The acquisition of mathematical concepts and processes*, (pp. 7-44). New York: Academic Press.

Evertz, R. (1982). *A Production System Account of Children's Errors in Fraction Subtraction*. (Tech. Report No. 28). Milton Keynes, U.K.: The Open University, CAL Research Group.

Davis, R.B. (1984). *Learning Mathematics. The Cognitive Science Approach to Mathematics Education*. NJ: Ablex.

Gelman, R., & Gallistel, C.R. (1978). *The Child's Understanding of Number*. Cambridge, MA: Harvard University Press.

Greeno, J.G., Riley, M.S., & Gelman, R. (1984). Conceptual competence and children's counting. *Cognitive Psychology, 16*, 94-143.

Hogben, L. (1936). *Mathematics for the Million. A Popular Self Educator*. London, U.K.: George, Allen & Unmin.

Kieren, T.E. (1976). On the mathematical, cognitive, and instructional foundations of rational numbers. In R.A. Lesh (Ed.), *Number and Measurement*, 101–145. Columbus, OH: ERIC Clearinghouse for Science, Mathematics, and Environmental Education.

Kieren, T.E. (1980). The rational number construct – its elements and mechanisms. In T.E. Kieren (Ed.), *Recent Research on Number Learning*, 125–149. Columbus, OH: ERIC Clearinghouse for Science, Mathematics, and Environmental Education.

Lyons, J. (1969). *Introduction to theoretical linguistics*. Cambridge, U.K.: Cambridge University Press.

Miller, G.A. & Johnson-Laird, P.N. (1976). *Language and perception*. Cambridge, MA: Harvard University Press.

Nesher, P. (1982). Levels of description in the analysis of addition and subtraction word problems. In T. Carpenter, J. Moser, & T. Romberg (Eds.), *Addition and subtraction: A Cognitive Perspective*. Hillsdale, NJ: Erlbaum.

Resnick, L.B. (1982). Syntax and semantics in learning to subtract. In T.P. Carpenter, J.M. Moser, & T. A. Romberg (Eds.), *Addition and subtraction: A cognitive perspective*, (pp. 136-155). Hillsdale, NJ: Erlbaum.

Resnick, L.B., & Omanson, S.F. (in press). Learning to understand arithmetic. In R. Glaser (Ed.), *Advances in Instructional Psychology*, (Vol. 3). Hillsdale, NJ: Erlbaum.

Romberg, T.A. & Carpenter, T.P. (1986). Research on teaching and learning mathematics: The disciplines of scientific inquiry. In M. C. Wittrock (Ed.), *Handbook of research on teaching* (3rd ed.) (pp. 850-873). New York: MacMillan.

Riley, M.S., Greeno, J.G., & Heller, J.I. (1983). Development of children's problem-solving ability in arithmetic. In H. Ginsburg (Ed.), *The development of mathematical thinking* (pp. 153-200). New York: Academic Press.

Rucker, W.E., & Dilley, C.A. (1981). *Health Mathematics*. Lexington, MA: D.C. Health.

Sawyer, W.W. (1964). *Introducing Mathematics. 1. Vision in Elementary Mathematics*. London: Penguin Books.

Tatsouka, K.K. (1984, January). *Analysis of Errors in Fraction Addition and Subtraction Problems*. (Tech. Report). Urbana, IL: University of Illinois, Computer-based Education Research Laboratory.

Thurstone, H.A. (Ed.). (1956). *The Number System*. New York: Dover Publications.

VanLehn, K., & Brown, J.S. (1980). Planning nets: A representation for formalizing analogies and semantic models of procedural skills. In R.E. Snow, P.-A. Frederico, & W.E. Montague (Eds.), *Aptitude, Learning and Instruction: Vol 2. Cognitive Process Analysis and Problem Solving*, 95–137. Hillsdale, NJ: Erlbaum.

Vergnaud, P. (1983). Multiplicative structures. In R. Lesh, & M. Landau (Eds.), *Acquisition of Mathematics Concepts and Processes*. New York, NY: Academic Press.

16 COMPUTERS TEACHING PROGRAMMING: AN INTRODUCTORY SURVEY OF THE FIELD

Benedict du Boulay and Christopher Sothcott

Cognitive Studies Programme
University of Sussex
Brighton, United Kingdom

1.0 INTRODUCTION

It seems entirely reasonable that we should delegate some of the burden of teaching students how to program to the computer itself. The machine, in some sense, would then become both the object of the student's study as well as the guide to that study.

It turns out, however, to be remarkably hard to build a system that can effectively mimic the activities of an insightful teacher: whether it be commenting on the way a student is developing a program, deciding on a sensible order for the introduction of new concepts, spotting a possible misconception underlying some syntactic or logical error, deciding whether a given program is a reasonable solution to an exercise, or even accurately pin-pointing where the errors are and making suggestions about how they might be corrected. This is hardly surprising. Good teaching borrows from many of our other human abilities and knowledge in the areas of, say, communication, interpersonal relationships and social skills, not to mention any abilities concerned specifically with the topics of instruction, such as understanding students' plans or the ways in which they might make mistakes in coding those plans. Building an effective surrogate teacher is, thus, a problem comparable in magnitude to that of the general Artificial Intelligence enterprise. In the context of Intelligent Computer Aided Instruction, these difficulties surface in such guises as representing tutorial goals, building a plan for the tutor to achieve those goals, building and maintaining a model of the student under instruction, monitoring the dialogue and deciding what to say next, recognizing a student's plan and noting deviations from such a plan, deciding how the it may be repaired, determining a teaching strategy, instantiating and then executing that strategy as a sequence of short-term teaching tactics, and being able to solve the problems that are being posed or answer unanticipated questions from the student.

Despite the difficulties, various systems have been built that partially address different aspects of the above issues in the domain of programming. We can divide these into three broad classes according to the educational roles they have attempted to play and the kinds of knowledge that they have deployed.

1. TUTORS: First there are systems which act as tutors in the sense that they make decisions about how, and in what order, programming concepts should be introduced, and attempt to monitor the student's progress in mastering the new notions. Typical examples are the systems by Anderson and his colleagues (1985), Cerri et al. (1984) and Elsom-Cook (1984), all of which teach Lisp, and to a lesser extent Bip (Barr et al., 1976), which teaches Basic.

   Coaches are a variant of tutors which simply monitor a student's problem-solving and so focus on a restricted part of the process of learning programming. Their job is to observe the way that the student tackles a problem and either comment when something seems to be going wrong, provide help when asked or, as in the case of Miller's (1978) initial Spade system, try to constrain the student to set about the problem in a particular way.

   Another possible way of distinguishing coaches from tutors is that coaches often give students some leeway to set their own goals and make mistakes, whereas tutors tend to react immediately to errors of both omission and comission and tend to be more prescriptive.

2. BUG FINDERS: The second class of systems, the bug finders, are those that are brought in after the event, as it were, to try to figure out what is wrong (and there is often something wrong) with the student's program and then provide advice about what to do. In some ways these may be considered as coaches, except that their advice has to be specifically sought by the student and they wait until the program is complete before attempting any analysis. Examples are the Laura system (Adam & Laurent, 1980), Goldstein's (1975) Mycroft and, more recently, Proust (Johnson & Soloway, 1983).

3. SUPPORT ENVIRONMENTS: The final class is more diffuse and consists of those systems that provide the means to make the interactions between the student and the programming system more effective or more understandable. Support environments include such tools as structure editors, debuggers, tracers, modelling aids, etc., which have been designed with novices in mind (see e.g., Green & Cornah, 1982; Eisenstadt, 1982). Many of the tutors mentioned in (1) above also incorporate tools, such as structure editors, that assist the programming process but which, in themselves, are neutral with respect to

issues of tutoring. The BIP system has several features which make it an early, interesting member of this class. More recent examples of environments include the Cornell Program Synthesizer (Teitelbaum & Reps, 1981) and the Pascal systems on the Apple Macintosh due to Vose (1984).

Strictly speaking, one might also include programming languages whose syntax and semantics have been simplified and tidied for novice consumption, such as Solo and various implementations of Logo. Although the system is not aimed at students, one of the developments of the Programmer's Apprentice (Rich & Shrobe, 1979), a knowledge-based editor called KBEmacs (Waters, 1985), also falls into this category, enabling a programmer to exploit programming "cliches" to speed up the program development process.

The Bridge system of Bonar and Cunningham (1986) provides an interesting contemporary development, in that it supports a number of explicit representations for a program that are based not on code but on the goals and plans that the student might have in mind. In some ways it is a kind of problem-solving monitor, in others it is a program-development tool that is tuned for use by novices, and so should be regarded as a support tool.

The above categories are not hard-and-fast for several reasons, though they do form convenient pegs on which to hang the literature. For instance, the distinction between a coach and a tutor is often somewhat blurred and may be as much a matter of teaching style as breadth of coverage. In any case, both must contain some kind of bug-finder if they are to make any comments about the student's incorrect code and both should, in principle, provide well-engineered support tools for doing programming.

The aim of this chapter is to provide an introductory survey of the capabilities of systems that fall mainly into the first two classes. Less attention will be paid to the third category, support environments, important though they are for teaching novices effectively. A related class of systems that will not be considered at all are those straightforward frame-based tutors ("frame" in the Computer Assisted Learning sense – not the Artificial Intelligence sense) that simply present textual information about programming and then ask questions on that material with little or no capability to either analyze the content of students' answers (programs) or respond in any kind of intelligent manner to the individual.

This chapter is in six parts. The next section discusses the general requirements for an intelligent teaching system for programming, by considering the kinds of knowledge that need to be represented in order to support insightful tutoring. Section 3 then goes on to consider several individual tutoring sytems. Section 4 examines bug finding systems, having first classified them into broad types according to the manner in which they represent the "correct" solution to the problem being tackled by the student. Section 5 examines Bridge and Bip as two interesting programming support environments. The final section draws the various strands together.

2.0 COMPONENTS OF A TUTOR FOR PROGRAMMING

The classic structure for a generic intelligent teaching system was set out by Hartley (1973). In his view, such a system is built around four knowledge sources:

1. A representation of the knowledge or skill that is to be taught. This provides the ability to solve the problems that are set to the student in order to either judge or comment on the adequacy of the student's answer or to answer questions posed by the student.

2. A set of teaching actions. These are actions such as making a positive or negative comment, providing an example, asking the student to explain some issue, stepping through an example with the student, setting a problem, asking the student to find a counter-example and so on. Setting a problem will involve a problem generator which may either retrieve a problem from a pre-stored file or dynamically fill out parameter values in some problem schema.

3. A model of the student's current state. This is the system's current understanding of the history, capabilities, knowledge, goals and motivation of the student it is teaching.

4. A set of means-ends rules that determine which teaching action should be deployed given the current goals of the system and the current state of the student model. These rules guide the behavior of the system and represent its tutorial model and so its knowledge of the whole class of students of which the particular student under instruction is presumed to be a member.

In addition to the above, other authors tend to add a "bug-catalogue" in which knowledge of standard programming mistakes is stored.

2.1 Knowledge of Programming

The received wisdom of ITS is that a system needs a representation of the skill or knowledge that it is attempting to impart. This is likely to be true in general, but there are cases where a human teacher (and so, in principle, an artificial teacher) can be an effective catalyst for learning, even though the teacher does not understand the content of the material to be learned. In these cases, the teacher is likely to be skilled in the social and motivational issues underlying learning, areas where artificial systems are notoriously poor, since they tend to concentrate on the domain of knowledge to be imparted. For example, the teacher may know that getting students to talk about their faulty programs may be all that is needed to help the students debug them without any specific advice being given at all. All the teacher need do in these cases is be a "good listener". Indeed, various people have jokingly suggested that an Eliza-like interface to a programming system might thus be very effective.

On the assumption that the tutor should understand what is being taught the following taxonomy can be regarded as both a set of requirements for knowledge available to the system as well as an overview of the classes of knowledge that the novice should be attempting to master.

Traditionally, knowledge of programming can be divided into (1) knowledge of the syntax and semantics of the language, (2) tactical and strategic knowledge of how to compose the givens of the language and of how to decompose the problem, as well as, (3) pragmatic knowledge of how to conduct an effective dialogue with the programming environment under all circumstances.

2.1.1 Syntax and Semantics

Syntactic knowledge includes all knowledge about the form that the programming language takes, i.e., how code is written. Novices often see this as the central aspect of learning to program. It is rarely regarded as such by educators, although several authors have noted errors by beginners that seem to be caused by syntactic over-generalizations or by interaction effects between, say, syntax and layout (see e.g., Shneiderman, 1980, for a review of these issues).

Semantic knowledge can be usefully subdivided into its procedural and declarative aspects. Procedural semantics is concerned with how the conceptual machine (sometimes called the notional machine) described by the programming language actually works, e.g., that a "while" loop in Pascal involves a check on a stated condition once on each cycle and is not some kind of software interrupt – as some novices apparently believe – (Soloway & Ehrlich, 1984). This is the knowledge that enables the system or the student to predict what behavior a piece of code will produce; it also enables the reverse link, from observed behavior back to the code that was responsible. Declarative semantic knowledge includes knowledge of the members and properties of the classes of entity described by the language, e.g., knowledge about the properties of data-structures and their types, for instance, the knowledge that "cdr" in Lisp is a function that takes one argument that is an s-expression and returns a result that is also an s-expression.

2.1.2 Tactics and strategy of decomposition

One of the issues that beginners have to grapple with is learning what kinds of problems are susceptible to solution by computer programs. Programming systems themselves do not need to know this (at present) because they work on the assumption that they will only be used when it is sensible, and need not concern themselves with such broad strategic issues.

Problem decomposition knowledge is largely tactical, it involves knowing how to decompose a problem into subproblems which can more easily be solved. Knowing that one should do this is commonplace, knowing how to do it for any given class of problems is rather trickier. These are related strategic issues, such as knowing how big a program is likely to be needed to solve a given problem, why the program is to be written, and who else will need to work with the program.

2.1.3 Tactics and strategy of composition

Program composition knowledge is also mainly tactical, it involves knowing how to link code to problems. This is the knowledge that is deployed in the planning of a program which determines choices among the available constructs and the methods of joining constructs together in a sensible and efficient manner. An example here is the set of production rules of Greaterp (Anderson & Reiser, 1985) that describe which construct should be used to achieve each programming goal. Equally important is the knowledge of standard chunks of code – or cliches – that are known to achieve certain classes of effect, and how to join such chunks together. For instance, these chunks are larger and more densely structured than just a "while" loop and more like partially filled-out, large-scale building blocks from which a program is constructed. This is the knowledge that is encoded in Proust (described in Section 3), in terms of "goals" and "plans".

2.1.4 Pragmatic knowledge

All the above areas of expertise need some glue to bind them together, and for the purposes of this paper they are lumped together under the heading of pragmatic knowledge. This is the knowledge of how to DO programming, i.e., how to have an effective conversation with the programming system, knowing what methodology should be adopted in developing a program, how to debug and test it, what to do when you don't know what to do, how to edit and compile and interpret the messages from the compiler, and so on.

2.2 Student Models, Tutorial Models and Teaching Actions

A student's knowledge is either a subset of that of the tutor, intersects with it or is disjointed, though the last of these is unlikely. Different systems have different expectations about this matter, and thus set about modelling the student's knowledge in different ways. The main issues are modelling the knowledge that the student and the tutor share, and modelling the knowledge that is peculiar to the student (this latter being the hardest and most interesting part of the problem). As the knowledge structures peculiar to the student is likely to be misconceptions, this kind of knowledge is often known as a "bug catalogue".

A model of the student which is expressed solely as a sub-set or sub-part of the knowledge being taught is known as an "overlay" model (Goldstein, 1982). A system employing such a model, e.g., Trill (Cerri et al., 1984), can only understand its student as a kind of expert with impoverished knowledge and can take no account of the fact that the student may have different, rather than simply less, knowledge or skill compared to the expert.

By contrast, a "differential" student model provides the capability, in principle, of recognizing and then acting upon a student's misconception, for example that "while" may be substituted for "if" in certain situations in Pascal, knowledge used by Proust (Johnson & Soloway, 1983), or that pieces of program plan may be systematically but incorrectly interleaved.

A further distinction can be drawn between an essentially static or declarative student model and an executable or procedural one. Most systems are built around the former, often consisting either of some vector of values, or tags in a network representing knowledge to be taught. While they may be the basis of some predictions about how the student will perform on further problems, they cannot usually provide a detailed account. A procedural model of the student is one that can be internally executed by the tutor to predict performance on a given problem or question. Differences between predicted and observed behavior can then used to refine the model (Self, 1974). Anderson et al.'s (1985) Lisp tutor is an example of this approach.

The above is only a brief discussion of the issue; for a more thorough review of student models see Clancey (1986).

In many ways, therefore, inferring (i.e., learning) the changing knowledge of the student can be considered as one of the most important sub-skills of a computer tutor (see e.g., Elsom-Cook, 1984; Cole et al., 1986). This view is not universal (see e.g., Ohlsson, 1986; Draper, 1986). Ohlsson has pointed out the relative lack of work on (2) and (4) and complains that many intelligent teaching systems are built around a rich representation of the knowledge and skills that they wish to impart but are handicapped because they can deploy only an impoverished set of teaching tactics. Furthermore, these tactics are not usually integrated into an overall teaching strategy. This has been partly due to our lack of an effective fine-structured educational theory that can determine what kind of teaching action should be conducted under various circumstances. There may well have to be a range of such theories, since classroom observation of human teachers shows that teachers adopt widely differing strategies, which are further modified by the teacher's personality. Furthermore, observation of learners shows that there may well be large differences in the cognitive style of individuals, which leads to marked differences in the effectiveness of a teaching strategy between individuals (see e.g., Pask, 1976). Given the opportunities for "individualizing" instruction promised by such intelligent systems, it is a shame that more has not been achieved in this direction.

Draper (1986) argues that it may be possible to produce equally effective learning in the student by enriching the set of teaching actions to include rules about how to recover from dialogue breakdowns, thus making them more sensitive to impasses, surprises and deviations from the planned tutorial dialogue. This would in some ways replace richness of understanding of the student under instruction with richness of understanding the process of instruction.

A more radical solution might be to attempt to finesse the whole issue by designing systems that are so comfortable to use and so readily learnable that the issue of explicit tutoring just does not arise. While intelligent application of Human Computer Interface (HCI) principles must be beneficial, these on their own are unlikely to be the whole solution. The main reason for this is that the novice is learning not just about new ways to solve old problems but also about a whole new space of problems. Evidence from more familiar and less complex machinery than the machinery of a programming language (e.g., cars, sewing-machines, videotape-recorders, washing machines) shows that instruction is still often needed.

2.3 Educational Philosophy

The various categories of systems mentioned in the introduction betray different, often implicit, prescriptive and descriptive models of the programming process and its support tools. A basic distinction can be made between those programming systems that attempt to monitor and support every aspect of the programming task, and those systems which assume that some part of the programmer's work will be performed off-line, or at least "out of sight" of the system. An example of the second type of system is Proust. It borrows a little of the traditional Pascal programming style by being a tool that novices can use or not as they wish and does not observe progress from initial idea to completed program but only attempts to debug the latter. The contrasting methodology, used for example in Bridge (Bonar & Cunningham, 1986) or Greaterp (Anderson & Reiser, 1985), has the novice develop a program completely under control of the system with, apparently, no "paper and pencil" or independent stage at all.

There are also distinctive styles in teaching programming to undergraduates. Many groups have developed their own well-established culture and set of prejudices on this issue. Some are very concerned to start students off in the way they wish them to continue and so discourage large amounts of programming ("hacking") at the start in favor of more formal exercises in algorithms, data-structures and logic. Others expect to base their teaching of these fundamental notions on the practical programming experiences that their students initially encounter. Within each of these camps there are many different approaches. In the "experience before theory" camp, some work their way systematically through the constructs of the chosen initial language, others provide high level functions and procedures as if they were primitives and then gradually reveal the way that these have been implemented in the chosen language. Further possibilities include basing the teaching on standard chunks or cliches, such as a loop to compute a sum and then show how such standard chunks can be reused and deformed for different purposes. There are, of course, many other methods and mixtures of methods. The point at issue here is that the systems that have been built to teach programming have usually been built within one of these cultures, often without justifying it, and so inherit its strengths and weaknesses. The other point is that our knowledge of both learning and teaching has not really developed to the point where we can make principled decisions between these different methods.

3.0 EXAMPLES OF TUTORS

This section describes a number of implemented tutors for a variety of programming languages and in each case attempts to summarize the tutor using Hartley's framework.

3.1 Malt

Malt was an early example of a computer tutor that worked in the domain of machine code programs (Koffman & Blount, 1975). Its teaching strategy was simple. It generated, and then presented, a problem, supplying comments as the student typed in a response which consisted of a sequence of machine-code instructions. The propensity of the system to interrupt the student became less as the student was deemed to be more expert, and the student was allowed to submit a larger number of program solution steps between each prompt.

The system could generate a problem, using a problem grammar, expressed as a tree of sub-problems, together with their breakdown into primitive tasks. Each sub-problem had several variants and each variant might be solved by a different sequence of primitive tasks, stored together with code for their solution. A top-down traversal of this and/or tree determined which problem was to be presented and at the same time constructed an ideal solution for matching against the student's attempt. The system had only a rudimentary model of the student's expertise, which consisted of probabilities attached to the sub-problem branches of the tree. During the traversal of the tree to generate a problem, these probabilities determined which sub-problems within the tree were chosen. The probabilities were affected in a global manner so that as the student became more experienced, harder sub-problem variants were generated. However, the system was not able to exploit its knowledge of the student's performance on a particular primitive task to affect the future choice of a sub-problem that required that task for its solution (e.g., by ensuring that a poorly performed task figured in future problems until it was performed satisfactorily).

The traversal of the problem grammar provided a particular breakdown of the problem into its constituent parts which the student was expected to follow. There were few difficulties in trying to understand the intent of arbitrary pieces of student code because the student was prompted for an answer to each primitive task. Assessment of the adequacy of the student's answer was based usually on direct matching to the system-generated solution or, in certain cases, arrived at by simulating the execution of the student's code to see if it performed correctly under the appropriate conditions.

It is not clear how far the solution-matching methods used by Malt are applicable to programs in high level languages where students are given more leeway to tackle the problem in their own way, though the method of giving immediate feedback is adopted in Anderson et al.'s (1985) system for Lisp. Whether or not it has any tutorial advantage, it certainly reduces the problem of keeping the tutor in synchronization with the student as any deviation from the expected solution is immediately flagged and the students are required to make their solutions conform to the tutor's. There is no real representation of a student's knowledge of machine code programming concepts, only a tally of the performance on particular sub-problems and primitive tasks. The tasks themselves are not separately organized, except in as much as they occur in particular sub-problems.

3.1.1 Summary

1. Programming Knowledge

   The main expertise consists of the grammar of sub-problems and primitive tasks together with their associated machine code solutions plus
   the ability to simulate code and cope with certain interactions between
   program fragments.

2. Teaching Actions

   There are really only two teaching actions. One is to generate a new
   problem and present it to the student piece by piece, already subdivided. The other is to comment on the adequacy (or otherwise) of
   the student's answer to a piece of the problem.

3. Student Model

   The model of the student consists of tags in the problem grammar,
   indicating the level of expertise on each sub-problem, plus a global
   parameter whose value indicates general expertise.

4. Means-Ends Rules.

   The means-ends rules are limited to applying the two teaching actions
   in (2) constrained by (3).

3.2 Trill and Impart

Cerri et al.'s (1984) system Trill is a tutor for a subset of Lisp. It represents
its knowledge of elementary Lisp in a semantic network and attempts to drill
students by retrieving pre-stored questions from nodes in the network. If an
answer is found to be incorrect, the system uses the network to determine
what are the underlying concepts needed to answer the question. The
system then traverses each of these concepts in turn, asking questions of
the student in order to localize the source of the student's confusion. This
process may be applied recursively to sub-concepts, if necessary, and the
ensuing dialogue has something of the "Socratic" flavor espoused in Why
(Collins et al., 1975). Once the student has answered questions about sub-
concepts correctly, questions about intermediate concepts are re-asked as
the system gradually unwinds the dialogue back up to the point where the
first error occurred.

Trill's most interesting feature is in the way it deals with incorrect
answers. The semantic network encodes the various dependencies between

different bits of Lisp, such as the fact that understanding "cdr" depends on being able to remove the first "s-expression" from an "s-expression", which in its turn depends on being able to identify an "s-expression" and so on. By generating and then asking supplementary questions, the system can determine whether an incorrect answer is due to a simple slip or due to a misunderstanding at a deeper level. As the system traverses the network representing an expert's knowledge of Lisp, it builds up a picture of the beginner's strengths and weaknesses that is used to guide what kind of question is generated next.

The system provides an overlay model of the student and thus has limited ability to cope with misunderstandings that do not conform to its expectations. It can only deal with elementary Lisp functions, such as "car" and "cdr", and so cannot deal with functions defined by the student. No doubt the semantic network could be expanded but it is not clear how well this representation of Lisp concepts could cope with more extensive programming knowledge.

Elsom-Cook's system Impart (Elsom-Cook, 1984) was more ambitious in several ways, though only parts of it have been completely implemented. It attempted to model the student's state of knowledge not only by reference to what the student has been told but also by considering the space of plausible inferences the student might have made about how Lisp works as a result of the behavior of the Lisp system in response to his or her attempts to type Lisp code. The tutoring system thus contained a procedural model of dynamic learning behavior of students that could be used to generate an initial set of hypotheses about the student being tutored. The system could present further examples that would, for example, constrain over-generalizations which it believed that the student might be entertaining.

The system did not work to a predetermined curriculum but allowed the student to experiment and then exploited those experiments in its later teaching, though it did not support mixed-initiative working to the extent that it could answer questions from the student. Reference back to earlier teaching episodes was handled by mechanisms that modelled conversations in general and tutorial conversations in particular.

An important aspect of Impart was that it used both an underlying operational semantic representation and a declarative representation of Lisp code for its analysis of the student's program. This gave it some ability to reason about the code rather than simply compare it with a specimen answer or execute it.

3.2.1 Summary

1. Programming Knowledge

   Trill encodes a hierarchy of elementary Lisp concepts but knows nothing about user defined functions. Impart makes use of declarative and procedural semantics that allows it to reason about the effect of simple user-defined functions.

2. Teaching Actions

   Trill has two teaching actions. One is to ask a question derived from its concept network, the other is to recursively traverse the network posing ever more fundamental questions in the attempt to establish the cause of a student error. Impart is much more sophisticated (in design) and includes the teaching action of keeping quiet and allowing the student to explore Lisp.

3. Student Model

   Both systems tag their concept networks indicating which concepts the students appear to have mastered. Impart generates descriptions of the students that are no part of the given concept network.

4. Means-Ends Rules

   Trill works its way through the network systematically unless a recursive exploration is triggered by a wrong answer. Impart attempts to model the hypotheses that the student could reasonably expect to entertain, given his or her experience of the system so far, and generates a comment or example where it suspects that an incorrect generalization might have occurred. This system also maintains rules for guiding the overall shape of the dialogue.

3.3 Anderson's Lisp Tutor, Greaterp

The most impressive current working tutor is that of Anderson and his colleagues (Anderson, Farrell & Sauers, 1984; Anderson & Reiser, 1985; Reiser, 1986). This can take a student through the first few hours of an extended Lisp lesson that consists of a graduated sequence of problems for the student to work on, though some of the burden of teaching is delegated to hard-copy lesson notes.

The system maintains a procedural model of both expert and novice programming ability expressed in terms of production rules. The novice rules represent standard mistakes that have been observed in novices. As the student enters a program, the system attempts to parse each new symbol either as an example of correct behavior, (matching the result of an expert rule), in which case it usually says nothing, or as an example of known incorrect behavior, (matching the result of a novice rule), in which case it constructs an appropriate error message. Failing either of these, the system immediately interrupts and presents the student with a number of alternatives (derived from the two sets of rules mentioned above) and invites a choice from the student, though it only allows further progress along what it considers to be a correct path.

The system is based on a theory of learning that suggests that mistakes by the student should be flagged as soon as they are detected. This gives it rather an authoritarian tutoring style, though this is justified by Anderson et al., who argue that students should not be allowed to persist in their errors for fear that they learn the error instead of the correct method, and that it increases the possibility that the student will be able to relate the advice to the current issue rather than getting advice much later about some earlier state of the problem that the student cannot now remember. By contrast, there is the argument that making mistakes and observing their consequences is an important, even crucial aspect of the learning process.

A computational advantage of the interventionist approach is that it dramatically reduces the usual combinatorics associated with mal-rules to simply deciding whether or not each new symbol is a legitimate (either legal or known illegal) continuation of the existing program. Despite this advantage, the system, as with most intelligent tutoring systems, is very heavy on processing power, though it can take a beginner through a substantial initial curriculum of Lisp topics.

The use of general purpose rules to encode programming knowledge and programming misunderstandings gives the system the power to generate its own solutions to problems, expressed as specifications, as well some ability to make sensible comments about a student's incorrect attempt at a problem that is so expressed. The system cannot undertake mixed-initiative dialogue, however, and it depends for its performance on the fact that it, rather than the student, selects the problem to be worked on. Unlike Impart, described above, this system has a fixed curriculum that the student is expected to work through.

Few of the rules in Greaterp's programming knowledge base are concerned with syntactic issues. The student enters his code via a structure editor, which handles mundane issues (such as bracket balancing) and which presents templates for code (such as a function definition) that the student later elaborates by replacing place-holders by Lisp code.

Anderson's Lisp tutor seems to suffer from the difficulty that it embodies a particular view about how a program should be organized and comments immediately that the student has started to depart from the prescribed path. Questions about how much a coach should interfere are still open in ITS with Anderson's view being at odds with the more taciturn and self-controlled coaching provided by some other systems (see e.g., Burton & Brown, 1982).

3.3.1 Summary

1. Programming Knowledge

   The system has a detailed-enough set of production rules so that it can solve for itself the problems that it sets the student. It also contains a problem generator and a syllabus that will take the student through the first few hours of hands-on Lisp experience.

2. Teaching Actions

   There are two main teaching actions: suggesting a problem that the student should work on and commenting on the unacceptability of the symbol that the student has just entered as part of the solution to that problem.

3. Student Model

   The system builds a differential model of the student solving a particular problem from a set of correct production rules that encode the kind of knowledge a good student should have and a set of "incorrect" production rules that model standard errors. These rules are fairly problem-specific and do not raise expectations about the increased (or possibly decreased) likelihood of that rule (or similar rules) being applicable in later problems.

4. Means-Ends Rules.

   The most important rules are (a) if an error is detected, say so and coerce the student to return to the correct path, and (b) if the system fails to understand the input at any point, stop the student and force him or her to return to the desired path.

3.4 Coach and Spade

Gentner's (1979) system, Coach for the language Flow, monitored students as they developed their programs for a simple Basic-like language.

Coach attempted to understand the significance of every keystroke, including mistypings, as well as understanding the pauses between keystrokes. This involved the hard problem of inferring the student's plan from an incomplete and growing program using a schema-based representation of programming knowledge and of errors. The system could make some assumptions because students were supposed to work from a specific course book, though it could only hypothesize that they were actually doing the problems set in the book.

Spade-0 (Miller, 1978) provided a system for the novice Logo programmer who wished to draw a particular picture (a wishing well) using the drawing primitives of that language. The system was primed with the programming problem under consideration and so avoided many difficulties that now beset those designing coaches that have no privileged information about the programmer (e.g., Jones et al., 1986).

The system was based on a theory of program planning which provided a vocabulary of planning actions that the student might carry out, such as "decomposing" a plan into sub-problems, as well as a vocabulary for parts of program plans, such as the "setup" step or the "cleanup" step. The student was expected to interact with the system using both these kinds of terms as well as the primitives of Logo. In other words, the novice was expected to have a dialogue with the system at the level of Logo primitives, in terms of chunks of program code and their relation to the overall problem, as well as in terms describing the process of doing programming.

Initial versions of the system attempted to lead the student through a classic top-down decomposition but would allow a determined student to depart from this regime and try to understand what might be going if such a departure occurs. Later versions were more relaxed and allowed students to develop programs in an order that seemed more matched to their wishes.

The student's terminal is divided into several windows showing the evolving plan, the interaction with Spade-0 and any drawings that were produced when code was run. One of the problems of the system was that it could not judge whether the code being entered by the student actually satisfied the program specification for the wishing well. Miller's aspirations to improve the system and produce Spade-1 and Spade-2 were ambitious, in that Spade-2 was intended to attempt to infer the programmer's plan from what was typed using a chart to hold the plan fragments, and Spade-1 was to check the adequacy of the student's solution (a problem partially solved for a limited class of similar programs by Goldstein's system Mycroft, see below).

3.4.1 Summary

1. Programming Knowledge

   The Spade systems have a rich knowledge of both composition of program structures and decomposition of problems.

2. Teaching Actions

   The main teaching action is to force the student to be explicit about how he or she is constructing and then debugging a program.

3. Student Model

   The model of the student is limited to a record of the history and current state of development of the program being built together with some expectations – "preference rules" – about the way students actually work when programming, derived from an analysis of student protocols taken from students working on programming patterns.

4. Means-Ends Rules

   There are two kinds of rules: those that decide when to interrupt the student and issue a warning when a possible error (or source of future errors) is detected, and those that drive the normal problem monitoring behavior of the system, e.g., requesting a command or planning action and responding in the appropriate manner.

4.0 EXAMPLES OF BUG FINDERS

All tutors have the problem of deciding whether or not a student has correctly answered a question or successfully solved a problem. In some subjects other than programming this difficulty can be reduced, for example, where an arithmetic problem which requires a numerical answer is given to the student, but in teaching programming, a system will not generally be able to decide easily whether a student's program fulfils the requirements of the problem set forth because of the difficulty of describing the required answer at the right level of detail and precision.

Most systems have concentrated on logical errors, rather than syntactic or semantic errors, leaving it to other devices, such as structure editors, to reduce or eliminate, e.g., syntactic errors. These systems adopt one of three different methods to isolate and localize bugs.

1. Match against a SPECIMEN ANSWER: Here a system, such as Laura (Adam & Laurent, 1980) is given a specimen answer to a problem

and also the student's answer. It has to find errors by attempting
to transform both programs until they can be made to tally. Crucial
difficulties with this method are that the system generally will have no
understanding of the goals of either the student's code, or the teacher's
code and so will be unable to reason sensibly about what the the code
is supposed to do in order to understand what the errors are. Also,
there may well be difficulties in isolating exactly where the errors are,
other than to say that the answer and the specimen fail to match at
certain points.

2. Match against a SPECIFICATION: In this method the system is provided with a high-level description of the goals of the student's code
and it checks to see to what extent the student's answer meets those
goals. In principle, this method can make much more insightful comments about errors, in that it may be able to relate errors it detects to
the original problem description which the student was working from.
Proust and Goldstein's Mycroft (1975) provide contrasting examples
of this approach.

3. Engage in a debugging DIALOGUE: This method has been exploited
for Prolog programs by Shapiro (1982). The system steps through the
(student's) code and asks a number of questions about what variations
of the sub-procedures were expected to do. Through an analysis of the
trace of calls of these procedures, and using the information provided,
it was able to isolate errors in such a way that a particular procedure
was specified.

4.1 Specimen answer: Laura

The Laura system takes a student program (in Fortran, though the methods
could be applied to other languages) and a specimen answer, expressed as
a program, and tries to bring them into correspondence through a series
of transformations. Irreconcilable differences are flagged to the student as
possible errors.

The first stage in the comparison process is to transform both programs into graphs. This has the effect of standardizing various control flow
variants into the same structure and normalizing arithmetic expressions.
The next stage is to standardize, as far as possible, the way that variables
are introduced and used, for instance, by removing redundant intermediate
variables. Finally, the graphs themselves are standardized, for example,
separating independent computations occurring in a single loop into a sequence of separate loops.

The next stage is to try to match the two graphs. The system builds
a series of hypotheses about the correspondences between nodes and arcs

in the two graphs and ranks them according to their plausibility. Having identified candidate corresponding parts of the two structures, the system then applies various transformations, such as permuting independent computation steps that do not change the overall action of the program. If there is no error in the student's program, then working through the allowable transformations for each of the sets of candidate correspondences should bring the two structures into exact correspondence.

Usually there are bugs in the student's program. In this case, the system tries to explain discrepancies between the two structures in terms of "minor" errors, such as the use of the wrong variable name, use of the wrong constant value, omission of a unary operator, error of sign and simple errors on branches and so on. Where even these do not explain the differences, the system prints out what it takes to be corresponding but unmatching parts of the two programs in the hope that the user will be able to spot the problem, given that the system has at least localized it.

The advantage of the above method is that it achieves a high degree of standardization of code, and is therefore less susceptible to being fooled by minor variants of the correct answer, as Proust is. Also, as the specimen answer is expressed as a program rather than as a complex set of assertions, the other user of such a system, the teacher, does not have to master a new program description language. But there are various problems. The system knows nothing about the high-level goals of the code and so it cannot relate errors back to such goals. Also, if the student makes use of the special properties of the problem domain to write an answer that is different in kind from the teacher's, the system would have no way of detecting this as it does not run the student's code and look at its output.

A minor shortcoming – that could be repaired – is that the system does not appear to have any particular expectations about the kinds of errors that students make and so it relies on a measure of syntactic similarity (e.g., wrong variable used) between the specimen answer and the students answer rather than on empirically derived differences.

4.2 Specification: Mycroft, Pudsy, Aurac and Proust

4.2.1 Mycroft

Goldstein's (1975) system, Mycroft, could detect and repair errors in fixed-instruction Logo programs designed to produce line drawings. It made the program conform to a set of assertions about the geometric properties of the drawing it was supposed to produce. It was able to relate inconsistencies between a program and the assertions, via theories of program planning and of errors in plans, and so repair the program.

The specification of what the program was intended to produce was called its "model". This was a set of assertions about the shape, connectivity and relative position of the parts that made up the drawing (e.g., the head body and legs of a stick man). The assertion language allowed complex shapes to be defined (and named) in terms of the primitive shapes known to the system such as "line" and so the model description took on some of the properties of a hierarchic decomposition of the overall drawing.

The system expected that the user would also have decomposed the drawing in a sensible manner and that sub-procedures would have been used in a way that bore some relation to this decomposition. The system also assumed that the procedures were very nearly correct and (like many humans) could not do very much with a very badly structured and incorrect program.

Mycroft started the debugging process by executing the user's program symbolically and annotating each line of code with comments that recorded changes of state of the turtle (the drawing device) as well as the properties of any shape that was produced. The system then tried to construct a plan, using these annotations, that accounted for all the steps in the program in terms of the original model. Various plausible and simplifying assumptions were made in the initial cycle of plan building. The most important of these were that the each model part was accomplished by contiguous sections of code and that the user's program accomplished the overall drawing by traversing it systematically, rather than hopping piecemeal from one part to another. The objective of the planning phase was to produce a plan with as simple a set of violations of the original model as possible. If it was not possible to produce a plausible plan using the above constraints, they would be relaxed, thus enabling the system to cope with the situation where a single drawing element was produced by two separated statements (e.g., a stickman line body interrupted by the stickman arms).

In the final phase, Mycroft used an imperative semantics to suggest and test changes to the code that would repair the model violations. The debugging steps were ordered in such a way as to minimize the chances that fixing one bug would make matters worse for the others. For instance, the system attempted to debug a violation of a geometric property of a part before working on relationships between parts. In the plan building phase, it attempted to identify which bits of the code were designed to produce parts of the drawing and which bits were "setup" steps designed to locate the turtle correctly before drawing such a part. This identification of roles was crucial in order to identify effectively where in the code to make the various kinds of changes.

Mycroft was an impressive bug finding system as described, although the choice of domain of turtle drawing gave it some advantages. In particular, these were the possibility of describing the intended outcome as a set of geometric assertions, the possibility of linking distinct entities in the drawing with sub-procedures and a semantics that enabled predictions to be made about the effects of insertions of code on the properties of the model. Useful techniques that might be generalized include the simplifying assumptions about "linear" code and the notion of ordering the repair of bugs, though the particular ordering criteria used in Mycroft were domain dependent.

4.2.2 Pudsy

Lukey's system Pudsy (1980) worked from an abstract specification and was able to eliminate a limited class of errors from small Pascal programs. These errors were mostly concerned with information flow rather than with control flow. The system engaged in two kinds of debugging. One kind was driven – or bottom-up – by clues in the code that suggested errors. The other kind of debugging was more systematic and showed how certain errors could be repaired by working backwards – or top-down – from a discrepancy between what the code did and what it was supposed to do.

The system started by sub-dividing the program into logical chunks corresponding to sub-tasks in the problem, using a pre-stored record of sub-tasks associated with the high-level abstract description of the program's goal. The system identified how information flowed into and out of each chunk as a preliminary step to identifying bugs.

In its first debugging pass, the system identified local clues that suggested errors in chunks, such as redundant assignments and use of variables, where the function of the variable was at odds with its name (e.g., a variable called count). These bugs were either repaired or noted as evidence to be used in the second pass. In this second pass, the system deduced low-level assertions about the values of variables on exit from each chunk of the program, and then amalgamated these low-level assertions into a high-level description which it could then match against a specification, also represented as high-level assertions. The low-level assertions were derived from stored schemata associated with certain constructs, such as the "for" loop, that were then adapted to the code in question.

If a mismatch was detected between the high-level specification and the high-level description, the system would examine the assertions it had built up – plus the reasons why each assertion had been derived – in an attempt to pinpoint the piece of code that was responsible for the high-level disparity between specification and description. Having identified a possible cause of the error, the system then used a generate-and-test method of proposing a plausible edit and testing it to see whether the consequent new high-level code description conformed with the specification.

Pudsy is, thus, not unlike Mycroft, except that its description of what the buggy code does is derived from the code itself rather than from the result of running that code (as in Mycroft). Lukey identified various problems with his system that included its lack of flexibility, its failure to make use of the run-time behavior and the slightly ad-hoc methods adopted. Another shortcoming of the system is that it had no particular expectations about the kinds of mistakes that it might find, and this would limit its applicability for use with novices.

4.2.3 Aurac

Hasemer's (1983) system Aurac was designed to debug programs written in the programming language Solo. This was a simple procedural language for manipulating a database of relations that was used in the Open University for teaching computational modelling within Cognitive Psychology to novice programmers. The system was based on an empirical study of expert debugging behavior and had a number of debugging strategies of varying complexity.

The system was designed to be used by the student after a program had failed to run as hoped. It was imbedded in a specially-designed programming environment, tuned for novices, that provided a number of support tools. When invoked by the novice, Aurac re-executed the program using a specially developed interpreter and examined the code for what Hasemer calls "higher-level syntactic errors". These corresponded to such execution errors as reference to a relation that did not exist at runtime, possibly produced by the use of an unbound variable – itself perhaps caused by a syntactic mistake in defining a procedure. This phase of the checking system was based on 12 production rules that looked for particular error conditions.

In the next phase of checking, the system attempted to match segments of the program against a library of cliches. Solo was a simple-enough language, and the problems undertaken by the students were sufficiently constrained that the system could store a set of programming cliches that would match most segments of the students' programs. Where only a partial match to a cliche could be achieved, the system treated this as a possible error and, after further analysis, printed out a message about the student's code that explained the deviation from the cliche.

The final stage of debugging involved a dataflow analysis that detected such errors as variables which were bound but never subsequently referenced. This stage was also able to recognize a limited class of simple algorithms and, thus, relate particular sgements of code to the high-level goals that they would achieve.

One of the interesting findings of this work was that a large amount of successful debugging could be achieved without a detailed understanding of the program submitted by the student (by contrast with the other systems described in this section), through the use of production rules primed to detect higher level syntactic errors and a cliche library to detect various forms of semantic and logical bug. However, this facility was partly due to the very restricted nature of the programming language involved and the limited number of problems that the students were known to be working on.

4.2.4 Proust

Proust is an impressive recent system (Johnson & Soloway, 1983; Johnson & Soloway, 1985; Johnson, 1985; Johnson, 1986) that can detect a wide variety of logical errors in student's Pascal programs. It makes use of data derived from an extensive (human) analysis of many students' answers to two problems sets as part of an initial Pascal course. The system is primed with what the teacher thinks the "goals" of a particular programming exercise are (i.e., what the program is intended to do). The system has available a repertoire of "plans" for achieving each of these goals. It systematically and exhaustively attempts to match the various plans onto the code it is presented with. It tries to understand discrepancies by deforming its plans in accordance with a large set of bugs that had previously been catalogued in the prior empirical studies.

The program specification is expressed as a sequence of goal statements. Each goal statement is associated with a frame-like object that stores declarative knowledge about that goal and contains the names of one or more plans that would fulfill that goal. Each plan is also stored in a frame that, among other things, contains a template for matching against Pascal code. The template is a mixture of actual Pascal code and pattern variables, which get bound during the matching process. Plans may contain further goals, so the matching process is recursive.

An advantage of the above approach is that system can relate chunks of code in the student's program to high-level goals and can, therefore, refer to an unfulfilled goal at that high level, if the requisite code is missing. Some of the error messages are quite impressive, though the behavior of the system is very much determined by the set of known plan deformation rules (and their associated error messages and suggested test data). The system can deliver messages, both about the submitted program's performance (for instance, suggesting test data that will cause the program to fail), as well as messages about hypothesized student misunderstandings (for instance, suggesting that a "while" statement has been used in place of an "if" statement).

The heart of the Proust system is a sophisticated matcher that finds a best fit between the student's program and the expected structure of goals and plans. Because students' programs contain bugs, such a match is not going to be exact and must make use of empirically derived expectations about the ways that students deform plans, omit goals, include extra goals or incorrectly interleave plans. Once these possibilities of matching are allowed, there will usually be a range of ways of accounting for the given code. The system chooses the match that minimizes the number of hypothesized violations and then reports these to the user.

The system runs quite fast, despite the horrendous matching problems, and covers a wide spread of errors in the programs that have been used. Impressive though the system is, it can deal only with a subset of Pascal, with only a limited range of problems, and can easily be fooled by pieces of code that are equivalent – but not identical to – those expected, for example, the use of a variable where a constant was expected. This kind of difficulty is a result of the way that plans are represented, as code intermixed with pattern variables, rather than using some underlying representation, such as dataflow diagrams that would provide a degree of canonical form. A further problem with the system is that it cannot work interactively with the student, for example, to help it choose between different interpretations of the code, and it cannot trace the execution of the code for the student to show exactly what happens under different circumstances.

4.3 Dialogue: Shapiro's system

Shapiro's system depends on the fact that the programs in question can be described in terms of a hierarchy of function or procedure calls that are free of side-effects. In principle, this system might be applied to a variety of languages but the examples Shapiro uses are all drawn from Prolog, where the function calls correspond to Prolog procedure goals. The system executes the program supplied by the user and builds a tree of the calling sequence of the procedures involved. It then examines this tree and asks the user questions about the desired and actual behavior of the procedures (i.e., their input and output values). By comparing actual values with desired values, it can determine which procedure definitions are in error. It makes use of an optimizing routine that substantially reduces the number of questions to be asked by narrowing down to the buggy procedures quickly.

The system as described relied on a human "ground oracle", i.e., it expected that the user could answer questions about the expected behavior of the program. In principle, the expected behavior of the program could be stored as a set of assertions, which could then be interrogated by the bug finding system. Thus, the system could be used by novices as a bug finder. In that case, it would have been not unlike Mycroft, but with the advantages that the declarative nature of Prolog makes easier the choice of how to relate changes in the code to desired changes in the program output and the lack of procedure side-effects removes the need to distinguish between "setup" steps and crucial drawing sequences.

The whole structure of the system relied very heavily on the special properties of the language chosen and it is not clear whether much of the methods used could be applied to a language like Pascal.

5.0 SUPPORT TOOLS

5.1 Bip and Bridge

In many ways Bip (Barr, Beard, & Atkinson, 1976) was a forerunner for many of the systems of support tools now available. It was designed for Basic and included a special interpreter with various graphic tracing facilities, a curriculum of programming problems and a task selection mechanism that mediated between the history of the performance of the student, the curriculum of problems, and the set of fundamental skills that the student was intended to learn. The system had a rudimentary answer-checking mechanism that compared I/O behavior of the student's program with that expected for the given problem, but only very limited facilities for identifying logical errors.

The support facilities included the ability to present a graphical step-by-step display of the working of a model answer to a problem, the graphical tracing and single-stepping of the student's answer and tracing of variables.

While the above facilities were impressive, and probably helpful, especially the ability of the system to present some of the workings of the underlying Basic notional machine, the system did not radically change the process of doing programming. Bridge (Bonar & Cunningham, 1986) is a system currently under development that provides the novice with a new way of thinking about Pascal programs and about their evolution from descriptions of problems in English through to code structures. It is based on a similar analysis to Proust, using goals and plans of the process of building programs.

The system is based on the notion of the interactive development of code through three phases. During each phase the system can supply hints on request. In the first phase, the student is given a problem in English, and is asked to construct a sequence of goals, picked from a menu of English phrases, as a solution to the problem. The phrases supplied enable a description of the problem at a number of different levels, the simplest of which simply indicates that the goal of the program is to print the answer.

By a process of further elaboration in this first phase, the student builds up the detail goal description corresponding to the model answer expected. Only when these goals have been correctly stated, is the student allowed to move to the next phase.

A special aspect of this system is that it allows the student to describe goals that will eventually involve some kind of program loop in a way that does not necessarily imply a loop, e.g., aggregating some quantity can be expressed as an aggregating action that makes no initial commitment at all to the need for a loop. Indeed, in some programming languages such actions might be primitive.

In the second phase, the student is expected to associate a plan from a menu of plans with each of the goal statements. The plans indicate a general method of achieving a goal and it is at this stage that the use of a loop, say for aggregating purposes, would be exposed. Again, a complete solution in terms of plans must be constructed before the student is allowed to move to the final stage.

In the final stage, the student chooses pieces of actual code to instantiate the plans, and so gradually builds the program itself with the help of a structure editor. The important issue being tackled by the Bridge system is the notion of providing the student with a number of different declarative representations of the original problem (e.g., as a sequence of goals, as a interlinked sequence of plans and as Pascal code). This may be contrasted with the Bip system's attempt to provide the student with an alternative procedural view of the code through the graphical tracing facilities.

Many issues remain to be solved in the Bridge system. These include the development of a wide range of problems and an appropriate set of English phrases. It is not clear at present how fast the set of phrases will grow with the introduction of each new problem. Other issues that the authors note as problematic are the difficulty that the students have in correctly selecting a plan to go with a goal statement and of selecting an appropriate piece of code to instantiate a plan. One of the difficulties of the latter is that the mapping from a general-purpose piece of code, such as an assignment, back to a plan is not at all obvious to the beginner.

6.0 CONCLUSIONS

In this survey we have attempted to indicate the main lines of development of systems that assist the learning of programming, either by engaging in teaching or by finding the bugs in students' code and commenting on them, or by providing tools for beginners to understand either the execution of their programs or the relation between code and problem description.

As was flagged by the negative remarks in the introduction, no system currently in existence does everything well, but some progress is being made. So, for example, Laura is good at standardizing a student program and a specimen answer and finding mismatches, but it cannot explain them as well as Proust. Proust works for only a limited number of problems and cannot be used interactively. Greaterp provides a comprehensive tutoring environment but is probably too prescriptive for some students. Bridge allows the student to describe his program at an intermediate level between English and code but has very limited diagnostics if the student makes serious errors.

Over the next few years we are likely to see the development of systems that combine the best features of the systems surveyed. Such a system would allow code to be described at a variety of levels, would monitor the student closely and effectively (if that was appropriate) or would keep quiet and allow the students to make what progress they can before undertaking the inevitable complex bug finding search.

ACKNOWLEDGEMENTS

We thank Mark Elsom-Cook, Derek Sleeman, Masoud Yazdani, Ashley Pinnington, Pat Fung, Anne Fletcher, George Haywood and Simon Buckland for helpful comments on an earlier draft of this paper. This work is supported by a grant from the Science and Engineering Research Council.

REFERENCES

Adam, A., & Laurent, J. (1980). A system to debug student programs. *Artificial Intelligence, 15,* 75–122.

Anderson, J. R., Farrell, R. & Sauers, R. (1984). Learning to Program in Lisp, *Cognitive Science, 8,* 87–129.

Anderson, J.R. & Reiser, B.J. (1985). The LISP Tutor. *BYTE, 10,* 4.

Barr, A., Beard, M., & Atkinson, R.C. (1976). The computer as tutorial laboratory: the Stanford BIP project. *International Journal of Man-Machine Studies, 8,* 567–595.

Bonar, J., & Cunningham, R. (1986). Bridge: an intelligent tutor for thinking about programming. *Proceedings of the ICAI Research Workshop,* Windermere, Cumbria.

Burton, R.R. & Brown, J.S. (1982). An investigation of computer coaching for informal learning activities. In *Intelligent Tutoring Systems,* D. Sleeman & J.S. Brown (Eds.), Academic Press, London.

Cerri, S.A., Fabrizzi, M., & Marsili, G. (1984). The Little Lisper, *AISB Quarterly Newsletter,* 50.

Clancey, W.J. (1986). Qualitative student models. *Proceedings of the ICAI Research Workshop,* Windermere, Cumbria.

Cole, A., Gilmore, D., O'Callaghan, L., & Self, J. (1986). The psychology of machine learning. *Proceedings of the ICAI Research Workshop,* Windermere, Cumbria.

Collins, A., Warnock, E.H., Aiello, N., & Miller, M. (1975). Reasoning from incomplete knowledge. In *Representation and Understanding,* D.G. Bobrow & A. Collins (Eds.), Academic Press, New York.

Draper, S. (1986). *Applying features of conversation to HCI.* Experimental Psychology,

University of Sussex.

Eisenstadt, M. (1982). *Design features of a friendly software environment for novice programmers* (Technical Report No. 3). Human Cognition Research Laboratory, Open University.

Elsom-Cook, M.T. (1985). *Design Considerations of an Intelligent Tutoring System for Programming Languages*. Department of Psychology, University of Warwick.

Gentner, D.R. (1979). Towards an intelligent computer tutor. *Procedures for Instructional Systems Development*, Academic Press, New York.

Goldstein, I.P. (1975). Summary of Mycroft: a system for understanding simple picture programs. *Artificial Intelligence, 6* 249–288.

Goldstein, I.P. (1982). The genetic graph: a representation for the evolution of procedural knowledge. In *Intelligent Tutoring Systems*, D. Sleeman & J.S. Brown (Eds.), Academic Press, London.

Green, T.R.G., & Cornah, A.J. (1982). *The programmer's torch*, (Working Paper). MRC/SSRC Applied Psychology Unit, University of Sheffield.

Hartley, J.R. (1973). The Design and Evaluation of an Adaptive Teaching System. *International Journal of Man-Machine Studies, 5*, 421–436.

Hasemer, T. (1983). *An empirically-based debugging system for novice programmers.* (Technical Report No. 6), Human Cognition Research Laboratory, Open University.

Johnson, W.L., & Soloway, E. (1983). *Proust: Knowledge-Based Program Understanding* (Technical Report 285), Department of Computer Science, Yale University.

Johnson, W.L., & Soloway, E. (1985). Proust. *BYTE, 10*, 4.

Johnson, W.L. (1985). Intention-based diagnosis of errors in novice programs. Computer Science Dept., Research Report No. 395, Yale University, New Haven, CT.

Johnson, W.L. (1986). Modelling programmers' intentions. *Proceedings of the ICAI Research Workshop*, Windermere, Cumbria.

Jones, J., Millington, M., & Ross, P. (1986). Understanding users' behavior. *Proceedings of the ICAI Research Workshop*, Windermere, Cumbria.

Koffman, E.B., & Blount, S.E. (1975). Artificial Intelligence and Automatic programming in CAI. *Artificial Intelligence, 6*, 215–234.

Lukey, F.J. (1980). Understanding and debugging programs. *International Journal of Man-Machine Studies, 12* 189–202.

Miller, M.L. (1978). A structured planning and debugging environment for elementary programming. *International Journal of Man-Machine Studies, 11* 79–95.

Ohlsson, S. (1986). Some principles of intelligent tutoring. *Instructional Science 14*, 293–326.

Pask, G. (1976). Styles and strategies of learning. *Br. J. Educ. Psychol., 46*, 128-148.

Rich, C., & Shrobe, H.E. (1980). Design for programmer's apprentice. In P.H. Winston & R.H. Brown (Eds.), *Artificial Intelligence: An MIT Perspective*. Cambridge, MA: MIT Press.

Self, J. (1974). Student Models in computer aided instruction. *International Journal of Man-Machine Studies, 6*, 261–276.

Shapiro, E.Y. (1982). *Algorithmic Program Debugging*. MIT Press, Cambridge, MA.

Soloway, E., & Ehrlich, K. (1984). Empirical studies of Programming Knowledge, *IEEE Transactions on Software Engineering*, SE-10:5, 595–609.

Shneiderman, B. (1980). *Software Psychology*. Winthrop Publishers, Cambridge, MA.

Teitelbaum, T., & Reps, T. (1981). The Cornell program synthesiser: a syntax-directed programming environment. *Communications of the ACM, 24*, 9, 563-573.

Waters, R.C. (1985). KBEmacs: a step toward the programmer's apprentice. AI Technical Report No. 753, MIT, AI Laboratory, Cambridge, MA.

Vose, G.M. (1984). Macintosh Pascal. *BYTE, 9*, 6.

17 GUIDON-WATCH: A GRAPHIC INTERFACE FOR VIEWING A KNOWLEDGE-BASED SYSTEM [1]

Mark H. Richer
William J. Clancey

Department of Computer Science
Stanford University
Stanford, CA 94305

ABSTRACT

GUIDON-WATCH is a graphic interface that uses multiple windows and a mouse to allow a student to browse through a knowledge base and view reasoning processes during diagnostic problem solving. This article presents methods for providing multiple views of hierarchical structures, overlaying results of a search process on top of static structures to make the strategy visible, and graphically expressing evidence relations between findings and hypotheses. We demonstrate the advantages of stating a diagnostic search procedure in a well-structured, rule-based language, separate from domain knowledge. A number of issues in software design are also considered, including the automatic management of a multiple-window display.

1.0 INTRODUCTION

An increasing number of Artificial Intelligence (AI) programs are implemented on high-performance workstations with a bit-map display, a mouse, and a keyboard. The programming environment (usually a dialect of LISP) generally provides support for displaying multiple windows and using menus that can be selected with a mouse. Importantly, a programmer can also specify arbitrary regions of a window (e.g., text items) to be selectable with the mouse. This means that a user can invoke an action by pressing or releasing a mouse button while the mouse cursor is in a selectable region. These features make it possible to create a user interface that is efficient and easy-to-use for viewing and browsing a complex system.

The GUIDON project at Stanford University is investigating how knowledge-based systems can provide the basis for teaching programs. NEOMYCIN (Clancey & Letsinger, 1984), a medical consultation system, has been

[1] Reprinted from: IEEE Computer Graphics and Applications, Vol. 5, No. 11, November 1985, pages 51-64.

developed for this purpose. This paper describes GUIDON-WATCH, a graphic interface to NEOMYCIN that uses multiple windows and the mouse to allow a user to browse the NEOMYCIN knowledge base and view reasoning processes during a consultation. The results reported include methods for providing multiple views of a database, techniques for illustrating dynamic processes including a search strategy, and some conclusions regarding automatic management of a multiple window display.

2.0 PROJECT GOALS

The ability to display and select information in several windows allows people to control and observe the behavior of an application program in an easy fashion. A graphic interface to a knowledge-based system can serve different kinds of users, including system designers, implementers, domain experts, students, and other end users.

In the GUIDON project, the end users will be medical students. We are currently collaborating with physicians and medical students to adapt NEOMYCIN, GUIDON-WATCH, and other programs for medical instruction. However, when this work began better tools were also needed to maintain the NEOMYCIN knowledge base and to debug program behavior. As a result, GUIDON-WATCH evolved into a tool for both programmers and medical students to use. We are just starting to make a clean separation between the functionality that is useful for students and that for programmers. We plan to develop user profiles that determine the interface behavior in a given situation. The current prototype can only be customized by making changes at the programming level.

GUIDON-WATCH is based on established principles for designing user interfaces on graphical workstations (Ingalls, 1981, Tesler, 1981; Foley & Van Dam, 1982, Card, et al., 1983; Foley et al., 1984). The design criteria for GUIDON-WATCH emerged from the conventional wisdom on the subject. The user interface is viewed as a conversation consisting of two languages (Foley, et al., 1984): (1) the language in which the user retrieves or requests information (with the mouse), and (2) the program's display and its interpretation by the user. We aim to maximize expressiveness, understandability, and efficiency for both languages. The user should be able to retrieve all information through one interface that is easy to understand and efficient to use. The display should include all relevant information, be easy to interpret, and update quickly when a user makes a request.

Several GUIDON-WATCH users have found the interface simple, consistent, and easy to use. However, those unfamiliar with NEOMYCIN have difficulty realizing exactly how and when the display can be useful. We have found that the display is the best means we have for explaining NEOMYCIN. Therefore, an on-line introduction to GUIDON-WATCH and NEOMYCIN is planned.

Informal evaluation with Stanford University medical students is scheduled for the Fall of 1985. Students will watch NEOMYCIN diagnose one or more patients. Data records of actual patients will be stored in files that can be accessed by NEOMYCIN during its questioning phase. A student will use GUIDON-WATCH to observe NEOMYCIN's reasoning processes during the consultation. NEOMYCIN will be able to explain in English why it asked a question (Hasling, 1984). Eventually, students will assist NEOMYCIN during a diagnosis in an apprenticeship setting.

The major results to date are summarized below:

- Multiple windows can provide several concurrent views of a knowledge-based system. They help users cope with the complexity of the system by highlighting and summarizing important reasoning events during a problem-solving session.

- Several methods for highlighting facts and events were found effective. These include using different font styles, reverse video, boxing, flashing, and graying regions. Using these techniques, dynamic information associated with a given patient can be overlaid on top of static structures such as a disorder tree or a table of evidence.

- Early results indicate that both programmers and medical users prefer to have GUIDON-WATCH manage screen space automatically. This includes the sizing, placing, and closing of windows. It is not trivial to do this with a large number of windows, particularly during development when changes to the system are frequent. A knowledge-based approach to window management is suggested.

3.0 The Development of NEOMYCIN

The GUIDON project has evolved from the MYCIN experiments (Shortliffe, 1976; Buchanan & Shortliffe, 1984) of the 1970s (Figure 3-1). MYCIN is a rule-based consultation program that recommends drug therapy for certain infectious diseases (e.g., meningitis). Because much of the functionality (e.g., the inference mechanism) of MYCIN does not depend on medical knowledge, it was possible to develop a domain-independent shell called EMYCIN (van Melle, 1981). MYCIN now consists of EMYCIN plus the MYCIN medical knowledge base. EMYCIN was used to develop several other knowledge-based systems, and is the basis for several commercial products.

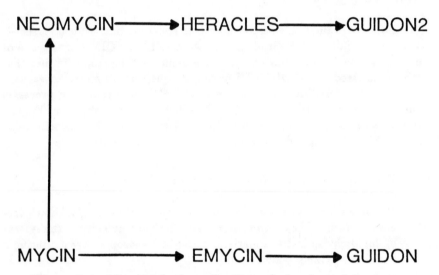

Figure 3-1: The Evolution of a Knowledge-based System

MYCIN evolved into EMYCIN, a domain-independent shell for building knowledge-based systems. The GUIDON tutoring system is a separate module that could be used with any EMYCIN system. EMYCIN was not found to be an adequate foundation for an instructional program. Therefore, EMYCIN and the MYCIN knowledge base were reconfigured into NEOMYCIN, a medical consultation system which is designed for enhanced explanation and tutoring capabilities. The domain-independent shell that NEOMYCIN is built with is called HERACLES. NEOMYCIN is the basis for GUIDON-2, a collection of instructional programs now in development.

In 1979 Clancey completed GUIDON (Clancey, 1983), an intelligent tutoring system that interfaces with EMYCIN. In theory, GUIDON can teach a student the rules in an EMYCIN knowledge base. However, Clancey found that the MYCIN rules were often difficult to understand because they combine a diagnostic procedure with medical facts in an opaque manner (Clancey & Letsinger, 1984). In a MYCIN rule the ordering of conjunct clauses in the premise might implicitly contain a strategy. For example, a rule might only apply if the patient is an alcoholic. One MYCIN rule premise begins with "if the patient is over 18 years of age and an alcoholic". The strategy that is implicitly represented in this rule premise is "don't ask a patient under 18 years of age if they are alcoholic".

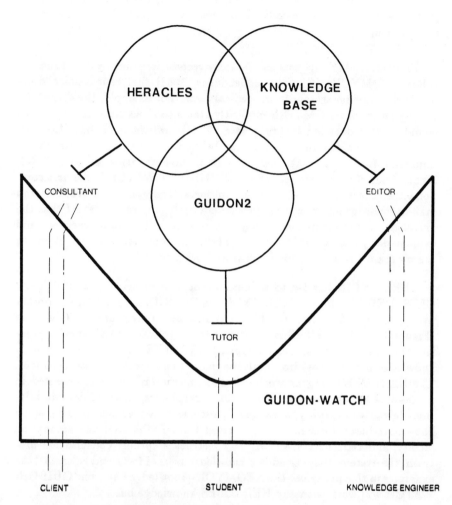

Figure 3-2: The HERACLES architecture.

The relationship between GUIDON-WATCH and three primary system modules is illustrated above. A consultation system consists of
HERACLES, a knowledge base, and GUIDON-WATCH. For instructional use, the GUIDON-2 module (now in development) can be added.
GUIDON-WATCH provides an interface for instructional use, to run
consultations, and to edit the knowledge base. Although there are differences in the interface for each type of user, in general, the interface
is very similar and represents a single program with several modes of
behavior. (The graphic editor is not described in this paper because
that interface has not been completey integrated with HERACLES.)

GUIDON demonstrated that satisfying the requirements for expert performance are not necessarily sufficient for the purpose of explanation and tutoring.

Therefore, MYCIN was significantly reconfigured into a new program called NEOMYCIN (Clancey & Letsinger, 1984) that represents a diagnostic strategy separately from medical facts. For example, the diagnostic strategy used in NEOMYCIN explicitly states to check for conditions that would make a question inappropriate. The knowledge base has also been expanded to include diseases that can be confused with meningitis (this is important for instruction). NEOMYCIN is the foundation for GUIDON-2, a new series of instructional programs. GUIDON-WATCH is the first component of the GUIDON-2 system. Importantly, interactive graphics can make knowledge and reasoning processes visible only to the extent that the knowledge is represented explicitly in a program. The well-structured and explicit design of NEOMYCIN provides many opportunities for exposing the program's reasoning to students and other users.

NEOMYCIN has led to a domain-independent system called HERACLES. HERACLES is to NEOMYCIN as EMYCIN is to MYCIN. In other words, NEOMYCIN consists of HERACLES and a medical knowledge base (Figure 3-2). HERACLES is a software tool applicable to diagnostic problems in many domains. For example, HERACLES was used to develop a knowledge base for cast iron fault diagnosis (Thompson & Clancey, 1986). The HERACLES program includes a diagnostic procedure represented in a rule-based declarative language, rule interpreters, a set of domain relations (e.g., causes, subtype, suggests), various software tools for developing knowledge-based systems (many derived from EMYCIN), an explanation facility, and GUIDON-WATCH. To construct a specific consultation program, the system designer adds a knowledge base of facts and rules. All the examples in this paper use the NEOMYCIN knowledge base, but GUIDON-WATCH will work with any HERACLES knowledge base.

4.0 DESCRIPTION OF THE GUIDON-WATCH DISPLAY

The windows and menus used in GUIDON-WATCH are described in detail in this section. First, the programming environment is briefly described to show what tools we used when we began the project. Then an overview of the interface is provided. The third section describes the window display facilities in detail.

4.1 Programming Environment

GUIDON-WATCH is implemented on Xerox 1100 Series workstations running Interlisp-D. The black and white display screen is 1024 pixels wide by

808 pixels high, with the density being approximately 75 pixels per inch.
Interlisp-D provides a window package that supports multiple overlapping
windows, scroll bars, and other window operations (Sannella, 1985). Many
graphics primitives are provided for drawing lines and curves, manipulating
bitmaps, filling and manipulating regions, checking the state and position
of the mouse, etc. In addition, a menu package, a grapher package (e.g.,
to display trees), and several default window functions (e.g., scrolling by
repainting) are provided. It required only a page of code to implement a
simple pull-down menu package using the window primitives.

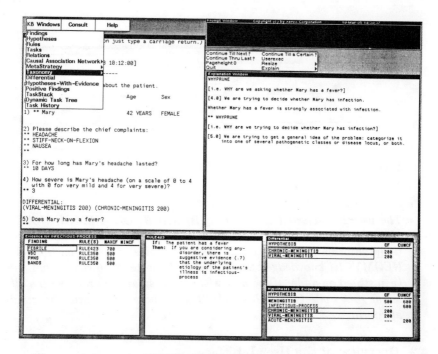

Figure 4-1:   A GUIDON-WATCH Display During a
               Consultation.

The user is running a consultation and the system has paused at question 5. The user has opened several windows to get information about the hypotheses that are being considered at this time. The use of pull-down menus is also illustrated. The user has selected the KB Windows menu and moved the mouse over the menu item Taxonomy. If the user releases the mouse button now, the Taxonomy window will be displayed.

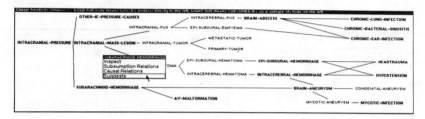

Figure 4-2: The Causal Relations Window.

The user has selected the node SUBARACHNOID-HEMORRHAGE with the left button and a pop-up menu displays options for additional information. This graph was automatically generated from the NEOMYCIN knowledge base, edited by hand to fit on the screen, and then stored on a file. If the user wished to display the graph with a different root node GUIDON-WATCH dynamically generates the graph at runtime.

4.2 Overview of the User Interface

Pull-down menus and a Prompt window are at the top of the GUIDON-WATCH display. (Figure 4-1). The Prompt window is a standard part of the Interlisp-D user interface that is used to print messages. Currently there are three pull-down menus of interest to a medical student: KB (Knowledge Base) Windows, Consult, and Help. The KB Windows pull-down menu displays a list of windows that can be opened for browsing the knowledge base or viewing a consultation. The Consult menu is used to start and quit a consultation. The Help menu allows the user to obtain information on the contents of a window.

4.2.1 Use of the Mouse

Xerox 1100 computers can be used with either a two- or three-button mouse (selecting the left and right button at the same time on a two-button mouse is equivalent to pressing the middle button on the three-button mouse). In GUIDON-WATCH, the mouse is used in a simple and consistent way. The left button is used to select all menu items and text items in a window. For example, in a window that displays a list of diseases, the user can select the name of a disease using the left button. A pop-up menu is displayed that allows a user to get more information in another window (Figure 4-2). Only those items that are currently relevant appear in the pop-up menu.

It has not been decided whether or not students will be asked to use more than the left button. In our current programming environment, the right button is used in the default manner provided by Interlisp-D, to manipulate windows (e.g., reshaping, closing). The middle button is sometimes used to display a pop-up menu with items that apply to the entire data structure in a window. For example, a user may want to highlight those items in a window that all have a certain property. We are considering the use of icons in a window for operations besides selecting menu or text items (e.g., closing a window). Therefore, the student interface may only use one button.

4.2.2 On-line Help

If the user selects Help window from the HELP pull-down menu, then a HELP icon attaches to the mouse cursor. The user can get help about a window by moving the HELP icon into a window and buttoning the window. A message associated with the selected window is printed in a special help window.

4.2.3 Management of Windows

The Interlisp-D graphics package provides functions for prompting users to position a ghost image of a window or to a shape a window. These prompts can be confusing to novices and distract from the task at hand. If it is possible to make a good decision regarding the size and position of a window, we can free the user from this chore. In addition, an automatic window-management system can often optimize the use of screen space better than a user. This is true in GUIDON-WATCH because there are a known set of windows whose contents are constrained to a certain form (e.g., a table).

To manage the window display, the screen is divided into logical units. The GUIDON-WATCH screen consists of top, middle, and bottom sections. The top section contains the pull-down menus and the Prompt window. The bottom and middle sections display knowledge base structures and have well-defined lower borders. Another logical division of the GUIDON-WATCH display provides vertical boundaries. For example, the width of the screen can be divided into equal or unequal regions. The current prototype uses three regions with two equal and one slightly wider than the other two. Furthermore, you can have a hierarchy of subdivisions (i.e., regions). Each window in GUIDON-WATCH is associated with one or more regions where it can be displayed.

GUIDON-WATCH decides where to place a window based on several considerations: (1) the default region of the window, (2) the other windows that are displayed and their position, and (3) the set of windows that the user would mostly likely prefer to remain in view. While the current window management system is effective, we would like to extend the flexibility of the interface. This would require a more complex scheme. It might be necessary to consider moving or reshaping windows that are already on the screen. Note that window systems that provide this capability do not consider the semantics of the contents of windows. Therefore, algorithms for scaling pictures and changing the font size of text are not sufficient when you have to decide where windows should beplaced and which windows should be closed or covered.

Although flexibility and control are relinquished by the user, the benefits of automatic screen management seem to outweigh potential disadvantages. Automatic window management saves the user time and maximizes the use of screen space. It is possible to allow the user to turn off automatic features, change defaults, or allow the user to use the move and reshape facilities. Furthermore, menus or icons can be used to allow the user to choose from a predefined set of sizes, positions, fonts, and so on, but then the implementation of the automatic window manager becomes increasingly complex. In our current implementation, when a window is displayed, a complex conditional in the window's display function is evaluated. This code is difficult to understand and modify. In addition, the situation has been complicated by the need for different user profiles. We are considering an approach where the behavior of the interface is specified separately and declaratively using knowledge representation formalisms (e.g., rules) and object-oriented programming.

4.2.4 Dynamic Updating of the Screen Display

Displaying dynamically changing information presents problems that are not unique to our application. For example, how often do you update the screen? Do you gray out regions that are out of date or immediately update them? Our philosophy is that users should be able to open and close windows at any time and that the display should accurately reflect the current state of the system or gray out regions that are not continuously updated. Regions that are grayed out can either be automatically updated at specified intervals or manually by the user simply buttoning the window to redisplay itself.

4.3 The GUIDON-WATCH Windows

Here we describe many of the windows available to the GUIDON-WATCH user and address important issues: What information in a HERACLES knowledge base is most important to display for programmers and for medical students? How can dynamic information be displayed? In the next section, we focus on static knowledge structures and the way they are displayed in GUIDON-WATCH. Subsequent subsections discuss the display of dynamic consultation knowledge.

4.3.1 What is There to Display in a Knowledge Base?

A HERACLES knowledge base (e.g., NEOMYCIN medical knowledge base) includes findings, hypotheses, rules, tasks, and relations. Findings are data that can be requested or inferred from rules. Generally findings can be observed or measured. Hypotheses can only be inferred from rules. In NEOMYCIN, hypotheses include diseases and pathophysiological states. Relations refer to predicate calculus relations and in HERACLES include subtype, causes, etc. Static knowledge includes facts about findings and hypotheses as defined by relations (e.g., meningitis is a subtype of infection, headache is a finding, etc.). It also includes the diagnostic procedure and domain rules (e.g., if the patient has double vision, then there is suggestive evidence for intracranial pressure). Dynamic knowledge is situation specific and refers to information that becomes known only during a problem solving session (e.g., "Mary's temperature is 102 degrees.").

NEOMYCIN uses a diagnostic strategy known as heuristic classification problem solving (Clancey and Letsinger, 1984). Given an enumerated set of solutions (e.g., diseases or possible diagnoses), NEOMYCIN heuristically maps a set of findings onto one or more possible solutions. This diagnostic procedure is provided by HERACLES (or Heuristic Classification Shell). It is represented as tasks, which are procedures that are stated in a declarative rule-based language (Figure 4-3). When a task is invoked, one or more of its metarules are applied (Figures 4-4, 4-5). Metarules in HERACLES are similar to conditionals in a procedure, but they are expressed as abstract rules.

Windows that display static knowledge include the Task, Metarules, and Rule windows in Figures 4-3, 4-4, and 4-5. They also include the Findings, Hypotheses, and Relations windows, which simply display an alphabetical ordering. Other windows display a graph to show the relationships between groups of objects. The Causal Relations window (Figure 4-2) is a lattice with causal and subtype links between findings and hypotheses; the Diagnostic Strategy window (Figure 4-6) shows the calling structure of the diagnostic tasks; and the Taxonomy window (Figure 4-7) represents a subtype hierarchy of disorders. In all of these windows the user may select an item to get more information.

```
Task PURSUE-HYPOTHESIS

ENDCONDITION:      STOP-PURSUING

TASK-TYPE:         SIMPLE

TASKGOAL:          PURSUED

FOCUS:             CURFOCUS

TASK-TRY-ALL?:     T

ACHIEVED-BY:       (RULE171 RULE590)

LOCALVARS:         ($BETTERHYP)
```

Figure 4-3: The Task Property Window.

Here the properties and values of the task Pursue-Hypothesis are displayed.

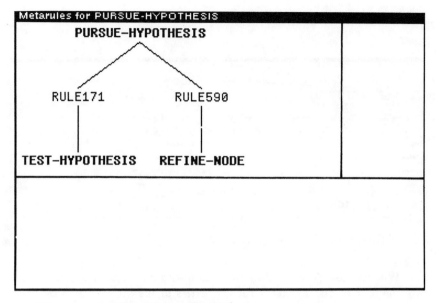

Figure 4-4: The Metarules Window.

Here the metarules that the task Pursue-Hypothesis calls are displayed.

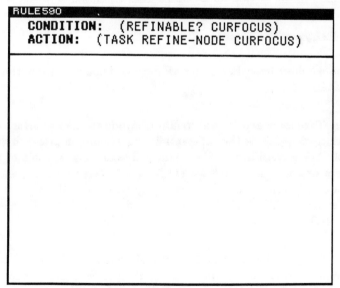

Figure 4-5: The Rule window.

Here a metarule of the task Pursue-Hypothesis is displayed.

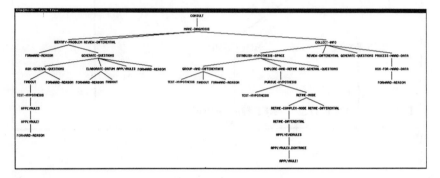

Figure 4-6: The Diagnostic Task Tree Window.

When a task is selected in this window, a menu pops up that allows the user to display either the properties of the task in the Task Property window (Figure 4-3) or the metarules that a task applies in the Metarules window (Figure 4-4). During a consultation the user can also choose to see dynamic information about task calls. This is described in the section on Dynamic Task windows.

4.3.2 Reifying the Process

The windows described below all display dynamic information during a consultation.

The Taxonomy and Causal Relations windows. An important concept in medical diagnosis is the differential, the set of competing hypotheses currently being considered. The etiological taxonomy is a tree of possible diagnoses or solutions in NEOMYCIN. The differential represents a cut through this solution space. Boxing the hypotheses in the Taxonomy window that are on the differential is a simple way to make this cut visible (Figure 4-7).

Flashing and boxing nodes in the Taxonomy and Causal Relations windows emphasize the dynamic search strategy. Whenever a hypothesis is added to the differential, its corresponding node label is flashed and then boxed. Whenever the hypothesis is removed from the differential, the box is redrawn with lighter lines, so that the hypotheses that had been considered previously are still highlighted, but the ones currently on the differential are more prominent (Figure 4-7). A student can observe NEOMYCIN looking up the disorder tree to group and compare categories of disorders before looking down to refine hypotheses. In essence, we are reifying (i.e., making more concrete) the process of problem solving.

Conclusions in a HERACLES consultation are associated with certainty factors that represent a degree of belief. They are not probabilities. In HERACLES, each hypothesis has both a certainty factor (CF) and a cumulative certainty factor (CUMCF). The CF represents the combined certainty of all rules that have concluded directly about the hypothesis. The CUMCF represents a combination of the CF of a given hypothesis (which may be zero) with CFs of its descendants in the disorder taxonomy. For example, evidence for meningitis (a positive CF) increases the CUMCF of infectious process because meningitis is a subtype of infectious process. (To be exact, negative CFs of ancestors are also combined; therefore, evidence against infection can decrease the CUMCF of meningitis.)

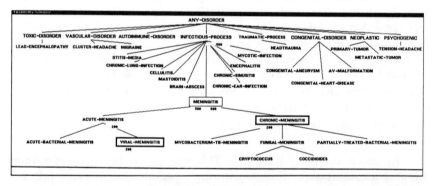

Figure 4-7: The Taxonomy Window.

The boxing, flashing, and printing techniques used in this window make the dynamic search strategy visible by displaying dynamic information on top of static knowledge structures, in this case the etiological taxonomy. The differential shown here is NEOMYCIN's internal differential and may not correspond precisely to a physician's differential. The differential shown to a student may differ from NEOMYCIN's internal list. This graph was generated, edited, and stored in the same manner as the graph in Figure 4-2. Note that Figures 4-7 through 4-10 correspond to the same state of the consultation as displayed in Figure 4-1.

When the CF or CUMCF is updated for a hypothesis, new values are printed below the node label corresponding to the hypothesis. The CF is printed on the left, the CUMCF on the right if it differs. The figures in this paper show the CFs printed as integers from -1000 to $+1000$; this is how they are represented internally. These numbers are far from precise and should be interpreted as falling in several categories: definite, strongly suggestive, suggestive, weakly suggestive or no evidence for (or against) a hypothesis. For students the internal CF values will not be printed; instead a graphic notation, such as zero to four pluses or minuses, could be used to indicate the degree of belief.

In the case in which a hypothesis window is not open, the printing, boxing and flashing of nodes is not done immediately. However, whenever the Taxonomy or Causal Relations window is opened during a consultation, the window is updated so that all the hypotheses are appropriately boxed, and certainty factors are printed. Therefore, the user is free to open these windows at any time. We describe several other windows that display dynamic information.

The Consultation Typescript window (Figure 4-1). This window is opened when a user starts a consultation using the Consult menu. The questions that are asked during a consultation are displayed in this window. Each question is followed by a response that is either supplied by the user or is retrieved automatically from a patient data file. Before an answer is retrieved the program pauses. The user can then use the mouse to select items or open any windows. A menu is provided that allows a user to proceed one or more questions further, receive textual explanations, resize the consultation window, and so on.

Evidence window (Figure 4-8). This window can be displayed without running a consultation. However, during a consultation dynamic information is overlaid onto static knowledge structures to show the current evidence relations between findings and hypotheses. All potential evidence for a hypothesis is displayed as a table in this window. The first column lists findings and hypotheses that suggest a hypothesis. The second column lists the rules that use these findings or hypotheses to make conclusions about the hypothesis. The third column shows the maximum CF in the rule's action, and the fourth column shows, if different, the minimum CF in the rule's action. Findings, hypotheses, and rules can be selected with the mouse to get more information. For example, a rule's premise and conclusion can be displayed in the Rule window (Figure 4-9).

During a consultation, GUIDON-WATCH employs boldfaced text and grayed-over regions to provide the user with additional information. The user may have displayed the evidence of meningitis because it was boxed in the Taxonomy window (Figure 4-7). Seeing that rule 424 succeeded (which is indicated by the bold text), the user can display the rule's premise and conclusion in the Rule window (Figure 4-9). A finding with a positive value is printed in bold; a negative finding is grayed over. Analogously, rules that have succeeded are printed in bold; rules that have failed are grayed over. Findings and rules that appear in normal print have not been investigated yet. This simple notation is an effective means of providing a great deal of information in a concise and understandable manner. Furthermore, it illustrates how dynamic information can be displayed on top of static knowledge structures that are displayed in a table format.

Evidence for MENINGITIS			
FINDING	**RULE(S)**	**MAXCF**	**MINCF**
TENSE-FONTANEL	RULE060	800	
SEIZURES	RULE060	800	
REDFLAG-CNS-FINDI	RULE323	700	
STIFF-NECK-ON-FLE	**RULE424**	500	
	RULE183	500	
HEADACHE	**RULE424**	500	
NEONATE	RULE183	500	
WBC	RULE131	−700	
CSFCELLCOUNT	RULE131	−700	
	RULE117	−800	
CSFPROTEIN	RULE117	−800	

Figure 4-8: The Evidence Window.

The findings and hypotheses displayed in this window are ordered so that the ones that may be most suggestive (have the highest MAXCF) are on top.

Positive Findings window (Figure 4-10). This window displays all the findings that have a positive value (i.e., the value is "yes", a number, or symbolic). Findings are printed in the first column, values in the second column, and CFs in the third (printed only if less than 1000). Findings are selectable, and when buttoned a pop-up menu is displayed. For example, a user may want to select a finding to see which hypotheses the finding may suggest.

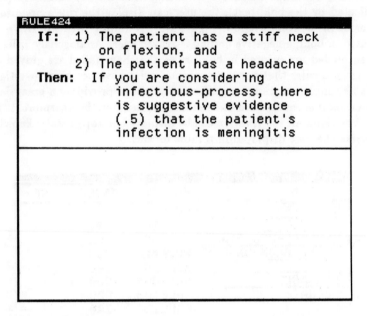

Figure 4-9: Rule window.

Here a domain rule is displayed.

FINDING	VALUE	CF
AGE	42	
SEX	FEMALE	
RACE	LATINO	
HEADACHE	YES	
STIFF-NECK-ON-FLEXION	YES	
NAUSEA	YES	
HEADACHE-DURATION	10	
HEADACHE-SEVERITY	3	
CNS-FINDING	YES	
STIFF-NECK-SIGNS	YES	
HEADACHE-CHRONICITY	CHRONIC	800
	SUBACUTE	300
CNS-FINDING-DURATION	10	

Figure 4-10: The Positive Findings window.

In this window items are printed incrementally during a consultation. If the Positive Findings window is open, new positive findings are printed in the window as soon as they are known. If the window is closed, the whole list of positive findings is printed when the window is opened. This feature provides flexibility for the user, who can open or close the window at any time during a consultation.

Differential window (Figure 4-11). Hypotheses on the differential are boxed when they appear in certain windows. However, the differential is such an important structure that a special window is provided for its display.

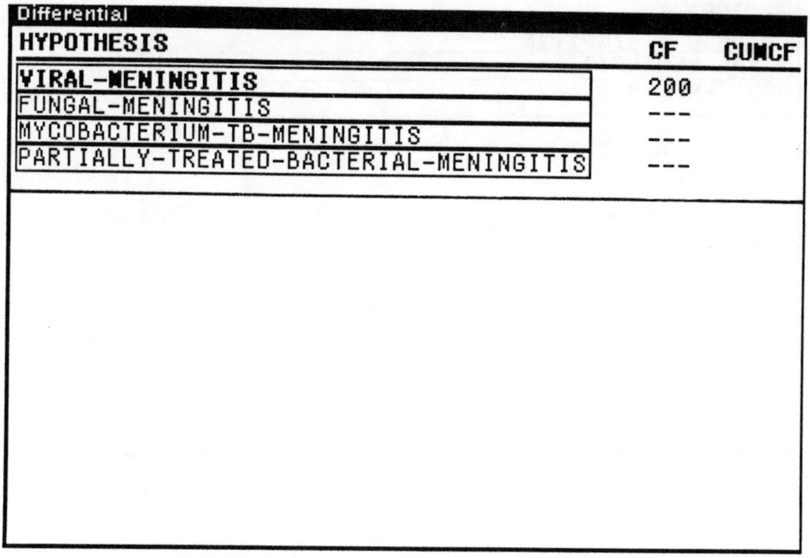

```
┌─────────────────────────────────────────────────────────────────────┐
│ Differential                                                         │
│ HYPOTHESIS                                              CF      CUMCF │
│ ┌─────────────────────────────────────────────────┐                 │
│ │VIRAL-MENINGITIS                                 │    200           │
│ │FUNGAL-MENINGITIS                                │    ---           │
│ │MYCOBACTERIUM-TB-MENINGITIS                      │    ---           │
│ │PARTIALLY-TREATED-BACTERIAL-MENINGITIS           │    ---           │
│ └─────────────────────────────────────────────────┘                 │
│                                                                      │
│                                                                      │
│                                                                      │
│                                                                      │
│                                                                      │
│                                                                      │
│                                                                      │
└─────────────────────────────────────────────────────────────────────┘
```

Figure 4-11: The Differential window.

This window is displayed several questions after the point shown in Figure 4-1. Subsequent figures all show windows as displayed at this later point.

Hypotheses-with-evidence window (Figure 4-12). However, not all hypotheses for which there is positive evidence are on the differential at a given time. This group includes hypotheses for which there is direct evidence (i.e., at least one rule concluded the hypothesis) and those for which there is belief when propagation is included (i.e., the CUMCF is above a certain threshold). Note that some of these hypotheses may not be on the differential at a given time, and additionally, hypotheses on the differential may not have evidence supporting them.

In both the Differential and Hypotheses-with-evidence windows, hypotheses that have direct evidence supporting them are printed in bold. These windows also contain columns for CF and CUMCF values. As usual, the hypotheses are selectable. These two windows, as well as the Taxon-

omy and the Causal Relations windows, illustrate how GUIDON-WATCH
provides multiple views of the same knowledge structures.

Hypotheses With Evidence		
HYPOTHESIS	CF	CUMCF
INFECTIOUS-PROCESS	700	880
MENINGITIS	500	600
CHRONIC-MENINGITIS	200	
VIRAL-MENINGITIS	200	
ACUTE-MENINGITIS	---	200

Figure 4-12: The Hypotheses-with-evidence Window.

Dynamic Task windows. These windows provide users with dynamic
views of the diagnostic strategy as it is instantiated during a consultation.
This is a challenging presentation problem because the abstract nature of
the diagnostic procedure as it is represented in the task and metarules is not
nearly as intuitive to people as are disorder hierarchies, causal networks,
domain rules, and lists of findings. Although the goal is to provide a view of
NEOMYCIN's reasoning that is understandable to medical students, the
model of the diagnostic strategy is in the form of a complex procedure
that is intimately tied to basic concepts of computing. For example, task
calls are very similar to procedure calls; a task may have a focus and local
variables. A focus consists of one or more findings, hypotheses, or rules
depending on the task. For example, Test-Hypothesis may have meningitis
or another disease as a focus in NEOMYCIN. Tasks invoke other tasks in
a chain, similar to procedure calls.

The three windows described here each provide a different view of the
dynamic diagnostic strategy by using three different graphic formats: a
stack, a tree, and a table. Although it has not yet been decided how they
will be adapted for instruction, they are already very useful for programmers trying to debug or understand NEOMYCIN's behavior. Programmers

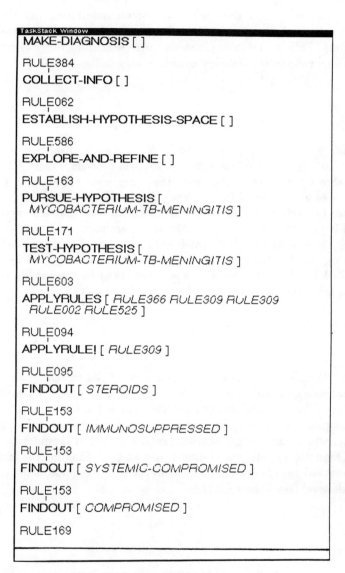

Figure 4-13: The Task Stack window.

By examining the task stack here, the user can see that NEOMYCIN is testing the hypothesis mycobacterium-TB-meningitis. As a result, a rule that was applied led to a series of calls to the task Findout. The last call, with the focus "compromised" finally resulted in a question to the user: "Is Mary a compromised-host?" The user would see this in the Consultation Typescript window.

can use these windows to find out exactly what NEOMYCIN is doing or
has done at a detailed strategic level. Consistent with Model's (Model,
1979) recommendations, these windows provide monitoring and debugging
tools at a level that corresponds to the program's design (e.g., tasks and
metarules). This is a great improvement over examining the low-level LISP
stack which reflects the strategy only in a very indirect way.

Task Stack window (Figure 4-13). This window displays the current
stack of task calls, which is similar to a stack of procedure calls. Its current
design shows the tasks in the order that they were called, with the first
task printed at the top of the window. If the task has a focus, it is printed
in square brackets after the task. The metarule that the task successfully
applied is printed below the task. Metarules are attached to the task they
invoke by a vertical line. Different font faces are used to distinguish tasks,
metarules, and foci from one another. Every rule, finding, and hypothesis
in the Task Stack window is selectable so that the user can quickly get more
detailed information on an item of interest.

The Task Stack window provides a view of the current path through
the diagnostic tree with metarules and foci instantiated. By examining the
task stack, the user can understand the reason for the current strategy.
For example, the user may be interested in why a question is being asked.
Students will be able to get textual explanations that should satisfy their
needs (Figure 4-1), but programmers may want to examine the task stack
to understand the computational reasons for a data request at the task and
metarule level (see Figure 4-13).

Dynamic Task Tree window (Figure 4-14). This window displays a
graph that shows all or part of the dynamic history of task calls. This
allows a user to view the overall structure of the diagnostic strategy that
NEOMYCIN is using during or at the end of a consultation. This capability
is useful because the static Diagnostic Task Tree window (Figure 4-6) shows
all possible paths in the task tree; this window shows only the paths that
are part of an actual diagnosis and reveals patterns of multiple calls of the
same task.

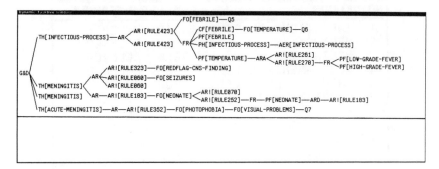

Figure 4-14: The Dynamic Task Tree window.

The node labels of tasks in this tree are abbreviated, but the user can see the full name expanded when a node is selected. TH is short for Test-Hypothesis in this tree. The figure above illustrates how the user can see multiple calls of a task and the resulting events in the Dynamic Task Tree window.

Task History window (Figure 4-15). This window contains a table of all the invocations of any given task during the consultation. It provides an alternate view (i.e., a slice at a time) of the information displayed in the Dynamic Task Tree window. In the first column, the invocation number of the task is printed, with the digit 1 meaning the first time the task was called. In the second column, the focus of the task call is printed; in the third column, the metarule that invoked the task is printed; and in the fourth column, the calling task is printed. As usual, rules, findings, hypotheses, and tasks are selectable. Additionally, the user can select an invocation number in order to display more information on the history of that task call. For example, the user can display a dynamic task tree with the chosen task invocation as the root.

Together, the three dynamic task windows provide a powerful aid for inspecting the current and past diagnostic strategy used during the consultation. It is clear that medical students would need some instruction in these concepts before the dynamic task windows would be meaningful to them. Part of the problem is that many of the task names are not commonly used in medicine. It is hoped that some of the problem can be alleviated by choosing names for the diagnostic tasks that are more familiar to students. Additionally, some tasks may be hidden from a student's view because they involve computational details of interest to a programmer only.

```
 Task History of TEST-HYPOTHESIS
 NO.  FOCUS                    CALLER  METARULE
  1   INFECTIOUS-PROCESS       G&D     RULE393
  2   MENINGITIS               G&D     RULE400
  3   MENINGITIS               G&D     RULE400
  4   ACUTE-MENINGITIS         G&D     RULE400
  5   CHRONIC-MENINGITIS       PUH     RULE171
  6   MYCOBACTERIUM-TB-MEN     PUH     RULE171
```

Figure 4-15: The Task History Window.

5.0   PRIOR AND RELATED WORK IN GRAPHIC INTERFACES

GUIDON-WATCH was influenced by a diverse collection of work stretching back to Vannevar Bush's seminal article, in which a desk-sized, electronic information device called a "memex" was proposed (Bush, 1945). Doug Engelbart and his colleagues pioneered much of the early work on information handling systems and provided the basis for the user interfaces commonly found on today's workstations (Engelbart, 1963, English and Engelbart, 1967, Engelbart, 1970: Engelbart, 1982). Alan Kay led the Learning Research Group (LRG) at XEROX PARC that brought similar ideas to fruition on personal workstations (Kay, 1977). Engelbart's group and the LRG shaped a view of the computer as a communications medium by which a user can store, retrieve, manipulate, and transfer information with ease. The LRG's vision of a dynabook (Goldberg, 1979: Borning, 1979; Weyer & Borning, 1984; Finzer & Gould, 1984) still remains an exciting dream in the spirit of Bush's memex.

The 1970s also brought many advances in Artificial Intelligence including the development of knowledge-based systems such as MYCIN. Starting from a different point of view, Seymour Papert led a group at MIT that explored the use of computer languages such as LOGO to teach subjects

such as geometry and physics in a new way (Papert, 1980). Papert offers
a provocative view of AI and computers in education; he influenced us to
consider how we can provide students with conceptual and software tools
to explore computational models (Papert, 1980). John Seely Brown further
inspired us to understand the potential of these ideas; his discussion of reifying the process of problem solving (Brown, 1985) is particularly relevant to
GUIDON-WATCH. To reify means to make real or concrete, or to mate-
rialize something that is abstract. GUIDON-WATCH makes the abstract
diagnostic procedure used in NEOMYCIN more concrete and visible.

Partly because bit-mapped raster displays have only recently been integrated with AI programming environments, little has been written about
graphic interfaces in AI programs. Some notable exceptions include Model
(Model, 1979), AIPS (Zdybel et al., 1981), the ONCOCIN project (Tsuji
& Shortliffe, 1983; Tsuji & Shortliffe, 1986; Lane, et al., 1986), and the
STEAMER project (Hollan et al., 1984; Stevens, et al., 1983). Model
demonstrated that graphic displays can facilitate the monitoring and debugging of complex programs (he used MYCIN for an early demonstration
of his work). Tsuji and Shortliffe investigated this idea further by implementing several graphic tools for constructing, monitoring, and debugging
ONCOCIN's knowledge base and inference procedures. (ONCOCIN is a
system that helps physicians administer experimental cancer therapy.) The
ONCOCIN group's strong commitment to the use of interactive graphics
has resulted in several graphic interfaces, including the ONCOCIN Inter-
viewer (Lane et al., 1986), a program that helps physicians enter patient
data.

STEAMER, an instructional program about power-plant operation,
uses interactive color graphics in a knowledge-based simulation. It is interesting to compare the use of interactive graphics in STEAMER and
GUIDON-WATCH. STEAMER emphasizes the construction of a visible,
interactive, and inspectable simulation. It displays the complex physical
processes of a steam-propulsion plant. NEOMYCIN, on the other hand, is a
computational model of diagnostic reasoning. GUIDON-WATCH provides
a user with a visible, interactive, and inspectable model of NEOMYCIN's
reasoning processes.

Several knowledge-base browsers similar to GUIDON-WATCH were
developed more or less concurrently. For example, ART, KEE, SRL+,
LOOPS, S.1, and STROBE provide interactive graphic displays that allow
programmers to browse class hierarchies and other general data structures
(Stefik et al., 1983; Kunz, et al. 1984; Williams, 1984; Richer, 1986). Sophisticated graphic editors may be provided; for example, STROBE has
an excellent knowledge base editor (Schoen & Smith, 1983). However, the

browsers provided in these systems are very general and are too complex for end users, requiring an understanding of the underlying knowledge representation framework. On the other hand, KEE and LOOPS do provide support for creating end-user iconic displays. These can be very useful for displaying the state of a complex device.

GUIDON-WATCH differs from other browsing programs because it is tuned to display specific kinds of knowledge structures (e.g., those found in a HERACLES system). For example, GUIDON-WATCH can display disease taxonomies, causal networks, evidence for a hypothesis, and positive findings in a way that is appropriate for end users such as medical students. Graphic techniques described in this paper illustrate an abstract diagnostic procedure during its actual use. To paraphrase, if a knowledge base is written for HERACLES, then an effective user interface is provided automatically.

6.0 FUTURE WORK

A continuing decrease in the price of hardware will provide more opportunities to use higher resolution screens, interactive pictures, color, animation, and interactive video. Certainly, we have only touched the surface in using graphics for viewing a knowledge-based system. Interactive and animated pictures can illustrate facts and processes. However, implementing interactive graphic displays is time-consuming. There is a need for high-level user interface kits that provide most of the common features that developers now have to implement over and over again. It is probable that an object-oriented programming system will be adopted as an extension to the Common Lisp standard (Bobrow & Stefik, 1986; Steele, 1984). This could provide the basis for a generic interface shell for lisp environments. Two examples of interface packages that successfully use the object-oriented approach include MacApp (Tesler, 1985) and EzWin (Lieberman, 1985); the latter is written in flavors, the object-oriented language within Zetalisp (Weinreb & Moon, 1981).

The discussion so far has focused on what interactive graphics can provide for AI systems. However, AI technology can contribute directly to more intelligent graphic interfaces. Current research topics include user modeling, intelligent presentation, and declarative languages for describing graphical interaction. Mackinlay (Mackinlay, 1986) is investigating some of these issues. For GUIDON-WATCH, we decided how to present information and hand-coded it. Instead, Mackinlay's program reasons on its own about how to present information. For example, it can decide to present data as a bar chart, a pie chart, a plot chart, a table, or a graph. It can also design several alternative sophisticated presentations from simpler ones and then use heuristics to choose one to display to the user.

Another important aspect of Mackinlay's work is that it uses a knowledge-based approach. Therefore, its reasoning is represented in an explicit, declarative language and not in opaque code. The use of a declarative representation results in programs that are easier to modify and understand. We found that the parts of our display code that are trying to be smart, such as the management of windows, are poorly represented in LISP. The code fails to make the underlying reasoning explicit, and it is difficult to modify. Another advantage of using a declarative representation is that it can be used in multiple ways. Mackinlay's current work addresses only the intelligent presentation problem, but eventually programs may be able to explain why a particular presentation was chosen. The graphic designer using an intelligent computer aid would want a justification for some design decisions. In intelligent tutoring systems, it would be useful if a program could automatically generate questions regarding a presentation on the screen.

The problems involved in developing intelligent interfaces are certainly very difficult, but if they are going to be solved, it seems likely that user interface behavior must be represented separately in a declarative language or a data base. Because the user interface is becoming an increasingly complex and important component of a software system, there are compelling reasons to make a clean separation between the user interface and the rest of a software system (Zdybel et al., 1981; Smith et al., 1984; Ciccarelli, 1984). There are several reasons to support such highly modular systems:

- they are easier to maintain and debug;

- they can be customized more easily;

- domain independence is possible; and

- an intelligent reasoning component can be interfaced with less difficulty.

In general, programs can be more attuned to individual users. Some users may prefer different configurations of the screen. The size of the fonts chosen in a window may be too small for some users. Optimizing screen space must not interfere with other concerns such as readability of the screen. Future versions of GUIDON-WATCH should allow users to customize the display to their liking while still providing automatic window management facilities. User models can play a role in smart interfaces that infer a user's preferences. However, a program must have an explicit model

of the user in order to reason about the user's preferences. We believe
that a knowledge-based approach (i.e., using declarative representations) is
necessary if a intelligent interface must combine general knowledge about
presentation with specific knowledge about a user. This is an area for
long-term interdisciplinary research in several areas of computer science,
psychology, linguistics, communications, education, and graphic design.

7.0 CONCLUSIONS

GUIDON-WATCH allows a user to view a knowledge-based consultation
system in an efficient way. The program demonstrates how multiple windows, menus, and a mouse can be used to achieve this goal. It also demonstrates that stating a diagnostic procedure in a well-structured rule-based
language facilitates developing a graphic interface for viewing and inspecting diagnostic problem-solving behavior. The most important principles
learned from this effort are as follows:

- Providing multiple views of the same knowledge or behavior can help a
  user understand a complex system. Tables, trees, pictures, animation,
  and other graphic formats can offer these different views. The current
  prototype of GUIDON-WATCH has made extensive use of trees and
  tables to display information in multiple, meaningful ways. Hierarchical relationships are naturally represented as trees, and lists of records
  with several fields are displayed as tables effectively. There are several
  important events in NEOMYCIN such as changes in the differential,
  conclusions about findings and hypotheses, and the task calls. Several
  windows with different formats can provide different views of these
  events. However, different classes of users may vary with regard to
  what constitutes an effective user interface.

- The use of bold fonts, boxing and graying items, and other graphic
  techniques can maximize information content and highlight facts and
  events in a way that is quickly understandable. The use of these simple
  techniques in the Taxonomy and Evidence windows illustrates their
  effectiveness (Figures 4-7 and 4-8).

- In well-constrained situations it is possible to manage the display and
  placement of windows automatically. Screen space is a precious resource, and each window must be designed, sized and placed to use
  space efficiently. However, this is a job that can be cumbersome for
  a user. Additionally, we want to avoid having a user concentrate on
  the motor activity of using the mouse to move and place windows on
  the screen. We believe that there is a fundamental difference between
  the constrained information-retrieval task that GUIDON-WATCH is

designed to perform and more creative and open-ended tasks such as programming or writing. For the latter category, the availability of overlapping windows that are usually shaped and positioned under the user's control may be more desirable.

By displaying information in multiple ways and allowing a user to interactively browse the dynamic state of a consultation, we have taken a first step towards reifying the process of reasoning during a NEOMYCIN consultation. Subsequent instructional programs now under development will ask students to explain, debug, and augment their own and program-generated problem-solving behavior. They will use graphic displays like GUIDON-WATCH to compare and contrast alternative solutions to problems.

8.0 ADDENDUM

After the original article appeared in IEEE Computer Graphics and Applications in November 1985, the GUIDON-WATCH interface was evaluated by our medical collaborators and medical students at Stanford University. Several significant changes and additions were made to the program, and they are briefly described here.

Mark H. Richer
William J. Clancey
January, 1987

8.1 Introduction

In the fall of 1985, Curt Kapsner, M.D., a visiting fellow at Stanford's medical school, and John Macias, a medical student at Stanford University with several years experience developing medical CAI programs, reviewed the GUIDON-WATCH interface. This began a cycle of evaluation including informal experiments with students followed by program modifications.

Related research efforts in medical AI and ICAI led us to add several additional features, most notably the patient-specific model graph, described below. Other important changes in GUIDON-WATCH and their motivation are also described. For the sake of brevity we omit a description of important changes in the NEOMYCIN knowledge base, the selection of patient cases for student use, and enhancements made to aid system developers, though these also evolved as a result of evaluating GUIDON-WATCH.

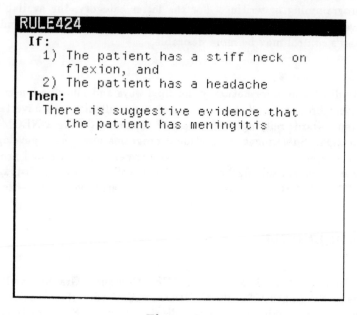

RULE424

If:
  1) The patient has a stiff neck on
     flexion, and
  2) The patient has a headache
Then:
  There is suggestive evidence that
     the patient has meningitis

Figure 8-1

8.2 Initial Changes to GUIDON-WATCH

One of the first suggestions was easily implemented, namely to omit some
of the existing GUIDON-WATCH windows for students. In particular, the
windows with tasks and metarules are not available when the program is in
"student mode". We believe that explaining the strategy that NEOMYCIN
is employing is interesting and important to a student, but the current task
and metarule windows are difficult for a student to understand without
training in the theory behind the program's design. Our goal is to improve
the explanation capabilities of the program so that the student can get relevant English explanations of NEOMYCIN's strategy (e.g., why a question
was asked). This development is still in progress and will not be discussed
further.

Initial changes to GUIDON-WATCH include improvements in the English translations of (medical) domain rules, the display of the differential,
and the elimination of numeric certainty factors from the student interface.

8.2.1 Rule Translations

Some of the rule translations in NEOMYCIN were verbose and awkward
(Figure 4-9). Improving these translations so that the rules are easier to

read and understand became an important priority. We were able to simplify many of the translations with a few changes to the translation code (compare Figure 8-1 and Figure 4-9). After the translations were improved we gained more confidence that the program was ready for use with medical students. We can now demonstrate that most NEOMYCIN rules are clear and simple, in contrast to many MYCIN rules which are difficult to understand because they contain implicit strategic knowledge.

8.2.2 The Differential

The term *differential* is commonly used in medicine, but there is no precise meaning that we can use in our programs that corresponds to every physician's or medical student's understanding of the concept. Internally NEOMYCIN's differential is a ranked set of competing hypotheses the program is considering, including only the most specific subtype in any path. For example, if chronic meningitis is added to the differential, its parent, meningitis, or any other more general hypothesis (e.g., infectious process) is not included. We refer to this as the *working differential*, in contrast, to the *final differential* or diagnosis.

Differential	
HYPOTHESIS	BELIEF
INFECTIOUS-PROCESS	+++
MENINGITIS	+++
ACUTE-MENINGITIS	+++
ACUTE-BACTERIAL-MENINGITIS	+++
INCREASED-INTRACRANIAL-PRESSURE	+++
INTRACRANIAL-MASS-LESION	++

Figure 8-2

The working differential as displayed in Figure 4-11 does not include infectious process, meningitis, chronic meningitis, or acute meningitis, but instead more specific subtypes. This was not intuitive to our medical collaborators because hypotheses with evidence often do not appear, whereas more specific subtypes without evidence do appear during hypothesis re-

finement before they are tested. We decided that the original Differential
and Hypotheses-with-evidence windows (Figure 4-12) should be replaced
with one window (Figure 8-2) that displays all the hypotheses with evidence in an outline format with more general hypothesis closer to the left
edge of the window and more specific causes or subtypes indented and below their parent. In subsequent evaluations medical students indicated that
the Differential window was understandable and useful.

```
 Summary of Evidence
 INFECTIOUS-PROCESS     +++
      febrile                            RULE423         ++

 MENINGITIS   +++
      headache                           RULE424         ++
      stiff-neck-on-flexion              RULE424         ++
      redflag-cns-finding                RULE323         ++

 ACUTE-MENINGITIS    +++
      photophobia                        RULE352          +

 INTRACRANIAL-MASS-LESION    ++
      focalsigns                         RULE365         ++
      increased-intracranial-pressure    RULE239         ++

 ACUTE-BACTERIAL-MENINGITIS     +++
      high-grade-fever                   RULE271         ++
      cns-finding-duration               RULE144         ++
      seizures                           RULE380          +
                                         RULE382          +

 INCREASED-INTRACRANIAL-PRESSURE    +++
      papilledema                        RULE209        +++
      seizures                           RULE262          +
```

Figure 8-3

8.2.3 Other Changes

The Summary-of-evidence window (Figure 8-3) is a table that shows supporting findings for each hypothesis with evidence. The user can select any
hypothesis, finding, or rule in the window to get more detailed information.
This became a very useful window. We also simplified other existing windows by removing information that a student did not generally need. For
example, we simplified the Evidence window for students (Figure 4-8) by
removing the minimum and maximum certainty factors.

8.3 Student Evaluations: Round One

We conducted five informal sessions with individual Stanford University students in late 1985 to evaluate the GUIDON-WATCH user interface. Sessions were recorded and transcribed. We found that students were consistent in their comments.

At the start of each session Dr. Kapsner explained the purpose of the program. He introduced the main menus, instructing the student on how to use the mouse to select a menu item. The student was told to start a consultation and choose one of the available patient cases. After the student observed NEOMYCIN ask several questions (answers were automatically retrieved from a stored patient file), Dr. Kapsner asked the student to open some of the windows starting with the Differential window. During the session Dr. Kapsner and Macias answered the student's questions about the program and requested feedback from the student. At the end of each session, the student was asked if the program was difficult to use, which windows were most useful, what he would like to see added or changed in the program, and so on.

We were surprised that the mechanical aspects of using the mouse and manipulating the windows presented less of a problem to students than understanding what would be useful to display when and how to get something displayed (what menu or window item to select with the mouse). The students independently agreed that it would not be obvious how to use the program without help or an instructional manual. However, given this they did not think the program was difficult to use. The excerpt below is indicative of student responses.

Although the informal evaluation indicated that the students found the program usable and understandable, many details remain to be resolved. It is clear that an introduction to the program is necessary along with on-line help. Some work in this area was subsequently done. In particular, we implemented GUIDON-TOURS, a facility for automatically demonstrating and explaining aspects of the program. The students also suggested new capabilities to be added to the program. For example, the students wanted to ask about previous questions in the consultation when they realized they misinterpreted what the program was doing.

Dr. Kapsner: In terms of just manipulating the windows and
                opening and closing them and selecting things
                from the menus, was that pretty easy to do?

Student: Once you know how to do it, it's easy to go back
                and forth very quickly [between windows and menus].

... a few questions later,

Dr. Kapsner: And finally the other windows, the
                Differential and the Taxonomy and the
                Evidence windows, could you understand
                those were they useful?

Student: They're very useful. It's a little hard
                to figure out which thing to punch to get
                to where, but once you figure that out,
                it's fine.

8.4 Patient-Specific Model Graph

Although it is clear that Neomycin has important limitations (e.g., it cannot diagnose multiple disorders), we decided that we would only make modifications to the basic framework and knowledge base that were necessary for our tutoring programs. A crucial shortcoming for teaching is that Neomycin cannot determine when a diagnosis is complete or satisfactory. A simple criteria is that a diagnosis is complete if it is consistent with all the known patient findings and is not in conflict with any of them (i.e., a finding does not rule out a hypothesis). We were influenced by related work that described a diagnosis as a causal or patient-specific model (Patil, et al., 1981), that is, an explanation of how the patient's abnormal state developed.

Another influential research project was the Geometry Tutor (Anderson, et al., 1985), which uses a graph to display a proof of a theorem as a complete or partial solution supported by axioms, other theorems and given information. We display the patient-specific model graph in a similar way (Figure 8-4), as an argument or proof showing the support for alternative hypotheses. Various opportunities for our tutoring programs emerge: using the patient-specific model as a form of explanation, as a tool for debugging an incomplete or faulty diagnosis, or as a notation a student can use to justify a hypothesis. In addition, recognition of incomplete knowledge to support a hypothesis can be the basis for automating knowledge-acquisition. Here we limit ourselves to describing the graphic tools available to a student using GUIDON-WATCH.

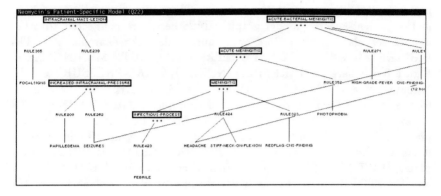

Figure 8-4

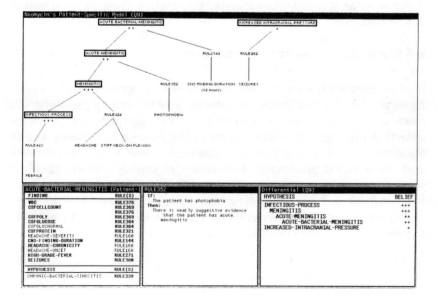

Figure 8-5

As shown in Figure 8-4, the most specific hypotheses or diagnoses are displayed at the top of the patient-specific model graph and abnormal patient findings are at the bottom. There are several kinds of links in the patient-specific model graph. Hypotheses are connected to other hypotheses via a subtype link or a causal rule. For example, ACUTE-BACTERIAL-MENINGITIS is a "subtype of" ACUTE-MENINGITIS in Figure 8-6, whereas INCREASED-INTRACRANIAL-PRESSURE can be "caused by" an INTRACRANIAL-MASS-LESION. Hypotheses are linked to one or more findings via a rule. For example, HIGH-GRADE-FEVER is "evidence for" or "suggests" ACUTE-MENINGITIS. A hypothesis "explains" a finding if it or any of its supertypes in the graph is connected to it via a rule node. For example, ACUTE-BACTERIAL-MENINGITIS explains PHOTOPHOBIA because RULE352 connects ACUTE-MENINGITIS and PHOTOPHOBIA, that is, acute meningitis is an explanation for the presence of photophobia.

8.5 "Rolling Back" the Display

A significant capability added to GUIDON-WATCH allows a user to display any window with the contents it would have had at the time of any question. This allows a user to go back to an earlier point in the consultation to view the differential, the patient-model graph, evidence for a hypothesis, and so on. Each window can be displayed at an earlier point independent of the other windows. In Figure 8-5, the Patient-specific model and Differential windows have been "rolled back" to Question 9. This feature was added in response to the students who requested information about earlier questions in a consultation.

8.6 Student Evaluations: Round Two

In June 1986 we ran some more informal sessions with medical students. Again students had difficulty remembering how to open up particular windows, that is, which window item or pull-down menu to select. It became clear that the organizational structure of the menus and windows was not obvious to students. Our informal experiments seem to indicate that students need verbal prompting to make use of available information. We propose that pop-up menus that prompt a student throughout a session with available and relevant options may be more effective than the global pull-down menus. A recent version of NEOMYCIN prompts the user with a menu of options whenever an explanation is requested (Figure 8-6).

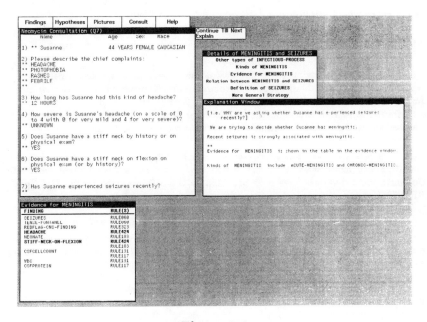

Figure 8-6

8.7 Conclusion

After the initial prototype of GUIDON-WATCH was developed, we entered the iterative process of evaluation, re-design, and re-implementation. We found that there are at least three sources of evaluation feedback: domain experts (including teachers), students or users, and the research community. Initially we underestimated some of the difficulties students would have with the program, in part because our medical collaborators had already become accustomed to way our thinking. Also some observers had overestimated the difficulty students actually had with the mechanics of the interface. Experiments with students quickly made these mis-judgements apparent. Other developments such as the addition of the patient-specific model graph resulted from our close contact with related research efforts.

To summarize, we found that students were able to learn the mechanics of the program with practice, but needed more help in understanding how the program could be used. Changes made to the Differential window, rule translations, and so on, seemed to help as students demonstrated they understood the contents of these windows. In this way we believe we made progress in bridging the gap between NEOMYCIN and a student's intuitive or learned notions about medical diagnosis. At this point, GUIDON-WATCH provides useful graphic displays for a medical student, but integrating these into an effective instructional program presents another research challenge.

ACKNOWLEDGEMENTS

Many people contributed to the evaluation, re-design and re-implementation of GUIDON-WATCH including Stephen Barnhouse, Curt Kapsner, M.D., David Leserman, John Macias, Naomi Rodolitz, and Bevan Yueh. Arif Merchant and David Wilkins also contributed to related efforts on the GUIDON project. We are particularly grateful to the medical students who helped us evaluate the program at different stages.

This research has been supported in part by ONR and ARI Contract N00014-79C-0302 and more recently by the Josiah Macy Jr. Foundation (Grant B852005). Computational resources have been provided by the SUMEX-AIM facility (NIH grant RR00785).

An earlier version of this paper appeared as Technical Report KSL-85-20, sponsored by the Knowledge Systems Laboratory at Stanford University. It subsequently was published in IEEE Computer Graphics and Applications in November 1985, Vol. 5, No. 11, pages 51-64.

REFERENCES

Bobrow, D., & Stefik, M. (1986). Perspectives on artificial intelligence programming. *Science, 231,* 951-957.

Borning, A. (1979). Thinglab – a constraint-oriented simulation laboratory. Technical Report SSL-79-3, Xerox Palo Alto Research Center, July.

Brown, J.S. (1985). Process versus product – a perspective on tools for communal and informal electronic learning. *Journal of Educational Computing Research, 1*(2). Also appeared in *Education in the Electronic Age,* proceedings of a conference sponsored by the Educational Broadcasting Corporation, WNET/Thirteen Learning Lab, NY, July, 1983, pp. 41-58.

Buchanan, B.G., & Shortliffe, E.H. (1984). *Rule-Based Expert Systems.* Reading, MA: Addison-Wesley.

Bush (1945). As we may think. *Atlantic Monthly, 176,* July, 101-108.

Card, S.K., Moran, S.K., & Newell, A. (1983). *The Psychology of Human-Computer Interaction.* Hillsdale, NJ: Lawrence Erlbaum Associates.

Ciccarelli, E. (1984). Presentation based user interfaces. Technical Report AI-TR-794, Artificial Intelligence Laboratory, Massachusetts Institute Technology, August.

Clancey, W.J. (1983). Overview of Guidon. *Journal of Computer-Based Instruction, 10*(1 and 2), Summer, 8-15. Also in *The Handbook of Artificial Intelligence,* Volume 2, Barr & Feigenbaum (Eds.), Kaufmann, Los Altos, CA, 1982, pp. 267-278.

Clancey, W.J., & Letsinger, R. (1984). NEOMYCIN: reconfiguring a rule-based expert system for application to teaching. In W.J. Clancey & E.H. Shortliffe (Eds.), *Readings in Medical Artificial Intelligence: The First Decade,* pp. 361-381. Reading, MA: Addison-Wesley.

Engelbart, D.C. (1963). A conceptual framework for the augmentation of man's intellect. In Howerton and Weeks (Eds.), *Vistas in Information Handling,* pp. 1-29. Washington, DC: Spartan Books.

Engelbart, D. (1970). Advanced intellect-augmentation techniques. SRI Project 7079, final report, Stanford Research Institute, July.

Engelbart, D.C. (1982). Toward high-performance knowledge workers. *Proceedings of* the *AFIPS Office Automation Conference*, pp. 279-290, April.

English, W.K., & Engelbart, D.C. (1967). Display-selection techniques for text manipulation. *IEEE Transactions on Human Factors in Electronics*, HFE-8(1), March, 5-15.

Finzer, W., & Gould, L. (1984). Programming by rehearsal. *BYTE*, 9(6), June, 187-210.

Foley, J.D., & Van Dam, A. (1982). *Fundamentals of Interactive Computer Graphics.* Reading, MA: Addison-Wesley 1982.

Foley, J.D., Wallace V.L., & Chan, P. (1984). The human factors of computer graphics interaction techniques. *IEEE Computer Graphics and Applications*, 4(11), November, 13-49.

Goldberg (1970). Educational uses of a Dynabook. *Computers and Education*, 3, 247-266.

Hasling, D.W., Clancey, W.J., & Rennels, G. (1984). Strategic explanations for a diagnostic consultation system. *International Journal of Man-Machine Studies*, 20, 3-19.

Hollan, J.D., Hutchins, E.L., & Weitzman, L. (1984). STEAMER: an interactive inspectable simulation-based training system. *AI Magazine*, 5(2), 15-27.

Ingalls, D.H. (1981). Design principles behind Smalltalk. *Byte*, 6(8), August, 286-298.

Kay, A. (1977). Microelectronics and the personal computer. *Scientific American*, 237(3), September, 230-244.

Kunz, J.C., Kehler, T.P., & Williams, M.D. (1984). Applications development using a hybrid AI development system. *AI Magazine*, 5(3), Fall, 41-54.

Lane, C., Differding, J., & Shortliffe, E.H. (1986). Graphical access to medical expert systems: II. Design of an interface for physicians. *Methods of Information in Medicine*, 25, 143-150.

Lieberman, H. (1985). There's more to menu systems than meets the screen. *Computer Graphics*, 19(3), July, 181-189.

Mackinlay, J. (1986). Automatic design of graphical presentations. Technical Report STAN-CS-86-1038, Computer Science Department, Stanford University.

Model, M. (1979). Monitoring system behavior in a complex computation environment. Technical Report STAN-CS-79-701, Computer Science Department, Stanford University, January.

Papert, S. (1980). *Mindstorms: Children, Computers, and Powerful Ideas.* New York: Basic Books, Inc.

Richer, M. (1986). An evaluation of expert system development tools. *Expert Systems.*

Sannella, M., Ed. (1985). Interlisp-D reference manual. Palo Alto, CA: Xerox Corporation.

Schoen, E., & Smith, R.G. (1983). Impulse, a display-oriented editor for strobe. *Proceedings of the National Conference on AI*, pp. 356-358, AAAI, August.

Shortliffe, E.H. (1976). *Computer-based Medical Consultations: MYCIN.* New York: Elsevier 1976.

Smith, R.G., Lafue, G.M.E., Schoen, E., & Vestal, S.C. (1984). Declarative Task Description as a user-interface structuring mechanism. *Computer*, 17(9), September, 29-38.

Steele, G.L. (1984). *Common LISP – The Language.* Burlington, MA: Digital Press.

Stefik, M., Bobrow, D.G., Mittal, S., & Conway, L. (1983). Knowledge programming in loops: report on an experimental course. *AI Magazine*, 4(3), Fall, 3-13.

Stevens, A., Roberts, B., & Stead, L. (1983). The use of a sophisticated graphics interface in computer-assisted instruction. *IEEE Computer Graphics and Applications*, 3(2), March/April, 25-31.

Tesler, L. (1981). The Smalltalk environment. *Byte*, 6(8), August, 90-147.

Tesler, L. (1985). *MacApp, Release 0.1.* Cupertino, CA: Apple Computer, Inc.

Thompson, T., & Clancey, W.J. (1985). A qualitative modeling shell for process diagnosis. *IEEE Software, 3*(2), March, 6-15.

Tsuji, S., & Shortliffe, E.H. (1983). Graphical access to the knowledge base of a medical consultation system. *Proceedings of AAMSI (American Association for Medical Systems and Informatics) Congress 83*, May, 551-555.

Tsuji, S., & Shortliffe, E.H. (1986). Graphical access to a medical expert system: I. design of a knowledge engineer's interface. *Methods of Information in Medicine, 25*, 62-70.

van Melle, V. (1981). *System Aids in Constructing Consultation Programs.* Ann Arbor, Michigan: UMI Research Press.

Weinreb, D., & Moon, D. (1981). *Lisp Machine Manual.* Cambridge, MA: Symbolics, Inc.

Weyer, S., & Borning, A. (1984). A prototype electronic encyclopedia. Technical Report 84-08-01, Computer Science Department, University of Washington, August.

Williams, C. (1984). Software tool packages the expertise needed to build expert systems. *Electronic Design*, August, 153-167.

Zdybel, F., Greenfield, N., Yonke, M., & Gibbons, J. (1981). An information presentation system. *Proceedings of the Seventh International Joint Conference on Artificial Intelligence*, August, 978-984.

18 TEACHING A COMPLEX INDUSTRIAL PROCESS

Beverly Woolf

Computer and Information Science
University of Massachusetts
Amherst, MA 01003

Darrell Blegen, Johan H. Jansen
and Arie Verloop

J.H. Jansen Co., Inc.
Steam and Power Engineers
18016 140 Avenue N.E.
Woodinville (Seattle), WA 98072

ABSTRACT

Computer training for industry is often not capable of providing advice custom-tailored for a specific student and a specific learning situation. In this paper we describe an intelligent computer-aided system that provides multiple explanations and tutoring facilities tempered to the individual student in an industrial setting. The tutor is based on a mathematically accurate formulation of the kraft recovery boiler and provides an interactive simulation complete with help, hints, explanations, and tutoring. The approach is extensible to a wide variety of engineering and industrial problems in which the goal is to train an operator to control a complex system and to solve difficult "real time" emergencies.

1.0 TUTORING COMPLEX PROCESSES

Learning how to control a complex industrial process takes years of practice and training; an operator must comprehend the physical and mathematical formulation of the process and must be skilled in handling a number of unforeseen operating problems and emergencies. Even experienced operators need continuous training. A potentially significant way to train both experienced and student operators for such work is through a "reactive computer environment" (Brown et al., 1982) that simulates the process and allows the learner to propose hypothetical solutions that can be evaluated in "real time." However, a simulation without a tutoring component will not test whether a student has actually improved in his ability to handle the situation. In addition, a simulation alone might not provide the conceptual fidelity (Hollan, 1984) necessary for an operator to learn how to use the concepts and trends of the process or how to reason about the simulation. For instance, evaluating the rate of change of process variables and comparing their relative values over time is an important pedagogical skill supporting expert reasoning; yet rate of change is a difficult concept to represent solely with the gauges in a traditional simulation.

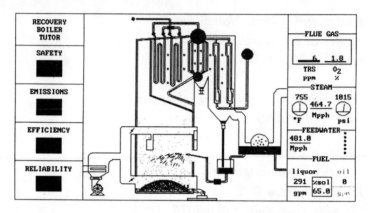

Figure 1: Sectional View of the Recovery Boiler

We have built a Recovery Boiler Tutor (RBT) that provides tools for developing abstract models of a complex process. The system does not actually represent the mental models that a learner might develop, rather, it provides tools for reasoning about that complex process. These tools include graphs to demonstrate the relationship of process parameters over time, meters to measure safety, emissions, efficiency, reliability, and safety, and interactive dialogues to tutor the operator about the ongoing process. The system renders a mathematically and physically accurate simulation of a kraft boiler and interacts with the student about those concepts needed for his exploration of the boiler. Our goal has been to couple the motivational appeal of an interactive simulation with the tutoring and modeling ability of an artificial intelligence system to direct the student in his experimentation.

The tutor was built in direct response to a serious industrial situation. Many industrial accidents, caused in part by human errors, have lead to dangerous and costly explosions of recovery boilers in pulp and paper mills. The American Paper Institute[1] built the interactive tutor to provide on-site training in the control room of recovery boilers. The tutor is now being beta tested in pulp and paper mills across the United States and is being prepared for nationwide distribution.

---

[1] The American Paper Institute is a non-profit trade institution for the pulp, paper, and paperboard industry in the United States.

2.0 THE RECOVERY BOILER TUTOR

A recovery boiler is an extremely complex machine found in hundreds of pulp and paper mills around the world. Figure 1, from the RBT screen, pictures a typical boiler and some of the meters used by an operator to control the process. The actual boiler can cost up to $70 million and can be up to 20 stories high. Its function is to processes the spent black liquor that can be produced in a pulp mill, up to 1500 tons/day, and to allow recovery and re-use of the pulping chemicals. It is a process in which hot and molten inorganic chemicals may lead to smelt/water and combustible gas explosions, endangering life and property.

The goal behind the tutor is to challenge an operator, to solve boiler problems and to maintain his incentive to continue to "play" with the tutor. The operator is encouraged to move setpoint controllers and to watch the results of his actions on the animated boiler or control board. The tutor monitors the operator's freewheeling trial-and-error behavior and provides help, hints, explanations, and tutoring when needed or requested.

An example interaction[2] between the student and tutor is shown in Figure 2. As the operator changes setpoint controllers and requests information about the boiler, the tutor selectively discusses the optimality of his actions (we show how in Section 3) and suggests how he might better focus his action or better utilize his data. An important feature to note about this dialogue is that at any point during the simulated emergency there are a large number of actions an operator might take and, as the problem worsens, an increasing number of actions that he *should* take to correct the operating conditions. Thus, an immediate and correct response might require only one action, such as rodding the primary air ports, but a delayed response causes the situation to worsen and requires the addition of auxiliary fuel.

The operator interacts with the tutor through a hierarchy of menus, one of which is shown in Figure 3. The first menu, (A), allows an operator to select a physical activity to be performed on the boiler, such as checking for a tube leak or rodding the smelt spout. The second menu, (B), allows the operator to select a particular computer screen, such as the alarm board or control panel board.

---

[2] The dialogue of Figure 2 was not actually produced in natural language; student input was handled through menus (Figure 3) and tutor output produced by cutting text from emergency-specific text files loaded when the emergency was invoked.

(Note: A partial blackout is in progress and it will lead to deterioration of the combustion process if no action is taken. Meters indicate that CO, SO_2, and O_2 readings are abnormally high.)

(An alarm buzzer sounds.)

Tutor: What action are you going to take?

Student: Check smelt spout cooling water.
              (Student's action does not result in a change in the boiler.)

Tutor: It looks as though the liquor isn't burning ...

Student: Help. What is going on?
              (Student requests help.)

Tutor: A partial blackout is occurring and this causes TRS, CO, SO_2, and O_2 to increase. Steam flow and steam temperature are dropping. I think part of the bed is not burning.

Student: Rod the primary air ports.
              (A small improvement in the boiler readings can be observed.)

Tutor: Your action is correct; however, at this time rodding alone is not effective ...

Student: Raise the liquor temperature.
              (Student's action does not reverse the emergency and a new alarm buzzer sounds).

Tutor: Rodding the air port apparently was not enough to undo the blackout.

Student: Increase the oil fuel supply.
              (Student's action reverses the emergency.)

Tutor: That solved the problem alright. Good thinking.

Analysis of the problem: You had a partial blackout caused by plugged primary air ports and a cold bed. Partial blackout can be effectively treated through a combination of rodding the primary air ports and adding more heat. The problem can be avoided by keeping the air ports clean.

Figure 2: Dialogue Between Tutor and Operator

Figure 3:   Menu to Select a Physical Task to
             Perform on the Boiler.

The student can initiate any of 20 training situations, emergencies, or
operating conditions (see Appendix 1). He can also ask that an emergency
be chosen for him or he might accidently trigger an emergency as a result
of his actions on the boiler. Once an emergency has been initiated, the
student should adjust meters and perform actions on the simulated boiler
to solve the emergency.

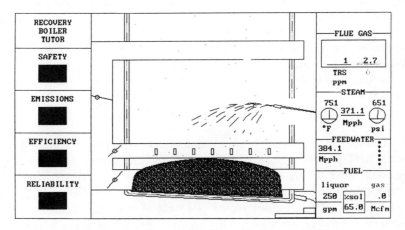

Figure 4: Focused View of the Fire Bed

For example, if the system has simulated a TRS reading of greater
than 15 ppm and if the amount of oxygen is less than 2%, then the student
is expected to increase the oxygen until it is 3.25%. If he does this, the level
of TRS will automatically be reduced to less than 5 ppm and the boiler will
return to a normal state. However, if he does not perform this action, a
critical situation will develop accompanied possibly by a blackout and, if
the situation is allowed to continue, a dangerous explosion.

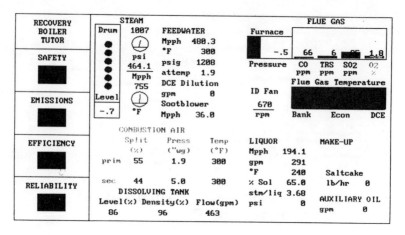

Figure 5: The Complete Control Panel

While the simulation is running, the operator can view the boiler from many directions and can focus in on several components, such as the fire bed in Figure 4. The tutor provides assistance through visual clues, such as a darkened smelt bed; acoustic clues, ringing alarm buzzers, textual help, explanations, and dialogues, such as that illustrated in Figure 2. The operator can request up to 30 process parameters on the complete panel board, Figure 5 or can view an alarm board (not shown). The tutor allows the student to change 20 setpoints and to ask menued questions such as "What is the problem?", "How do I get out of it?", "What caused it?", and "What can I do to prevent it?."[3] The operator can request meter readings, physical and chemical reports, dynamic trends of variables. All variables are updated in real time (every 1 or 2 seconds).

In addition to providing information about the explicit variables in the boiler, RBT provides information about implicit processes through *reasoning* tools, with which an operator can understand and reason about the complex processes. One such tools is composite meters (left side of Figures 1 and 5). These meters record the state of the boiler using synthetic measures for *safety, emissions, efficiency,* and *reliability* of the boiler. The meter readings are calculated from complex mathematical formulae that would rarely, if ever, be used by an operator to evaluate the same characteristics of their boiler. For instance, the safety meter is a composition of seven independent parameters, including steam pressure, steam flow, steam temperature, feedwater flow, drum water level, firing liquor solids,

---

[3] These four questions are answered by cutting text from a file which was loaded with the specific emergency. These questions do not provide the basis of the tutor's knowledge representation, which will be discussed in Section 3.2

and combustibles in the flue gas. Meter readings allow a student to make inferences about the effect of his actions on the boiler using characteristics of the running boiler. These meters are not presently available on existing pulp and paper mill control panels; however, if they prove effective as training aids, they could be incorporated into actual control panels.

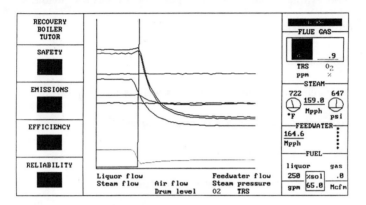

Figure 6: Trends Selected by the Operator

Other reasoning tools include trend analyses, Figure 6, and animated graphics, such as shown in Figures 1 and 4. Trend analyses show an operator how essential process variables interact in real time by allowing him to select up to 10 variables, including liquor flow, oil flow, and air flow, etc, and to plot each against the others and time. Animated graphics are provided as a part of every view of the boiler and include realistic and changing drawings of dynamic components of the boiler, such as steam, fire, smoke, black liquor, and fuel.

Each student action, be it a setpoint adjustment or proposed solution, is recorded in an accumulated response value. This value reflects an operator's overall score and how successful, or unsuccessful, his actions have been and whether the actions were performed in sequence with other relevant or irrelevant actions. This accumulated value is not presently used by the tutor, but the notation might be used to sensitize the tutor's future responses to the student's record. For instance, if the operator has successfully solved a number of boiler emergencies, the accumulated value might be used to temper subsequent tutoring so that it is less intrusive. Similarly, if a student's past performance has been poor, the accumulated value could be used to activate more aggressive responses from the tutor.

3.0 MULTIPLE REPRESENTATIONS OF KNOWLEDGE

Multiple concepts and processes were represented in ARBT, some procedurally, some declaratively, and some in both ways. For example, emergencies in the steam boiler were first represented as a set of mathematical formulae so that process parameters and meter values could be produced accurately in the simulation. Then these same emergencies were encoded within the tutor's knowledge base as a frame-like data structure with slots for preconditions, optimal actions, and conditions for solution satisfaction so that the tutor could evaluate and comment upon the student's solution.

RBT can recognize and explain:

- equipment and process flows,

- emergencies operating problems as well as normal conditions,

- solutions to emergencies and operating problems,

- processes for implementing solutions, and

- tutoring strategies for assisting the student.

Four modules were used to represent this knowledge: *simulation, knowledge base, student model, and instructional strategies.* Development of the last three components was inspired by prior work in intelligent tutoring systems (Brown et al., 1982; Anderson et al., 1985, Sleeman, 1982; Slater et al., 1985; and Woolf and McDonald, 1984a, 1984b).

3.1 Simulation of Equipment and Process Flow

The *simulation* uses a mathematical foundation to depict processes in a boiler through meter readings and four animated views of the boiler. It reacts to more than 35 process parameters and generates dynamically accurate reports of the thermal, chemical, and environmental performance of the boiler (not shown) upon request. An alarm board (not shown) represents 25 variables whose button will turn red and alarm sounded when an abnormal condition exists for that parameter.[4] The simulation is interactive and inspectable in that it displays a "real time" model of its process, yet allows the student to "stop" the process at anytime to engage in activities needed to develop his mental models (Hollan et al., 1984). The operators who tested RBT mentioned that they like being able to stop the process to ask questions or to explore boiler characteristics.

If a student working on a problem inadvertently triggers a second problem, the least serious problem will be placed on a stack and held in abeyance

---

[4] Engineering details about the steam and chemical parameters in RBT and the boiler simulation capabilities can be found in (Jansen et al., 1986).

while the student is coached to solve the more serious problem. After the more serious problem is solved, the student is coached to solve the remaining one. Thus, the simulation provides facilities for handling multiple instantiations of emergencies.

One advantage of a formal representation of the process is the availability of a "database" of possible worlds into which information, based on typical or previous moves, can be fed into the simulation at any time (Brown et al., 1982) and a solution found. In this way, a student's hypothetical cases can be proposed, verified, and integrated into his mental model of the boiler.

3.2 Knowledge Base of Emergencies and Operating Conditions

The *knowledge base* contains preconditions, postconditions, and solutions for emergencies or operating conditions, described as *scenarios*. Scenarios are represented in frame-like text files containing preconditions, postconditions, and acceptable solutions for each scenario. For example, in Lisp notation, a true blackout would be described as:

> preconditions:
> (or   ($\leq$ blackout_factor 1)
>   ($<$ heat_input 5000))
>
> postconditions:
> (or   (increasing O_2)
>   (decreasing steamflow)
>   (increasing TRS)
>   (increasing CO)
>   (increasing SO_2))
>
> solution_satisfaction:
> (and ($=$ blackout_factor 1)
>   ($>$ heat_input 5200))

Scenarios in RBT have been teased apart to represent successively more serious problems. For instance, a smelt spout pluggage is represented as separate scenarios depending on whether the solution requires rodding the spout, applying a portable auxiliary burner, removing the liquor, or a combination of all three. Again, formalized knowledge of the domain made it easy to represent and evaluate graduated scenarios, as well as multiple operator actions.

The efficiency of the student's action is evaluated both through the type of action performed, such as *increasing O_2* or *increasing steamflow* for a true blackout, and the effect of that action on the boiler. Thus, if an inappropriate action, nevertheless, resulted in a safe boiler, the student would be told that his action worked, but that it was not optimal. For example, a partial furnace blackout requiring manual rodding of the air delivery system can be alleviated by shutting down the boiler. However, this is an expensive and unwarranted action and the student will be advised to use an alternative approach.

3.3 Student Model to Monitor the Operator's Solution

The *student model* records actions carried out by the student in solving the emergency or operating problem. It recognizes correct, as well as incorrect actions and identifies each as relevant, relevant but not optimal, or irrelevant.

The tutor compares the student's actions with those specified by the knowledge base and uses a simplified differential model to recognize and comment about the difference between the two. For instance, if a partial blackout has been simulated, the black liquor solids are less than 58%, and the operator adjusts the primary air pressure, the tutor might interrupt with a message such as:

"Primary air pressure is one factor that might contribute to blackout, but there is another more crucial factor – try again."

or

"You have overlooked a major contributing factor to blackouts."

The student model is currently the weakest component of the tutor. We intend to incorporate inferences about patterns of student errors and possible misconceptions[5] as a way to increase the tutor's ability to reason about what the operator has accomplished so far and what possible misconception he has. For example, we would like to test presumed misconceptions and use future operator actions to verify the existence of those misconceptions. To do so, the student model would have to link misconceptions with scenarios and to record all common errors and evidence for possible misconceptions.

3.4 Instructional Strategies to Assist the Student

---

[5] Misconceptions will be compiled by J.H. Jansen Co., Inc., Steam and Power Engineers, who, in addition to being the authors of RBT, have extensive operating experience with boilers in the U.S.A. and Canada.

The *instructional strategies* contain decision logic and rules to guide the tutor's intervention of the operator's actions. In RBT, the intent has been to "subordinate teaching to learning" and to allow the student to experiment while developing his own criteria about boiler emergencies. The tutor guides the student, but does not provide a solution as long as the student's performance appears to be moving closer to a precise goal.

Represented as if/then rules based on a specific emergency and a specific student action, the instructional rules are designed to verify that the student has "asked" the right questions and has made the correct inferences about the saliency of his data. Responses are divided into three categories:

Redirect student: "Have you considered the rate of increase of O_2?"
"If what you suggest is true, then how would you explain the low emissions reading?"

Synthesize data: "Both O_2 and TRS have abnormal trends."
"Did you notice the relation between steam flow and liquor flow?"

Confirm action: "Yes, It looks like rodding the ports worked this time."

The tutor selects from within each category a response that address both the operator's action and his apparent ability to solve the problem. Special precautionary messages are added to the most specific tutor responses to alert an operator to when a full-scale disaster is imminent.

The instructional strategies are designed to encourage an operator's generation of hypotheses. Evidence from other problem solving domains, such as medicine (Barrows & Tamblyn, 1980), suggests that students generate multiple (usually 3 – 5) hypotheses rapidly and make correct diagnoses with only 2/3 of the available data.[6] The RBT tutor was designed to be a partner and co-solver of problems with the operator, who is encouraged to recognize the effect (or lack of same) of his hypotheses and to experiment with multiple explanations of an emergency. No penalty is exacted for slow response or for long periods of trial and error problem solving.

This approach is distinct from that of Anderson et al. (1985) and Reiser et al. (1985), whose geometry and Lisp tutors immediately acknowledge a incorrect student answers and provide hints. These authors argue that erroneous solution paths in geometry and Lisp are often so ambiguous and

---

[6] Medical students have been found to ask 60% of their questions while searching for new data and obtain 75% of their significant information within the first 10 minutes after a problem is stated (Barrows & Tamblyn, 1980).

delayed that they might not be recognized for a long time, if at all, and then the source of the original error might be forgotten. Therefore, immediate computer tutor feedback is needed to avoid fruitless effort.

However, in industrial training, the trainee must learn to evaluate his own performance from its effect on the industrial process. He should trust the process itself to provide the feedback, as much as is possible. In RBT we provide this feedback through animated simulations, trend analyses, and "real-time" dynamically-updated meters. The textual dialogue from the tutor provides added assurance that the operator has extracted as much information as possible from the data and it establishes a mechanism to redirect him if he has not (Burton & Brown, 1982; Goldstein, 1982).

4.0 DEVELOPMENTAL ISSUES

RBT was developed on an IBM PC AT (512 KB RAM) with enhanced graphics and a 20 MB hard disk. It uses a math co-processor, two display screens (one color), and a two-key mouse. The simulation was implemented in Fortran and took 321 KB; the tutor was implemented in C and took 100 KB.

Although we tried to implement the tutor in Lisp, we found extensive interfacing and memory problems, including segment size restrictions (64K), incompatibility with the existing Fortran simulator, and addressable RAM restrictions (640K). To circumvent these problems the tutor was developed in C with many Lisp features implemented in C, such as functional calls within the parameters of C functions. Meter readings and student actions were transferred from the simulation (in Fortran) to the tutor (in C) through vectors passed between the two programs.

The approach taken here can be extended to other engineering and industrial training problems. Factors that are likely to be considered in building a training system are availability, cost, and appropriateness of software and hardware for the scope of the task. In our case, decisions were made to ensure swift production of a simulation and tutor, given approximately 18 months development time.

5.0 EVALUATIONS

The tutor has been well-received thus far. It is presently used in actual training in the control rooms of several pulp and paper mills throughout the U.S. Formal evaluation will be available soon. However, informal evaluation suggests that working operators enjoy the simulation and handle it with extreme care. They behave as they might at the actual control panel of the pulp mill, slowly changing parameters, adjusting meters through small intervals, and checking each action and examining several meter readings before moving on to the next action.

Both experienced and novice operators engage in lively use of the system after about a half-hour introduction. When several operators interact with the tutor, they sometimes trade "war stories" advising each other about rarely seen situations. In this way, experienced operators frequently become partners with novice operators as they work together to simulate and solve unusual problems.

6.0 CONCLUSIONS

Several fundamental lessons about building an intelligent tutor were learned from this project. The first and foremost was the need for "in-house" expertise; in our case the programmer, project manager, and director of the project were themselves chemical engineers. More than 30 years of theoretical and practical knowledge about boiler design and teaching was incorporated into the system. Had these experts not previously identified the chemical, physical, and thermodynamic characteristics of the boiler and collected examples of sucessful teaching activities, development time for this project would have been much longer.

A second critical lesson was the need to clarify and implement the components of a teaching philosophy early in the development process in order to ensure full realization of a tutor in the completed system. For example, in order to manifest a philosophy of subordinating teaching to learning, we had to build up the system's ability to recognize partially-correct as well as irrelevant actions (in the knowledge base), to custom-tailor its responses to each type of answer (in the instructional strategies), and to quietly monitor the operator while judiciously reasoning about when to interrupt him (in the student model). The need to limit authoritarian responses from the system and to restrict it to giving only as much help as absolutely needed, meant that tutoring was not tacked onto the end of an expert system, but rather was developed as an integral part of components of the expert system. We suggest that silence (inactivity) on the part of a computer system is, in itself, a recognition of the learner's role in the training process and provides an expression of our confidence in his progress.

A third and most surprising lesson learned from this project was that a teaching system can be designed for multiple students. The system is now being used with groups of operators who work with each other and with the computer to solve problems; pedagogically wholesome things are beginning to happen among them. For example, novice and experienced operators, who might otherwise not be comparable in training and ability, can share their problem solving knowledge and experience; each teaching and learning in a non-evaluative environment.

Several issues remain unresolved in our work to improve the compter tutor's ability to respond to the student. We need to to sort out those skills or processes that a student has learned from those that he is still trying to learn and to sort out those concepts he has grasped from those he still has problems with; we also need to recognize which techniques have been effective in helping him. Currently, the tutor can not do this and we have suggested how we might extend the student model to incorporate inferences made about the student's knowledge, his errors and potential misconceptions to make progress along these lines.

ACKNOWLEDGEMENTS

The authors thank Jeremy Metz, Bradford Leach, and the A.P.I. Recovery Boiler Committee for their encouragement and support.

This work was supported by The American Paper Institute, Inc., a non-profit trade institution for the pulp, paper, and paperboard industry in the United States, Energy and Materials Department, 260 Madison Avenue, New York, NY, 10016. Preparation of this paper was supported by the Air Force Systems Command, Rome Air Development Center, Griffiss AFB, New York, 13441, and the Air Force Office of Scientific Research, Bolling AFB, DC, 20332, under contract No. F30602-85-C-0008. This contract supports the Northeast Artificial Intelligence Consortium (NAIC).

REFERENCES

Anderson, J., Boyle, C., & Yost, G. (1985). The geometry tutor. *Proceedings of the International Joint Conference on Artificial Intelligence*, Los Angeles.

Barrows, H.S., & Tamblyn, R.H. (1980). *Problem-Based Learning: An Approach to Medical Education*. New York: Springer Publishing Co.

Burton, R., & Brown, J. (1982). An investigation of computer coaching for informal learning activities. In D. Sleeman & J.S. Brown (Eds.), *Intelligent Tutoring Systems*. Cambridge, MA: Academic Press.

Brown, J., Burton, R., & deKleer, J. (1982). Pedagogical natural language, and knowledge engineering techniques in SOPHIE I, II, and III. In D. Sleeman & J.S. Brown (Eds.), *Intelligent Tutoring Systems*. Cambridge, MA: Academic Press.

Goldstein, I. (1982). The genetic graph: a representation for the evolution of procedural knowledge. In D. Sleeman & J.S. Brown (Eds.), *Intelligent Tutoring Systems*. Cambridge, MA: Academic Press.

Hollan, J., Hutchins, E., & Weitzman, L. (1984). STEAMER: an interactive inspectable simulation-based training system. In *The A.I. Magazine*, Summer.

Jansen, J., Verloop, A., & Blegen, D. (1986). Recovery boiler tutor: an interactive simulation and training aid. In *Proceedings of the Technical Association of the Pulp and Paper Industry Engineering Conference*, Seattle, WA, (in print).

Reiser, B., Anderson, J., & Farrell, R. (1985). Dynamic student modelling in an intelligent tutor for Lisp programming. In *Proceedings of the International Joint Conference on Artificial Intelligence*, Los Angeles, CA.

Slater, J., Petrossian, R., & Shyam-Sunder, S. (1984). An expert tutor for rigid body mechanics: Athena cats - MACAVITY. In *Proceedings of the Expert Systems in*

Government Symposium. IEEE and MITRE Corp., October.

Sleeman, D. (1982). Assessing aspects of competence in basic algebra. In D. Sleeman & J.S. Brown (Eds.), *Intelligent Tutoring Systems*. Cambridge, MA: Academic Press.

Woolf, B., & McDonald, D. (1984). Context-dependent transitions in tutoring discourse. *Proceedings of the National Conference on Artificial Intelligence*, (AAAI), Austin, TX, August 1984a.

Woolf, B., & McDonald, D. (1984). Design issues in building a computer tutor. *IEEE Computer*, September 1984b.

The A.P.I. Recovery Boiler Reference Manual. Prepared by J.H. Jansen Co., American Paper Institute, New York, NY, 1982.

APPENDIX 1
Emergencies & Operating Problems
Simulated by the Tutor

Emergency Situations:

Smelt/Water Explosion
Combustible Gas Explosion
Tube Rupture (various locations)

Operating Problems:
High Drum Water Level
Low Drum Water Level
Loss of Steam Header Pressure
Nozzle Pluggage
Liquor Supply Loss
Smelt Spout Pluggage
Heavy Smelt Run-off
ID Fan Failure
FD Fan Failure
Carryover & Pluggage
Depleted Weak Wash Flow
Low Liquor Firing Solids
Partial Blackout
Complete Blackout
Instrument Air Failure
Electrical Power Failure

INDEX